PLANNING AND MANAGING HUMAN RESOURCES

STRATEGIC PLANNING FOR HUMAN RESOURCES MANAGEMENT

Second Edition
Completely Revised and Updated

WILLIAM J. ROTHWELL ✧ H. C. KAZANAS

HRD Press   **Amherst, Massachusetts**

Published by Human Resource Development Press, Inc.
22 Amherst Road
Amherst, Massachusetts 01002

1-800-822-2801 (U.S. and Canada)
1-413-253-3488
1-413-253-3490 (fax)
http://www.hrdpress.com

ISBN 0-87425-718-2

Production services by CompuDesign
Cover design by Eileen Klockars
Editorial services by Suzanne Bay, Robie Grant, and Sally Farnham

CONTENTS

List of Figures ix
List of Activities xiii
Preface xv

Chapter 1 **Introduction to Planning and Managing Human Resources:**
Strategic Planning for Human Resources Management 1
What Is Strategic Planning for Human Resources (SPHR)? 2
How Did Human Resources Planning (HRP) Evolve? 3
What Do We Mean by *Strategy*? 4
Why Is Strategic Planning for Human Resources Needed? 6
What Makes Strategic Planning Difficult in Organizations? 20
How Can the SPHR Process Be Described? 22
What Are the Roles of HRP Practitioners? 24
What Is Role Theory? 26
What Do We Know about HRP Roles? 28
How Can HRP Roles Be Conceptualized? 29
How Are the Roles of HR Planners Related to the SPHR Model? 31
How Is This Book Structured? 31
Activities 33

Chapter 2 **The Human Resources Organizational Coordinator** 41
What Does the HR-Organizational Coordinator Do? 41
Why Is It Important to Link Organizational Plans and HR Plans? 42
What Are the Purposes, Goals, and Objectives of the Organization? 42
What Are the Purposes, Goals, and Objectives of Strategic Human
    Resource Plans? 46
Alternative Methods of Linking Strategic Business Plans with HR Plans 48
Activities 54

Chapter 3 **The Human Resources Work Analyst** 63
What Does the HR Work Analyst Do? 63
What Specialized Terms Are Associated with Work Analysis? 64

Why Is Work Analysis Important? 66
What Should Be Analyzed? 68
How Is Work Analysis Traditionally Conducted? 71
How Is General Background Information Collected? 71
What Results Do Analysts Hope to Obtain? 73
What Are Some Approaches to Work Analysis? 73
What Are Some Data-Collection Methods for Work Analysis? 77
How Can the Work Analysis Process Be Carried Out? 87
How Are Results Verified? 87
How Are Internal and External Conditions Monitored? 88
How Are Competencies Identified, and How Are Values Assessed? 89
Activities 91

Chapter 4   The Human Resources Workforce Analyst 103
What Does the HR Workforce Analyst Do? 104
What Specialized Terms Are Associated with Workforce Analysis? 104
Why Is Workforce Analysis Important? 106
What Should Be Analyzed? 106
How Is Workforce Analysis Traditionally Conducted? 107
How Are Job Specifications Prepared? 109
What Is the Link Between Workforce and Work Analysis? 110
Why Are Employee Performance Appraisals Important? 112
What Should Be Evaluated? 113
How Should Evaluation Be Carried Out? 119
What Problems Exist with Traditional Employee-Appraisal Methods? 123
How Can Problems with Employee Appraisals Be Overcome? 125
How Are Appraisal Results Used in Human Resources Planning? 128
Activities 133

Chapter 5   The Human Resources Auditor 137
What Does the HR Auditor Do? 137
How Is the HR Audit Conducted? 138
Deciding on Issues to Examine 139
Deciding, Tentatively, How to Conduct the Audit 142
Selecting People to Assist with the Audit 143
Collecting Background Information 144
Finalizing the Audit Plan 148
Collecting Audit Information 149
Compiling Audit Results 160
Activities 163

Chapter 6   The Human Resources Environmental Scanner 175
What Does the HR Environmental Scanner Do? 175
Why Is Environmental Scanning Important? 176

How Is the Environmental Scanning Process Conducted? 176
Identifying Future Trends 177
Problems with Environmental Scanning 179
Assessing the Effects of Future Trends 186
Conducting Future-Oriented Work Analysis 187
Selecting a Means to Conduct Future-Oriented Work Analysis 196
Verifying Results of Future-Oriented Work Analysis 197
Conducting Future-Oriented Workforce Analysis 200
Scanning for the HR Department 203
Determining Desired Effects of Environmental Factors 205
Activity 207

Chapter 7   The Human Resources Forecaster 209
What Does the HR Forecaster Do? 209
What Are Some Models of Forecasting? 210
What Are Some Reasons for Demand Forecasting? 215
Forecasting Methods 216
What Are Some Reasons for Supply Forecasting? 221
Supply Forecasting Methods 223
Forecasting External Labor Supply 226

Chapter 8   The Human Resources Planning Formulator 229
What Does the HR Planning Formulator Do? 229
Bringing It Together: Conceptual Models for Strategic Planning for HR 230
Four-Factor Condition/Criteria Analysis 231
Other Methods of Analysis 236
The Range of HR Grand Strategies 242
Weighing Strategic Alternatives 245
Selecting an HR Grand Strategy 253
Activities 255

Chapter 9   The Human Resources Integrator 267
What Does the HR Integrator Do? 267
Developing HR Objectives 269
Providing Leadership 271
Matching Rewards and Controls to HR Strategy 274
Devising HR Policies Consistent with Strategy 277
Coordinating HR Practice Areas 280
Matching Structure to Strategy, and Strategy to Structure 284
Activities 292

Chapter 10   Career Planning and Management 301
The Role of Career Planning and Management in Implementing
    HR Grand Strategy 301

Contents

The Traditional Approach to Career Planning 304
The Traditional Approach to Career Management 305
Problems with Traditional Approaches to Career Planning and
    Management 312
Strategic Career Planning 312
Strategic Career Management 323
Activities 328

Chapter 11 Recruitment and Selection 333
The Role of Recruitment and Selection in Implementing
    HR Grand Strategy 333
The Traditional Approach to Recruitment and Selection 335
Problems with the Traditional Approach to Recruitment and Selection 347
Strategic Recruitment and Selection 348

Chapter 12 Training 353
What Is Training? 353
The Role of Training in Implementing HR Grand Strategy 354
The Traditional Approach to Training 356
Problems with the Traditional Approach to Training 367
Strategic Training 368

Chapter 13 Organization Development 373
The Role of OD in Implementing HR Grand Strategy 374
The Traditional Approach to OD 379
Problems with the Traditional Approach to Organization Development 389
Strategic OD 389

Chapter 14 Job Redesign 393
What Is Job Redesign? 394
The Role of Job Redesign in Implementing HR Grand Strategy 394
Organization and Job Design 395
Traditional Approaches to Job Redesign 396
Problems with the Traditional Approach to Job Redesign 409
Strategic Job Redesign 409

Chapter 15 Employee Assistance Programs 415
The Role of Employee Assistance Programs (EAPs) in Implementing
    HR Grand Strategy 417
The Traditional Approach to EAPs 418
Problems with the Traditional Approach to EAPs 429
Strategic EAPs 429

Chapter 16 Labor Relations 435
    The Role of Labor Relations in Implementing HR Grand Strategy 437
    The Traditional Approach to Labor Relations Programs 438
    Problems with the Traditional Approach to Labor Relations 445
    Strategic Labor Relations 446

Chapter 17 Compensation and Benefits 451
    Key Terms in Compensation and Benefits 452
    The Role of Compensation/Benefits in Implementing
     HR Grand Strategy 453
    The Traditional Approach to Compensation/Benefit Programs 454
    Problems with the Traditional Approach to Compensation/
     Benefit Programs 464
    Strategic Compensation/Benefit Programs 466

Chapter 18 The Human Resources Planning Manager 477
    What Does the HR Planning Manager Do? 477
    How Is the HR Planning Manager's Role Carried Out? 478
    Establishing HR Department Goals and Objectives 478
    Creating Department Structure 480
    Staffing the HRP Department 484
    Issuing Orders 489
    Resolving Destructive Conflicts 490
    Communicating within and between Departments 492
    Planning for Needed Resources 495
    Dealing with Power and Politics 497
    Activities 503

Chapter 19 The Human Resources Planning Evaluator 507
    What Does the Human Resources Planning Evaluator Do? 507
    How is Evaluation Carried Out? 507
    Purposes of HR Evaluation 508
    Control Systems 513
    Criteria 518
    Carrying out the Evaluation Process 522
    Feeding Back the Results of Evaluation 525
    Activities 533

    References 539

    Index 551

LIST OF FIGURES

Figure 1   Strategic Planning for Human Resources Management:
              The Plan of the Book xx

Figure 1-1   Occupations with the Largest Job Growth, 1994–2005
              (*in thousands*). 8

Figure 1-2   Fastest Growing Industries (*in thousands*). 10

Figure 1-3   Change in Employment by Education and Training Category,
              1994–2005. 11

Figure 1-4   Major Laws and Cases Dealing with Human Rights. 13

Figure 1-5   The Aging U.S. Population 15

Figure 1-6   A Simplified Model of SPHR (Strategic Planning for
              Human Resources). 25

Figure 1-7   A Model of Variables Involved in Organizational Roles. 28

Figure 1-8   The Many Roles of the HR Planner 30

Figure 1-9   The Relationship between the Steps in a Simplified
              SPHR Model and the Roles of an HR Planner. 32

Figure 2-1   Strategic Four-Factor Diagram 45

Figure 3-1   Selecting the Appropriate Focus for Work Analysis 69

Figure 3-2   How to Conceptualize Differences in Perceptions
              about Work Activities, Using the Johari Window 70

Figure 3-3   Steps in the Traditional Work-Analysis Process 72

Figure 3-4   A Summary of Approaches to Work Analysis. 78

Figure 3-5   A Summary of General Data-Collection Methods for Job Analysis . . . 79

Figure 4-1   Selecting the Appropriate Focus for Workforce Analysis 107

Figure 4-2   Steps in Traditional Workforce Analysis 108

Figure 4-3   The Process of Converting a Job Description to a Person
              Specification 110

Figure 4-4   A Behaviorally Anchored Rating Scale for an Auditor 117

Figure 4-5   A Sample Employee Performance-Appraisal Form. 131

Figure 5-1   A Simplified Model of the HR Auditing Process 140

Figure 5-2   A Simple HR Audit Plan 149
Figure 5-3   Steps in Carrying Out a Document Review Using Content Analysis . 152
Figure 5-4   A Conceptual Model for Diagnosing HR Discrepancies 156
Figure 5-5   A Findings Sheet 159
Figure 5-6   A Summary of HR Department Strengths and Weaknesses 162
Figure 6-1   A Simplified Model of the Environmental Scanning Process 178
Figure 6-2   Identifying a Strategic Gap in HR 181
Figure 6-3   The Internal and External Environments. 183
Figure 6-4   Internal and External Factors Influencing the HR Subsystem 186
Figure 6-5   Linkage of Events in a Cross-Impact Analysis for Work Analysis 191
Figure 6-6   Advantages and Disadvantages of Data-Collection Methods for
              Future-Oriented Work Analysis 198
Figure 6-7   An Interview Guide for HR Department Scanning 204
Figure 6-8   Key Questions to Consider in Strategic Planning for HR. 206
Figure 7-1   A Simplified Model of the HR Forecasting Process 211
Figure 7-2   Methods of Forecasting Supply 224
Figure 8-1   A Simplified Model of the HR Formulation Process 231
Figure 8-2   Four-Factor Condition/Criteria Analysis: A Model 232
Figure 8-3   A BCG Growth/Share Matrix. 239
Figure 8-4   A Performance/Potential Matrix for Classifying Employees 240
Figure 8-5   A Summary of HR Grand Strategies 244
Figure 8-6   The Relationship between the Corporate Strategy and Human
              Resource Grand Strategy 249
Figure 9-1   A Simplified Model of the HR Integration Process 268
Figure 9-2   Objectives and Levels of HR Planning. 270
Figure 9-3   The Time Frames, Change-Orientation, and Focus of HR
              Practice Areas 281
Figure 9-4   A Functional Structure for the HR Department. 288
Figure 9-5   Divisional Structures for the HR Department: Some Alternatives . . . 290
Figure 10-1   The Four Environments Faced by Individuals in Career Planning
              and Management 315
Figure 10-2   A Summary of Career Strategies as They Relate to Different
              Environments. 319
Figure 10-3   A Sample Outline for a Career Planning Workshop 326
Figure 11-1   The Recruitment/Selection Process. 336
Figure 12-1   The Training Process. 357
Figure 12-2   The Role of Instructional Objectives 361
Figure 12-3   Training Delivery Methods and Strategies 365
Figure 13-1   Driving and Restraining Forces 377

Figure 13-2   Steps in Action Research in OD Interventions. 380

Figure 13-3   A Summary of OD Interventions 387

Figure 14-1   The Job Redesign Process 396

Figure 14-2   Components in a Simplified Model of Performance. 400

Figure 14-3   Job Enlargement: Add More of the Same Kind of Tasks. 403

Figure 14-4   Job Enrichment: Add More Tasks of a Higher Level 404

Figure 14-5   Work Flow Rearrangement: Rotate Tasks. 405

Figure 14-6   Steps in Strategic Job Redesign 412

Figure 15-1   The Employee Assistance Process 420

Figure 15-2   Pointers for Planning and Conducting a Counseling Interview
              with a Problem Employee 424

Figure 16-1   The Role of Interpretation in Contract Administration 443

Figure 17-1   The Compensation Process 455

Figure 17-2   Methods of Communicating about Compensation:
              Advantages and Disadvantages. 465

Figure 17-3   Steps in the Strategic Compensation Process. 467

Figure 17-4   Strategic Approaches to Job Evaluation 470

Figure 17-5   Forecasting Compensation/Benefit Trends. 472

Figure 17-6   Incentive Plans. 474

Figure 17-7   Types of Rewards. 476

Figure 18-1   The HRP Management Process 479

Figure 18-2   Steps in Implementing Management-by-Objectives in an
              HR Department 481

Figure 18-3   Goal and Value Differences 491

Figure 19-1   Steps in the HRP Evaluation Process. 508

Figure 19-2   Human Resources Planning Evaluation 510

Figure 19-3   Meetings Associated with Strategy. 525

Figure 19-4   The Strategy Hierarchy 527

Figure 19-5   The Evaluation Cycle in Strategic Human Resources Planning 532

LIST OF ACTIVITIES

Activity 1-1   Case Study 33
Activity 1-2   A Self-Diagnostic Survey of HRP Skills 34
Activity 2-1   Case Study 54
Activity 2-2   A Worksheet for Identifying the Purpose of Strategic Planning for
                Human Resources. 55
Activity 2-3   Case Study 56
Activity 2-4   A Self-Diagnostic Survey on Linking Strategic Business Planning
                to Strategic HR Planning 58
Activity 3-1   Work Analysis Role Play 91
Activity 3-2   An Interview Guide Form for Job Analysis 99
Activity 4-1   Conducting an Appraisal Interview 133
Activity 4-2   Case Study 135
Activity 5-1   Issues to Consider in a Stakeholder Analysis for an HR Audit 163
Activity 5-2   An Initial Diagnosis Worksheet for an HR Audit 165
Activity 5-3   An Interview Guide for Assessing the Strengths and Weaknesses
                of the HR Department 171
Activity 5-4   An Interview Form to Collect Information about Critical Incidents
                Pertinent to HR Department Strengths and Weaknesses. 172
Activity 5-5   Case Study 173
Activity 6-1   Future-Oriented Work Analysis 207
Activity 8-1   Worksheet for Summarizing, Using Four-Factor Condition/
                Criteria Analysis 255
Activity 8-2   A Worksheet For Four-Factor Condition/Criteria Analysis 257
Activity 8-3   A Worksheet Based on WOTS-Up Analysis 258
Activity 8-4   A Worksheet for Classifying Jobs, People, and the
                HR Department. 259
Activity 8-5   A Worksheet for Considering an HR Grand Strategy 260
Activity 8-6   A Worksheet for Evaluating an HR Grand Strategy. 262

Activity 8-7   Case Study 264
Activity 8-8   Case Study 265
Activity 9-1   A Worksheet for Developing HR Objectives 292
Activity 9-2   A Worksheet for Assessing Management Support for the
                 HR Grand Strategy 293
Activity 9-3   A Worksheet for Matching Rewards to the HR Grand
                 Strategy 294
Activity 9-4   A Worksheet for Assessing the Influence of a New Program
                 Initiative in One HR Practice Area on Other Areas 296
Activity 9-5   A Worksheet on HR Department Structure 297
Activity 9-6   Case Study 298
Activity 10-1   A Worksheet for Assessing Career Strengths and Weaknesses 328
Activity 10-2   A Worksheet for Scanning the Career Environment 329
Activity 10-3   A Worksheet for Identifying the Range of Career Strategies 330
Activity 10-4   A Worksheet for Implementing an Individual Career Strategy 331
Activity 10-5   A Checklist for Evaluating a Career Strategy 332
Activity 18-1   The HRP Department Structure 503
Activity 18-2   Reducing Resistance to Implementation of HR Plans and
                 Grand Strategy 505
Activity 19-1   Success Factors and HR Strategy 533
Activity 19-2   Evaluative Measures 534
Activity 19-3   An Interview Guide for the Evaluation of HR Practice Areas 535
Activity 19-4   Case Study 536

PREFACE

This book is intended for human resource (HR) practitioners, HR or personnel managers, specialists in HR planning, and students interested in this field. We saw a need for a book, designed for practitioners, that would go beyond traditional and heavily quantitative approaches to HR planning. This book is focused on HR as a tool for implementing organizational strategic plans. We define **strategic planning for human resources** (SPHR) as *the process of anticipating long-term HR supplies and demands relative to changing conditions inside and outside an organization, and then crafting HR programs and other initiatives designed to meet the organization's needs for knowledge capital.*

The broad goal of this book is to help practitioners improve their skills in strategic thinking and planning. Top managers want HR practitioners who anticipate problems, rather than merely react to them. Some authorities in the HR field believe that the future career success of practitioners will increasingly hinge on how skilled they are at strategic thinking and planning. Others note that firms that develop and implement workforce strategies consistently outperform their more short-term, crisis-driven competitors.

The approach we have taken is to (1) describe a simple but generalizable model of SPHR and (2) derive practitioner "roles" from each step in the SPHR model. Some readers might object that the model and the roles we describe are not found in practice. In part, at least, they are right. The reader seeking practitioners who bear job titles like "HR Scanner," "HR Policy Formulator," or "HR Organizational Coordinator" will not find them. Nor will it be easier to pinpoint specific organizations using all steps in the SPHR model.

However, individual pieces of the SPHR model we describe can no doubt be found in some organizations. Regardless of job titles, HR practitioners do try to:

1. Help link the long-term purpose, goals, and objectives of the HR function (department) and/or HR plans with organizational plans.
2. Examine what people are presently doing in their jobs in the organization.
3. Examine what kind of people are doing the work at present.
4. Analyze the HR department and/or HR practices in the organization to identify present strengths and weaknesses.
5. Identify future trends, the likely impact of those trends, and the desired impact of those trends.
6. Estimate numbers of people and jobs needed by an organization to achieve its objectives and realize its plans.
7. Compare present and future jobs, people, and HR department practice areas.
8. Implement HR Grand Strategy, a long-term direction for all HR efforts in the organization.
9. Lead the HR department, unit, or function.
10. Monitor whether HR Grand Strategy will work, is working, and has worked.

Each activity we link to a role or function of the HR Planner, defined here as one who is involved in the SPHR process.

The chapters of this book are sequenced to lead the reader through steps in SPHR:

1. Chapter 1 provides background information about strategic business planning, explains the need for SPHR, and describes roles of the HR practitioner in a strategic context.

2.   Chapters 2 through 9 and 18 through 19 focus on how HR practitioners enact their roles, and how they and their organizations can carry out the steps in the SPHR model.

3.   Chapters 10 through 17 treat HR "practice areas" of career planning, career management, recruitment and selection, training, and organization development as ways to implement an HR Grand Strategy (see Figure 1 for a depiction of the plan of this book).

We have attempted to make the content of this book as practical and concrete as possible. We provide many case studies and exercises for readers to use in practicing, discussing, and carrying out the SPHR process. The result, we hope, is a book that will at once be useful to HR practitioners and to college students enrolled in courses in HR planning, management, and development.

Acknowledgments

Few books are the work of a single author. This book is no exception to that rule. The authors would like to acknowledge the assistance of many individuals and institutions who have given freely of their time and information during the preparation of the manuscript. The authors also extend their sincere appreciation to Hong Lin and to Yu Zhanghai for their assistance with this book.

Finally, the authors would like to acknowledge the understanding and support of their family members, who have stood firm in their commitment to see their work completed. We want to thank our spouses, Marcelina Rothwell and Nuria Kazanas, particularly because they sacrificed their time with us as we devoted our attentions to this book.

William J. Rothwell, Ph.D.
State College, Pennsylvania

H. C. Kazanas, Ph.D.
Naples, Florida

Figure 1: Strategic Planning for Human Resources Management: The Plan of the Book

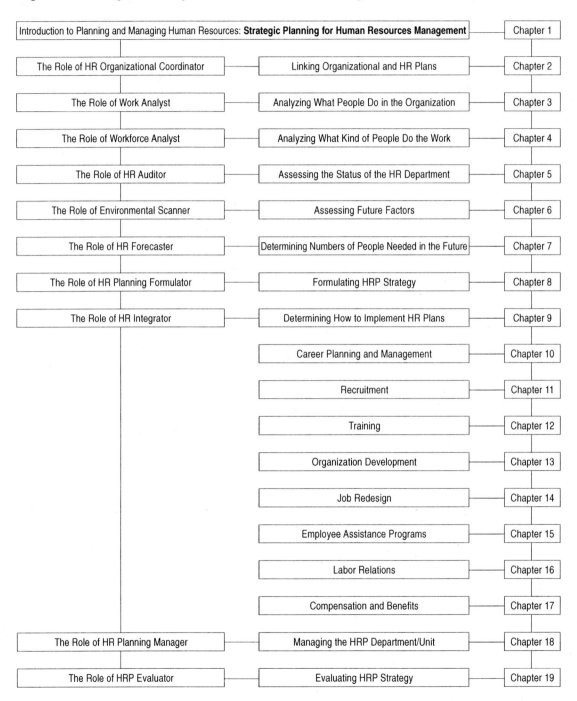

Introduction to PLANNING AND MANAGING HUMAN RESOURCES: STRATEGIC PLANNING FOR HUMAN RESOURCES MANAGEMENT

Practitioners and academicians are devoting increasing attention to strategic planning for human resources.* (See, for instance, Becker and Huselid, 1999; Brockbank, 1999; Fields, Chan, and Akhtar, 2000; Gratton et al., 1999; Chew and Chong, 1999; Wagner, 1999.) Some contemporary observers of the business scene attribute this stepped-up interest to a desire by HR professionals to become more involved in strategic business planning (SBP) as a way of increasing their own importance. At the same time, however, top managers often say they want proactive HR professionals who can participate meaningfully in strategic business planning and who can play a strategic leadership role in helping their organizations attract, retain, and develop the intellectual capital and human talent that is increasingly important to business success in a fiercely competitive global marketplace (Rothwell, Prescott, and Taylor, 1998). While other resources can be acquired easily, it is human talent that has emerged as the most difficult to acquire, yet it is key to competitive success and is the energy that founds new businesses, invents new products, discovers new markets, and serves customers.

---

* We shall use the terms *SPHR, HRP,* and *HR* planning synonymously throughout the text. We recognize that not everyone will agree that they are—or should be—the same.

What is **strategic planning for human resources** (SPHR)? How did human resources planning (HRP) evolve? What is strategy? Why is SPHR needed? What makes SPHR difficult in organizations? How can the SPHR process be described? How is this book structured? This chapter addresses these questions and thereby introduces the book.

What Is Strategic Planning for Human Resources (SPHR)?

There is no single definition of human resources planning (HRP) with which everyone agrees. Many definitions and models of HRP exist. Many HRP practitioners* prefer to focus on the *technical side*—that is, the mathematical and behavioral methods of forecasting HR needs. Others prefer the *managerial side*—that is, the way decision-makers tackle human resource issues affecting an organization. Still others distinguish between *strategic HRP,* undertaken to formulate and/or implement an organization's long-range plans, and *operational HRP,* undertaken to guide daily HR decisions. To complicate matters even more, some HR practitioners distinguish between *HRP for an organization,* which focuses on planning solely to meet organizational demands, and *HRP for individuals,* which focuses on the implications of such plans for individual career planning.

Despite these differences, most HR practitioners would probably agree that Human Resources Planning focuses on analyzing an organization's HR needs as the organization's conditions change, and then supplying strategies to help respond proactively to those changes over time. HRP helps ensure that the right numbers of the right kinds of people are available at the right times and in the right places to translate organizational plans into reality. This process becomes *strategic* when some attempt is made to *anticipate* long-term HR "supplies and demands" relative to changing conditions facing the organization, and then to use HR department programs in an effort to meet these identified HR needs. There is good reason to pay attention to this issue: organizations that manage HR strategically tend to outperform competitors who do not do so (Lam and White, 1998).

---

* We shall use the terms *personnel practitioner, HR planner,* and *HRP practitioner* synonymously throughout this book.

How Did Human Resources Planning (HRP) Evolve?

In the early days of industrialization, managers rarely had to think ahead about the numbers and kinds of people required to get the work out: Conditions outside organizations were relatively stable. Most work demanded little by way of specialized training and expertise. And managers could find all the people they needed on short notice, provided they were willing to pay competitive wages.

However, there must have been some HR planning going on, even in earliest times. It is hard to imagine that the builders of the Great Pyramids or of Stonehenge completely disregarded planning those superhuman exertions that were required to erect these monuments of antiquity over many generations. Yet records from that time do not exist to reveal how managers planned for their human resources.

The origin of *manpower planning,* the predecessor of modern HR planning, predates the beginnings of twentieth-century management theory. Among the first to raise the manpower-planning issue was the Frenchman Henri Fayol (1841–1925). His famous fourteen points of management are still considered valid today. One point had to do with what Fayol called *stability of tenure of personnel.* For Fayol, administrators bear responsibility to plan for human resources, ensuring that "human and material organization is consistent with the objectives, resources, and requirements of the business concern" (Fayol, 1930, p. 53). This point resembles some modern definitions of HRP.

A deep recession in the late 1950s sparkled the need for a new way of thinking about management. People were increasingly viewed as assets—*human resources*—that could be either developed or wasted. This way of thinking became even more pronounced during the 1960s and 1970s, when the focus was on finding ways to design organizations and jobs to permit individuals greater latitudes of self-expression. Human creativity and job satisfaction are still two of the most important concerns of management.

The 1960s also spawned the term *manpower planning.* Initial manpower planning efforts were typically tied to annual budgeting, as is still the case in some organizations. The implication was that people are expense items, since wages, salaries, and employee benefits constitute a major cost of doing business. Early planners were more often found in planning and budgeting departments than in personnel or HR departments, but they did manage to devote some attention to forecasting manpower demands. However, it was a need to budget, not a desire to stimulate creativity or increase productivity, that spurred them.

As the Human Resources school of management thought grew in importance throughout the 1970s, manpower planning activities gradually shifted to personnel departments. At the same time, the term *human resources planning* supplanted *manpower planning*. Likewise, personnel departments were renamed *human resource departments,* reflecting a new and more pronounced emphasis on the *human* side of the enterprise.

Human resource practitioners and other contemporary observers of the management scene have expressed a growing awareness ever since the 1990s that people represent a key asset in competitiveness. While Western nations have long placed enormous faith in the power of technology to enhance productivity, the fact is that the greatest competitive gains stem from the exercise of human creativity to identify new products and services, find new markets and applications for existing products and services, and make use of the possible gains to be realized from technology. Without the creative application of human knowledge and skill, organizations would not be formed and would not thrive for long. Human beings thus represent intellectual capital to be managed, just like other forms of capital (Brown, 1998).

What Do We Mean by *Strategy*?

The new way of thinking about people and people planning that took place in the 1960s and 1970s coincided with a new way of thinking about the role of top managers and the nature of long-range organizational planning.

Organizations before 1980 tended to operate in relatively stable external environments. Most of them offered a single service or product line to a clearcut group of customers in a geographically limited sphere of operations. Planning for changes in the external environment was less important then than coordinating such *internal functions* as finance, marketing, operations/production, and personnel. Top managers therefore devoted most of their time to *policy making,* an activity intended to ensure coordination inside an organization. Long-range planning, to the extent that it was carried out at all, was based on the assumption that the future would resemble or even represent a mere continuation of the present or past.

In the early 1950s, organizations began to diversify into new businesses, expanding their range of products and services. They served increasingly diverse customers and increased the geographical scope of their operations into other countries and cultures. It soon became apparent that policies suited for a single-product organization were not necessarily well-suited to a diversified corporation that operated simultaneously in different industries, faced a range of contrasting environmental factors, dealt with diverse and more demanding customers, and handled multiple product lines. Nor were policies appropriate to firms limited to domestic U.S. operations necessarily appropriate to a company operating in several nations with varying laws, social customs, and economic climates. Simple policy-making proved inadequate for coordinating functions and activities across a corporate portfolio of businesses. Long-range planning based on an assumption of environmental stability likewise proved inadequate for dealing with an increasingly dynamic external environment where the uncertain future was often nothing like the present or past. At this point, strategic business planning emerged as a way of coping with increasing environmental and organizational complexity. Top managers discarded older notions of planning and policy-making in favor of a strategic view.

The word *strategy* means "general" in Greek and, in a military sense, is linked to the planning of battles and military campaigns. It differs from *tactics,* which refers to more limited planning to achieve immediate objectives. Though people continue to argue about the meaning of "strategy" in a business setting, most would probably agree that it has to do with long-term, large-scale plans for future-oriented, competitive success. Strategic issues are mostly the concern of top managers. These issues involve allocation of organizational resources. They exert significant influence on the organization's success or survival; they focus on anticipating the future; and they require consideration of the world outside one organization's boundaries.

In large corporations consisting of multiple businesses under one corporate umbrella, strategy often exists on at least three levels: (1) *corporate,* involving the entire organization; (2) *business,* involving a single enterprise in the corporation; and (3) *functional,* involving managers of different products, geographical areas, or activities (such as finance and HR). *Corporate strategy* is the responsibility of the highest-level decision-maker in the corporation. *Business strategy* is the concern of the chief executive in one part of the organization. (A single business is sometimes called a *strategic business unit* [SBU] to reflect its relative autonomy.) *Functional strategy* is the concern of the highest-level decision-maker in one business segment.

Some studies have shown that organizations with formal strategic business planning processes outperform those without them, depending on the type of environment confronting the organization (Brew, 1999). Yet true comprehensive planning remains more elusive than the management literature leads people to believe. Where it does exist, expert observers give it only mixed reviews for quality. One reason is that not enough attention is paid to long-term HR planning issues, since too many managers still operate under the mindset that people are a commodity that can be used and discarded. Another reason there is not more comprehensive planning is that as business conditions become even more dynamic and fast-paced, it is often necessary to rethink the role of strategic planning, from preparing plans to encouraging managers to think strategically better in real time (Mintzberg, 1994).

Why Is Strategic Planning for Human Resources Needed?

The same environmental uncertainties that originally led to the evolution of comprehensive strategic business planning have also made strategic planning for human resources an increasing necessity. Changes in economic, technological, geographic, demographic, governmental, and social conditions necessitate a way to anticipate long-range HR and talent needs, instead of merely reacting to short-term needs to replace workers.

Economic Conditions

The U.S. economy has a direct and obvious influence on employment and on the HR needs of organizations. Cyclical economic downturns have touched off waves of layoffs and firings as businesses cut back on employment levels to save money on salaries when production demands declined. On the other hand, cyclical economic upturns produce massive callbacks and hirings as businesses gear up for higher production levels.

The problem with relying on those historic patterns is that few workers want to remain unemployed for long. Laid-off workers look for new jobs, and some become discouraged and give up—or else start their own businesses, sparked by a distinct disdain for large, impersonal companies. As business conditions improve, companies must recruit and orient new workers who are not as qualified or skilled as those who were given early retirement, an early out, a buyout, or a layoff. The additional costs of recruitment and orientation are usually ignored or overlooked, though, because they rarely show up directly (though lower productivity of inexperienced workers often does).

Cutting back on people in economic downturns and hiring frenzies when the economy kicks up does bring short-term cost savings to organizations. When most people work in blue-collar, unskilled, or semi-skilled jobs, the costs associated with recruiting, selecting, and orienting people are simply not that great; employers can sometimes get away with viewing people as expendable machine parts that can be easily replaced.

Today, such short-sightedness no longer works. There are several reasons why: (1) fewer people are willing to work as unskilled labor; (2) human factors like creativity are becoming more important, as organizations struggle to out-produce cheaper foreign labor; and (3) the U.S. economy has become more service- and knowledge-oriented, and thus more labor-intensive.

The U.S. economy is changing dramatically: Just look at the occupations with the largest expected job growth (see Figure 1-1), the fastest growing industries (see Figure 1-2), and the projected changes in employment by education and training category (see Figure 1-3).

Figure 1-1: Occupations with the Largest Job Growth, 1994–2005 (*in thousands*)

Occupation	Employment Change, 1994–2005 (projected)			
	1994	by 2005 (projected)	Numerical	Percent
Cashiers	3,005	3,567	562	19%
Janitors and cleaners, including maids and housekeeping staff	3,043	3,602	559	18%
Salespersons, retail	3,842	4,374	532	14%
Waiters and waitresses	1,847	2,326	479	26%
Registered nurses	1,906	2,379	473	25%
General managers and top executives	3,046	3,512	466	15%
Systems analysts	483	928	445	92%
Home health aides	420	848	428	102%
Guards (security)	867	1,282	415	48%
Nursing aides, orderlies, and attendants	1,265	1,652	387	31%
Teachers, secondary	1,340	1,726	386	29%
Marketing and sales worker supervisors	2,293	2,673	380	17%
Teacher aides and educational associates	932	1,296	364	39%
Receptionists and information clerks	1,019	1,337	318	31%
Truck drivers, light and heavy	2,565	2,837	271	11%
Secretaries, except legal and medical	2,842	3,109	267	9%
Clerical supervisors and managers	1,340	1,600	261	19%
Child care workers	757	1,005	248	33%
Maintenance repairers, general utility	1,273	1,505	231	18%
Teachers, elementary	1,419	1,639	220	16%
Personal and home health care aides	179	391	212	119%
Teachers, special education	388	593	206	53%
Nurses, licensed practical	702	899	197	28%
Food service and lodging managers	579	771	192	33%

Figure 1-1: *(continued)*

Food preparation workers	1,109	1,378	187	16%
Social workers	557	744	187	34%
Lawyers	658	839	183	28%
Financial managers	768	950	182	24%
Computer engineers	195	372	177	90%
Hand packers and packagers	942	1,102	160	17%

Source: Bureau of Labor Statistics (BLS) 1995f. *Occupations with the Largest Job Growth, 1994–2005.* Unpublished work. Presented at http://stats.bls.gov/emptb2.htm. Washington, D.C.: U.S. Department of Labor.

Technological Conditions

Americans place great faith in technology to increase productivity. The trouble is that technological change tends to change people's needs. It heralds skill obsolescence for some people and new opportunities for others.

According to one authority ("Technology influences training needs," 1996, *http://www.shrm.org/issues/0596b.htm*):

> At the same time they make communications easier, technological advances create new employee training needs that will have to be met by human resource professionals. As telecommuting continues to grow, for example, training programs to facilitate the transition from "management by sight" to "management by product" will become increasingly important. Employees will look for assistance in setting up home offices, mastering the technology that enables them to telecommute, adjusting to a new work location, managing their productivity, and balancing work/life issues while working at home. Managers will need help learning to measure employee performance in terms of product rather than attendance.

Technology thus creates new problems even as it solves old ones. It will necessitate additional (and nearly continuous) training, new management working styles, and special skills among technology users (Rothwell, 1999b).

Figure 1-2: Fastest-Growing Industries (*in thousands*)

Industry	Employment Change, 1994–2005 (projected)			
	1994	2005	Numerical	Projected Annual Increase
Health services	1,032	1,900	868	5.7%
Residential care	602	1,100	498	5.6%
Computer and data-processing services	950	1,610	660	4.9%
Individual and miscellaneous social services	779	1,314	535	4.9%
Miscellaneous business services	1,741	2,932	1,191	4.9%
Personnel supply services	2,254	3,564	1,310	4.3%
Child daycare services	502	800	298	4.3%
Services to buildings	854	1,350	496	4.2%
Miscellaneous equipment rental and leasing	216	325	109	3.8%
Management and public relations	716	1,049	333	3.5%
Nursing and personal care facilities	1,649	2,400	751	3.5%
Amusement and recreation services	1,005	1,434	429	3.3%
Job training and related services	298	425	127	3.3%
Museums and botanical and zoological gardens	79	112	33	3.2%
Water and sanitation	213	300	87	3.2%
Automobile parking, repair, and services	796	1,118	322	3.1%
Personal services	225	314	89	3.1%
Miscellaneous transportation services	195	270	75	3.0%
Offices of health practitioners	2,545	3,500	955	2.9%
Legal services	927	1,270	343	2.9%

Source: Bureau of Labor Statistics (BLS). 1995d. *Fastest Growing Industries.* Unpublished work. Presented at http://stats.bls.gov/emtab-4.htm. Washington, D.C.: U.S. Department of Labor.

Figure 1-3: Change in Employment by Education and Training Category, 1994–2005

Description: This exhibit presents the projected change in employment by education and training category, 1994–2005 *(numbers in thousands)*

Education Category	1994		2005		Projected Change, 1994–2005		Job Openings Due to Growth and Net Replacement, 1994–2005	
	Number	Percent	Number	Percent	Number	Percent	Number	Percent
Total	127,014	100.0	144,708	100.0	17,693	100.0	49,631	100.0%
First professional degree	1,702	1.3	2,076	1.4	374	22.0	657	1.3%
Doctorate degree	976	.8	1,156	.8	180	18.4	467	.9%
Master's degree	1,500	1.2	1,927	1.3	427	28.5	658	1.3%
Work experience, plus a bachelor's or higher degree	8,191	6.5	9,494	6.6	1,303	15.9	3,062	6.2%
Bachelor's degree	14,007	11.0	17,771	12.3	3,764	26.9	6,684	13.5%
Associate degree	3,956	3.1	4,919	3.4	963	24.3	1,594	3.2%
Post-secondary vocational training	7,102	5.6	7,845	5.4	743	10.5	2,378	4.8%
Work experience	9,994	7.9	11,325	7.8	1,331	13.3	3,554	7.2%
Long-term on-the-job training	13,672	10.8	14,904	10.3	1,229	9.0	4,754	9.6%
Moderate-term on-the-job training	16,219	12.8	17,083	11.8	864	5.3	5,670	11.4%
Short-term on-the-job training	49,695	39.1	56,208	38.8	6,513	13.1	20,152	40.6%

Source: Bureau of Labor Statistics (BLS). 1995c. *Change in Employment by Education and Training Category, 1994–2005.* Unpublished work. Presented at http://stats.bls.gov/emptab08.htm. Washington, D.C.: U.S. Department of Labor.

Government/Legal Conditions

Government exerts a pervasive influence on employment. Each year it seems that this influence becomes greater, as: (1) laws are passed at the federal, state, and local levels; (2) courts hand down rulings with obvious implications for employers; (3) executive orders are written at the federal and state levels; and (4) regulations affecting employment are established by such agencies or quasi-judicial bodies as the National Labor Relations Board, the Equal Employment Opportunity Commission, the Office of Federal Contract Compliance, the Occupational Health and Safety Administration, and their counterparts at the state, county, and city levels. The tendency of the Federal government in recent years has been to increase its mandates governing employers and employment. Notable examples include enactment of the Americans with Disabilities Act and the Family Medical Leave Act, and the issuance of workplace regulations affecting immigration reform, workplace safety, and ergonomics.

Governmental influence in employment is pervasive, but three areas are of prime importance to HR planners: (1) equal employment and affirmative action, (2) labor laws and regulations, and (3) employment-at-will. In order for organizations to comply with the law, they will have to start doing human resources planning: HR plans help coordinate the entire HR function of an organization. They also ensure that such activities as hiring, training, and performance appraisal are carried out in compliance with laws and other governmental requirements, as well as with business requirements.

Equal employment opportunity (EEO) refers to activities intended to accord protection to people in special groups specified by law, regulation, court decision, or executive order. Figure 1-4 summarizes a few sources of legal protection. Managers and employers are obligated to avoid *disparate treatment* (meaning unequal and unjustified treatment) or *disparate impact* (meaning the application of otherwise neutral employment practices that, in fact, lead to discriminatory results) on members of protected groups. The appreciation of diversity must thus be considered in HR planning for legal reasons. Additionally, employers face public relations problems even if it looks as if they are discriminating. Such public perceptions can adversely impact the organization's ability to attract, retain, and develop promising, diverse talent who have the skills needed to help the organization compete.

Affirmative action programs are related to equal employment efforts. They set forth specific goals for hiring, training, compensating, and promoting members of protected groups. They help ensure that discrimination does not occur, building in goals to guide and control other HR planning efforts.

Labor laws exist to protect rights of employees to unionize and bargain collectively. They are important because the advent of unionization in an organization requires new HR strategies. Labor laws can affect hiring, firing, promoting, and compensating workers. *Employment-at-will* is the legal principle that employ-

Figure 1-4: Major Laws and Cases Dealing with Human Rights

Law/Case	Summary of Provisions
Equal Pay Act (1963)	I For employers dealing with interstate commerce I Prohibits pay discrimination based solely on the sex of the employee
Civil Rights Act (1964) [Amended 1972] (Title VII of Act is most relevant to employers)	I For employers with more than 15 employees; labor unions; employment agencies I For employers with more than 15 employees; labor unions; Outlaws discrimination on basis of color, religion, sex, race, or national origin in most employment practices
Age Discrimination in Employment Act (1967)	I For employers with more than 20 employees; unions numbering more than 25 in membership; employment agencies I Forbids discrimination on basis of age for those between age 40 and 65
Griggs vs. Duke Power Co. (1971)	I Focuses on the impact (results) of employment practices I Forbids employment practices that exclude minorities unless "business necessity" can be shown I Employer has burden of proof to show "business necessity" I Employment tests must be based on job requirements
Vocational Rehabilitation Act of 1973 (Sec. 504)	I Covers federal contractors with contracts exceeding $2,500 I Prohibits discrimination against the handicapped
Vietnam Era Veterans Readjustment Act (1974)	I Covers federal contractors with contracts exceeding $10,000 I Prohibits discrimination against Vietnam veterans
Albemarle Paper Co. vs. Moody (1975)	I Employment tests must be validated for all jobs for which they are used I Personnel actions must be nondiscriminatory, both in result and in intent
Washington vs. Davis (1976)	I Court favored measures of training as standards in validation studies
Weber vs. Kaiser Aluminum (1976)	I Preferential hiring of minorities may be defended when the purpose is to rectify evidence of past discrimination

ers have the ability to discharge employees for any reason, a bad reason, or no reason. The first restriction of this principle occurred in 1935 with passage of the Wagner Act. It limited termination stemming from union activity. More recently, courts have restricted the principle further by ruling in favor of discharged workers when the cause resulted from violations of public policy (such as firing a worker who refuses to steal when ordered to do so by a supervisor) or when employee handbooks implied a contractual arrangement between employer and employees.

Increasingly, judges are acting on the basis that employees have "property rights" in their jobs. As a result, it is becoming more difficult to discharge people. HR planners need to consider this issue, and indeed they are: many are using so-called alternative employment arrangements in which an organization's staffing needs are met by some combination of full-time workers, part-time workers, contingent workers, consultants, outsourced work, telecommuted work, and a host of other options.

Demographic Conditions

Changing conditions in the U.S. population generally and in the labor force specifically will pose special problems for managers and HR planners in the future. Four trends are perhaps especially important. These are (1) more older workers, (2) more immigrants, (3) more women at work, and (4) more contingent, temporary, and part-time workers.

Of particular importance to HR planning is the aging U.S. population, which is creating a quiet crisis in leadership succession in many organizations (Rothwell, 2000b). The statistics tell the story:

> Fifteen years from now, the first of the Baby Boomers will turn 65. By 2025, after most of the Baby Boomers have surpassed the 65 year mark, 62.2 million Americans will be classified as senior citizens, up from 33.6 million in 1995 and a projected 40 million in 2005. The aging of this generation, combined with several other emerging trends, will have serious consequences for employers. Such an influx would profoundly affect

workforce planning, employee benefits, compensation, and litigation (Aging 1996).

Figure 1-5 depicts the aging population characteristics of the U.S. workforce over time.

Figure 1-5: The Aging U.S. Population

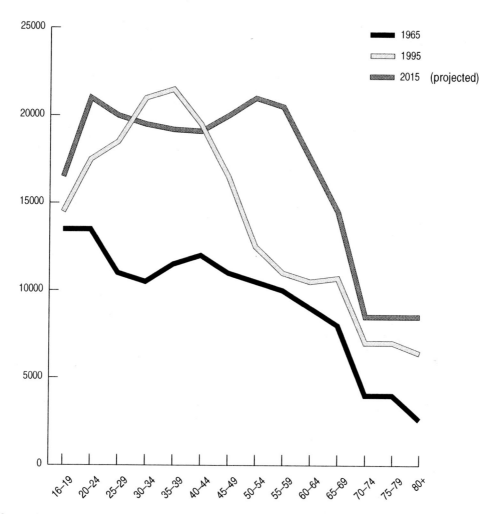

Source: Poulos, S., and Nightingale, D. The Aging Baby Boom: Implications for Training Programs. Washington, D.C.: The Urban Institute. Prepared under contract for the U.S. government.

Immigrants have been a traditional source of labor during times of labor or skills shortage, and this will continue. Despite increasingly restrictive immigration policies in recent years, the United States has experienced nearly a 40 percent increase in work-related immigration since 1996. "The number of persons who immigrated for job-related reasons increased from slightly more than 85,000 in 1995 to nearly 117,500 in 1996" (Leonard, 1997, p. 10). As noted in Rothwell (1999), this trend will have important implications for employers:

A continuing influx of immigrants into the United States has several implications for employers. First, employers will continue to be a major focus of government efforts to regulate immigration. Since increased earnings is a primary reason for immigration, the U.S. government will continue to view employers as an excellent point of contact for monitoring, regulating, and restricting immigration. Second, employers are likely to find the continuing debate about English-only rules to intensify. (An *English-only rule* is a work policy prohibiting workers from speaking in languages other than English while in the workplace.) And yet increasing pressures to meet global competitive challenges will make multilingualism a prized skill among future U.S. workers.

Indeed, the contributions of immigrants, including ethnic populations heretofore unrepresented in the U.S. workforce, are considerable. The complicated issues related to such diversity must be addressed by individual organizations as they arise. Communication in the workplace is among those critical issues.

More women will work in the U.S. labor force. The U.S. Bureau of Labor Statistics predicted that between 1994 and 2005, women would represent a slightly greater portion of the labor force in 2005 than in 1994—increasing from 46 to 48 percent. Female participation in the labor force is actually outstripping male participation. That will likely increase pressures to address perceived gender-gap compensation practices and address work/life balance programs, among other challenges (Whelan-Berry and Gordon, 2000).

Finally, employers are relying increasingly on *contingent workers,* understood to mean individuals who work full- or part-time for an employer and/or "on call" but who do not consider themselves to have an implicit or explicit long-term contractual relationship with one employer. Contingent workers are also not typified by a certain level as they once were when they used to be associated with "day laborers," "unskilled workers," or "blue-collar laborers." Today's contingent worker can be a professional, a manager, or a technical worker—or even a CEO hired by the hour, day, week, or month. In 1995, between 2.2 and 4.9 percent of all workers in the U.S. were positioned in what could be classified as contingent work. An additional 8.3 million workers (6.7 percent) called themselves "independent contractors," 2.0 million (1.7 percent) worked on call, 1.2 million (1.0 percent) worked for temporary-help agencies, and 652,000 (0.5 percent) worked for contract firms that provided the worker's services to one customer at that customer's worksite. In short, as much as 14.8 percent of the entire U.S. workforce was then contingent (Bureau of Labor Statistics, 1995).

Contingent workers pose a special challenge to organizations. While the cost of their benefits is lower to the organization—a major attraction for using such workers—they also have less loyalty than other workers. At the same time, decision-makers are more reluctant to invest money in the training and development of contingent workers, who might be "here today and gone tomorrow."

Geographic Conditions

HR planners are well advised to consider two key issues having to do with geography over the next ten years. The first key issue is the population shift occurring within the United States. As the year 2000 census revealed,

> The U.S. population increased by 13.2 percent between the 1990 and year 2000 census. The population is 281.4 million in 2000. But the growth was not uniform across all States: the South grew by 14.8 million; the West grew by 10.4 million; the Northeast grew by 2.8 million; and the Midwest grew by 4.7 million. (U.S. Population Soars 2000)

While most journalists focus on the political implications of this population shift, it also has important implications for HR planners: Finding and keeping labor in slow-growth states will be more difficult than it is in high-growth locales such as Nevada or Florida.

The second key issue has to do with the transfer of jobs outside the United States. It is a result of cheaper and more plentiful unskilled labor in developing nations. Indeed, the economic growth over the next decade will chiefly occur outside of the United States and Europe as growth booms continue in China, the Pacific Rim, and much of South America. U.S. corporations have already started shifting resources to these non-U.S. markets (Globalization 1996).

To cope with these trends, HR planners must take more time assessing labor availability in areas surrounding their facilities, wherever those facilities are located. Telecommuting capabilities will allow U.S. employers to take advantage of skilled labor in countries where wage rates are lower. Improved videoconferencing technology permits employers positioned in developing economies to tap the skills of those in the developed economies whenever the need arises.

Employers moving outside the United States will find cheaper unskilled labor, though skilled talent will no doubt be much harder to come by. Those moving to the American sunbelt will find more plentiful employment supplies, but also gradually increasing costs as taxes and wages slowly rise due to competition.

Of special note is this geographically related issue:

A key concern for human resource professionals operating in this global economic environment will be the shortage of global managers. During the next decade, the need for global managers will grow more acute, and according to several recent studies, multinational companies may not have enough managers with international experience to meet their needs in the coming years. In one survey of 1,000 CEOs in thirty countries, less than half of the respondents said they have successfully filled their international management positions. In another survey, one-third of the 440 European executives who responded said it was difficult to find global managers with sufficient international experience. More than 70% said they expect the problem to persist in the future (Globalization 1996).

To cope with this trend, organizations will need to devote more attention to *localization,* the process of raising the skills of local managers to international standards through intensive (and sometimes accelerated) leadership development efforts.

Social Conditions

Two social trends are likely to pose special challenges for HR planners over the next twenty years. They include (1) significant underemployment of the college-educated, and (2) the decline of the traditional family. The first trend poses a special problem: With the increased supply of well-educated contenders for a constant or decreasing number of spaces in middle and upper echelons of U.S. organizations, career advancement is no longer a matter of which path to take: There is more competition as early retirees choose to pursue second careers to supplement their retirement incomes. That will place them in competition with younger workers, if only on a part-time basis. The increasing number of retirees might reduce some of this pressure, however.

The decline of the traditional family has quite different implications, though by no means better ones. Good interpersonal skills, crucial to the top manager's role, are likely to be harder to find because fewer people will have experienced sustained, intimate relationships in which to develop them. Effective human relations skills were never the strong suit of individualistic and frequently authoritarian American managers and they will become more rare, just when we need "high touch" workplaces to offset "high tech."

These trends—economic, technological, governmental, demographic, geographic, and social—solidify our argument for long-term HR planning. It is an increasing necessity: Only by planning for talent can decision-makers anticipate threats and opportunities in the labor force affecting the ability of their organizations to attract, retain, and develop the numbers and kinds of people needed for success or even survival.

What Makes Strategic Planning Difficult in Organizations?

Most everyone in the HR field understands the importance of making HR more future-oriented and giving HRP practitioners an expanded role in formulating organizational strategy. After all, organizations are composed of people! To be truly effective, plans must take into account the present abilities and future capabilities of people. Leadership—a human factor—is of key importance in strategy formulation and implementation. At the same time, business plans imply human skills that have to be developed in present employees or sought outside the company. SPHR simply makes good business sense, but it must be both continuous and consistent (Baron and Kreps, 1999; Leibman, Bruer, and Maki, 1996).

Convincing others to accept SPHR will not be easy, however.

Top managers do not necessarily perceive a need for it. This poses a chicken-or-the-egg problem: Which should come first, financial support, or a program deserving of it? An SPHR effort is unlikely to get off the ground until it receives organizational support.

There are several ways to address this problem. First, HRP practitioners can champion the idea: They can talk about it. They can give those who will lend half-an-ear an ear full, and they can educate superiors on what SPHR is and how it will help them meet *their* needs and deal with *their* problems. Second, they can pounce on problems stemming from short-sighted HR thinking: When a key executive leaves, for example, there is usually much scrambling about to find a replacement (Rothwell, 2000b). An event like that opens a "window of opportunity" because decision-makers will be especially receptive to solutions that might keep this problem from re-occurring. Third, HR practitioners can include information about SPHR in training programs: If the company offers organized in-house training, incorporate SPHR, too. By doing this, practitioners build grassroots support for SPHR from people outside the HR department or HRP unit. Fourth and finally, HR practitioners can analyze the objections of those who oppose SPHR. What accounts for their opposition? Can their fears be laid to rest? Can sore points be negotiated?

It is especially important to prepare an action plan for an SPHR program while these efforts are under way. There will certainly be later modifications of the program, as decision-makers gain understanding of it and experience with it. A concrete description of a course of action—any course of action—will give decision-makers something tangible to react to at the point when someone expresses interest. On the other hand, nothing is more potentially devastating to the credibility of HRP practitioners than a response like this: "We need more time *to study* the issue." Be ready with a concrete proposal when someone asks for it. It will expedite action.

A second barrier to the acceptance of SPHR is that HRP practitioners are sometimes perceived to be "HR experts" and not "experts in the *business*." Historically, the personnel function had its origins in record keeping. With the advent of social legislation aimed at protecting certain groups, HRP practitioners became more adept at dealing with employment laws, and gained higher visibility. They mastered a technical specialty area—the HR craft—often to the exclusion of mastery in the business itself. Professional values and organizational requirements came into conflict.

HRP practitioners must be given a credible role in strategy formulation, but this will only happen if the organization believes they are competent in the business of the company. It is much easier to recognize this need than to meet it. In too many cases, HR professionals are accorded junior, not senior, executive status, and are thus ineligible to participate in strategic planning.

There is no simple solution to a credibility problem. One approach is to take the initiative: identify the needs of major stakeholders, and then work deliberately to meet those needs. One highly visible success is worth a dozen quiet efforts, so it is best to pick a thorny problem and tackle it. In time, HR practitioners can then gain the credibility necessary to be included in the ranks of senior decision-makers.

A third barrier to the acceptance of SPHR is that HR information is sometimes incompatible with other information used in strategy formulation. Strategic planning efforts have long been oriented toward financial or market forecasting, often to the exclusion of other information.

To demonstrate the value of SPHR, develop financial measurement methods for it. Some approaches include doing human-asset accounting and portfolio analysis of HR assets. The best approach is probably to negotiate measurements for HR with other decision-makers in the organization. In this way, they will be most likely to accept them.

A fourth barrier to the acceptance of SPHR are the conflicts that arise between short-term and long-term HR needs. Many managers continue to function as though any HR need can be met immediately because all skills are available in the external labor market as long as salaries and wages are competitive. They fail to recognize that by approaching hiring or promotion decisions on the basis of short-term requirements alone, they neglect long-term issues. It is this kind of thinking that was so effectively criticized in the classic *Peter Principle* (Peter and Hull, 1969): People tend to rise to their level of incompetence because superiors mistakenly assume that successful performance at one job indicates potential success for the next higher-level job.

For example, Harry Jones was a very good accountant. He had been with his employer for many years. On the basis of his seniority, technical competence, and obvious loyalty, he was promoted to chief accountant in charge of a staff of ten.

Harry turned out to be a disappointment. A technical whiz, he wanted to do all the work himself. He spent so much time absorbed in details that his staff suffered from lack of direction. When he realized that he was overburdened with too much work, he had nobody to delegate it to, because no one had been developed to a sufficient level of competence. Harry had to be retired early in order to make way for someone with the interpersonal skills so crucial for a successful supervisor.

The moral: Conflicts do exist between short-term HR needs (such as pressure to get the work out on time) and long-term needs (such as preparing people for assuming greater responsibility). An important responsibility of the HR planner is to help keep managers "honest" by making them consider long-term as well as short-term HR needs.

How Can the SPHR Process Be Described?

Models depict objects, situations, or processes that are otherwise more complex. There are various kinds: (1) *scale models* represent objects (for example,

a toy automobile is a model of a real one); (2) *analog models* represent phe-
nomena lacking physical appearance (for example, a watch is an analog model
for time; a thermometer is a model for temperature); (3) *mental models* represent assumptions and norms, and managers rely on such models to make decisions (for example, what results will be produced by an action? Are they consistent
with what is desired?); (4) *mathematical models* represent quantitative relationships between variables (for example, what has been the relationship between
turnover and absenteeism, turnover and productivity, measures of turnover and
employee satisfaction, measures of turnover and employee performance); and
(5) *simulation models* are quantitative (that is, mathematical) or qualitative (that
is, mental) representations of a dynamic process over time. Beginning with
known relationships between variables, decision-makers project trends into the
future to see what will happen.

Models are quite simply aids for decision-making. Some merely describe
what is (existing conditions), while others prescribe *what should be* (desired conditions). With this information by way of background, we can describe a simplified model of the SPHR process. Working with others, HR practitioners should:

1. Link the purpose, goals, and objectives of the HR department and/or
   HR plan to the purpose, goals, and objectives of the organization.
2. Assess the present status of HR in the organization by analyzing
   work done in jobs, positions, or job categories; the people in jobs,
   positions, or job categories; and the HR department.
3. Scan the environment to assess how jobs, positions, or job categories
   will probably change over time; how people in those jobs, positions,
   or job categories will probably have to change over time to keep up
   with job changes, and how the HR department will probably be
   affected by changes inside and outside the organization over time.
4. Compare the present work being done in jobs/positions to the
   expected future work that will probably be done in the future (the
   result is a *planning gap in the work*), and then present people doing
   the work and those who will be needed in the future. The result will
   be a *planning gap in the workforce*.

5. Consider the range of long-term HR strategies that will help close planning gaps in the work and workforce, and then select one. This becomes your *HR Grand Strategy*.

6. Implement HR Grand Strategy through coordination of such HR practice areas as career management programs, training, recruitment, job design, organization development, labor relations, employee assistance programs, and compensation/benefits.

7. Manage the HR function so that it is an effective vehicle for helping implement HR Grand Strategy by changing people and jobs.

8. Evaluate HR Grand Strategy before, during, and after implementation. The results of evaluation are fed back to Step 1. These steps are illustrated schematically in Figure 1-6.

It is important to understand that this model is a simplified one representing a contingent process. It is not intended to imply an inflexible, unwavering, step-by-step approach. Instead, it implies a *process* of planned change on a large scale. As a process, SPHR is not entirely linear: Steps can, and do, overlap and can occur simultaneously and even in real time. Organizational politics also affect goals, objectives, strategies, and outcomes.

What Are the Roles of HRP Practitioners?

Human Resource planners have traditionally been specialists in the HR field, often focusing on matching labor demand and supply and on forecasting HR needs. Yet in a completely different sense, HR planning can be considered the HR department's counterpart to strategic business planning. When it is, the HR planner's role is like that of the chief executive: bearing major responsibility for establishing direction or strategy. The difference between the two roles is one of focus: the CEO focuses on the whole business, while the HR planner focuses on *the human side* of the enterprise. In this way, HR planning is associated with the role of the highest-level HR executive, just as strategic business planning is associated with the CEO's role.

Figure 1-6: A Simplified Model of SPHR (Strategic Planning for Human Resources)

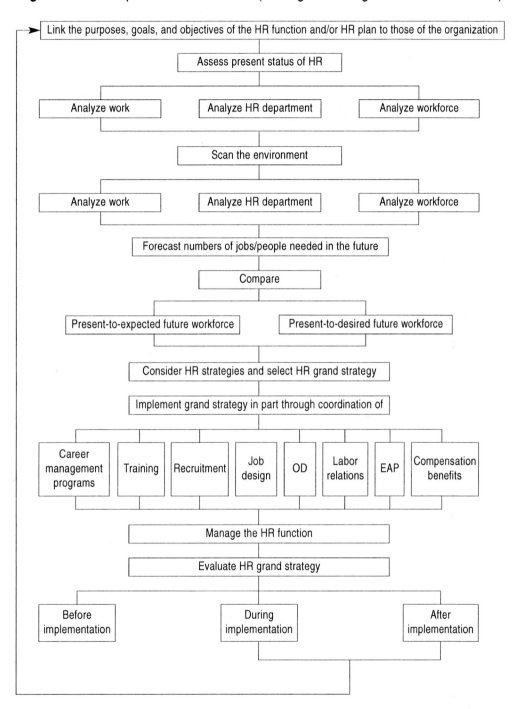

Of course, what HR planners are expected to do varies widely across organizations. Differences depend on:

1. Management philosophy and culture. *(What do managers in the organization want from HR planners? What norms of behavior are accepted or desired in the organization?* See Duane, 1996.*)*
2. Practitioner skills. *(What kind of people occupy jobs as HR planners? What are they able to do?)*
3. Organizational size *(Is the firm large enough to afford a highly specialized unit to focus solely on HRP?)*

Perhaps organizational size is the single most important factor. After all, HR practitioners in small organizations wear many hats. They tend to be generalists and typically bear titles like "HR manager." As firms increase in size, however, the HR department itself also increases in size, and practitioners are given titles like "compensation specialist," "technical trainer," "learning officer," and "recruiter." The title "HR planner" or some variation of it is only rarely found in small or medium-sized firms.

In the broadest sense, of course, people do not have to work in a job with the title of "HR planner" in order to be involved in strategic planning. In the smallest organizations, HRP practitioners deal with some form of HRP regularly, though perhaps they do not call it by that name. Some people are not aware that establishing long-term direction for the HR department *is* SPHR, and that it helps ensure that the right people will be in the right places at the right times to meet organizational needs. The same tendency is also evident in some larger organizations.

We contend that it really makes more sense to speak in terms of *roles* rather than *job titles;* all HR practitioners at one time or another probably engage in at least some activities associated with the SPHR model.

What Is Role Theory?

What is meant by "role theory"? What have researchers found out about HRP roles? How can the roles of HR planners be linked to the SPHR model? This section of the chapter will answer these questions.

Role does not mean the same thing as "job title"; rather, it connotes an organized set of behaviors belonging to an identifiable office or position (Rothwell and Sredl, 2000). Individual personality can affect *how* a role is performed, but not *that* it is performed. Thus, actors, managers and others play roles that are predetermined, although individuals interpret them in different ways. The nature of an individual's job creates certain expectations about *work methods* (how the job is carried out) and *work results* (what outcomes might be expected). However, individuals affect how well work methods are applied, and how much work and what quality of work results in desired outcomes.

As Katz and Kahn (1978) explain, role behavior is a function of such variables as

1. *Individual attributes.* What are the unique strengths or talents and weaknesses or shortcomings of the role incumbent? (A *role incumbent* is someone who plays a role.)
2. *Interpersonal factors.* What feelings exist between the role incumbent and others with whom he or she must deal?
3. *Organizational factors.* What explicit and implicit norms affect behavior and role expectations? (Explicit norms are written and formal rules governing behavior; implicit norms are unwritten and informal "rules of engagement" among people.)
4. *Role senders.* What do those who interact with a role incumbent expect from him or her by way of methods or results? (What do they communicate to him or her about those expectations?)
5. *The role receivers.* How does the role incumbent interpret role communications received from senders? (What behavior does the role incumbent engage in?) Relations between these variables are depicted in Figure 1-7.

This model illustrates how the focal person or role incumbent receives messages from others about how to behave. He or she interprets them, in turn, within the context of personal attributes and interpersonal relationships, which are affected by organizational factors. As the focal person acts, he or she influ-

Figure 1-7: A Model of Variables Involved in Organizational Roles

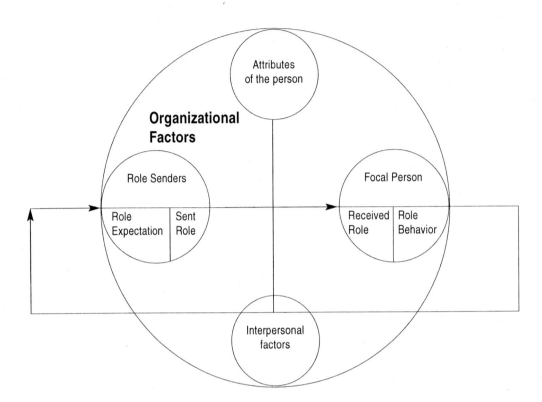

ences the expectations of others and the role messages they send. At the same time, interpreted role messages affect behavior.

Organizations are not just a context for role enactment. Instead, they are *role systems* in which the behaviors and perceptions of others affect individuals. All the while, individuals are role players who not only enact a role, but attempt to manipulate the role messages and expectations of others.

What Do We Know about HRP Roles?

Despite growing interest in HRP as a vehicle for helping engineer achievement of long-term organizational plans, relatively little has been written specifically about how the roles of HR planners differ from the roles of HRM practitioners. One possible reason is that not everyone agrees on what HRM practitioners should do *generally,* let alone what roles should be played *specifically* by HR planners (see: Blancero, 1996; Bolman, 1984; Brown, 1997; Condodina, 1997; Conner, and Ulrich, 1996; Gorsline, 1996; Kochanski, 1996; Lawson, 1996; Martell, 1995; McMahan, 1996; Morris, 1996; National Academy of Public Administration, 1996; Patton, 2000; Ulrich, 1985; Ulrich, 1995; Ulrich, Brockbank, Yeung, and Lake, 1995; Wright, 1998; Yeung, 1994; Yeung, 1996).

Yet if one role in the HR field requires extra care to clarify, it must certainly be that of HR planner. The reason is that HR planners do more than act as technical specialists (which they can be); they also act as the highest-level decision-makers in their respective departments. The HR plan integrates activities and initiatives of the personnel department and those of the organization, while simultaneously integrating such discrete HR practice areas as career planning/management, recruitment, training, and compensation/benefits. The HR planner is a linking pin across HR specialties and between hierarchical levels in the organization. He or she helps match people, jobs, and HR activities over time.

How Can HRP Roles Be Conceptualized?

We propose a new model for thinking about roles enacted by HR planners and potentially by all HR practitioners engaged at one time or another with activities associated with HRP. These roles are

- HR-organizational coordinator
- Work analyst
- Workforce analyst
- HR auditor
- Environmental scanner

- HR forecaster
- HR planning
- HR integrator
- HR planning manager
- HRP evaluator

This is what HR planners can do (Figure 1-8). Of course, any job in the HR field can encompass one or more of these roles at different times.

Figure 1-8: The Many Roles of the HR Planner

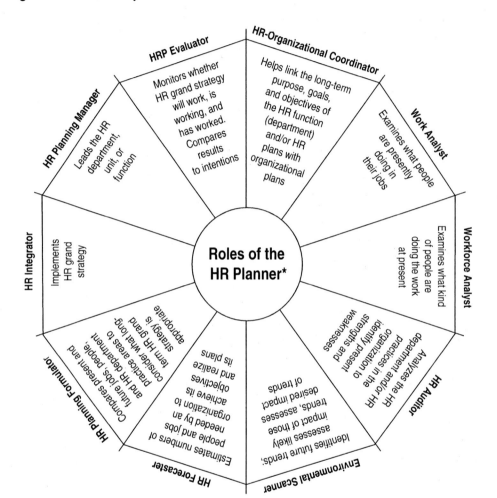

HRP Evaluator
Monitors whether HR grand strategy will work, is working, and has worked. Compares results to intentions

HR-Organizational Coordinator
Helps link the long-term purpose, goals, and objectives of the HR function (department) and/or HR plans with organizational plans

HR Planning Manager
Leads the HR department, unit, or function

Work Analyst
Examines what people are presently doing in their jobs

HR Integrator
Implements HR grand strategy

Roles of the HR Planner*

Workforce Analyst
Examines what kind of people are doing the work at present

HR Planning Formulator
Compares present and future jobs, people, and HR department practice areas to consider what long-term HR grand strategy is appropriate

HR Forecaster
Estimates numbers of people and jobs needed by an organization to achieve its objectives and realize its plans

Environmental Scanner
Identifies future trends; assesses likely impact of those trends, assesses desired impact of trends

HR Auditor
Analyzes the HR department and/or HR practices in the organization to identify present strengths and weaknesses

* An individual can enact any or all of these roles.

A model of this kind is useful because it can aid practitioners in specifying what they do for the benefit of managers in other parts of the organization, so as to furnish a common base of information for communicating. It is also useful because it provides an HR descriptive tool for (1) preparing job descriptions or establishing HR competency models; (2) preparing special selection instruments—such as tests, interview guides, and weighted application blanks—for hiring or promoting HRP practitioners; (3) devising long-term training, education, and development plans for HRP practitioners; (4) devising specialized performance appraisal methods for HRP practitioners; and (5) facilitating individual career planning for HR practitioners. Though untested and normative, this model is more concrete and specific than many models previously described by others.

How Are the Roles of HR Planners Related to the SPHR Model?

Each role of the Human Resource planner we described corresponds to a step in the strategic planning model in Figure 1-9. Hence, we base our conception of the HRP practitioner's duties, responsibilities, and behaviors on activities associated with SPHR. These roles thus match up to many activities that have frequently and typically been linked to HRP. In this respect, then, the roles make sense intuitively. Figure 1-9 illustrates the relationship between steps in a simplified SPHR model and roles of the HR planner.

Throughout this book, then, we shall closely link the roles of HR planners with the steps in the model. But remember: roles are not job titles. As a consequence, perhaps nobody in the "real world" will actually have a title like "HR-organizational coordinator" or "HR integrator." Yet behaviors associated with these roles might, in fact, be exhibited in many organizations, some not even using job titles like "HR planner" or having specialized units engaged full-time in HR planning.

How Is This Book Structured?

Despite the shortcomings of any model as a description of a complicated process, the one we have proposed for SPHR is helpful when thought of as a "flight plan" for reaching a desired destination. As any pilot knows, a flight plan describes where the flight is headed, but does not necessarily specify at what altitude; it thereby provides some flexibility in reaching the destination. Of course, in the

Figure 1-9: The Relationship between the Steps in a Simplified SPHR Model and the Roles of an HR Planner

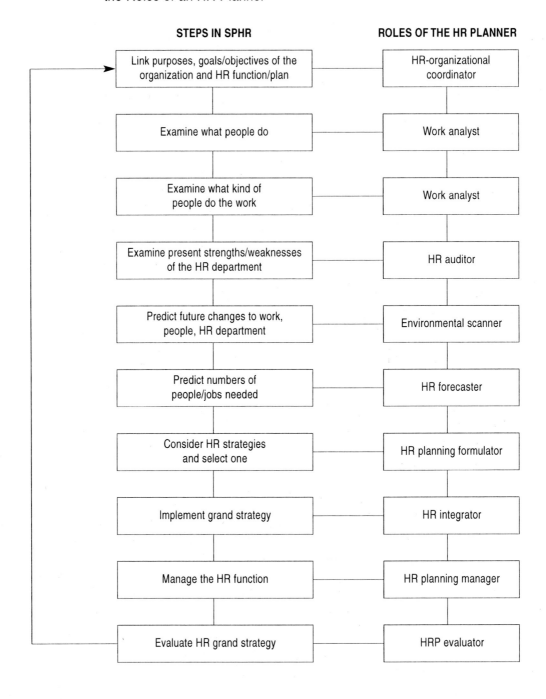

STEPS IN SPHR	ROLES OF THE HR PLANNER
Link purposes, goals/objectives of the organization and HR function/plan	HR-organizational coordinator
Examine what people do	Work analyst
Examine what kind of people do the work	Work analyst
Examine present strengths/weaknesses of the HR department	HR auditor
Predict future changes to work, people, HR department	Environmental scanner
Predict numbers of people/jobs needed	HR forecaster
Consider HR strategies and select one	HR planning formulator
Implement grand strategy	HR integrator
Manage the HR function	HR planning manager
Evaluate HR grand strategy	HRP evaluator

context of SPHR, the "destination" means having the right number and kinds of people available at the right times and in the right places to facilitate achievement of organizational plans. The book is structured around the model shown in Figure 1-9; Chapters 2 through 8 correspond to steps 1 to 7 of the model; Chapters 9 through 17 correspond to steps 7 and 8 of the model; and Chapters 18 and 19 correspond to steps 8 and 9 of the model.

Activity 1-1: Case Study

Directions: Read through the case that follows, and then answer the questions at the end. (This case is entirely fictitious.)

John P. McQuillan, age 21, is a student majoring in business administration at a large state university in a medium-sized city (population 100,110) about 200 miles from the nearest metropolitan area. He is interested in a career in personnel management and, in particular, a specialty in HRP.

John has decided to talk to an HR planner as part of his research for a term paper in his graduate seminar in Human Resources Planning. The first problem is finding one. John has telephoned the personnel departments of large local employers, but has had no luck so far in locating an HR planning specialist. In fact, he has been unable to find a single organization in which HRP has been made a distinct structural component of an organization.

John is confused. The assigned readings for the graduate seminar imply that HRP is common, and that state-of-the-art techniques in organizations are quite sophisticated. Yet John has found no evidence of real-world operations like those described in textbooks and academic articles.

Questions:
1. What accounts for John's problem?
2. How might John go about finding HRP by virtue of roles enacted by practitioners? Where should he look for them in organizations that do not possess a formal HR planning department? Why do you think so?

Activity 1-2: A Self-Diagnostic Survey of HRP Skills

Directions: Use this activity to do some self-diagnosis about your present strengths/weaknesses in HRP roles, and the skill or role areas in which you would like to improve.

In the left column in Part 1 below, you will find a list of skills associated with roles of the HRP practitioner. In the right column, mark the space above the scale that indicates your present level of ability. Then mark the space below the scale that indicates your desired level of ability.

When you finish Part 1, complete the questions in Part 2.

Part 1

Skill/Ability	Level of Skill Ability		
How well are you able to . . . ?	*No ability*	*Merely adequate ability*	*Expert ability*

(HR-Organizational Coordinator responsibilities)

1. Participate meaningfully as a member of formal organizational and HR Planning groups   0 1 2 3 4 5 6 7

2. Assess information pertaining to HR   0 1 2 3 4 5 6 7

3. Communicate information pertaining to HR in simple language   0 1 2 3 4 5 6 7

4. Establish interpersonal relationships with managers at all levels   0 1 2 3 4 5 6 7

5. Maintain effective interpersonal relationships with managers at all levels   0 1 2 3 4 5 6 7

(Work Analyst responsibilities)

6. Collect information about job families, jobs, and positions in the organization   0 1 2 3 4 5 6 7

7. Decide what results you hope to obtain (generally) from work analysis   0 1 2 3 4 5 6 7

8. Select an approach to work analysis from among several alternatives   0 1 2 3 4 5 6 7

9. Select a means to gather information about the work being done   0 1 2 3 4 5 6 7

Activity 1-2: *(continued)*

	Skill/Ability	Level of Skill Ability								
	How well are you able to . . . ?	*No ability*		*Merely adequate ability*			*Expert ability*			
10.	Conduct work analysis by drawing out information from job incumbents	0	1	2	3	4	5	6	7	
11.	Compile results of work analysis	0	1	2	3	4	5	6	7	
12.	Verify results	0	1	2	3	4	5	6	7	
13.	Monitor conditions inside and outside the organization that might reveal a need for work analysis	0	1	2	3	4	5	6	7	
	(Workforce Analyst responsibilities)									
14.	Infer, from job descriptions, the education, experience, and personal characteristics needed by job incumbents	0	1	2	3	4	5	6	7	
15.	Select what characteristics of employee performance to evaluate	0	1	2	3	4	5	6	7	
16.	Select the means by which to evaluate employee performance	0	1	2	3	4	5	6	7	
17.	Identify problems with evaluation methods/criteria	0	1	2	3	4	5	6	7	
18.	Attempt to solve problems with employee performance appraisal methods	0	1	2	3	4	5	6	7	
19.	Collect results of employee appraisals	0	1	2	3	4	5	6	7	
	(HR Auditor responsibilities)									
20.	Get others to articulate what should be examined in an HR audit	0	1	2	3	4	5	6	7	
21.	Draft a rough plan to guide an HR audit	0	1	2	3	4	5	6	7	
22.	Identify the people best suited to conduct the HR audit	0	1	2	3	4	5	6	7	
23.	Collect background information on an auditee	0	1	2	3	4	5	6	7	

Activity 1-2: *(continued)*

Skill/Ability	Level of Skill Ability							
How well are you able to . . . ?	No ability		Merely adequate ability			Expert ability		

24. Finalize an HR audit plan	0	1	2	3	4	5	6	7
25. Collect audit information	0	1	2	3	4	5	6	7
26. Compile audit results	0	1	2	3	4	5	6	7
27. Use audit results	0	1	2	3	4	5	6	7

(Environmental Scanner responsibilities)

28. Identify important trends outside the organization	0	1	2	3	4	5	6	7
29. Identify important trends inside the organization	0	1	2	3	4	5	6	7
30. Assess likely effects of trends on								
a. Work	0	1	2	3	4	5	6	7
b. Workforce	0	1	2	3	4	5	6	7
c. HR department	0	1	2	3	4	5	6	7
31. Assess desired effects of trends on								
a. Work	0	1	2	3	4	5	6	7
b. Workforce	0	1	2	3	4	5	6	7
c. HR department	0	1	2	3	4	5	6	7
32. Describe								
a. What will probably be in the future	0	1	2	3	4	5	6	7
b. What should be in the future	0	1	2	3	4	5	6	7

(Forecaster responsibilities)

33. Categorize employees	0	1	2	3	4	5	6	7
34. Categorize positions	0	1	2	3	4	5	6	7
35. Identify predictors of outputs by staffing level	0	1	2	3	4	5	6	7
36. Forecast HR demand by using appropriate techniques	0	1	2	3	4	5	6	7

Activity 1-2: *(continued)*

Skill/Ability	Level of Skill Ability		
How well are you able to ...?	No ability	Merely adequate ability	Expert ability
37. Forecast HR supply by using appropriate techniques	0 1 2 3 4 5 6 7		
38. Compare HR supply and demand to determine HR needs	0 1 2 3 4 5 6 7		
(HR Planning Formulator responsibilities)			
39. Summarize information about present and future			
a. Work	0 1 2 3 4 5 6 7		
b. People	0 1 2 3 4 5 6 7		
c. HR department practice areas	0 1 2 3 4 5 6 7		
40. Identify alternative long-term HR grand strategies	0 1 2 3 4 5 6 7		
41. Select appropriate means to weigh pros and cons of each possible HR Grand Strategy	0 1 2 3 4 5 6 7		
42. Weigh pros and cons of each possible HR Grand Strategy	0 1 2 3 4 5 6 7		
43. Select appropriate HR Grand Strategy	0 1 2 3 4 5 6 7		
(HR Integrator responsibilities)			
44. Develop long-term HR objectives	0 1 2 3 4 5 6 7		
45. Develop intermediate-term HR objectives	0 1 2 3 4 5 6 7		
46. Develop short-term HR objectives	0 1 2 3 4 5 6 7		
47. Provide leadership to the HR department	0 1 2 3 4 5 6 7		
48. Provide leadership to HR efforts of the entire organization	0 1 2 3 4 5 6 7		
49. Make sure that organizational rewards are consistent with HR Grand Strategy	0 1 2 3 4 5 6 7		

Activity 1-2: *(continued)*

Skill/Ability	Level of Skill Ability							
How well are you able to . . . ?	*No ability*		*Merely adequate ability*			*Expert ability*		
50. Make sure that organizational controls are consistent with HR Grand Strategy	0	1	2	3	4	5	6	7
51. Devise HR policies that are consistent with HR Grand Strategy	0	1	2	3	4	5	6	7
52. Coordinate HR practice areas	0	1	2	3	4	5	6	7
53. Match HR department structure to strategy	0	1	2	3	4	5	6	7
54. Match HR strategy to structure	0	1	2	3	4	5	6	7
(HR Planning Manager responsibilities)								
55. Develop goals and objectives	0	1	2	3	4	5	6	7
56. Create a structure for the HRP unit	0	1	2	3	4	5	6	7
57. Recruit HRP staff	0	1	2	3	4	5	6	7
58. Select HRP staff	0	1	2	3	4	5	6	7
59. Develop HRP staff	0	1	2	3	4	5	6	7
60. Issue orders	0	1	2	3	4	5	6	7
61. Resolve destructive conflicts within the department	0	1	2	3	4	5	6	7
62. Resolve destructive conflicts between the HRP department/unit and other departments or units	0	1	2	3	4	5	6	7
63. Communicate with people inside and outside the department	0	1	2	3	4	5	6	7
64. Budget for the department	0	1	2	3	4	5	6	7
65. Deal with power issues in the organization	0	1	2	3	4	5	6	7
(HRP Evaluator responsibilities)								
66. Decide on the purpose(s) to be served by evaluation	0	1	2	3	4	5	6	7

Activity 1-2: *(continued)*

Skill/Ability	Level of Skill Ability							
How well are you able to . . .?	*No ability*			*Merely adequate ability*			*Expert ability*	
67. Establish HR control systems	0	1	2	3	4	5	6	7
68. Select criteria for evaluation in line with purpose(s)	0	1	2	3	4	5	6	7
69. Carry out evaluation								
a. Before HRP implementation	0	1	2	3	4	5	6	7
b. During HRP implementation	0	1	2	3	4	5	6	7
c. After HRP implementation	0	1	2	3	4	5	6	7
70. Feed results of evaluation back into								
a. The organization's strategic planning process	0	1	2	3	4	5	6	7
b. The HRP process	0	1	2	3	4	5	6	7
c. Activities in HRP practice areas	0	1	2	3	4	5	6	7

Part 2

71. List the skills and abilities in which the greatest discrepancy exists between your present and desired levels of ability.

72. Describe how you can increase your level of ability in each skill/ability listed in item 71.

73. Provide a timetable or deadline for achieving the level of skill/ability you listed in item 71.

CHAPTER 2

THE HUMAN RESOURCES ORGANIZATIONAL COORDINATOR

Chapter 1 defined strategic planning for human resources, described steps in a simplified model of it, and summarized major roles enacted by human resources planning (HRP) practitioners. In this chapter, we turn our attention to an in-depth look at the first of these roles: *HR-Organizational Coordinator* (HROC).

What Does the HR-Organizational Coordinator Do?

This coordinator links the long-term purpose, goals, and objectives of the HR function or department and/or HR plans with strategic business plans. People enacting this role deal with major stakeholders inside and outside the organization on HRP-related issues. As a consequence of the status typically equated with this responsibility, incumbents of this role frequently occupy the highest decision-making position in the HR department or HRP unit. An *HRP unit* or *division,* as we use this term, is part of the HR department staffed by specialists who devote a majority of their time to forecasting and other activities unique to HRP. This degree of specialization is usually not found in small organizations.

Why Is It Important to Link Organizational Plans and HR Plans?

A link means "anything serving part of a thing with another; a bond or tie." Similarly, *linkage* means "the act of linking; the state or manner of being linked." A linkage between the organizational and the HR function thus refers to the process of tying them together or aligning them. This link helps ensure that the right numbers and right types of people are available with the right talents at the right times and in the right places to help achieve organizational goals. It also helps to address a pressing skill shortage that is hampering growth in many organizations (Greengard, 1998).

HR practitioners have frequently been advised to work toward coordinating their efforts closely with strategic planners. There are good reasons for doing so. First, successful firms in every industry are more likely than poor performers to deal strategically with HR (Barney and Wright, 1998; Lam and White, 1998). Second, top managers in many organizations, as a group, want HR professionals who are capable of dealing proactively, anticipating rather than just reacting to organizational needs, particularly needs for *management* talent consistent with strategy requirements (Bennett, Ketchen, and Schultz, 1998). Third, the career success of HR professionals depends increasingly on their ability to think strategically and act decisively. The use of HR data during the strategic business planning process is an important characteristic associated with state-of-the-art HRP programs. HRP can, in fact, be linked to strategic business planning and business mission or purpose. We explore the ways next.

What Are the Purposes, Goals, and Objectives of the Organization?

One place to begin linking organizational and HR plans is to examine the *purpose* of each of them.

Historically, the strategic business planning process has been viewed as emanating from two quite different starting points. One is a decision made by key strategists to harvest, maintain, or build *market share* (that is, the competitive position of the business relative to its environment). Once this decision is made, it implies subsequent and related decisions about human and financial resources. For instance, a decision to harvest should prompt cutbacks in spending and in staffing. In short, it is a downsizing, smartsizing, or rightsizing decision.

A second possible starting point is to define the purpose of business that builds value-added in the customers' eyes. Defining business purpose is a much more difficult and creative process than making decisions about market share. Indeed, decisions about market share should themselves stem from such a sense of purpose or mission (the terms *purpose* and *mission* are used synonymously).

Purpose is important because it helps decision-makers understand how their organization is positioned relative to the environment and competitors, and even how parts inside the organization are interrelated. It helps suggest how the overall business will change when, for example, managers consider adding a new line of products, dropping an old line, or diversifying the firm.

At this point, it might help to clarify just what it is we mean by "purpose." A *purpose statement* stems from a vision (Grensing-Pophal, 2000). It broadly identifies the organization's type of operation or business, its intended areas of service, its targeted customers or users, its approach to providing service, and any special philosophical views about how the organization should conduct business. Each part of the organization should also have a purpose statement that is rationally related to the organization's purpose statement; the statement should spell out the department's unique contribution, the functions it serves, the work it performs, and the philosophy to which it adheres. A purpose statement thus reflects a sense of organizational identity amid the turbulence of a dynamic environment.

Much like an individual's sense of identity, organizational purpose is relatively enduring. However, it can be affected by four considerations that were well-explained in a classic, and still relevant, treatment by Abell (1980):

1. What the organization might do (in other words, with what opportunities or threats will it face as a result of external environmental conditions?)
2. What the organization can do (what strengths or weaknesses does it possess relative to its environment?)

3. What decision-makers want or value (in other words, what are the values and personal preferences of key executives?)

4. What the organization *should do* (what social, political, and ethical considerations, etc., should be considered?)

These points are interrelated. The information, in fact, will help shape formal statements of company purpose and strategic business plans stemming from those statements.

An organization's purpose statement is much too general to provide adequate guidance in daily decision-making. For this reason, it is typically converted into goals and objectives. A *goal* is a broad, timeless, and unmeasurable statement of desired results. *Objectives* are derived from goals. They are capable of being measured and are expressed in terms that make the time period specific. To cite some examples, a goal is a statement like "Company X will retain its commanding lead in the market for widgets." An objective is more concrete. "Company X will increase its market share in widgets by 5 percent each year for the next 5 years."

Once we concede the importance of preparing an organizational purpose statement, we must then ask this question: How do we prepare one? There is no simple answer to this question. Several methods are possible. One approach is for top managers to meet, as a group, and address such questions as these: What is our business? What should it be? What products/services do we offer? What should we offer? What groups do we serve? How do we offer our products/services? How do we serve the groups we intend to serve? What values do we especially embody? What values do we want to embody? This approach is often counterproductive because the resulting purpose statement does not inspire workers. Purpose statements resulting from this approach are likely to emphasize a profit motive to the exclusion of such equally important and potentially conflicting aims as promoting social justice, preserving the environment, improving quality of work life for employees, and acting as a responsible corporate citizen in the community.

Another approach focuses on different issues: values, external environment, internal environment, funding sources, and organization structure. Rowe et al.

Figure 2-1: Strategic Four-Factor Diagram

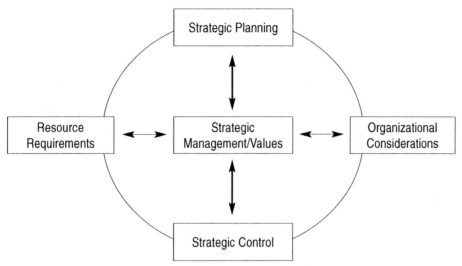

(1986) called this approach *strategic four-factor analysis.* Basing it on a classic scheme first espoused by Churchman (1968), they advocate that it be used as a starting point for considering major strategic issues and interrelationships (see Figure 2-1). A purpose statement is then based on how decision-makers in an organization view their firm in relation to these issues.

The approach to be used in building a purpose statement should depend on the reason for the exercise. Is the intent to clarify existing values, strengthen specific values, or change values? A different approach should be used in each case. One interesting idea is to hire a consultant for an anthropological expedition through the firm. The consultant asks old-timers whether the firm has a culture, and what that culture is. The consultant then analyzes results and emerges with a purpose statement that avoids the many pitfalls that can mar management exercises in preparing such a statement. "Old war stories" are particularly rich sources of beliefs, values, and core purpose.

A sense of purpose—even if it is not formalized in a written statement—is a necessary precondition to formulating organizational strategy and clarifying the role of the HR function. Goals and objectives stem from purpose.

They express results sought. Goals are desirable outcomes or results sought, while objectives are precise and measurable targets to be achieved over a fixed timespan. They focus on *what* and *when,* but not on *why* or *how.* It is essential to establish goals and objectives (the ends) before deciding on organizational strategy (the means).

What Are the Purposes, Goals, and Objectives of Strategic Human Resource Plans?

We begin creating strategic human resource plans in much the same way we start creating strategic business plans: defining purposes, goals, and objectives. It has seldom been thought of in this way. You must consider these things before attempting to forecast HR demands or assess supplies:

1. What HR needs are implied by the nature of the business?
2. What HR needs are implied by the products/services offered?
3. What HR needs are implied by the groups served by the organization?
4. What HR needs are implied by the ways that products/services are offered and the ways that consumer or constituent groups are served?
5. What HR needs are implied by values prized in the organization?

Despite the progress made by HR planners in large firms, relatively few organizations make any systematic attempt to anticipate and provide for human implications of strategic business plans. Strategists have a tendency to establish overly ambitious goals and objectives that call for too much social change in too little time, without regard to the skills and resources needed to achieve them. At the same time, managers—particularly at lower levels, where strategic plans are implemented—are forced by daily pressures to adopt short-sighted, reactive-based practices to get the work out. The strategic business plan is easily lost sight of as each short-term problem cries out for attention.

Matters are complicated in that *purpose,* in the context of strategic planning, has a somewhat different meaning from its customary usage in the context of organizational strategy-making. It refers to *needs served.* The central questions of SPHR's purpose thus revolve around issues of *who, what, when, where,* and *how much* or *how well.* Consider these points:

1. *Who* is responsible—and how much—for coordinating the development of SPHR? Implementation? Evaluation?

2. *Whose* HR needs are to be met? The organization's needs only? Individual needs for growth and development? Some combination of organizational and individual needs?

3. *What* HR needs are to be met? For numbers of people, or jobs? For types of people, or jobs? For skills for what people *might* do? For what people *can* do? For what people *want to* do? For what people *should* do?

4. *When* are HR needs to be met? Over what time frame? How might short-term, intermediate-term, and long-term HR needs conflict? What should be done about such conflict?

5. *Where* are HR needs to be met? Over what geographical scope? How might needs differ by location?

6. *How much* or *how well* are HR needs to be met? What performance indicators should be associated with HRP?

The first question affixes the major responsibility for SPHR. This issue might well be the most important one, and it can be related to the *life-cycle stage* of HRP in the organization. There are four such stages:

1. At the most basic and least sophisticated level, manpower planning is driven by strategic business plans. HR needs are forecast purely on the basis of expenditures.

2. At the next level, HRP is shifted to the personnel department. At this point, "manpower planning" or purely cost-oriented HR demand forecasting is transformed to the more comprehensive approach.

3. At the third level, HRP becomes the integrative function that ties together all HR activities. In this respect, HRP is said to become vertically integrated (Rothwell, Prescott, and Taylor, 1998).

4. At the fourth and most sophisticated level, vertically integrated HRP affects and is in turn affected by strategic business plans. It thus

becomes simultaneously integrated across HR practice areas and vertically (that is, up and down). HRP is transformed to the future-oriented perspective associated with SPHR.

Note that the change that occurs between levels is closely associated with the individual(s) bearing responsibility. At the least sophisticated level, personnel practitioners have little or no say; at the most sophisticated level, they share responsibility with strategists at other levels.

Other questions about SPHR are also important. *Whose* needs to meet is a question of emphasis; *what* needs to meet is one of focus; *when* to meet these needs establishes the planning horizon; *where* to meet these needs establishes priorities by location or by segment of the organization or its environment; and *how much* or *how* well to meet these needs provides measures for use in subsequent evaluation. If these questions have been adequately addressed, goals and objectives for SPHR can be devised easily enough.

The process of defining the purpose, goals, and objectives for SPHR can be handled in a manner appropriate to lifecycle stage. In the first stage, the process will not be carried out at all because human resource issues are not valued. In the second stage, attention will most likely center on what the HR department can do for others. In the third stage, attention will center on what the HR department can do and on what each *practice area* of HR can do within that framework. At the most sophisticated level, attention will focus on what the HR department can do; what practice areas within the department can do; and what impact these efforts have had on strategic business planning outcomes or should have on future strategic business planning outcomes. To clarify these distinctions, see Activity 2-1 at the end of this chapter. It will help you work through this process in your organization, and help you link strategic business plans and HR plans based on purposes, goals, and objectives.

Alternative Methods of Linking Strategic Business Plans with HR Plans

Generally speaking, three approaches can be used to link strategic business plans and HR plans. First is the *formal,* which ensures linkage through explicit and institutionalized processes or rituals and specifically delegated work methods or structure. Second is the *informal,* which ensures linkage through interpersonal interactions of top management strategists and those responsible for strategic planning for HR. This approach is based on leadership relations. Third is a *combination of formal and informal approaches,* in which varying degrees of linkage depend on formal methods and informal leader relations. To a considerable extent, *organizational culture* is the determining factor in any setting as to which approach will most likely be successful. We shall have more to say about culture later.

Formal Approaches

In most cases, an organizational plan implies long-term change, a gradual narrowing of a gap between *what is* (or present conditions) and *what is desired* (intended future conditions). If we view organizations as rational, then we can confidently place reliance on structure and methods to help bring about change. The idea is simple enough: If we want something to be done on any regular basis, we must create a structure for carrying it out and assign the responsibility for doing it to somebody specific. By extension, if we want HRP to be done, we must create a means to do it and place somebody in charge of seeing that it is carried out.

Most academic and professional literature on HRP stresses this approach. In part, that accounts for the extraordinarily large number of HRP models: They help conceptualize a means for conducting HRP and tying it to strategic business plans. Most of these approaches are based on a few key elements:

I   Linking HR plans to strategic business plans (SBPs)
I   Analyzing internal and external environments
I   Designing and considering HR programs
I   Evaluating results.

In one classic treatment of the subject of HRP that is still relevant today, Dyer (1984) relied on his personal experience to suggest the most specific approaches of any to link HRP and SBP. He finds that "linkages are always made, but not always in the same companies" (p. 80). Nine methods are possible, he believed, though not all are necessary in any one company at any one time. One link takes place before the strategic business planning process begins. Working alone or with others, HR planners assess external environmental conditions pertaining to HR, such as labor union trends or employment-related legislation. They then prepare written summaries of the likely impact of each condition on the firm and distribute the summaries to key strategists before they begin strategic business planning (SBP). The intent is to make strategists aware of key issues, so they can consider them during the SBP process. The same approach can be used in a less formal way, where meetings or discussions with strategists take the place of written summaries. Dyer considered this informal approach a second link between human resources planning and SBP.

A third link is made during the process of creating the Strategic Business Plan. Strategists obtain specific information from HR planners and insert it into prepared planning forms, and then consider HR issues as part of the business plan. A related approach and the fourth link is to leave it up to corporate planners to determine when specific HR issues are relevant; they would not be required to consider HR, but could do so.

A fifth link takes place shortly after this SBP process: Tentatively prepared strategic business plans are reviewed by staff groups—including HRP practitioners—before being placed before top managers for final approval. The top decision-maker in the HR department expresses formal concurrence or nonconcurrence with the plan, because the idea is to build consensus. In most cases, HR planners are given initial input in business plans, so review serves only to strengthen their desire to implement the plans.

A sixth link takes place after the Strategic Business Plan is written. It is submitted to HR practitioners, so that they can work in consultation with others to do the following: identify specific, potentially critical, HR issues requiring attention; designate task forces to study specific issues in depth; and prepare action plans for the HR function based on more intensive study of specific issues. Of course, a task force has a highly structured activity confronting it and can draw on the expertise of people from various hierarchical levels.

A seventh link is very similar to the sixth described above. Action planning is substituted for task force study. In other words, HR practitioners are asked to prepare very specific plans to deal with critical HR-related issues. Dyer believes this approach is rarely used.

The eighth and ninth links between strategic business planning and HR planning are closely related. One is not often thought of: The same people are involved in both processes. Hence, business strategists are familiar with HRP because they participate in it as a process separate from SBP. Linkages occur in their minds, not in written plans.

The ninth and final link occurs when separately prepared HR plans and business plans are reviewed by top managers at the same time. In short, they have a common review point and are thereby linked.

Dyer believes that the most popular approaches are the fifth and sixth—what he calls *interpretation*. As Dyer (1984, p. 83) noted, "If you are only going to link at one point. I think it makes sense to use interpretation because it provides an opportunity to demonstrate that you can take action and contribute to the business plans that managers are trying to accomplish. Without this credibility, it is very difficult to make use of the other linkage points." To achieve linkage between SBP and HRP, Dyer (1984, p. 79) had simple advice: Practitioners should "discover how business strategy is actually formulated, determine how much consideration is given to HR, decide how much consideration should be given to HR, and close the gap."

Informal Approaches

Advocates of the so-called behavioral school have done a convincing job of demonstrating that organizations are at least as political as they are rational. In one particularly well-known and classic treatment, March and Simon (1958) showed that *process*—that is, *how* decisions are made—is much more revealing about the values and beliefs of top managers than decisions or even results. Mintzberg (1979), in another classic and still-relevant treatment, argued that formulation of business goals and strategies is really a political process in which different people and groups jockey for power. In fact, power is an end in itself, and a means to achieve self-interested goals. Research has demonstrated that as much as 60 to 75 percent of organizational planning is informal, falling outside the purview of formal processes or rituals, but inside the political sphere (Dyer, 1984).

Several writers in the HRP field have avoided models, preferring instead to focus on specific issues and offer general advice about how to link organizational and HR plans. Some "models" will not transfer well across organizations. Hence, general advice might be more useful in that it can be used to create an approach in unique settings.

To be more effective in linking HRP to organizational planning, HR practitioners should:

I   Be more professional in approach and behavior.
I   Be more familiar with the business.
I   Be more willing to lead others by suggesting new ideas while doing "the basics" well.
I   Be more willing to act as team players in dealing with others.
I   Be more willing to influence others by setting a good example.
I   Be more vocal.
I   Be more successful in avoiding surprises.
I   Be more willing to take a stand on some issues and fight for them.
I   Be more willing to maintain integrity, even in the face of unfavorable odds.

These suggestions sound more like a code of professional ethics than principles for linking SBP and HRP, but they do imply that personal credibility is a helpful source of power for achieving linkage between SBP and HRP. The importance of credibility as a key competency for HR leadership has been supported by recent research (Rothwell, Prescott, and Taylor, 1998).

Organizational Culture

How can HRP practitioners select one specific approach to linking strategic planning and HR planning? How can they enact the role of HR-organizational coordinator to best effect? These questions defy simple answers. The reason is that corporate cultures differ: What works in one setting will not or might not work in another. Approaches to linking HRP and SBP must be appropriate to the culture. Likewise, role behaviors of HRP practitioners must be similarly adapted.

What is *culture*? The term typically denotes a system of shared *values and beliefs* that produce *norms* of behavior. Values (what is important) and beliefs (how things work) interact to cause norms (how we *should* do things). Managers are at once the chief stakeholders in and apologists for culture, because they customarily embody the values prized in the organization. According to popular mythology, the best-run firms in the United States have distinctive corporate cultures.

Although corporate culture is difficult to put a finger on, it is quite clear that some firms and organizations have distinctive ways of operating. This viewpoint was once expressed eloquently by an anonymous wag: "There's a right way, a wrong way, and an Army way." To diagnose culture for human resources in your firm, consider the following questions drawn from the classic treatment of the topic (Deal and Kennedy, 1982):

- What physical evidence, if any, exists to indicate that employees are valued?
- What do company publications state about employment with the firm generally and about the potential for career advancement, promotions, evaluations, and terminations?
- How much time do supervisors and managers claim they spend on training employees, counseling employees about career matters, and negotiating long-term career plans with employees?
- To what extent do employees agree with the answers of supervisors and managers to the previous point?
- What do insiders say about the general status of HR planning in the firm, about the desired status of HR planning in the firm, the status of HR planners in the firm, and about how to get promoted? What about turnover and absenteeism? What kind of people leave? Why do they leave? How are hiring and firing decisions made?

By considering these and related questions, HR planners can assess the existing culture as a first step in comparing it to what they believe it should be. They can then select strategies—both formal and informal—to link HRP and culture.

Activity 2-1: Case Study

Directions: Read through the case that follows and answer the questions at the end. (This case is entirely fictitious.)

The Lectro Mining Company is a small firm, employing 400 people. Its annual sales from coal mining are $63 million. Of this amount, $3 million per year is profit.

The company's purpose is set forth in annual reports, the employee handbook, and budget documents. It is to "extract and refine coal for use by utility companies, manufacturing firms, and schools, while contributing to the quality of working life for employees and to a clean environment." Company goals are thus implicit in the purpose statement. They are (1) to extract and refine coal, (2) to contribute to the quality of working life for employees, and (3) to contribute to a clean environment.

The chief executive of the company recently hired a consultant to help top managers plan for the human resource needs of this non-unionized firm. The CEO and her immediate subordinates met for two days at a resort located 100 miles from the company's nearest coal mine. At that meeting, they crafted the wording for a role statement for HRP. They stated that role as follows:

> The purpose of human resource plans and development activities at Lectro Mining is to improve the quality of working life of employees through efforts geared to help them prepare for future promotion in the company.

The top executives decided that HRP had not been systematically handled, but that it should be. Responsibility for HRP initiates was delegated to a committee consisting of the CEO, the vice president of personnel, one line manager, and two experienced miners.

Questions
1. Do you think that the purpose statement for HRP was a good one? Why or why not?
2. What sort of culture do you think is evident in this company? Why?
3. How successful do you think this effort will be? Why do you think so?
4. Do you see any relationship between the purpose of the company and that of HRP?
5. What questions about HRP do you think will have to be addressed in the near future?

Activity 2-2: A Worksheet for Identifying the Purpose of Strategic Planning for Human Resources

Directions: Using information from your own organization, work through this sheet. Answer the questions on a separate sheet. The results of this activity should help clarify key issues about SPHR in your organization. (If your organization makes no attempt at this time to plan for HR, then answer these questions in terms of how it should do so.)

1. Who is responsible for coordinating
   (a) development of the strategic business plan (SBP)?
   (b) implementation of the SBP?
   (c) evaluation of the SBP?

2. Who is responsible for coordinating
   (a) development of strategic plans for human resources (SPHR)?
   (b) implementation of SPHR?
   (c) evaluation of SPHR?

3. Whose needs does the organization meet?

4. Whose HR needs does the strategic HR plan meet?

5. What needs does the organization meet?

6. What HR needs does the strategic HR plan meet? Consider needs for
   (a) numbers of people.
   (b) types of people.

7. When does the organization meet the needs of those it serves?
   (a) Over what time frame?
   (b) How might short-term, intermediate-term, and long-term issues conflict?

8. When are HR needs to be met?
   (a) Over what time frame?
   (b) How might short-term, intermediate-term, and long-term HR needs conflict?

9. Where does the organization function?

10. Where are HR needs to be met?

11. How much or how well
    (a) does the organization presently meet the needs of those it serves?
    (b) should the organization meet the needs of those it serves?
    (c) should the organization meet the needs of those it serves in the future?

Activity 2-2: *(continued)*

12. How much or how well
    (a) does the SPHR function presently meet the needs of the organization? Individuals?
    (b) should the SPHR function meet the needs of the organization? Individuals?
    (c) should the SPHR meet the needs of those it serves in the future?

13. What is the purpose of the organization?

14. How do human resources help the organization serve its purpose?

15. What is the purpose of SPHR in the organization?

16. How does SPHR help the organization serve its purpose?

17. How should SPHR help the organization serve its purpose?

Activity 2-3: Case Study

Directions: Read through the case that follows and answer the questions at the end. (This case is entirely fictitious.)

The Texarkana State University is a small state-supported liberal arts college. The college's purpose statement is published in university catalogues, student recruitment literature, and in budget documents prepared for the state legislature. It is to "prepare students for a productive life as citizens of the state through a liberal arts education." Organizational goals are implicit in this statement. The first is to prepare students "through a liberal arts education." But the ultimate goal is to "prepare students for a productive life."

After a series of meetings, the formal purpose for the human resource plan of the school was stated as follows:

> The purpose of human resource plans and development activities at Texarkana State is (1) To provide for the cost-efficient operation of the school by possessing the right number of people at the right times and with the right skills to meet the needs of the school and its students. (2) To foster an interdisciplinary approach to learning through teaching, research, and community activities intended to link different subject areas for purposes of integrating knowledge.

The goals of the SPHR effort are implicit in the statement: priority is given first to economic considerations ("cost-efficient operation") and then second to a theoretical issue ("foster an interdisciplinary approach").

Activity 2-3: *(continued)*

The university president appointed a blue-ribbon faculty panel to prepare a human resource plan that would clarify what outcomes were to be achieved over a five-year period and by what means progress would be measured, and other such matters.

After several months, the panel submitted a report that set objectives such as the following ones: (1) to hire qualified faculty as needed; (2) to foster the sharing of information about research in the university community; and (3) to foster faculty development through limited funding for attendance at professional conferences.

This report was rather quickly returned to the panel, with the following remarks from the president: "What you have submitted is not a plan but an expression of desirable goals. Reword the goals so they are stated in measurable terms over a definite time period."

Questions
1. Critique the sample objectives provided by the panel. What do they leave out?
2. Revise one of the objectives (you choose which one) so that it addresses such questions as: How much? How well? How soon? How will achievement be measured? Who bears responsibility for achievement?
3. For what reason do you think that setting SPHR objectives at a university might be somewhat different from doing so in a business firm? For what reasons do you think they might be similar?
4. Critique the purpose statement for SPHR. What might be better language?

Activity 2-4: A Self-Diagnostic Survey on Linking Strategic Business Planning to Strategic HR Planning

Directions: In column 1 below, you will find a list of general conditions that are associated with linkages between strategic business plans and strategic plans for human resources. In columns 2 and 3, you will find rating scales. Rate, in column 2, how much the condition exists in your organization at present; rate, in column 3, how much you feel the condition should exist in your organization at some time in the future. In column 4, jot down some notes on how to close the gap (if any exists) between columns 2 and 3. Use more paper if necessary.
  Use the following scale for columns 2 and 3:

0 means that the item does not apply in your organization
1 means very little
2 means little
3 means somewhat
4 means much
5 means very much

Column 1	Column 2	Column 3	Column 4
To what extent in your organization . . .	*How much does the condition exist at present?*	*How should it be in the future?*	*How can the gap between columns 2 and 3 be closed?*
	Very Little Very Much	*Very Little Very Much*	
1. Is there a process to assess external environmental conditions pertaining to HR?	0 1 2 3 4 5	0 1 2 3 4 5	
2. Do HRP practitioners prepare written summaries of the likely impact of external environ-mental conditions?	0 1 2 3 4 5	0 1 2 3 4 5	
3. Do HRP practitioners distribute summaries of environmental conditions to strategists before the SBP process?	0 1 2 3 4 5	0 1 2 3 4 5	

Activity 2-4: *(continued)*

Column 1	Column 2	Column 3	Column 4
To what extent in your organization	*How much does the condition exist at present?*	*How should it be in the future?*	*How can the gap between columns 2 and 3 be closed?*
	Very Little Very Much	*Very Little Very Much*	
4. Do strategists obtain specific information from HRP practitioners as a required part of completing SBP forms?	0 1 2 3 4 5	0 1 2 3 4 5	
5. Are tentatively prepared SB plans reviewed by HR planners before final approval by top managers?	0 1 2 3 4 5	0 1 2 3 4 5	
6. Does the top HR decision-maker have to express formal concurrence or nonconcurrence with draft SB plans?	0 1 2 3 4 5	0 1 2 3 4 5	
7. Are specific, potentially critical HR issues singled out?	0 1 2 3 4 5	0 1 2 3 4 5	
8. Are task forces commissioned to study specific, potentially critical HR issues in depth?	0 1 2 3 4 5	0 1 2 3 4 5	

Activity 2-4: *(continued)*

Column 1	Column 2	Column 3	Column 4
To what extent in your organization . . .	*How much does the condition exist at present?*	*How should it be in the future?*	*How can the gap between columns 2 and 3 be closed?*
	Very Little Very Much	*Very Little Very Much*	
9. Are detailed action plans prepared to deal with specific, potentially critical, HR issues?	0 1 2 3 4 5	0 1 2 3 4 5	
10. Are the same people involved in Strategic Business Planning and HRP?	0 1 2 3 4 5	0 1 2 3 4 5	
11. Are draft SB plans and HR plans, prepared separately, reviewed at the same time by top managers?	0 1 2 3 4 5	0 1 2 3 4 5	
12. Are human resource dimensions evident in the organization's purpose statement?	0 1 2 3 4 5	0 1 2 3 4 5	
13. Are human resource dimensions explicitly considered in the organization's SB planning process?	0 1 2 3 4 5	0 1 2 3 4 5	
14. Do effective linkages exist between organizational and HR decision-making?	0 1 2 3 4 5	0 1 2 3 4 5	

Activity 2-4: *(continued)*

Column 1	Column 2	Column 3	Column 4
To what extent in your organization . . .	How much does the condition exist at present?	How should it be in the future?	How can the gap between columns 2 and 3 be closed?
	Very Little Very Much	Very Little Very Much	
15. Does the office of chief executive provide the climate for integrating SBP and HRP?	0 1 2 3 4 5	0 1 2 3 4 5	
16. Is responsibility established at all levels for HR issues?	0 1 2 3 4 5	0 1 2 3 4 5	
17. Are initiatives of HR relevant to the needs of the business?	0 1 2 3 4 5	0 1 2 3 4 5	
18. Does HR identify environments in which the organization is or will be doing business?	0 1 2 3 4 5	0 1 2 3 4 5	
19. Do HR practitioners interact with those outside the organization who represent environments in which the organization is or will be doing business?	0 1 2 3 4 5	0 1 2 3 4 5	
20. Other (specify) _____ _____	0 1 2 3 4 5 0 1 2 3 4 5	0 1 2 3 4 5 0 1 2 3 4 5	

THE HUMAN RESOURCES WORK ANALYST

Chapter 2 introduced the first of ten roles enacted by HR planners: HR-organizational coordinator (HROC). As you will recall, the HROC serves as a linking pin between the organization and the HR function. This chapter introduces the second of these ten pivotal roles, that of the *HR work analyst*.

What Does the HR Work Analyst Do?

Perhaps one of the best places to begin human resources planning is with what people are doing at present. After all, it is hard to plan future action if nobody is sure about what is being done at present. The work analyst role of the HR planner studies the methods (means) used and results (ends) achieved by all people in the organization sharing the same job title. Work analysts direct their attention to finding out what people *are doing* and what they *should be doing*. More and more HR planners are also going steps beyond that to look at what competencies distinguish best-in-class (exemplary) performers from the fully successful ones (Dubois and Rothwell, 2000). Another issue also attracting attention is the difference in values that distinguish the successful from the unsuccessful workers (Laabs, 1997).

Traditional work analysis is probably an inadequate tool by itself for anticipating future organizational needs, for reasons which will be treated at length in Chapter 6 (see Schneider and Konz,

1989). At this time, however, we shall summarize traditional methods of work analysis because of their crucial importance to customary HR efforts.

What Specialized Terms Are Associated with Work Analysis?

Before we begin our discussion about work analysis, we need to first clarify what the associated terms mean. Otherwise, they will be a source of confusion for those unfamiliar with them.

- *Work* simply means purposeful physical and/or mental activity.
- A *task* is a work activity with a definite beginning and end.
- A *position* consists of a distinct cluster of related tasks carried out by one person in only one organization or work setting. A firm employing 1,000 people has 1,000 positions.
- A *job* refers to similar positions. All secretaries in an organization share a common job, for example, though each secretary occupies a different position.
- A *job family* is a series of related jobs. Common distinctions between job families are made by level of difficulty or by amount of experience or education. Secretary I, Secretary II, and Secretary III *are job titles* for related jobs in the same family. At the same time, all "clericals" are part of a common job family, which is distinct from such others as "technicals," "professionals," "supervisors," " managers," and "executives."
- *Work analysis* is the systematic investigation of work.
- *Task analysis* refers to methods for studying activities within a position or job. Methods can be classified according to focus: what people actually do when carrying out a task; what people should do; what abilities are required of the person; and what conditions elicit appropriate behavior from a performer.
- *Position analysis* is an investigation of tasks performed by one person in one organization, usually at one point in time.

- *Job analysis* is the study of tasks, duties, and responsibilities shared by similar positions.
- A *competency* is any characteristic that is essential to achieve desired work results (Dubois and Rothwell, 2000).
- *Competency identification* is the process of discovering the characteristics that underlie successful work performance (Dubois and Rothwell, 2000).
- A *position description* is the product of a position analysis that describes major work tasks performed.
- A *position specification* is based on a position description, and lists knowledge, skills, and abilities needed by an employee to function in that capacity with minimum acceptable performance.
- *Job descriptions* and *job specifications* are similar, except that their focus is on tasks and abilities shared across similar positions.
- A *job incumbent* is a person occupying a job.
- A *job cycle* refers to the length of time separating a job incumbent's recognition that action is necessary, and the decision of what action to take, action itself, examination of the consequences of the action, and evaluation of whether consequences resulting from the action satisfy intentions and initial reasons for taking action. The simpler the job, the shorter the job cycle. Generally, jobs at the lowest level of an organization's hierarchy of authority have the shortest cycles, while those at the highest level have the longest cycles. The cycle of a chief executive can extend over many years, for instance.
- A *value* is a belief about what is right or wrong—or good or bad (Flynn, 1997).
- *Validity* means that a method of analysis actually relates to characteristics associated with performance.
- *Reliability* means that a method of analysis yields consistent results upon subsequent use.

Why Is Work Analysis Important?

Every organization exists for at least one reason—and usually several reasons—and can only survive when some advantage is gained by its transactions with the environment. Advantages are of different kinds: profitability (in business) or satisfaction of perceived constituent needs (in government and not-for-profit sectors).

Jobs are the link between individuals and the organization, and between organizational structure and outputs (Hupp, 1995). While some observers have predicted the end of the traditional "job" (Bridges, 1994), work never seems to go away. When employees act in capacities that make good use of their abilities, the organization is able to gain through its transactions with the environment. Productivity is greater, and the organization is profitable and/or satisfies perceived societal needs.

From the standpoint of HR planners, work analysis is the basic process on which most other HR activities depend. Its aim is to provide managers with detailed information about how the organization performs its functions and thus goes about achieving its goals and objectives. It is the traditional foundation for all other HR initiatives, providing a foundation for recruiting, hiring, orienting, training, appraising, compensating, transferring, and promoting individuals.

There is an implicit link between work analysis and strategic business planning. Organization planning is concerned basically with role prescriptions at the upper levels and with defining expected behavior within the managerial hierarchy. Job analysis carries this process down through the rest of the organization. Job analysis, like organization planning, is a method of establishing a base against which the actual behavior of a firm's employees can be evaluated. It helps to provide a picture of each job and the interrelationships between jobs. In short, *what people do* and *how they do it* is related to *what the organization does* and *how well plans are ultimately realized*.

Nor does the matter end there. Work analysis provides the basis for establishing or reassessing the following points:

1. *Organizational structure* (sometimes called *organizational design*): How should the overall tasks of the organization be divided into entities like strategic business units, divisions, departments, work groups, and jobs?

2. *Job structure:* How should tasks be clustered in positions, jobs, and job families?

3. *Degrees of authority:* How should authority for decision-making be allocated?

4. *Span of control:* How should reporting relationships be established? How many and what kinds of people should report to each superior?

5. *Equal employment opportunity goals:* How should protected groups be represented in various jobs and job families?

6. *Performance standards:* How should measures be created over time to assess individual performance, group performance, and organizational performance?

7. *Succession plans:* How should succession be planned for?

8. *Career plans:* How should individuals prepare themselves to realize career aspirations?

9. *Selection criteria:* How should people be selected for jobs? How does a job constrain the kind of people appropriate for it?

10. *Training plans:* How should gaps between actual and required knowledge, skills, and abilities be rectified over time? How should people be prepared for high level responsibilities and upward mobility or lateral mobility?

11. *Organization development programs:* How should interpersonal relationships be handled between those in the same or different jobs, considering the potential conflict stemming from different values, goals, and objectives? What relations should exist within and between groups?

12. *Employee assistance programs:* How should conflicts be handled between individuals and between individuals and job requirements?
13. *Labor relations programs:* How should relationships be handled between management, as a class or group, and other classes or groups that have banded together for the purpose of collective bargaining?
14. *Compensation and benefit programs:* How should people be rewarded?

In short, work analysis yields crucial information of importance in every facet of organizational and HR planning (Clifford, 1994). It reveals needs that HR initiatives are intended to rectify or even anticipate.

What Should Be Analyzed?

Work analysis is undertaken to invent what people do. But it's not really as simple as this. *What people do* can be defined in more than one way, depending on one's perspective. Before beginning the work analysis process, the analyst will have to decide which perspective or perspectives are needed to provide the kind of information decision-makers require.

At least eight perspectives are possible (Walker, 1980):

1. *Reality:* What do people really do?
2. *Perceptions:* What do people believe they do?
3. *Norms:* What should people do?
4. *Plans:* What do people intend to do in the future?
5. *Motivation:* What do people want to do?
6. *Ability:* What are people able to do?
7. *Capability:* What do people have the potential to do that they are otherwise not doing?
8. *Forecast:* What do people expect to do in the future?

In a classic and still relevant treatment, Walker (1980) pointed out that there is a tradeoff between validity/reliability and expense: The greater the need for high validity and reliability—that is, a focus on reality—the greater the time and cost of obtaining information. Each perspective is appropriate for particular uses. They are summarized in Figure 3-1.

Figure 3-1: Selecting the Appropriate Focus for Work Analysis

Focus On	When You Want to
Reality: What do people really do?	Obtain very reliable and valid information
Perceptions: What do people believe they do?	Obtain information quickly and at relatively low cost
Norms: What should people do?	Clarify/compare employee and supervisory expectations
Plans: What do people intend to do in the future?	Clarify individual (or group) career intentions
Motivation: What do people want to do?	Identify factors in job/task design that motivate individuals, as a means of pinpointing useful improvement efforts Identify factors in job/task design that demotivate individuals, as a means of pinpointing barriers to productivity
Ability: What are people able to do?	Collect information about present behavior/performance common in a job
Capability: What do people have the potential to do that they are otherwise not doing?	Identify fruitful areas for productivity improvement
Forecast: What do people expect to do in the future?	Plan for future job requirements/activities

Traditionally, work analysts collect information based on *perceptions* of job incumbents and their superiors. Information of this kind is relatively inexpensive to obtain. It is used, in turn, to develop a normative statement of what people in a given job category are expected to do. As a consequence, most job descriptions differ from the reality of what individuals do in their positions in at least three key respects: job descriptions are often based on mere perceptions rather than reality; they reflect what is desired (norms) rather than what is (actual conditions), and they are more general than position descriptions. Job descriptions focus more on key similarities rather than on key differences between positions. In addition, job descriptions typically have a bias toward what people are doing or have been doing rather than what they will probably be doing in the future or should be doing at that time. That bias is particularly troublesome. The Americans with Disabilities Act (1990) requires the employer to make *reasonable accommodation* in such a manner as to make it possible for a worker with a disability to be employed, unless it poses an *undue burden* on the employer. While there are many forms of reasonable accommodation that an employer can make, an important one with implications for HR planners is called *job restructuring.* Job restructuring includes reallocating or redistributing marginal job functions that an employee is unable to perform because of a disability; and altering when and/or how a function, essential or marginal, is performed. To do that, of course, the employer must have a good sense of how often and how important that job function is to the employee's work.

Matters are further complicated in that perceptions about what people do frequently differ between job incumbents and their superiors. Indeed, these differences can be conceptualized by using the well-known Johari window (see Figure 3-2). On some matters, everyone agrees; on some, only the job incum-

Figure 3-2: How to Conceptualize Differences in Perception about Work Activities, Using the Johari Window

		Employee (Job Incumbent) Knows what to do	Employee (Job Incumbent) Does not know what to do
S U P E R V I S O R	Knows what employee does	Area of Agreement in Perceptions (Employee and supervisor agree on what should be done.)	Supervisors think they know what employee does, but employee does not perform in this area. (Supervisor perceives requirements that the employee is unaware of.)
	Does not know what employee does	Employees think they are expected to perform in this area, but supervisor does not know of this belief. (Employee perceives requirements that the supervisor is unaware of.)	Blind Spot Employee does not know what to do in this area; supervisor does not know what employee does in this area. Those outside the department might notice actions in this area. (Neither employee nor supervisor knows what should be done in this area.)

bent superior or the supervisor believes action is being taken; and on others, nobody agrees on what is being done. One major benefit of work analysis is that it establishes a common base of expectations on which job incumbents and their superiors can agree. As many studies have shown, common goals and expectations can produce major benefits in productivity improvement.

How Is Work Analysis Traditionally Conducted?

Think of the traditional work analysis process as consisting of seven steps. Analysts:

1. Become familiar with the position, job, or job family to be investigated. Work analysis is usually conducted for one job (i.e., secretary, supervisor, auditor) at a time.
2. Decide what kind of results are desired.
3. Select an approach to analysis that is best suited to yield the desired results.
4. Select a means to gather information.
5. Carry out work analysis by collecting information.
6. Compile and verify results.
7. Monitor conditions inside and outside the organization to determine when work analysis should be repeated to gather updated information. Figure 3-3 illustrates these steps in a simple flowchart.

How Is General Background Information Collected?

The starting point for any position or job analysis is to collect general background information. (We shall limit our discussion to job analysis. Essentially the same steps are used in examining a position.) Work analysts are seldom familiar with the details of any job until they do background research on it (Hackett and Williams, 1993). They need this information if they are to do effective analysis. They obtain information by collecting and reviewing past job descriptions used in the organization; contacting colleagues in other organiza-

Figure 3-3: Steps in the Traditional Work-Analysis Process

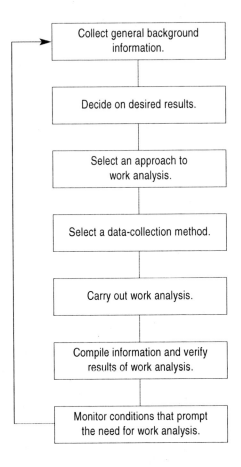

tions to request copies of any job descriptions they might have; looking for information about the job in specialized books, such as the *Dictionary of Occupational Titles,* or websites such as *http://www.doleta.gov/programs/onet/* or *http:// www.stepfour.com/jobs/* and in general books containing information about job descriptions; contacting associations representing people who share common job occupations across organizations in order to obtain sample descriptions and any other information that might be pertinent to job analysis; speaking informally with job incumbents or their superiors; and touring the work site to observe working conditions, tools, or equipment used and other jobs with which incumbents come in frequent contact. Though all these steps are not always necessary, work analysts should begin with a good, basic grasp of the job or position that they will examine.

What Results Do Analysts Hope to Obtain?

Before undertaking any study, analysts should decide tentatively what results they hope to obtain. By doing so, they will save themselves considerable time and effort collecting the information most valuable to decision-makers. In fact, before collecting the data, decide on the format in which results will ultimately be reported. If a standardized format is used for job descriptions throughout the organization, then the general appearance of the end product is already clear. Of course, a standardized format is only appropriate when the information it sets forth is useful to decision-makers (Grant, 1989).

Job analysis typically sets out to answer such questions as the following: What is the title of the job? What should it be? What is the general purpose of the job? How does the job relate to goals and objectives of the organization? What other job titles report to job incumbents? To what other titles do job incumbents report? What tasks are usually performed by the incumbents? What are the major duties and responsibilities of incumbents? More intensive work analysis projects—particularly those focused on reality more than perceptions— might require analysts to address the following questions: What tasks or activities occupy the most time of job incumbents? What tasks are most critical to successful job performance? With what behaviors or results are tasks associated? What activities take the longest for new job incumbents to learn? And what results or outputs are yielded by work activities? Answers to each question are appropriate for such uses as establishing performance standards, setting the length of probationary periods, and identifying where productivity can be improved.

What Are Some Approaches to Work Analysis?

Several approaches to work analysis are relatively common. They include Functional Job Analysis, the Position Analysis Questionnaire, the Position

Description Questionnaire, the Job Information Matrix System, the Job Element Approach, the Task Inventory Approach, the Occupational Analysis Inventory, and the Work Performance Survey System.

Functional Job Analysis (FJA), one of the best known, was first used by the U.S. Air Force and is popular in the public sector. Key assumptions:

1. The work analyst must distinguish between *what gets done* (results) and *what workers do to get things done* (procedures, work processes, behaviors).
2. Work process involves the action of people, data, and things.
3. All jobs involve some use of people, data, and things.
4. Though behavior and results can be described in many ways, only a handful of definite "functions" are involved.
5. The functions performed relative to people, data, and things can be classified on a taxonomy arranged from simple to complex (McCormick 1979).

Functional Job Analysis is the foundation for many HR systems. However, critics complain that it is too costly, relies too much on verbal descriptions, and applies to manual jobs more than to managerial/professional jobs.

The Position Analysis Questionnaire (PAQ) is a highly structured survey that categorizes jobs in terms of 187 elements, organized in six divisions:

1. *Information input* (where and how the worker gets information used in performing a job)
2. *Mental processes* (what reasoning, decision-making, planning, and information-processing activities are involved in performing a job)
3. *Work output* (what physical activities the worker performs and with what tools or devices)
4. *Relationships with other persons* (the relationships with other people that are required to perform a job)
5. *Job context* (in what physical or social context is the work performed)
6. *Other job characteristics* (what activities, conditions, or characteristics other than those described above are relevant to perform-

ance). Each job can be rated on each element, using six different rating scales in the survey instrument (McCormick, 1979, p. 144).

The Position Analysis Questionnaire has been widely used, so its results can be compared with those obtained in other organizations. The capability for comparison is one advantage; another is that responses are coded on optical scan sheets, which lend themselves easily to computer analysis. The PAQ might not be easily tailored to unique situations, organizations, or conditions (Walker, 1980).

The *Position Description Questionnaire* (PDQ) is also widely used. A creation of Control Data Corporation, it lends itself easily to quantification of results and thus to computer analysis. Unfortunately, it is costly to tailor to unique requirements of specific organizations.

The *Job Information Matrix System* (JIMS) is another approach to analysis, but it has not been applied to all occupations. This system is designed to collect information on such issues as what the worker *does* on the job, what equipment or tools the worker *uses,* what the worker *has to know,* what the worker's *responsibilities* are, and *under what conditions* the worker has to perform. This matrix system can be completed by supervisors and/or workers (McCormick, 1979).

The Job Introduction Matrix System is standardized, and that is an advantage. Responses to each module can be computerized, but a Work Analyst will still be needed to monitor analysis. This system can be used to great effect with some occupations. Its major disadvantage is that it does not lend itself well to analysis of white-collar jobs.

The *Job Element Approach* to analysis was the creation of Dr. Ernest Primoff. It was designed to help select employees for the U.S. Civil Service. An *element* is an item of knowledge, a skill, an ability, or a personal characteristic linked somehow to job success. Initially, Primoff envisioned 62 such elements, all applicable to manual jobs. A group of supervisors and experienced employees rate jobs according to these elements. A simple three-point scale indicates whether the specific element is not present in the job, is present but is not important, or is present and is important (McCormick, 1979).

The chief advantage of the approach is simplicity. Since the response scale is numerical, results for each job can be analyzed by computer. The disadvantage is that, in this form, the job element approach is not useful for white-collar occupations.

The *Task Inventory Approach* does not have a standardized format. It consists of two parts. The first part is a list of tasks, often as comprehensive as possible. Each task is phrased in terms of what is done by the incumbent. It does not focus on the cause for acting or on specific procedures. The second part is a scale for responding, allowing those using the survey to indicate how important the task is, how often it is performed, or how much time is devoted to the task. Naturally, a task inventory implies that a detailed task analysis has already been performed, using any one of several standard approaches. In addition to the primary rating scale, other scales can be used to gather additional information about job complexity, length of training time required, or supervision time needed for incumbents.

Task inventories are very helpful for most occupational fields and organizations. They are quite flexible and can be quantified to allow for computer analysis. Though useful for designing training, they do have drawbacks. First, they are time consuming and thus expensive to develop. Second, they require technical expertise in task analysis, which is not always available. Third, they work best for manual jobs and less well for professional, technical, and managerial ones that do not lend themselves easily to observation. Jobs of the latter type are better handled through creation of competency models. Much attention has been devoted recently to task complexity in work (Campbell, 1998).

The *Occupational Analysis Inventory* (OAI) was the creation of Dr. William Cunningham. He started out trying to find a way to cluster occupations for preparation of educational programs. In many respects, it is quite similar to the Position Analysis Questionnaire, except that it includes job-oriented elements as well as worker-oriented ones. It also covers work goals. The inventory uses over 600 elements organized in five divisions: information received, mental activities, work behavior, work goals, and work context. These elements are rated on three scales: significance, occurrence, and applicability. The first two scales are six-pointed; the last one, dichotomous.

The Occupational Analysis Inventory is advantageous in that it is more comprehensive than the Position Analysis Questionnaire. In this respect, results are more specific, but the sheer number of elements is a drawback, making it unwieldy to use. While results do lend themselves well to an assessment of training needs, other approaches are preferable for such other uses as establishing pay schedules. The results of OAI are simply *too* specific for many uses.

The *Work Performance Survey System* (WPSS) was developed by AT&T as part of a project initiated in 1973. It represents a half-way point between unstructured task inventory approaches and a structured format. It is appropriate when many people perform the jobs under analysis, when people are widely scattered geographically, when quantitative data are desired, when computer analysis will be used, and when specific information is needed. Task statements are developed from frequently mentioned job activities found on previous job descriptions, observations of job incumbents, and interviews with job incumbents and their superiors. The chief source of information is the interview.

The approaches to work analysis are briefly summarized in Figure 3-4. In recent years, too, various innovative approaches have been explored (Belbin, Watson, and West, 1997). Special approaches have been applied to teams (Caudron, 1994), and research has compared the relative value of different work analysis approaches (Clifford, 1996). Work has also been analyzed for the values required for it (Laabs, 1997), and it has also been examined for the unique requirements necessary to comply with organizational policies on quality (Siegel, 1996).

What Are Some Data-Collection Methods for Work Analysis?

If the work analyst is interested in comparing their results to those from other organizations, he or she will most likely select a standardized approach like those described in the previous section. On the other hand, if they wish to adapt their methods to unique conditions prevailing in their organization, they can design their own specialized forms and procedures for collecting information through job observations, surveys, interviews, work diaries, and content

Figure 3-4: A Summary of Approaches to Work Analysis

Approach	Brief Description	Advantages	Disadvantages
Functional Job Analysis	I Work analyst distinguishes between what gets done and what workers do	I Based on a good conceptualization scheme	I Too costly I Relies too much on verbal descriptions I Less applicable to white-collar than manual jobs
Position Analysis Questionnaire	I Highly structured survey to be completed by the work analyst	I Results can be compared to those obtained in other organizations	I Requires high levels of reading comprehension I Difficult to tailor
Position Description Questionnaire	I Another highly structured survey	I Results lend themselves to computer analysis	I Costly to tailor to unique requirements in one setting
Job Information Matrix System	I Designed to collect information on what people do, what they use, what they have to know, what responsibilities they have, and under what conditions they perform	I Standardized I Results can be computerized	I Does not lend itself well to white-collar jobs
Job Element Approach	I Uses a three-point scale to rate jobs	I Simple I Results can be computerized	I Does not lend itself well to white-collar jobs
Task Inventory Approach	I Consists of a list of tasks and a scale for responding	I Flexible I Results can be computerized	I Time consuming and expensive I Requires special expertise I Does not lend itself well to white-collar jobs
Occupational Analysis Inventory	I Uses over 600 elements, rated on three scales	I Comprehensive I Results are very specific	I Number of elements makes it unwieldy to use
Work Performance Survey System	I Represents a half-way point between structured and unstructured surveys	I Appears to balance flexibility and structure	I None noted

Figure 3-5: A Summary of General Data-Collection Methods for Job Analysis

Method	Variations	Brief Description	Advantages	Disadvantages
Observations	Structured	▪ Watch people go about their work; record frequency of behaviors or nature of performance on forms prepared in advance	▪ Third-party observer has more credibility than job incumbents who may have reasons for distorting information ▪ Focuses more on reality than on perceptions	▪ Observation can influence behavior of job incumbents ▪ Meaningless for jobs requiring mental effort (in that case, use information-processing method) ▪ Not useful for jobs with a long job cycle
	Unstructured	▪ Watch people go about their work; describe behaviors/tasks performed		
	Combination	▪ Part of the form is prepared in advance and is structured; part is unstructured		
Surveys	Structured	▪ Ask job incumbents/ supervisors about work performed, using fixed responses	▪ Relatively inexpensive ▪ Structured surveys lend themselves easily to computer analyses ▪ Good method when survey sample is widely scattered	▪ Depends on verbal skills of respondents ▪ Does not allow for probing ▪ Tends to focus on perceptions of the job
	Unstructured	▪ Ask job incumbents/supervisors to write essays to describe work performed		
	Combination	▪ Part of the survey is structured; part is unstructured		

Figure 3-5: *(continued)*

Method	Variations	Brief Description	Advantages	Disadvantages
Diaries	Structured	■ Ask people to record their activities over several days or weeks in a booklet, with time increments provided	■ Highly detailed information can be collected over the entire job cycle ■ Quite appropriate for jobs with a long job cycle	■ Requires the job incumbent's participation and cooperation ■ Tends to focus on perceptions of the job
	Unstructured	■ Ask people to indicate in a booklet over how long a period they work on a task or activity		
	Combination	■ Part of the diary is structured; part is unstructured		
Individual interviews	Structured	■ Read questions and/or fixed response choices to job incumbent and supervisor; must be face-to-face	■ More flexible than surveys ■ Allows for probing to extract information	■ Depends heavily on rapport between interviewer and respondent ■ Possible problems with validity/ reliability
	Unstructured	■ Ask questions and/or provide general response choices to job incumbent and supervisor; must be face-to-face		
	Combination	■ Part of the interview is structured; part is unstructured		

Figure 3-5: *(continued)*

Method	Variations	Brief Description	Advantages	Disadvantages
Group interviews	Structured	■ Same as structured individual interviews, except that more than one job incumbent/supervisor is interviewed	■ Groups tend to do better with open-ended problems than individuals ■ Chance that reliability/validity is higher than with individuals because group members cross-check each other	■ Costs more because more people are taken away from their jobs to participate ■ Like individual interviews, tends to focus on perceptions of the job
	Unstructured	■ Same as unstructured individual interviews, except that more than one job incumbent/supervisor is interviewed		
	Combination	■ Same as combination individual interviews, except more than one job incumbent/supervisor is interviewed		
Content analysis	Structured	■ Use a form, created through unstructured content analysis, to record frequency of mention of tasks or activities in a job	■ Avoids influencing behavior of job incumbents (as observation is prone to do) ■ Minimizes reliance on perceptions of job incumbents	■ Depends heavily on choice of documents, previous descriptions ■ Tends to focus on norms, rather than on reality
	Unstructured	■ Identify common duties/tasks/activities of a job through examination of documents; create a form		
	Combination	■ Use a form created through unstructured content analysis for same activities associated with a job; create a form for other activities		

analysis. Each approach to collecting job information has distinct advantages and disadvantages, which are summarized briefly in Figure 3-5.

Historically speaking, the first work analysis methods were based on observation. Frederick Taylor advocated early in this century that managers should watch their experienced employees while they work. By doing so, managers could learn productive short cuts that could be taught to newcomers. Frank and Lillian Gilbreth turned observation into a science. Using photographs taken in quick succession, they were able to dissect physical movements of laborers and reassemble them in more efficient and productive ways. When time as well as movement was considered, modern *work measurement*—otherwise known as *time and motion study*—was born.

While appropriate for analyzing jobs requiring physical effort and observable behaviors, work measurement has been less appropriate for white-collar occupations relying on mental effort to produce results. Examples of such occupations include medicine, law, and management. More appropriate in these cases is the *information-processing approach*. Work analysts tag along with experienced job incumbents as they work.

To summarize basic steps in this process, the analyst: (1) watches job incumbents as they work; (2) asks questions about what is happening; (3) probes about the necessary order of events to find out why one task or sequence of tasks is carried out before others; (4) defines procedures and decision criteria; (5) constructs a flowchart of activities and decision points; and (6) presents the flowchart to a panel of job incumbents and their superiors for verification. Obviously, the focus is less on what is done than on what criteria are used in decision-making. Though difficult to distill into a job description, results of such analysis provide much useful information for training and career planning (Zemke and Kramlinger, 1982).

However, more general approaches to *work observation* can also be used. For example, a work analyst can watch job incumbents as they engage in typical duties. Analysts record the type or frequency of behaviors on an "observation sheet." First, *structured observation sheets* are prepared in advance. Analysts mark behavioral observation scales, representing the frequency of common or important behaviors. Obviously, some other method—such as task analysis—

must be used first to identify what behaviors to record. Second, *unstructured observation sheets* are filled out as the job incumbent is working. They can be used as a starting point for designing more structured observation methods. In other words, the analyst tries to identify categories of behavior while the behavior is occurring. Unstructured observation sheets are of limited value because it is hard to define categories of behavior while simultaneously recording the frequency of their occurrence. Third, *partially structured and partially unstructured sheets* lend themselves to analyzing jobs characterized by diversity of behavior.

Most observation methods are superior to written surveys or face-to-face interviews for collecting job information. One reason is that recording the frequency of behavior is bound to be more accurate than asking incumbents or their superiors to estimate frequency. Even incumbents can have a distorted sense of how much time they spend on certain activities. In addition, third-party observers usually have no stake in the results of job analysis, while incumbents are often aware that results might affect things like salary or performance standards. Unfortunately, observation is expensive to use because of the cost of paying an observer. Moreover, some jobs—particularly white-collar ones—do not lend themselves well to observation. They require other methods.

The *written survey* is another common approach to data collection. We have already discussed two standardized ones: the Position Analysis Questionnaire and the Position Description Questionnaire. However, managers in some firms prefer to develop their own surveys to collect information of particular value to them. Developing and using job analysis questionnaires is not significantly different from the process used in developing any questionnaire. However, it is sometimes hard to ensure that self-designed surveys are valid and reliable. Indeed, the same problem holds true for any do-it-yourself approach (Urbanek, 1997).

Much like general observation methods, surveys can be of three types. In *structured surveys,* respondents check a scale already provided, fill in blanks, or circle a multiple-choice response. In *unstructured surveys,* respondents write essays on specific questions. In *partially structured and partially unstructured surveys,* respondents complete a structured part of the survey and then write

essays in other parts. Activity 3-1 at the end of the chapter gives you an opportunity to examine an interview form that can be easily converted to an unstructured written survey.

Job-analysis surveys are usually completed by one or more job incumbents
and then reviewed by their supervisors. They tend to focus on perceptions of
work activities more than on reality. They are relatively inexpensive to administer and are particularly useful for gathering information from large samples of
geographically scattered job incumbents. Disadvantages of using them include
their heavy reliance on the verbal ability of respondents—especially when
unstructured—and the potential for misinterpretation or deliberate manipula-
tion of questions and answers.

Interviews are similar to surveys in many respects. The work analyst meets
with a job incumbent and later with the supervisor to pose questions and record
answers about work activities. Group interviews with job incumbents and/or
supervisors are also possible. Much like general observation methods and surveys, interviews can be:

1. *Structured:* A list of questions and/or answers called an *interview
   schedule* is prepared in advance of the interview. A schedule resembles a structured survey. Questions are in a fixed order and have
   fixed wording from which the interviewer cannot stray. Maintaining
   this wording is important, because it helps preserve consistency
   across interviews.

2. *Unstructured:* A list of topics called an *interview guide* is prepared.
   The list is a general one about work. The interviewer makes up specific questions on the topics during the interview. Topics need not
   be treated in a fixed order. Respondents are asked about the equipment they use, the jobs with which they interact, their most important duties, and how much time they spend on various aspects of
   the job.

3. *Partially structured and partially unstructured:* In this format, the
   interviewer relies on a combination of the other two. Part of the interview is structured; part is unstructured.

A sample job analysis interview form is illustrated in Activity 3-2 at the end of the chapter.

The major advantage of the interview is its potential for probing and give-and-take between work analyst, job incumbent, and his or her superior. The interview leads to a deeper understanding about the person than do written surveys. Major disadvantages include the following:

1. Interviewing is time consuming and thus expensive.
2. It does not lend itself well to widespread coverage of a large, scattered population, due to the cost of travel and time needed to conduct interviews.
3. Unstructured interview results do not lend themselves easily to quantification for subsequent computerized analysis.

Interviews, like written surveys, tend to tap perceptions about what people think they do and not so much what they really do.

A work diary or log is yet another way to collect data. The job incumbent is asked to record his or her activities at regular intervals (every 15, 30, or 60 minutes, for instance). A diary, as its name implies, is a booklet that looks much like a personal diary or account ledger. There is a page or two for each day. Each page has time recorded in increments along the left margin and blank columns for activities and remarks.

For jobs covering a relatively long cycle, diaries are effective for recording activities but are not so useful for assessing consequences of those activities. Their chief disadvantages are that they rely heavily on the cooperation of the job incumbent, and they concentrate on activities rather than results. If the job incumbent forgets to make or complete an entry, the results will be inaccurate because recollections tend to be selective. At the same time, how important is it to know, for instance, that an executive spends three hours per day on the telephone? When activity is the focus of attention, as it is in a diary, those are the kinds of things that will be recorded. Much more important for analyzing the executive's job is to find out what was discussed on the phone, what results stemmed from it, and how well results matched up to intentions.

Content analysis is a fourth approach to data collection. Simple as it appears, research has generally shown that it can be as accurate as factor analysis (a statistical test), without the mathematics. Of course, it has been applied to a broad range of problems in the humanities and social sciences.

One way to use correct analysis is to form a team or panel consisting of the analyst, job incumbents, and their superiors. Team members then collect information about the job from previous and outside job descriptions, procedure manuals used by incumbents, training materials, and any other documents that shed light on work activities related to the job being studied. They then write task statements, derived from the documents, on slips of paper or on notecards. Each team member does this separately; only one statement should appear on each card, and a task statement indicates one activity, observable actions, the context or job conditions in which the activity is carried out, and an outcome. The next step is to sort statements into clusters, based on similarities of tasks (each team member does this separately) and then compare the clusters developed across individuals on the team. The group achieves consensus about clusters of tasks, and names each cluster. This approach is called *unstructured content analysis*. Its purpose is to develop clusters of tasks for use in preparing, updating, or otherwise modifying job descriptions.

Once clusters are developed, work analysts can then use them to create much more structured survey, interview, or observation forms. For instance, a form can be devised as an aid in conducting future job-analysis studies. If the original list of tasks is fixed and allows for no modification, it serves as a guide for future *structured content analysis* of the job.

Content analysis is advantageous in that it is not based on mere perceptions, the way surveys, diaries, and interviews are. Nor does it have the potential to change the behavior of job incumbents as the job-analysis process is being carried out (a problem that can plague observations). Compared with interviews and observations, content analysis is relatively inexpensive to conduct. However, it does suffer from one major drawback: It depends heavily on the quality of materials selected for review. If they are inaccurate, outdated, invalid, or unreliable, then the analysis will be, too.

How Can the Work Analysis Process Be Carried Out?

Few books discuss how to carry out work analysis in much detail.

The most important point to remember is that the work analyst is a disinterested third party. Surely work analyses are sometimes requested for reasons other than a dispassionate desire for information. Often there is a hidden agenda. Employees might be interested in magnifying their own importance in an effort to get higher pay, titles, and status. Managers sometimes go along with this ploy, especially when they fear loss of an experienced worker with whom they enjoy a good and productive relationship. The appropriate role of analyst is not to function as a confederate in a conspiracy; rather, it is to gather and assess facts objectively and impassionately, and convey recommendations to decision-makers.

Though work analysts should seek rapport with those with whom they deal, they should not do so at the expense of professionalism. To act as a confederate in a conspiracy to inflate the pay and/or status of an employee or job category is not the act of a professional. In addition, serving as a "rubber stamp" for decisions already made is to risk the credibility not only of work analysis but of the entire HR function.

How Are Results Verified?

No single method of job analysis is entirely satisfactory alone. Each suffers from a major drawback. Generally speaking, the more reliable and valid the results, the higher the cost to obtain them. Hence, the analyst must consider how important it is to seek highly reliable and valid information.

Several methods can be used to increase the validity and reliability of results.

1. *Use more than one approach.* By combining approaches, the drawbacks of each can be minimized.
2. *Use more than one job incumbent.* If only one job incumbent is studied, he or she might or might not be representative of an entire group

of employees; hence, it is appropriate to sample the incumbents and study individuals as part of a group.

3. *Use multiple raters.* Job incumbents and their superiors rarely agree completely on actual or desirable job duties, tasks, or methods. For this reason, it is appropriate to involve both an incumbent and a superior in the job analysis process for double checking and for establishing a common ground of expectations.

As a further step in verification, the analyst should feed results back to participants for their review. If participants do not agree with results, further refinement might be needed. Though seeking consensus is time consuming, costly, and often frustrating, it is essential if incumbents and their superiors are to agree on what work is being done and should be done at present.

The results of traditional work analysis are important indeed. They are variously used to develop job descriptions, prepare job specifications, carry out salary surveys, develop pay schedules, assess training needs, establish individual performance appraisals, facilitate organizational and job design decisions, allocate authority for decision-making, establish appropriate numbers and kinds of people reporting to each supervisor, establish or monitor equal employment opportunity goals in compliance with law, improve use of existing employee talent, devise succession plans, develop training plans for job clusters, facilitate individual career planning, and much more.

In short, traditional or present-oriented work analysis is a key step in strategic planning for HR because it helps to describe the work that is being done and establishes a norm about the work that should be done. By itself, it is inadequate for strategic HR planning. But when compared to forecasts of the future— a topic treated in a later chapter—this information provides a basis for long-term planning.

How Are Internal and External Conditions Monitored?

There are no guidelines that address how often positions, job classes, or job families should be analyzed. It depends solely on the organization. However, work analysts should consider establishing a regular cycle so that every so often each job class is routinely analyzed. In this way, managers always have reasonably accurate and up-to-date information about what employees are doing.

Clearly, whenever there is a major change inside or outside the organization, some jobs should be reviewed. Internal changes include reorganizations, reallocations of authority, and selection of new long-term strategies. External changes include mergers with or purchases of or takeovers by other firms, and any other dramatic or unexpected event that poses a threat or opportunity to the business. One impact of changes like these is that they will alter somewhat how people approach their work, and what they do. Work analysis can help deal with change by identifying shifts in work patterns that are likely to occur, are occurring, or have occurred at every level throughout the organization. For this reason, work analysts should watch for changes and take action on them.

Who initiates work analysis? It varies. Theoretically, any major group—job incumbents, supervisors, and work analysts—should have the right to *request* review. Others might veto the request, putting it off or squelching it completely. In more practical terms, however, analysis might not be discretionary. Collective bargaining agreements can make it difficult to carry out and even more difficult to act on results, especially when they are unfavorable for job incumbents whose pay and title depends on results.

To avoid these problems, the work analyst must be at once technician and expert in interpersonal skills. Technical skill is crucial in carrying out the process itself; interpersonal skills are essential to any study of what people do because you must demonstrate that compelling reasons justify it.

How Are Competencies Identified, and How Are Values Assessed?

In recent years, professional work analysis has been energized by a new view of what is necessary to achieve successful performance in organizations. Competencies are now the focus. Going a step beyond simply listing work activities, duties, or responsibilities, *competency identification* is the process of discovering the key differences between best-in-class and average workers in any job category (Dubois and Rothwell, 2000). While there are many approaches to performing competency identification (Rothwell and Lindholm, 1999), most share in common the assumption that successful performance has to do with differences between people, rather than between jobs or work activities. Hence, "competency" is a broad term that encompasses not just knowledge, skill, and attitude, but also personality characteristics, levels of motivation, and other factors that distinguish one person from another. Most often, competency identification is focused on a group, such as a job category, occupation, or department. The goal of a competency identification effort is to move beyond job descriptions to identify all the factors that distinguish the most successful from the average performers. Then, the behaviors linked to those competencies are identified.

But outstanding performance is not enough: Organizations also require moral leadership. For that reason, some organizations have gone beyond traditional work analysis to review the work in terms of its moral dimensions. This is called *values identification*. What values are necessary for successful performers to be effective? While performance can be achieved at the expense of morals and ethics, the price is often too high in terms of long-term impact on the organization or industry.

The recent addition of competency identification and values identification represents new dimensions against which to examine work efforts. They are important because competency identification recognizes that performance (results) involves more than just the work activities that people do—or even the knowledge, skills, and attitudes necessary to carry out those activities. It focuses on differences between individuals, and between the best-in-class workers and those who are average. Values identification adds yet another dimension—a moral and ethical dimension—to work analysis.

Activity 3-1: Work Analysis Role Play

Purpose
This activity is intended to simulate one way of performing work analysis.

Group Size	*Time Required*
Recommended for groups of three people each	Approximately 100 minutes
Materials Needed	*Special Seating Requirements*
Pen or pencil	Movable chairs and tables are desirable, but not essential

Introduction
Work analysis can be somewhat more challenging in reality than when discussed in the abstract. This activity gives you an opportunity to try your hand at it.

Procedure
Step 1: 5 minutes

1. In each group of three people, one person should play the role of work analyst, a second should play the role of a job incumbent, and a third should play the dual roles of observer and the job incumbent's immediate supervisor.
2. The work analyst will interview the job incumbent (first), using the structured questionnaire/interview schedule provided. (If the activity is conducted in a university setting, the job incumbent's position can be that of student; if the activity is conducted in a work setting, the job incumbent's position should be the same as that in real life.)
3. The observer will take notes during the interview on how well the interviewer is able to elicit complete and meaningful answers.
4. When the work analyst has completed the interview with the job incumbent, he or she will then interview the "supervisor" (played by the observer) by using the questions provided on the last two pages of the structured questionnaire/interview schedule.

Step 2: 60 minutes

The work analyst should conduct the interview with the job incumbent while the observer takes notes. Make up answers to any questions for which you have no real ones.

Job Analysis Study

(Interviewer: Begin by asking the interviewee to provide answers for each blank below)

Employee Name _____

Position _____

Date Hired _____

Date of Last Evaluation _____

Time in Position _____

Supervisor's Name _____

Today's Date _____

Activity 3-1: *(continued)*

Position Interview Schedule
Part 1

Instructions: This section of the job analysis study is designed to gather general information about your job.

1. (If applicable) Do you perform special duties or use special skills that you think are probably unlike those of others with your job title? If so, describe your special duties or skills, and outline the experience or education needed for them.

2. If you are a manager, list in the spaces below the *position titles* that report directly to you. (If you are not a manager, skip to question 3.)

3. If you are not a supervisor, but are recognized periodically as someone who directs the work of others, check here ( ) and complete the following list:

Position Title Reporting to You

_____

_____   Estimate the total amount of time *in hours* you
                                            spend annually on issuing orders and/or instruc-
_____   tions to other people.

_____   _____

_____

_____

4. List your *major* duties, expected results of those activities, the estimated amount of time that you devote to each duty, and how long it would take your immediate supervisor to detect *substandard* performance. Try to limit the list so that it includes only those duties you believe are most critical to successful job performance. In addition, rank the activities so that the most important ones are listed first. Use a piece of paper to organize your thoughts before answering.

Duty (briefly describe)	Expected results (briefly describe)	Percentage of time	Length of time needed to detect substandard performance
1.			
2.			
3.			
4.			

Activity 3-1: *(continued)*

Duty (briefly describe)	Expected results (briefly describe)	Percentage of time	Length of time needed to detect substandard performance
5.			
6.			

7. List the major sources of information to which you *frequently* refer during the normal course of your duties, (Example: a clerk-typist might refer to style manuals in the typing of letters; an auditor might refer to ledgers, audit standards, etc.)

8. At what stage of completion are assignments typically given to you? (Examples: near completion, far from completion.) What decisions about how to treat a job assignment have already been made when you receive it?

9. Describe those areas in which you regularly *take action* without higher approval.

10. List the most typical tangible outputs of your work. (Examples: computer print-outs, memos, letters, statistical summaries.)

11. List each item of equipment that you *frequently* use in your work. (Examples: typewriter, calculator, microfiche reader, computer terminal.)

    1. _____

    2. _____

    3. _____

    4. _____

    5. _____

    6. _____

    7. _____

Activity 3-1: *(continued)*

12. If your job has changed *significantly* since the last analysis (or as it appears on the present job description), specify duties, responsibilities, or activities that have been added, substantially changed, or phased out.

13. Do you foresee any changes in your position *within the next year* that might result from changes in work flow? If so, describe them.

14. What people *within the organization* do you regularly contact in the performance of your job? Indicate how often such contacts are made by checking one of the columns below. Finally, describe the purpose of these contacts.

Frequency of Contact
(check (✓) appropriate box)

(A) many times daily (B) once or twice daily (C) once or twice a week
(D) once or twice a month (E) once or twice a year.

Position Title	A	B	C	D	E	Purpose of Contact
_____	( )	( )	( )	( )	( )	_____
_____	( )	( )	( )	( )	( )	_____
_____	( )	( )	( )	( )	( )	_____
_____	( )	( )	( )	( )	( )	_____
_____	( )	( )	( )	( )	( )	_____
_____	( )	( )	( )	( )	( )	_____
_____	( )	( )	( )	( )	( )	_____
_____	( )	( )	( )	( )	( )	_____

Activity 3-1: *(continued)*

15. What people outside of your organization do you regularly come in contact with in the performance of your job? (In some cases it might be a group: e.g., the general public, the press.) Indicate how often these contacts are made:

Frequency of Contact
(check (✓) appropriate box)

(A) more than twice daily (B) once or twice daily (C) once or twice a week (D) once or twice a month (E) once or twice a year.
Finally, describe the purpose of these contacts

Position Title/ Organization	A	B	C	D	E	Purpose of Contact
_____	( )	( )	( )	( )	( )	_____
_____	( )	( )	( )	( )	( )	_____
_____	( )	( )	( )	( )	( )	_____
_____	( )	( )	( )	( )	( )	_____
_____	( )	( )	( )	( )	( )	_____
_____	( )	( )	( )	( )	( )	_____
_____	( )	( )	( )	( )	( )	_____

16. What specific college or training courses would be *essential* for starting in your job?

_____

_____

_____

_____

_____

_____

_____

Activity 3-1: *(continued)*

17. What specific background *experience* would be *essential* for starting your job? Estimate *how much* of this experience you think would be needed.

Essential background experience	How much?
_____	_____
_____	_____
_____	_____
_____	_____
_____	_____
_____	_____

18. Given the education you specified above, what is the *least* amount of experience necessary before a new employee should be assigned to your job and function at your present level of performance?

19. Given the education specified above, what would a new employee be *compelled to learn* before he or she could work satisfactorily?

20. What personality traits do you believe are *particularly* important for successful performance in your job?

21. Describe the most *frequently recurring problems* you encounter in your job.

22. Do you have recommendations to make in order to improve the nature of your job or your job duties? If so, what are they?

Feel free to add any other comments you wish to make.

Activity 3-1: *(continued)*

Step 3: 15 minutes

The work analyst should conduct the interview with the job incumbent's supervisor.

To be asked of the supervisor

Directions to Interviewer: Ask the employee's supervisor to review the employee's answers to questions on the Job Analysis Survey. Then pose the following questions:

1. In general, do you feel this employee (check a box below the item)

   Is a high producer?   Is a moderately high producer?   Is a somewhat low producer?   Is a low producer?

   ☐   ☐   ☐   ☐

   Remarks: _____

   _____

2. The best mix of education and experience for this specific position is

3. Based on past experiences, an employee at this level needs about how much time before he/she is expected to perform at the same level of efficiency as seasoned employees with the same job title?

4. Before operating at a level of efficiency comparable to more experienced employees, what specific information or skills would a new employee have to learn?

5. From your observations, what are the most *frequently recurring problems* encountered by the employee in conducting his or her work?

6. Comment on any substantive areas of disagreement with the employee's summary of his or her job duties, activities, responsibilities, etc.

Supervisor's signature _____

Date _____

Activity 3-1: *(continued)*

Discussion

Discussion Questions

1. Will observers from each group summarize their observations?
2. What common problems were apparent in the conduct of these interviews? What could be done to avoid them in the future?
3. What can be done with results of the work analysis?
4. How well do you think this work analysis would work for production employees? Clerical/secretarial workers? Managers? Technical personnel? What makes you think so in each case?
5. How might the results of this work analysis be used?

Notes

Activity 3-2: An Interview Guide Form for Job Analysis

Name of Job Incumbent	Name of Supervisor
Name of Work Analyst	Date of Interview
Job Title	Department
Length of Time in Job	Division
	Location

Purpose

1. In one sentence or so, please summarize the major reason that your job exists. In short, what is its *main purpose*?

Supervision Received

2. What is the job title of your supervisor?

3. Do you sometimes report to more than one person? If so, what are the job titles of these other individuals? How often—that is, what percent of the time—do you report to them?

Titles	Percent of Time

Supervision Exercised

4. What job titles report to you?

5. How many people do you supervise?

6. What percent of your time is spent on directing or overseeing the work of other people?
   _____%

Tools/Equipment

7. List major tools or equipment you frequently use in your work. (Be sure to include, when appropriate, such tools as computers, typewriters, calculators, etc.)

Activity 3-2: *(continued)*

Working Conditions

8. What work activities occupy most of your time? Briefly describe what you do and how you do it. Begin with the most time-consuming duty first.

Duty	Process
a.	
b.	
c.	
d.	
e.	
f.	
g.	

9. Which of these duties are most important for successful performance? List the most important duties below. Then explain in the right column why you believe each is important.

Duty	Process
a.	
b.	
c.	
d.	
e.	
f.	
g.	

10. Which of these duties took the longest to learn how to perform successfully?

Education

11. What kind of education would you consider essential, as a bare minimum, to start in your job? Explain your reasoning.

Experience

12. What kind of experience would you consider essential, as a bare minimum, to start in your job? Explain your reasoning.

Activity 3-2: *(continued)*

Personal Qualities
13. What personal qualities would you consider essential, as a bare minimum, to start in your job and perform successfully? Explain your reasoning.

Comments
14. What additional comments do you have?

Supervisor's Remarks
15. On what responses provided by the job incumbent do you disagree? Identify them and explain.

CHAPTER 4

THE HUMAN RESOURCES WORKFORCE ANALYST

In the previous chapter, we suggested that the best place to begin strategic planning for human resources (SPHR) is by examining *what people are doing at present*. This process is called *work analysis*. Traditionally, it involves gathering information from job incumbents and their superiors based on their perceptions of work activities. The information is used to form idealized or normative statements about what job incumbents should be doing. These statements are called *job descriptions*. Work analysis, we noted, has traditionally been crucial in establishing and maintaining appropriate organizational structure, job design, allocation of authority, and span of control. Indeed, results of work analysis are valuable because of the norms they provide for all facets of human resources, including the establishment of selection criteria, assessment of training needs, and preparation of competitive pay schedules.

However, work analysis provides only part of the information that decision-makers need to plan for the organization's long-term future. A related issue has to do with *what kind of people are doing the work of the organization at present*. This chapter addresses this issue and thus introduces the third of the ten roles of HR planners: the *workforce analyst*.

What Does the Workforce Analyst Do?

The workforce analyst is the term used to refer to the role of HR planner associated with *establishing norms for the kind of people to be selected for jobs, devising methods for assessing individual performance, and taking inventory of knowledge, skills, and attitudes of workers in the organization.* Traditional workforce analysis—like traditional work analysis, its counterpart—is inadequate for anticipating future organizational needs for reasons that will be treated at length in Chapter 7. However, we shall focus attention at this time on traditional methods of workforce analysis, because of its importance in HR.

What Specialized Terms Are Associated with Workforce Analysis?

There are only a few terms associated with workforce analysis. To save time later and facilitate economical expression, we shall begin with definitions.

- A *position specification* is a list of concrete requirements inferred from a position description—educational, experiential, and personal. These requirements are considered minimum entry-level knowledge, skills, and abilities necessary for one position in one organization.
- A *job specification* lists the human characteristics that are deemed essential to learning the job. It translates the general work requirements found on the job description into the necessary educational, experiential, and personal requirements needed by someone to do the job.
- A *person description* is similar to a job specification, but it is more detailed. It translates each task listed on a job or position description into the skills needed by an individual to carry out the task.
- A *job performance standard,* sometimes called simply a *work standard,* is a norm that establishes *how well* an activity should be performed. Based on work analysis, it is a yardstick against which individual performance is to be assessed.

■ *Employee performance appraisal,* sometimes called *performance appraisal* or *performance evaluation,* assesses or measures how well individuals are performing their jobs over a specific time period. While a job description sets forth what people are supposed to do, employee appraisal evaluates how well an individual actually carries out those job description activities, duties, or responsibilities over a given time.

■ *Performance management* is the process of establishing a work environment where people want to perform, and where they receive continuous feedback about their performance. Performance appraisal is usually included as part of a more comprehensive performance-management system.

■ *360-degree appraisal* is a process by which individuals are rated by those who surround them (as in a circle). *360-feedback systems* can be used for development or for appraisal (Lepsinger and Lucia, 1997). At present, this method is probably used more for appraisal in the United States than in other nations (Fletcher, 1998). In fact, it is so widely used for appraisal, some observers call it a fad (Waldman, Atwater, and Antonioni, 1998).

■ A *skill inventory* is a general term referring to any manual or computerized catalogue of human characteristics available to the organization. This enables decision-makers to find out what kinds of people are available, usually within the organization. (For a recent directory of skill inventory software, see Fryer, 1999). A particularly sophisticated skill inventory is used by Xerox (Reid, 1995).

■ A *human resource information system* (HRIS) is a comprehensive, almost always computerized database that contains information for many purposes. It differs from a skill inventory in that it is more complete, containing all personnel and payroll information in a form capable of nearly infinite cross-indexing and matching.

Why Is Workforce Analysis Important?

Organizations are human institutions, and jobs are carried out by people. For both reasons, the talents of people in the jobs and in the organization exert tremendous influence on how well the organization can achieve its goals, objectives, and long-term plans. Through comparisons of *what people are doing and should be doing* (work analysis information) and *what kinds of people are doing the work and should be doing the work* (workforce analysis information), decision-makers begin to obtain data about human strengths and weaknesses of the organization. These data can be compared subsequently to predictions about the future talent needs of the organization as a means of devising strategic plans for human resources that will facilitate realization of strategic business plans.

What Should Be Analyzed?

The focus of workforce analysis, like that of work analysis, can vary. Indeed, for each possible focus of work analysis, there is a corresponding one for workforce analysis: *reality* (What kind of people are really present in the organization?); *perceptions* (What kind of people are believed to be in the organization?); *norms* (What kind of people should be in the organization?); *plans* (What kind of people are intended to be in the organization in the future?); *motivation* (What do people want to become?); *ability* (What are people able to become?); *capability* (What do people have the potential to become?); and *expectations* (What do people expect to become in the future?).

Individual performance is usually assessed by using norms based on supervisory perceptions. The trouble is that supervisors who rate performance differ in their perceptions. What is "excellent" to one supervisor is "satisfactory" or even "poor" to another. People "perceive" the same performance in various ways. Even worse, some managers assume that every work group is normally distributed, and that for every exemplary worker, a correspondingly poor one must also exist. This problem is called "rating error," and it poses a major challenge to any employee performance-appraisal system (Bowman, 2000).

Figure 4-1: Selecting the Appropriate Focus for Workforce Analysis

Focus on . . .	When you want to . . .
Reality: What kinds of people are really present in the organization?	∎ Obtain information that is free of bias
Perceptions: What kinds of people are believed to be in the organization?	∎ Obtain information quickly and at lower cost than with a focus on reality
Norms: What kinds of people should be in the organization?	∎ Clarify/compare employee self-perceptions and supervisory expectations
Plans: What kinds of people are intended to be in the organization in the future?	∎ Clarify supervisory or top-management intentions arising from organizational plans
Motivation: What do people intend to become?	∎ Identify career objectives and how people plan to achieve them
Ability: What are people able to become?	∎ Identify personal traits/qualities that are impeding/encouraging future growth
Capability: What do people have the potential to become?	∎ Assess the likelihood that people will realize their potential
Expectations: What do people expect to become in the future?	∎ Plan for future performance levels

Each focus for workforce analysis is appropriate for a particular circumstance. They are summarized in Figure 4-1.

How Is Workforce Analysis Traditionally Conducted?

Think of traditional workforce analysis as a process that consists of six steps. The analyst:

1. Infers from job descriptions the education, experience, and personal characteristics needed by job incumbents to do the work.

2. Selects what characteristics of performance to evaluate (in consultation with others).

3. Selects how to evaluate employee performance (in consultation with others).

4. Identifies any problems with evaluation methods and criteria.

5. Attempts to solve problems with employee performance-appraisal methods.

6. Collects the results of employee appraisals, and includes them with other information about the organization's workforce.

These steps are illustrated schematically in Figure 4-2.

Figure 4-2: Steps in Traditional Workforce Analysis

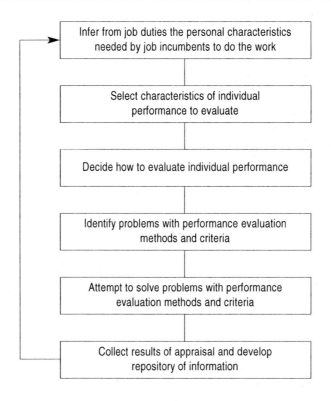

How Are Job Specifications Prepared?

Job specifications are given scant attention by most authorities on Human Resource Management. One reason is that traditionally ways of dealing with them do not tell us much. They merely describe, in a few sentences, the education, experience, and other basic requirements necessary for an individual to begin a job. Another reason for giving them little attention is that they do not necessarily bear any relationship to actual educational, experiential, and personal qualities of successful job incumbents. All janitors in a company might possess Ph.D.s in English or history, but that has little to do with the minimum educational requirements for conducting the janitor's job, at least theoretically.

Job specifications are important, however, because they furnish the basis for screening and selection as well as for appraisals of how well people perform once they are hired. Without clear and concrete specifications, screening/selecting and appraising are more likely than not handled on highly subjective grounds. There have been several successful court challenges to various selections and appraisal practices on the basis of unrealistically high educational requirements, but employers continue to use them, as well as unrealistically high experience requirements (*qualifications inflation*).

One way to deal with the problem of subjectivity and possible legal vulnerability is to create so-called *person descriptions*. Each task or responsibility on a job description is translated into corresponding knowledge, skill, and personal characteristics needed to carry out the task. Of course, job descriptions are themselves products of traditional work analysis.

Ideally, so-called person descriptions should be highly detailed and linked directly to actual work requirements. The more that they are, the greater the likelihood that they will pinpoint what is needed to perform successfully. This will serve to minimize subjective and potentially discriminatory or political judgments by supervisors who are charged with screening and selecting. At the same time, they will furnish potential incumbents with a realistic view of what they can expect when they are hired. As a result, turnover rates will decrease because absenteeism and turnover are frequently linked to unclear or unrealistic job expectations.

To prepare person descriptions, workforce analysts merely list the major tasks or duties of the job and translate them from normative statements of *what is done* to normative statements of *what kind of person does them*. Figure 4-3 illustrates how this process is handled.

Of course, it is possible to make each item on a person description more specific than shown in Figure 4-3. To do so, workforce analysts will need to address such questions as

I   How is the skill exhibited?
I   How well does the skill have to be exhibited?
I   What tools are needed to exhibit the skill?

As each task is converted into a corresponding skill and each skill is expressed in terms of behaviors or results, it becomes increasingly possible to measure employee performance from specific items on person descriptions.

What Is the Link Between Workforce and Work Analysis?

Work analysis furnishes information about *what* people do. From it, managers infer *what kind of people* are needed to do the work. In addition, work analysis provides the basis for job or performance standards. Workforce analysis is essentially a continuation of work analysis, which adds such questions as *how*

Figure 4-3: The Process of Converting a Job Description to a "Person Description"

If the job description reads: *An Auditor shall . . .*		Then the corresponding person-description reads: *The job incumbent . . .*
1. Gather data pertinent to audits	⟶	1. Will be able to collect data pertinent to audits
2. Write audit reports	⟶	2. Will be able to write audit reports
3. Conduct background research on auditee entities	⟶	3. Will be able to conduct background research on auditee entities
4. Prepare work papers of facts collected during an audit	⟶	4. Will be able to prepare work papers containing facts collected during an audit
5. Write audit findings in compliance with specified policy	⟶	5. Will be able to write audit findings in compliance with specified policy

many? and *How well?* following initial answers to questions dealing with *What do people do?*

From a list of job tasks and corresponding employee skills, managers sort out what issues are most important for achieving high work productivity and for helping realize organizational plans. Alternatively, workforce analysts collect, synthesize, and verify such information from job incumbents, their subordinates, peers, and supervisors. This process is the starting point for an employee performance-appraisal system and a comprehensive control system that reveals substantial performance discrepancies and helps pinpoint their cause and significance and evaluation of possible corrective action.

There are really two employee-appraisal systems operating side by side. The first is a *formal one,* usually an outgrowth of workforce analysis and associated with forms prepared by the HR department. The second is an *informal one,* embodied by the daily behavior and feedback of the supervisor and others about an employee's work. As long as these two systems are compatible, employees have a powerful incentive to perform according to job requirements and supervisory expectations. However, when the two systems are at odds, employees become confused and experience role stress, frustration, and decreasing work satisfaction. These conditions can, in turn, produce performance problems. This leads to declining morale and increases the possibility of union grievances, absenteeism, and turnover.

Differences between formal and informal appraisal systems stem from inconsistencies in *official and operative organizational goals.* Managers say they seek one set of goals when, in fact, their behavior indicates that they hold another set of priorities. Inconsistencies in *work group goals* are visible when top managers value one group of activities in line with one set of goals, supervisors value a conflicting group of activities, and employees are placed in the middle of the conflict. There can also be inconsistencies in *ideology and reality* where appraisals suggest a "wish list" different from actual expectations or managers want appraisals to "look good" to justify their own subjective and biased reasoning. There is a difference between what the formal appraisal appears to mean and what it really means. These and other problems distort employee appraisals and complicate efforts to establish, implement, and follow up on them.

Why Are Employee Performance Appraisals Important?

Most organizations have some kind of formal employee performance-appraisal system. Indeed, it is almost a ritual in some settings. Supervisors are required to fill out forms and meet with their subordinates at least once a year. They do not greet that chore with enthusiasm, however, even when the approach is automated to make it less burdensome (Hulme, 1998; Meade, 1999). In some settings, there are appraisals after completion of projects lasting a month or more.

There are at least six common reasons for having a formal appraisal system:

1. To validate selection methods. *To what extent is the organization choosing the right kind of people for jobs?*
2. To identify candidates for promotion. *Who is ready now for advancement? How soon will others be ready?*
3. To validate appraisal methods. *To what extent is the organization using appropriate yardsticks to evaluate performance?*
4. To provide evaluative feedback on individual performance. *How well have individuals been carrying out duties assigned to them?*
5. To determine training needs. *What specific learning experiences will help individuals improve their future job performance? Prepare for promotion?*
6. To allocate rewards. *Considering individual contributions, what rewards should be given to them?*

Appraisals can also serve to document performance for legal purposes, should employees later decide to sue their employer.

This all sounds good. The trouble is that an employee appraisal system cannot be all things to all people. Maintaining the appraisal system is often considered an HR responsibility, and it is difficult to do successfully in the long term (Martin and Bartol, 1998). In fact, if not handled well, the annual employee appraisal can actually lead to poorer rather than better performance. The reason is that appraisal interviews, where supervisors discuss the appraisal, contain either too much criticism or none of it. In addition, appraisals tend to focus on *past* performance, prompting arguments between appraisers and employees about interpretations and causes of past events (Kikoski, 1999).

For this reason, it might be best to concentrate formal appraisals on some purposes—development, for example—while providing daily concrete feedback on specific performance problems. Much can be learned by studying appraisal in best-practice firms where appraisal is focused and managed continuously (Grote, 2000; Hodges, 1999; Lecky-Thompson, 1999).

What Should Be Evaluated?

The first thing that should be done when designing any formal employee appraisal system is to determine the purpose. How will results be used? If the intent is to compensate people for their output, then the system should be directed at assessing job results. On the other hand, if the intent is to improve future performance, then the system should be directed at assessing work behaviors and methods. It is essential to select evaluative measures that will yield results of value for subsequent decisions.

The issue of what to evaluate has traditionally been approached through ratings based on traits, outputs, critical incidents, behaviors, and objectives. Each is worth a brief summary.

Trait Rating

A *trait* is a personality attribute, a descriptive term useful in labeling. Examples of such terms include *ambitious, creative, decisive, tenacious*, and *cooperative*. With a little thought and a good thesaurus, we can generate many such terms.

Early leaders in scientific management first stimulated interest in traits. They tried to identify qualities from great people of the past that could be associated with management ability. For instance, effective leaders might be more intelligent, taller, and heavier built than ineffective ones. In addition, they might exhibit a greater willingness to initiate action.

Trait rating is advantageous in that it appears to furnish a common basis for evaluating all people in an organization, regardless of their jobs or locations. We can, for instance, rate a janitor and a chief executive on such traits as dependability, decisiveness, and creativity, but that is also a disadvantage because the same traits have different meanings for different people. Nor are all traits of equal importance, assuming that agreement can be reached on common meanings. To complicate matters further, effective performance is likely to be associated with exhibiting many traits in combination, rather than just one or two. Finally, and worst of all for using trait ratings, they do not make specific exactly what a person must do to influence the organization's success as measured by profitability, growth, or market share. For this reason, trait ratings are rarely defensible when employees file lawsuits on the grounds that appraisal results were used improperly.

Output Ratings

An *output* is a tangible work product or work result. Examples include the number of orders taken, the number of units made, or the number of people served. Outputs can also include ratings or measures of quality as well as quantity, such as the number of complaints received, the number of errors, or the number of rejected units.

Output ratings are, as a rule, easily verifiable. Two employees and two supervisors can examine the same information and compute the same output. The objectivity of output ratings, in fact, is a major advantage to using them over trait ratings, which can vary substantially across raters.

Frederick Taylor, the father of scientific management, was the first to advocate use of output ratings. Each employee would be assigned a "job standard" for each day of work. The standard was to be based on the average output of an experienced worker operating at a normal pace. Any production over the standard output, Taylor believed, should be compensated above the usual hourly rate.

Unfortunately, the piecework system Taylor advocated has not produced the high levels of output that might be expected. Several reasons account for its failure: First, peers exert pressure to keep production low so that everyone looks good to management. Second, individuals might not be able to affect the rates of output that depend on a coordinated group or team effort. Third, not every job lends itself to easy quantification of important outputs. (The job of college professor is an example.) Finally, employees complain—often with justification—that when they exceed standards, managers simply raise the standards until they are so high that nobody could ever achieve them.

Critical Incident Rating

A *critical incident* is a statement that describes very good or very bad performance. The method originated during World War II as a means to reduce pilot error. Experienced pilots were asked to relate stories revealing exceptionally appropriate or inappropriate behavior under circumstances with which they had been confronted. The phrase "critical incident" was most descriptive, because respondents were asked to relate information about situations in which improper responses could lead to critical life or death consequences.

The same basic approach to developing critical incident ratings has remained essentially unchanged since the first time it was used.

Workforce analysts use the following procedure:

1. Select for participation only those who have directly observed behavior of job incumbents (participants on a critical incident panel of raters can include supervisors, job incumbents, peers, or even subordinates of the job incumbents).
2. Explain the aim of the project.
3. Explain exactly what the panel is to report (data can be collected on surveys or through individual or group interviews).
4. Collect data by asking participants to relate information about a specific incident, such as when it occurred, how it represented especially good or bad performance, and what specific observable outcomes resulted from the behavior.

5. Develop a method of classifying incidents into nonoverlapping categories, sometimes using a "clustering" approach to content analysis in which multiple raters sort incidents and arrive at a consensus
on a classification system.

6. Select a rating scale. An alternative method is for the rater (supervisor or peer) to keep a log of individual behavior and cite specific,
actual incidents at regular intervals.

The major advantages of the critical incident rating method are that they
bring greater objectivity to the process than trait ratings; the potential is greater
than output ratings for dealing with jobs that have hard-to-define outputs
(examples include research scientists, auditors, medical doctors, and HR planners); and the method is a greater source of information than either trait or
output ratings.

The drawbacks of the critical incident rating method include its heavy
reliance on observers, the subjectivity of categories, and the high cost of collecting information. Perhaps more seriously, the traditional approach to developing critical incidents tends to emphasize *past* behaviors, which might not be
appropriate under future—and largely uncertain—job conditions (Fenwick and
De Cieri, 1995).

Behaviorally Anchored Ratings

A *behaviorally anchored rating scale* (BARS) consists of a list of common behaviors ranging from those deemed most to least desirable, presented in a scaled
format. (A simple example of such a scale is shown in Figure 4-4.) This approach
to performance appraisal is especially appropriate when you need to focus on
work behaviors or processes (how should the work be done?) but not so much
on *work results* (what outcomes resulted?).

To create a behavioral rating scale for each job in the organization, workforce analysts take the following steps:

1. Select experienced supervisors and job incumbents to participate
in the project.

2. Divide participants into three separate groups.

3. Ask those in the first group to list major activities for the job to be evaluated with BARS and then prioritize activities in order of perceived importance for successful performance.

4. Ask those in the second group to describe critical incidents for the top twelve or so activity areas (these incidents should represent very good or very bad behaviors).

5. Ask those in the third group to rate each incident along a continuum.

6. Compile results, thereby creating BARS.

7. Verify the scales with the three groups.

There are, of course, other ways for developing BARS.

The advantages this behavioral rating scale has over other employee appraisal methods is that it minimizes subjectivity in ratings, provides the basis for specific feedback on performance to job incumbents, and clarifies supervisory expectations in ways likely to improve future performance. Employees actually prefer appraisals that are more behaviorally focused and based on observable

Figure 4-4: Behaviorally Anchored Rating Scale for an Auditor

Performance Dimension

Work paper preparation: documents information obtained during the course of an audit. This auditor could be expected to:

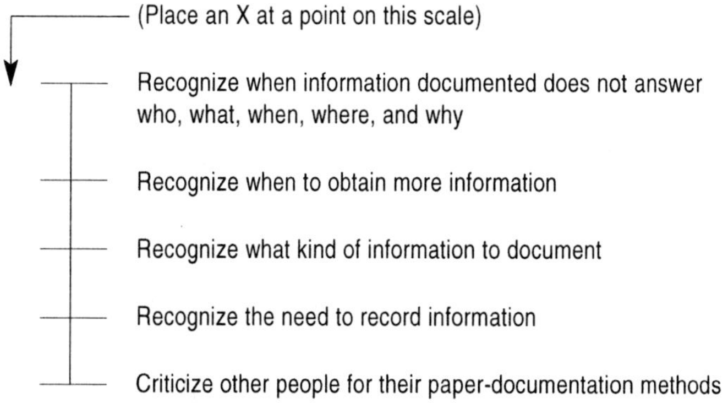

(Place an X at a point on this scale)

Recognize when information documented does not answer who, what, when, where, and why

Recognize when to obtain more information

Recognize what kind of information to document

Recognize the need to record information

Criticize other people for their paper-documentation methods behaviors (Tziner, Joanis, and Murphy, 2000). The BARS is especially well-suited to use with *competency models* (Dubois and Rothwell, 2000)—the narrative descriptions that result from competency identification—and with value statements, the codification of expected values in an organization that are the typical outputs of value clarification. However, disadvantages of BARS include its high cost to prepare and the limited number of behavioral categories it covers. Like the critical incident approach, it tends to focus attention on past rather than future performance.

Management by Objectives (MBO)

Unlike BARS or critical incident ratings, management by objectives focuses on *work results or outcomes* more than on *work processes;* unlike trait ratings, it lends itself to objective verification; and unlike output ratings, it can be used with jobs with hard-to-define outcomes. Early advocates of this approach included Peter Drucker (1954) and Edward Schleh (1955). In the phraseology of MBO, an objective is a statement of a measurable result to be achieved (Morrisey, 1976). Objective-setting is an organization-wide process; one laudable aim is to link each person's targeted work results to the organization's targeted competitive results.

When appraisers meet with appraisees (managers) to set up objectives, the standards by which the achievement of the objectives is measured are also jointly set. These appraisees—who are themselves upper-level managers—in turn set up objectives (both quantitative and qualitative) for their own subordinate managers (middle level), thereby dismantling the objectives into parts. These parts are, in turn, assigned to each middle-level manager. Since the setting and splitting of objectives continues until the lowest level of management is reached, the end result is that the objectives set for each level of the organization are closely interrelated.

Management by objectives thus resembles the interlocking conference approach to organizational change made famous by Rensis Likert. He used it in feeding back results of attitude surveys and using them as a means to stimulate joint action planning between managers and their subordinates. But MBO is used instead for creating performance targets.

Various approaches to MBO share common features:

▎ Managers and their subordinates meet, individually, to establish measurable objectives (these objectives are negotiated).

▎ Objectives are future-oriented, quantifiable, and related to organizational objectives and plans.

▎ Performance related to objectives is reviewed periodically.

Advocates of MBO point to such advantages as its potential future-oriented thrust, its reliance on participative decision-making, its capability to motivate people to achieve goals they have helped establish, and its fairness arising from the negotiated nature of objectives. To some, it is a means of enriching jobs.

Opponents are less enthused. Its critics say that management by objectives is too often a specious attempt to force people to accept goals established at the top. In many cases, it fails because its participative assumptions make it incompatible in authoritarian settings where it is used. In fact, if MBO is successfully implemented in an authoritarian setting, the culture itself will undergo change. And, worst of all, MBO has a tendency to create a paperwork bureaucracy of highly detailed objectives.

While some people might say that this approach is "dead," several recent cases exist where it has been applied with great success (Ingham, 1994; Ingham, 1995).

How Should Evaluation Be Carried Out?

Let us turn to two factors that should be considered when you are deciding how evaluation should be carried out: scaling and determining who will carry out evaluations. Each warrants some attention.

Scaling

A *scale* is a means of measuring that assigns by category. The most widely accepted taxonomy of scaling was set forth by Stevens (1951). He describes four levels of measurement:

1. The *nominal scale*. It is the most primitive, involving categorization by qualities, rather than quantities. Categories are different and mutually exclusive. Numbers can be used, but they have meaning only as they represent categories. For example, males are represented by the number 1; females, by the number 2.

2. The *ordinal scale*, slightly more sophisticated than the nominal scale, involves positioning people, objectives, or performance results relative to some attribute. An order is implied, but distance between positions on the scale is not. As in a nominal scale, numbers can be used, but only in connection with ordering.

3. An *interval scale* is one in which the amount of an attribute as well as the order is implied by position on the scale. (A thermometer is an interval scale because temperatures are arranged from low to high. Each degree is the same distance from the one preceding and the one following it.)

4. A *ratio scale* is the most sophisticated. It has a true zero point. It also exhibits the qualities of an interval scale.

Scaling is important because employee performance has to be rated relative to *something*. That *something* is a scale. The most popular scales used in employee appraisals are nominal. Common examples include traits rated relative to quality. Qualitative scales include the following:

-   A *five-point scale*. Positions are "outstanding," "good," "satisfactory," "fair," and "unsatisfactory." One variation: "far above standard," "above standard," "meets standard," "below standard," and "far below standard."

-   A *seven-point scale similar to those listed above.* For example: "far exceeds expectations," "clearly exceeds expectations," "somewhat exceeds expectations," "meets expectations," "falls somewhat below expectations," "clearly falls below expectations," and "falls far below expectations."

-   A *four-point scale with no "average" position.* An example: "very good," "good," "poor," "very poor."

The problem with these scales is that they do not provide sufficient detail about each objective. An employee receiving a "far exceeds expectations" rating on an item like "loyalty" has good reason to wonder what it means. To complicate matters even more, a number can be assigned to each position on the scales above. The supervisor then averages the scores to assign pay increases and assess, say, an individual's eligibility for promotion. (Of course, this can cause major problems in rating and end up demotivating workers. See Campbell, Campbell, and Chia, 1998.)

An alternative to scaling is to rank employees. It is simple, inexpensive to use, and readily understandable. The supervisor or other rater simply lists all employees reporting to him or her, and then ranks them in one or two ways. One way is by *alternation*: The highest and lowest people are selected. Then the second highest and second lowest, and so on until everyone is listed. A second way is by *paired comparison*: A matrix is set up with names of all employees along the top and left margins. Each pair is considered; the person receiving the most favorable comparison status is ranked first. While useful for small groups, ranking is not practical for large ones. Imagine trying to use alternation ranking for 100 people! Even worse, paired comparisons of 50 employees will require 1,225 separate reviews.

As can be seen, neither the scaling nor the ranking approach simplifies the task of appraisers. At the same time, neither yields information of much value for assessing past performance or coaching for future improvement.

Determining Who Will Handle Evaluations

Supervisors usually handle evaluations. However, there are alternatives: Job incumbents can appraise themselves; their peers can do so; subordinates can do so; or a combination of groups can participate in the process to create the increasingly popular full-circle, multi-rater assessment (Dubois and Rothwell, 2000).

When job incumbents appraise themselves, the results can be quite revealing. For example, suppose that the manager simply asks a subordinate to answer—in narrative form—four basic questions: What did you do over the last appraisal period? How well did you do it? What should you do over the next appraisal period? How well should you do it? Answers to these questions will not only point out special contributions—only some of which the manager will remember or be aware—but will also highlight what the employee considers important. Self-appraisal relies on writing skills, so be careful not to let it become a forum for self-interested grandstanding. It can furnish managers with information about employee perceptions and expectations, however—information that can later be used to coach for improved performance and self-development.

Variations on self-appraisal are possible. Job incumbents can rate themselves on traits or critical incidents. Their responses can then be compared to supervisory ratings. In this way, self-perceptions can be compared with those of a supervisor.

Peer appraisals, as their name implies, involve the conduct of employee performance evaluations by colleagues. They can be more accurate and frequently more concrete than ratings conducted by superiors. One approach is to ask people in a work unit to rate each other anonymously. Completed forms are then placed in a box. The supervisor compiles scores for each employee and can even include his or her own independent (and previously prepared) ratings in the composite. In some firms, the approach is even carried through the appraisal interview, which can be conducted by a superior or a panel of one's peers.

Subordinate appraisals can be revealing, but they are as threatening to supervisors as traditional appraisals are to workers. People are usually reluctant to give their supervisors honest feedback for fear of possible future retribution. Yet there is little doubt that major benefits can result from such appraisals, particularly in the area of improving the human relations skills of supervisors.

Using a third person for subordinate appraisals is a good idea. An external consultant or a member of the HR department can serve this purpose. This person interviews employees or collects anonymous rating forms from them and then gives superiors detailed, concrete advice about how to improve their supervisory skills based on employee opinions and perceptions. The choice of who carries out evaluations depends solely on the purpose evaluations are intended to serve. Supervisors should do appraisals, since they have a major influence on employee work skills, allocation of pay increases, or promotions. Other people whose opinions are especially important should participate in the appraisal process.

Finally, *full-circle, multi-rater assessment*—sometimes called *360-degree appraisal*—is an approach to rating an individual performer who uses the people who interact with them. (The term "360 degrees" comes from the number of degrees in a circle.) A full-circle, multi-rater assessment is meant to address the problem of rater bias by smoothing out the biases through many raters. It is thus possible to have an individual rated by one or more organizational superiors, one or more organizational peers, up to five subordinates, and perhaps other raters as well—including representatives of customer groups, company suppliers, company distributors, and even family members of the individual. Full-circle, multi-rater assessment is practiced widely now in Fortune 500 companies. They generally use competencies for the job category or department as the basis for the rating (Dubois and Rothwell, 2000). Full-circle, multi-rater assessments can be purchased from many vendors, but the competency models on which those ratings are based might not be representative of requirements in one corporate culture, so proceed with caution. Many full-circle, multi-rater assessments are conducted through web-based data collection, since the data analysis chore of such a system can be daunting when more than a few people are rated. While the use of full-circle, multi-rater assessment systems is not likely to diminish in the future, it is likely that many organizations will use 180-degree assessments to economize on data collection and still gain some of the benefits.

What Problems Exist with Traditional Employee-Appraisal Methods?

We have already described advantages and disadvantages of the most popular employee-appraisal methods. As we have seen, none is foolproof; rather, each is characterized by its own unique drawbacks. Trait ratings tend to be highly subjective for assessing past performance and are of limited value in coaching to improve future performance. Output ratings are useful only for jobs with tangible outcomes. Critical incident ratings and behavioral anchored rating scales are expensive and time consuming to prepare. Management by objectives has been used improperly to force goals on employees without first going through the negotiation process so staunchly advocated by its proponents.

Nor are these problems the only ones. Others include mismatches or conflicts between the appraisal method and the purpose or goals of the organization, the way it is used, the person or people using it, and the uses to which results are put. In short, those who use appraisals are more important to the success of a system than the system itself.

It seems obvious that an appraisal system should be compatible with the purposes and goals of the organization. However, that is not always easy or simple to do. One reason is that organizations rarely have a single purpose or goal. A business clearly exists to make a profit. Yet how is profit defined? More than simply for profit making, a business also exists as a social institution with responsibilities to the community, state, nation, and its employees. Goals can stem from each purpose, and some goals conflict. Moreover, managers value some goals more than others. Hence, we should not be surprised that it is difficult to fit the performance of an individual into a crazy quilt of otherwise conflicting business purposes and goals. And what is to be done about the outstanding performer whose job is related to a purpose and goal area not highly valued by management?

Any appraisal system also suffers when it is not used as originally intended. For instance, evaluators who are not trained can spoil almost any appraisal system. Training is essential to

I   Communicate the purpose of the system;
I   Ensure some consistency across raters;
I   Anticipate problems likely to come up during administration of the system and grapple with solutions before the problems actually arise; and
I   Deal with problems that do come up.

Most issues are related directly to the people carrying out the process. Workforce analysts must, on a regular basis, ask these questions about their managers or supervisors:

■ Are they motivated to appraise employee performance accurately?

■ Are they being held accountable for their ratings?

■ Do they perceive that outcomes of the appraisal process will be important? (How do they feel appraisal outcomes will be used?)

■ Do they have a stake in outcomes? (Do supervisors feel that low employee ratings reflect on their own ability? Do supervisors feel that criticism of employees is avoided so as to preserve rapport with their subordinates?)

■ Do the results of the formal appraisal system match the results of the informal ones? (How well have supervisors been giving feedback to employees throughout the year?) Answering these questions every few months will help you identify problems with the appraisal system and work toward corrective action.

Finally, how will evaluation results be used? To what degree (if any) will they affect pay increases, promotions, assessments of training needs, and expectations established for future ratings? What primary purpose will they serve? It is essential that they yield information of use to decision-makers. However, the kind of information decision-makers need will vary, so pay particular attention to the priorities set in the appraisal system itself. HRP practitioners can make a major contribution to employee appraisal by coordinating this priority-setting process and communicating priorities to supervisors and employees.

How Can Problems with Employee Appraisals Be Overcome?

Most problems having to do with performance appraisals stem from two sources: ideas about appraisals, and the people who use them.

To deal with the first problem, decision-makers need to look beyond thinking of appraisals as a once-a-year activity. A better idea is to think of a *performance management system* that establishes a work environment where people want to perform to their peak and are given the resources and feedback necessary to assess and improve their own performance. To that end, HRP practitioners are often tasked to think creatively about ways to build in feedback to performers directly from those they serve. One example is a customer feedback survey given frequently, with results fed back to the workers.

To deal with the second problem, it makes sense to direct solutions at the people who do appraisals. Action in two areas can yield significant improvement: (1) how appraisal interviews are carried out and (2) how supervisors deal with employee performance generally, rather than with formal performance appraisals specifically.

The Appraisal Interview

An appraisal interview is the face-to-face discussion between a rater and an employee during which performance is reviewed and objectives for the future are formally agreed on. The purpose is to open a dialogue for mutual negotiation. Three conditions make for effective interviews: First, the supervisor should be thoroughly familiar with what the subordinate does and how well he or she has been doing it. Second, the supervisor should be perceived as supportive of the worker, and not punitive. Finally, the subordinate should be encouraged to participate openly and honestly in the discussion.

Evaluators use one of three general approaches in an appraisal interview (Maier, 1976). The first is the *tell and sell approach*. Employee performance is reviewed, and the evaluator attempts to convince the person who is rated to perform better. This approach is usually most appropriate for new employees because it encourages them while also giving them guidance and coaching for improvement. The second is the *tell and listen approach*. Employee performance is reviewed, and then employees are allowed to vent their feelings. The evaluator uses counseling methods to help employees accept responsibility for their actions and commit to improved future performance. The third is the *problem-solving approach*. Through open dialogue, employee and evaluator explore forces that impede effective performance and forces that impel improved performance. A force is, of course, any condition that influences performance. Working together, employee and evaluator identify means by which to weaken performance impediments and strengthen forces leading to improvements. Obviously, the third approach is most participative and thus most likely to produce outcomes to which most employees feel committed.

How should the interview be carried out? Evaluators must decide, in advance, whether (1) to focus on past performance or (2) to focus on future improvement. They should focus next on a broad summary of actual performance, if overall performance has been satisfactory or if future prospects are good. If the reverse is true, avoid an overall summary and begin with the most favorable aspects of performance. Sandwich the most negative aspects in the middle of the interview and end on a positive note. Evaluators should then discuss in concrete terms what can be done to improve future performance, emphasizing the evaluator's willingness to listen and help. Finally, they should close the interview on an upbeat note, focusing on the positive and on the future. During the interview, evaluators should minimize interruptions (privacy is quite important), be very specific in describing employee behavior (cite actual incidents if possible), avoid personal remarks and focus only on behavior, avoid arguments, make specific recommendations for improvement, and let the employee do most of the talking.

To get employees to talk, ask open-ended questions beginning with words such as *what, when, where, how, for what reason,* and *could.* Avoid close-ended questions that do not prompt discussion. They begin with words such as *is, are, was, were,* and *does or did.*

Training

Training can improve the skills of those who conduct performance appraisals. Indeed, it improves consistency across raters, improves consistency between the organization's priorities and those of the raters, and might even help avoid legal battles and cope with union opposition.

Training on employee appraisals usually has a twofold purpose. It provides evaluators with information about the purpose of the system and how results are used. It also builds skills in appraising performance and in carrying out appraisal interviews. Some organizations meet the first of these needs by preparing a handbook on evaluation to explain, in detail, the purpose of the system, how to use it, and what to do with results. Training might still be needed as a management control to ensure that raters have read the handbook and understand it.

Building appraisal skills requires a different approach. Perhaps the most promising is *behavior modeling,* in which evaluators literally learn to model or imitate effective appraisal behaviors. Training depends on this model, and it has been quite successful in many companies. The trainer begins with instructional objectives that help learners understand what behavior they will learn and how well they can exhibit it. He or she follows with (1) a brief discussion of each skill used in appraising performance, conducting interviews, and providing direction and coaching to employees; (2) an illustration of wrong behaviors to use (they are shown on videotape); (3) a discussion of why and how these behaviors are inappropriate; (4) an illustration of appropriate behaviors on videotape; (5) a discussion of why these behaviors are appropriate; and (6) role plays in which evaluators practice behavior and receive feedback on how well they demonstrate them. Finally, the trainer concludes with an action plan in which participants contract for improved performance in how they will appraise employees.

How Are Appraisal Results Used in Human Resources Planning?

From the beginning of this chapter, we have stressed that employee performance appraisal results can be used for many purposes. Most notably, they can lead to improved individual performance and can furnish information to guide salary actions, assess training needs, serve as a quality control check on recruitment practices, and assess readiness for promotion. Of course, before they can be used at all they must be put in a form that allows for easy access and examination by workforce analysts. It is in this respect that skill inventories and human resource information systems (HRISs) are important. Appraisals provide guidance for many decisions about individuals.

Skill Inventories

During the 1960s, HR departments began keeping track of the various skills that could be put to use within the organization in the form of "skill" inventories. They are essentially record-keeping systems, either computerized or manual, that list skills and the names of employees possessing them. Much of this information is already available in personnel files, but files are not generally organized to make it easy to find one person who possesses the right skill to meet a specific need.

Skill inventories can be based on written surveys sent to employees. Literally thousands of "skills" can be listed. Respondents check each skill they believe that they possess. Examples might include foreign language proficiency, familiarity with computer languages, or an ability to operate special machines or equipment. The surveys are then returned to the HR department, where data are recorded and meticulously cross-referenced. Results of performance appraisals can also be included in the inventory.

An alternative approach to the traditional skill inventory is to compile a biography, resembling a résumé or basic biodata sheet, on each employee. This information is in turn cross-referenced to yield specific reports *by skill*. A simpler method than the first, it stores computerized information that will typically have to be investigated further before it can be relied on to make specific decisions for assigning staff to projects.

The Human Resource Information System

Personal computers and automated payroll systems have enabled HRP practitioners to begin taking a more comprehensive approach to keeping records and even to forecasting HR needs. A human resource information system (HRIS) is based on a broader conception of HR data needs than skill inventories. Indeed, an HRIS is a repository for *all* information pertaining to HR.

A computer-based HR Information System serves several purposes: (1) to describe the organization's present workforce and (2) to aid in forecasting the future and modeling possible effects of changes in HR policies and programs. It thus serves as a sort of HR balance sheet, containing information about the organization's present workforce and possible future one. Most large companies with over 1,000 employees have been using some variation of this for some time.

Think of a comprehensive HR information system as consisting of four subsystems. Each subsystem has the capability to store, manipulate, and retrieve information. These subsystems are, in turn, linked by a general retrieval system, which allows for information to be pooled between them.

One important use of any such information system is to allow for matching suitable candidates to job openings as they appear. With the machine-scoring capabilities of computers, HR planners are able to compare not just employee skills and job requirements, but also other variables such as employee career preferences of employees. Of course, performance appraisal information is often included because it is an important indicator of an individual's past track record.

Designers of these HR information systems also include otherwise objective measures, such as payroll, EEO/AA data, and general personnel records. More subjective measures—such as employee attitude survey results—do not appear to be included in many such systems, but we believe that the systems can be more effective and useful if subjective measures are included in the process of matching open jobs and prospective candidates for them. See Figure 4-5 for the kind of performance-appraisal data that should be included.

The creation of an HR information system is an important starting point for any HR planning effort. It combines all that is known about the organization's workforce in one place. Its creation and management is thus an important responsibility of the workforce analyst.

Figure 4-5: A Sample Employee Performance-Appraisal Form

Annual Evaluation

Employee Name	_____	Position	_____
Period covered	_____	Evaluator	_____
Date of evaluation	_____	Experience in position	_____

Part 1. Rating

Instructions: Rate employee performance over the appraisal period by using the following scale:

1. Totally inadequate for time in rank
2. Generally poor and/or occasional serious lapses, considering time in rank
3. Needs improvement, considering time in rank
4. Meets requirements for time in rank
5. Above average for time in rank
6. Superior performance for time in rank
7. Exceptional for time in rank

Task Requirements*	Rating
1. _____	_____
2. _____	_____
3. _____	_____
4. _____	_____
5. _____	_____
6. _____	_____
7. _____	_____
8. _____	_____
9. _____	_____
10. _____	_____
11. _____	_____
12. _____	_____
13. _____	_____
14. _____	_____
15. _____	_____
16. _____	_____
17. _____	_____
18. _____	_____

* List task requirements representative of your job or of one you know about.

Figure 4-5: *(continued)*

	Rating
19. Other _____	

Total points received   _____

(Divide by) number of qualities evaluated   _____

Mean Score   _____

Part 2. Unique Contributions

20. Describe any particular strengths or weaknesses exhibited by the job incumbent during the evaluation period. Refer to any unique contributions of the employee.

Part 3. Training Needs

21. What training, education, or other development needs should be addressed by the job incumbent, in the evaluator's opinion?

Part 4. Remarks

22. Add any other remarks. *(Attach more paper if necessary.)*

Part 5. Acknowledgment of Review

I have reviewed this document and discussed the contents with the evaluator. My signature means that I have been informed of my performance and does not necessarily imply that I agree with the ratings or comments. I have been informed of my rights to attach my written response to this evaluation.

Employee signature   _____   Date   _____

Evaluator signature   _____   Date   _____

Activity 4-1: Conducting an Appraisal Interview

Purpose

This activity is intended to give you an opportunity to practice conducting a performance appraisal interview.

Advance preparation

1. Read (or reread) the section of this chapter on conducting the appraisal interview.
2. Obtain a copy of an employee appraisal form used in your organization and fill it out however you wish. (If you do not have easy access to such forms, fill out and use the form immediately following this section.)

Group size

This activity is recommended for groups of 3.

Time required

Approximately 45 minutes.

Materials needed

1. Pen or pencil.
2. Paper for the observer.
3. Copy of a completed employee performance-appraisal form.

Special seating requirements

Use this form if you must. Photocopy it in advance and complete it however you wish.

Activity 4-1: *(continued)*

Introduction

The interview is an essential part of any employee performance-appraisal system. At this time, employee and supervisor meet to discuss past behavior and/or plan for future performance improvement. As noted in the chapter, most employee appraisals either have a negative effect or no effect on behavior, depending on how much criticism it contains. Use this exercise to try your own hand at practicing the employee appraisal interview.

Procedures

Step 1: 5 minutes

1. Divide your large group into smaller ones of three people each. In each small group, one person will play employee, one will play supervisor, and one will play observer.
2. Using the employee appraisal form that has been completed, the "supervisor" will begin the interview. (Be creative in how you play your role.)
3. During the interview, the observer will take notes. The observer should note key phrases used by both participants. Record any noticeable body language, such as jiggling the foot or leg, looking at the appraisal more than at the employee, or any other noticeable behavior. Jot down what you observe as it happens and be prepared to report what took place to the larger group of people.

Step 2: 20 minutes

The supervisor should conduct the appraisal interview with the employee. If time allows, switch roles and repeat the interview.

Step 3: 20 minutes

Discussion. Answer the questions that follow in the large group.

Discussion Questions

1. Observers, what observations did you make about the interview?
2. What "supervisory" behaviors were especially effective? What behaviors were especially negative and likely to be ineffective?
3. Should methods of interviewing differ by:
    a. The employee's level in the hierarchy?
    b. Experience in the job?
    c. The amount of education possessed by the employee?

Discuss these issues.

Notes

Activity 4-2: Case Study

Directions: Read through the case that follows, and then answer the questions at the end. (This case is entirely fictitious.)

Peter Roe, age 43, is director of human resources planning for the Wade Company, which operates a large chain of retail shoe stores in a dozen states. He was hired only three months ago from a smaller chain in the retail-shoe industry.

Peter completed a review of the company's personnel practices. He is particularly concerned about the lack of performance appraisals. From what he can tell, only a few of the larger stores in the chain make any effort at all to appraise employee performance in any systematic way. Nor is he completely surprised: Many of the shoe clerks are part time and earn minimum wage. What bothers him is that nobody makes any effort to appraise store managers, yet division managers and, ultimately, the top executives in the firm are promoted from the ranks of store managers.

Peter wants to initiate an appraisal system to assess employees at all levels. Top executives will appraise division managers who will, in turn, appraise store managers. In all but the smallest stores, even part-time hourly clerks will be appraised on an annual basis.

Not everyone is as enthusiastic about this project as Peter is. In fact, the senior vice president for operations was quite vocal in his dissent. At one meeting, he said this:

"Employee appraisals are only trappings of bureaucracy. I know my people; they know me. I expect my subordinates to have the same relationship with those reporting to them. We don't need forms for this purpose. Nor do we need forms to decide on who should be promoted when openings exist. We already know who the best candidates are."

Questions:
1. How should Peter go about setting up the performance appraisal system he envisions?
2. Do you feel that the very first appraisal system implemented in an organization has special significance? Why or why not?
3. Assume that the opinion expressed by the senior vice president for operations is one shared generally by other senior managers (except for Roe).
   What special problems are created by open, vocal opposition?
   How can these problems be overcome?
4. Based on what you read, what should be the primary purpose for the new employee appraisal system? Why?
5. How might a change in company strategy complicate the selection process for an employee appraisal system? Implementation of it?

CHAPTER 5

THE HUMAN RESOURCES AUDITOR

The human resource (HR) *auditor* analyzes the Human Resources department in the organization to pinpoint its existing strengths and weaknesses, and there are indeed weaknesses. Serious mistakes are quite costly to the company, so a comprehensive audit is imperative. The results of an HR audit can be compared with predictions about conditions inside and outside the organization. Together, this information will provide the basis for the future selection of a strategic plan for HR (Adler and Coleman, 1999; Willer 1997; Yeung 1997). We will explore the role of HR auditor in this chapter.

What Does the HR Auditor Do?

The auditor analyzes *what kinds of HR practice areas will help match people and work over time.* (A *practice area* is a relatively enduring effort, such as recruitment, training, labor relations, and organization development.) The auditor's role is associated with that of human resources planning (HRP) evaluator, who is responsible for monitoring whether HR strategy will work, is working, or has worked. The two roles are different: Auditors evaluate an HR department at present to uncover existing strengths and weaknesses, at the operational and strategic levels (Hussey, 1995). Evaluators, on the other hand, examine how well an existing HR plan has been working in order to guide HR activities. In short, the auditor examines the HR department and its programs *before* HR strategy is chosen; the evaluator most often makes an examination *after* choice and implementation of HR strategy. These roles can overlap, however.

How Is the HR Audit Conducted?

The *human resource audit* is a systematic assessment of the organization's HR policies and practices (Spognardi, 1997). It can focus on such matters as (1) how well the HR department's present purpose and strategy support those of the organization, (2) how well the department's structure enhances its ability to function, and (3) how well staffing and policies of the department are compatible with its purpose in the organization. These issues are important because department efforts in such *HR practice areas* as recruitment, training, compensation, and benefits—among others—are tools for influencing "goodness of fit" between people and positions. In other words, each practice area is a long-term change strategy in its own right that helps match up what kind of work is being done and the kind of people available to do the work.

Another scheme to guide an HR audit that can prove useful is the so-called balanced scorecard approach (Kaplan and Norton, 1996), which is also described in Chapter 19 as a tool for evaluating HR strategy. When this scheme is used, the HR auditor focuses attention on the HR function's finances, operations, customer relationships, and strategic capability.

But regardless of what scheme is chosen to guide the HR audit, HR planners should follow these steps:

1. Decide what to examine in an HR audit.
2. Tentatively decide how to conduct the audit by drafting a rough audit plan.
3. Select people to assist in the audit.
4. Collect background information on any or all of the following areas: the HR department, the HR plan, or practice areas; the organization; linkages between the HR department and organization; or specific issues to be investigated.

5. Finalize the audit plan.
6. Collect audit information, comparing *what is* (actual conditions) to *what should be* (criteria). For each *discrepancy* between what is and what should be, auditors try to determine cause (what is the reason for the discrepancy?), significance (how important is the discrepancy?), and corrective action (what should be done to rectify the discrepancy?).
7. Compile audit results and use them to identify present strengths and weaknesses of the HR department and to pinpoint fruitful areas for long-term action in order to improve the existing status of the HR department.

These steps are illustrated schematically in Figure 5-1. In many respects, the HR audit is thus the personnel department's counterpart to an organizational appraisal that is typically undertaken prior to strategic planning.

Deciding on Issues to Examine

HR auditors begin by deciding on what issues they want to focus and how extensively they want to collect information. Will the audit be (1) *comprehensive,* focusing on interactions between the organization and HR department; (2) *programmatic,* focusing on specific HR practice areas such as recruitment, training, job design, compensation, and benefits; or (3) *restricted,* focusing on a single issue such as turnover or absenteeism or accident rates? These questions have to do with *scope,* meaning what the audit will encompass.

A comprehensive HR audit spans the full range of HR department activities. It yields information so a long-term plan can be chosen to guide the department. The audit itself assesses *how well* the department, its practice areas, or a previously adopted HR plan is achieving the results it was intended to achieve.

On the other hand, programmatic or restricted HR audits are not so ambitious nor far reaching. Programmatic audits are directed at a single practice area (training or recruitment, for example). Restricted audits examine how well the HR department is dealing with an issue that overlaps practice areas. Most often,

Figure 5-1: A Simplified Model of the HR Auditing Process

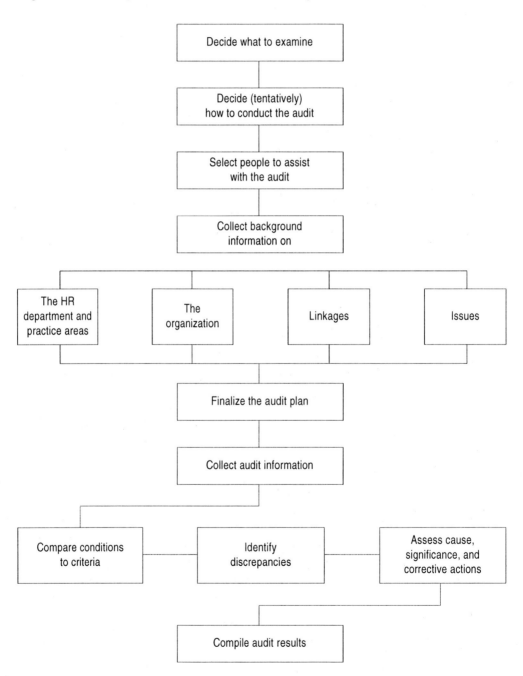

programmatic audits help establish long-term plans for a single practice area, while restricted audits help establish specialized efforts to deal with such issues as turnover or absenteeism.

Once the question of scope has been answered, auditors consider *on what basis* they will identify a strength or weakness. Choices vary. For example, they can decide to use any or all of the following:

1. *Comparative (or competitive) analysis:* The organization's HR department is compared to others in the community or industry, or to those of major competitors. In this context, a discrepancy is any variation between what HR departments in other organizations are doing and what this department is doing.

2. *External analysis by a consultant:* An HR specialist from outside the organization is asked to examine and critique the HR department. In this context, a discrepancy is any variation between what the HR department is doing and what the consultant believes it should be doing.

3. *Statistical analysis by insiders or outsiders:* A team of HR specialists from inside and/or outside the organization examines ratios or measures. Ratios or measures focus on *performance* (for example, unit labor costs per unit of output), *satisfaction* (for example, employee satisfaction with specific HR programs), *turnover, absenteeism,* or *accident rates.* The assumption is that the organization should compare favorably with similar ones if the HR department is functioning as it should be. In short, a discrepancy is any major deviation between what ratios/measures are expected or desired and what are actually found.

4. *Compliance analysis:* This approach assumes that the HR department is responsible for ensuring organizational compliance with laws, rules, and regulations in such areas as equal employment opportunity, occupational health and safety, and employment law. Auditors create checklists of governmental requirements applicable to the firm and then compare actual practices/policies to those required by law.

5. *Management by objectives (MBO):* Auditors can compare employee performance objectives to results when auditing the HR department. Discrepancies between objectives established and results subsequently achieved are analyzed to identify the causes.

Each approach implies a major focus or point of emphasis. Comparative analysis, for example, views an HR department *strength* as an area in which it functions better than corresponding departments within similar firms in the industry; a *weakness* is an area not functioning as well. External analysis relies on a consultant's opinion of state-of-the-art methods, regardless of their prevalence in industry, as the basis for a strength; a weakness is business-as-usual for the HR department. Statistical analysis compares national or industry averages on turnover, training costs, and absenteeism (and more) to those of the organization under audit. When the comparison is favorable, it is an *HR department strength*; when unfavorable, it is an *HR department weakness*. Compliance analysis views conformity with law as a strength and nonconformity (or inaction) as a weakness. Finally, MBO views achievement of objectives as strength and nonachievement as weakness.

Deciding (Tentatively) How to Conduct the Audit

Auditors will need to devote some thought early on to how they plan to conduct the audit. By doing so they can gather data efficiently. Of course, this planning is not always easy to do when, as in the case of outside consultants, auditors are not as familiar as insiders with the HR department and the kind of organization of which it is part. A *tentative audit plan* is useful as a starting point. It is nothing more than an informal description of what the audit will look at, what information will be needed, what the end product will look like (report? presentation?), and what resources by way of money, time, and staff will be needed. A tentative audit plan is subject to change as more information is gathered.

Depending on the scope of the audit, auditors begin by finding out more about (1) HR departments in other organizations for comparative or competitive analysis; (2) state-of-the-art methods in each HR practice area; (3) appropriate ratios and measures for the organizations; (4) applicable laws, rules, and regulations affecting the organization; and/or (5) existing management-by-objective plans and methods. Collection of this information is guided by the tentative audit plan, which can undergo modifications as auditors learn more about the auditee.

Several sources can help auditors with scope and focus: (1) past personnel audits and procedures used in them; (2) readings on management auditing generally; (3) readings on the general theory of personnel auditing; and (4) general guides for carrying out personnel audits. Other good places to get ideas: (1) the corporate board of directors; (2) senior managers, particularly those involved in strategic planning; (3) HRP practitioners themselves; and/or (4) employees. Members of these groups will no doubt have their own ideas about what HR issues are worth examining. In fact, they might have been the ones to request an HR audit in the first place, and thus constitute the primary audience for audit results.

Selecting People to Assist with the Audit

Typically, audits are conducted by a team. Team members should collectively possess knowledge about the organization, HR plans, the HR department, HR practice areas (preferably in the industry), data-collection methods to be used, and any special analytical methods that will be applied to the data once it is gathered. An HR audit can begin with only one or two people who construct the tentative audit plan and then collect background information. However, once it is more clear what work will be involved in the audit itself, then other members of the audit team can be selected on the basis of the kinds of knowledge and skills that are required. They can come from inside the HR department, from the organization outside the department, from outside the organization, or from some combination of these sources.

Collecting Background Information

Once an audit team is assembled and a tentative audit plan has been prepared, the next step is collecting background information. Auditors simply need to find out more about the purpose of the audit, key decision-makers, the auditee, and conditions they will face during data-gathering. This research is our background information.

In Chapter 2 we touched briefly on the importance of *stakeholder analysis,* the examination of what interested parties expect or desire from the organization. The same issues are important in an HR audit: Who suggested it? Why? What do they hope to find out? Obviously, the audit will not serve a useful purpose if it does not answer the questions that led to it in the first place. See Activity 5-1 at the end of the chapter for a worksheet to use in identifying issues to consider in a stakeholder analysis for an HR audit.

Another issue to address in the early stages of collecting background information is *Who or what should be audited?*: (1) *the HR department only*; (2) *HR activities in the organization,* spanning both what the HR department does and what line managers do; (3) *an HR practice area in the department,* such as training, recruitment, or compensation and benefits; or (4) *an issue cutting across the HR department and perhaps across the line organization as well.* For instance, turnover control is a matter that does not fall under the domain of any specific group inside most HR departments. What line managers do can affect turnover to a considerable extent, too. If an issue will be examined, auditors will have to decide how to handle overlapping responsibilities.

For purposes of a comprehensive HR audit, the auditee is usually the HR department and its practice areas. Various models can be used for initial diagnosis of an HR department and its practice areas. Each provides a starting point for investigation. A few of these models—each of which is classic and has a long history associated with it—are briefly described next.

The Clinical Approach of Levinson (1972)

Auditors collect historical data about the HR department. They review *factual data* (documents describing activities), *outside information* (interviews with those knowledgeable about the department), *structure* (the organization chart), *activities* (services offered, types of problems addressed by the department, service delivery methods, and methods of controlling the behavior of individuals or groups), *impressions* (how auditors feel about the setting), and *task patterns* (how each member of the department contributes to overall department purpose, how group members interact with each other, and how they interact with those from outside the department or unit).

The Six-Box Model of Weisbord (1976, 1978)

Auditors collect data about the following: how work is divided up; the match between tasks and incentives; ways of coordinating between activities; ways of resolving conflicts between competing interests or priorities within the organization or between the auditee and the host organization; and the match between the purposes, goals, and objectives of the auditee and the backgrounds and beliefs of those in charge of the HR department or organization. The six-box model is still widely used (Stahl, 1997), and it focuses attention on six specific categories for the HR audit: purposes, structure, relationships, rewards, leadership, and helpful mechanisms.

The Nadler and Tushman (1977) Model

Auditors focus attention on the following:

- *Environment outside the auditee,* both external to the organization and to the HR department or other auditee
- *Resources available to the auditee:* money, people, equipment, etc.
- *History,* or patterns or events that have influenced activities of the auditee
- *Strategy,* or how the HR department or other auditee is presently going about offering *services*
- *Functioning,* or how the department is meeting its objectives, using resources available to it, and adapting to or anticipating change;

group relations, or how people within the department are interacting

- *Individual performance,* or backgrounds of department employees, their attitudes, and feelings
- *Relationships with other units,* or how the department interacts with those outside its boundaries
- *Work flow,* or how the work comes in and goes out

The Hornstein and Tichy (1973) Model

Auditors extract from audited organizations what issues *they* consider important, and then use the categories thus defined to develop a profile of auditee status. Alternatively, the auditors provide guidance to auditees, who develop their own profile of strengths and weaknesses. A simple approach using this model, for instance, might simply be to interview a representative cross-section of managers and workers, asking such questions as: (1) what is the HR function doing especially well in this organization, and why do you think so? and (2) what could the HR function improve in this organization, and why do you think so?

The Lawrence and Lorsch (1967) Model

HR auditors examine how the HR department assesses pressures from outside the organization or department, how work is divided up, how coordination between activities is handled, how the auditee handles competing priorities or interests, and how well individuals within groups or between groups get along.

The Kotter (1978) Seven Circle Model

Another way for auditors to begin surfacing issues is to survey *formal organizational structure* (reporting relationships of the HR department or other auditee), the *dominant coalition* (what key strategists say they want), the auditee *environment* (outside the department but inside or outside the organization), *technology* (equipment and methods used by the auditee), the *social system* (cultural conditions affecting the auditee), *employees* (members of the audited organization relative to their work requirements), and *key organizational processes* (communication and decision-making within the HR department or between it and other parts of the organization).

The Glueck (1980) Internal Appraisal Model

Auditors collect information on the extent to which the HR department contributes to organizational strengths and weaknesses. For example, how does the HR department affect the organization's financial condition, marketing practices, production, or service methods? These questions can be quite difficult to answer, but the answers link contributions of the HR department to organizational activities.

The Rothschild (1976) Principles of Resource Analysis

Auditors adapt the general principles of this approach, intended for use in organizational planning, to specific diagnosis of HR department strengths and weaknesses. Typical questions used in this approach might include these: How much is the department able to come up with new approaches to problems? Deliver services? Influence others in the HR area? Obtain necessary resources? Handle current activities efficiently and effectively? The answers to these questions provide clues to current conditions and future improvement opportunities.

The Generic Models of HR Department Activities

Auditors also rely on generic models of what HR departments should be doing. Such models are prepared by analyzing the tables of contents of textbooks on personnel/human resources. For example, a comprehensive audit of the HR department can include examination of recruitment and selection, training, HR planning, career planning, employee performance appraisal, job analysis and design, compensation, benefits, health and safety, equal employment opportunity, labor relations, organization development, employee assistance, HR research, and HR information systems.

Any model mentioned in this section can help members of an HR audit team collect background information, by providing structure for the investigation of the unknown or the unfamiliar. Use Activity 5-2 at the end of the chapter to consider issues for review in an HR department audit.

Before beginning data collection, auditors should consider how the results will be reported. In fact, they can economize their effort by preparing segments of the report as they proceed. Methods of reporting include completed check-lists, oral presentations to interested parties, and reports. No one method is appropriate for all situations. Auditors should select a method with the wishes of those who initially requested the audit. This person or group constitutes the primary audience, so it is only right that the report be geared to the preferences of that person or group.

Finally, during the early stages of collecting background information, audi-tors must assess how much cooperation they think they will get in subsequent stages. In organizations characterized by low levels of trust or high levels of competition, cooperation doesn't always come easily. Some people never indi-cate what they really think under any circumstances when asked about HR department strengths and weaknesses; some will do so only with the most vig-orous promises of confidentiality. In such cases, HR auditors will probably have to use more than one method of data collection, build in ways to double-check results, and plan on using more time than when people are more will-ing to speak their minds.

Finalizing the Audit Plan

Auditors should complete the background research stage with a strong grasp of what issues should be examined. At this point they are ready to revise the tentative audit plan, transforming it into a final version adequate for guiding the collection and analysis of information.

The final audit plan (1) lists tasks to be performed; (2) provides estimated time frames, usually expressed in days, weeks, or months; (3) indicates which members of the team will be doing what tasks and when; and (4) helps estimate the time and resources needed to carry out the HR audit. An example of a sim-

Figure 5-2: A Simple HR Audit Plan

(What to do?) Task	(How long to do it?) Time Frame												(Who does it?) Responsibility
	J	F	M	A	M	J	J	A	S	O	N	D*	
1. Determine the formal purpose of the HR department													Team members Johnson and Smith
2. Assess (a) Goals of the HR department													Team members Horton and Clay
(b) Measurable objectives of the HR department													Team members Johnson, Smith, and Clay
3. Examine programs in the HR department— specifically: (a) Training (b) Recruitment (c) Compensation													Team members Horton, Johnson, Smith, and Clay

*   Letters stand for months of the year, in chronological sequence.
This audit plan is only the first page of a longer document.

ple audit plan is illustrated in Figure 5-2. Of course, software programs for project management can also be helpful for organizing this information.

Collecting Audit Information

The heart of any HR audit? The data-collection effort. At this point, members of the audit team accumulate information consistent with the requirements specified in the final audit plan. What kind of information is collected? The answer to this question depends on:

1. *Audit scope.* In a comprehensive HR audit, data collection centers on such issues as purpose, goals, objectives, structure, activities, and results of the HR department. A programmatic HR audit examines a single component of the department, such as training, recruitment, or compensation. A restricted audit focuses on one issue, such as how the HR department is controlling turnover, encouraging employee health and safety, handling drug and alcohol abuse, or encouraging employee training and development.

2. *Audit focus.* Will the emphasis be on *comparison?* How well does the HR department compare to its counterparts in the industry, its counterparts in the organization's chief competitions? Will the emphasis be on *theory?* How well do practices compare to state-of-the-art theories? Will the emphasis be on *statistics?* How well does the organization's measures of performance, satisfaction, turnover, absenteeism, and accident rates compare to historical averages compiled on an annual basis? What trends are discernible? Will the emphasis be on *compliance?* Is the organization acting in conformity with applicable laws, rules, and regulations? Will audit emphasis be on *objectives and results?* How well are people within the department achieving pre-established performance objectives? What problems account for failure to meet objectives?

3. *Stakeholder needs.* What information will satisfy those who initiated the audit?

4. *Expected applications of results.* If results will be used in strategic business planning, they will have to be presented in a form lending themselves to comparison with other types of information.

Data-collection methods include observations, interviews, focus groups, questionnaires, document reviews, and unobtrusive measures.

People can be observed, for example, as they do their work. Observations are then recorded on sheets specially constructed as aids for categorizing and aggregating data. This approach to data collection is usually of limited value, however, in assessing *departmental* strengths and weaknesses. The reason is that assessments of a department depend more on *interactions between people and programmatic results achieved* than on *observable actions of individuals* carrying out daily tasks.

Interviews and written surveys are probably more appropriate than observation for collecting information on broad matters of departmental strengths and weaknesses. People at different hierarchical levels with different perspectives can be sources of valuable information about what the HR department has been doing well, has not been doing well, has been doing but should not be doing, and has not been doing but should be doing. Activity 5-3 at the end of the chapter provides a simple example of an audit interview guide prepared for the collection of such information. Of course, information of the same kind can also be collected through written surveys.

Focus groups are simply group interviews. They are more appropriate than observation for collecting information on broad matters of departmental strengths and weaknesses. In fact they are more efficient than interviews because data from many people can be gathered at once. They are disadvantageous because if individuals dominate the discussion, this will skew results.

Document reviews can also yield information about HR department activities. Documents include employee handbooks, annual reports, recruitment brochures, catalogs of training courses, brochures describing company benefits, and similar publications. Prepared for broad distribution, they are usually written from the standpoint of *intentions*. They thus reveal what HRP practitioners are trying to accomplish. Compare them to results during the audit process to help identify significant departures from intentions and significant accomplishments. Figure 5-3 illustrates basic steps in carrying out a document review by using content analysis.

Document reviews need not be limited merely to publications intended for broad distribution. In fact, informal communications between members of the HR department or between them and others in the organization can frequently be more revealing. Examples of documents include MBO plans for the department, budgets, letters, memoranda, and meeting agendas.

Figure 5-3: Steps in Carrying Out a Document Review Using Content Analysis

1. Identify key words from audit tasks. (Develop topic categories.)
2. Prepare a sheet that lists key words.
3. Go through HR documents—those prepared for broad distribution and those for limited distribution.
4. Record the frequency (i.e., number of times key words appear in the documents).
5. Draw inferences about what HRP practitioners consider important. List key words by frequency, first listing those used most often.

Auditors use content analysis

■ To develop categories of topics or problems raised in the documents
■ To count the frequency of references to each topic
■ To devise a checklist from the topics, giving priority to those frequently mentioned
■ To investigate how many times the same problems were raised in informal communication, how many problems were apparently acted on and how many were not, and what results stemmed from auditee action and inaction.

Auditees can participate in this process by helping develop topic categories, counting frequencies, reviewing the checklist developed, and investigating subsequent results.

The advantage of this approach is that HR department strengths and weaknesses are examined from information familiar to practitioners, not from issues imposed by outsiders. For this reason, practitioners are more likely to accept results and use them as a basis for subsequent corrective action. On the other hand, the disadvantage is that these strengths and weaknesses are not necessarily related to matching people and positions or to realizing strategic business plans. Indeed, you might have to superimpose categories developed for checklist preparation on documents. This will help you see how much attention the department's practitioners are paying to business plans or people- and position-matching.

Another way to collect data on departmental strengths and weaknesses is through *unobtrusive measures,* so named because the data-collection process is not readily noticeable to auditees. Observations, surveys, interviews, and document reviews are sometimes obtrusive because they involve direct interaction with people whose work is being audited. Not so with unobtrusive measures. They include records on employee performance, satisfaction, turnover, absenteeism, and accident rates. This information comes from reviewing employee files and other documents. (Few people need to know about these file searches.) You will be able to figure out ratios and other measures of department performance and subsequently compare them with desires of top managers or to historical trends in the organization.

This approach is appropriate when the focus of the HR audit is on statistical or comparative analysis. The chief advantage is that unobtrusive measures rarely prompt changes in the behavior of people whose work is under scrutiny, unlike more obvious ways of collecting information. The chief disadvantage is that ratios are difficult to translate into broad descriptions of departmental strengths and weaknesses. They are also limited to results rather than behaviors, programs, or intentions, and seldom furnish reasons for data. Further, the HR department bears only some of the responsibility for employee performance, satisfaction, and turnover. Using unobtrusive measures, auditors have a tough time affixing degrees of responsibility, an issue that *can* be examined by other data-collection methods.

Other approaches can be used in more limited ways to collect data about strengths and weaknesses of an HR department. They include the critical incident process, the so-called "organization mirror," and the Delphi technique.

The *critical incident process* is a simple but powerful approach that lends itself to HR auditing, analyzing work, and assessing training needs. When applied to HR auditing for identifying HR departmental strengths and weaknesses, HR auditors interview or survey HRP practitioners and line managers about *important situations* ("critical incidents") in which HR department programs have especially helped or hindered organizational performance or progress toward realizing organizational strategic plans. Activity 5-4 at the end of the chapter provides a simple interview form designed to yield information of this kind.

Critical incident data is collected from all segments of the organization. If interviews are used, time and cost constraints might limit the number of people who are asked to provide information. Auditors select a small random sample to interview from the organization as a whole—different departments, divisions, strategic business units, or even a cross-section of the corporate hierarchy. If written surveys (or electronic surveys) are used for data collection, more people can be solicited for information, though what they provide is often less detailed than what can be obtained through face-to-face or telephone interviews.

Content analysis is applied to results of surveys or interviews in much the same way it is used in document reviews. Auditors, working as a team, develop individual categories of HR department strengths/weaknesses, compare them in their team, and reach consensus on how to classify incidents. They can then count frequencies, listing HR department strengths that correspond to situations in which the department helped achieve strategic plans and weaknesses that correspond to situations in which the department hindered or did not contribute to realization of plans.

The *organizational mirror,* first described by Fordyce and Weil (1971), is another approach to data gathering. It overlaps with others. It is a means for providing feedback to a group or department about how others perceive its activities or its performance. Hence, the "organization mirror" is useful because it reflects department image. When applied to the HR audit, people outside the HR department are asked such questions as the following ones:

I   What do you think about the HR (personnel) department generally?

I   In what ways do you feel that the department is functioning well? What are its present strengths?

I   In what ways do you feel that the department could improve its usefulness? What are its present weaknesses?

I   How do you feel the department could help your part of the organization improve operations in line with long-term strategic plans?

Answers to these questions are then analyzed, placed in categories developed through content analysis, fed back to HRP practitioners, and used as the basis for subsequent departmental planning.

The *Delphi technique* lends itself not only to HR auditing but to other applications as well. To use it to assess strengths and weaknesses of the HR department, Auditors (1) prepare a written survey and send it out to a small number of people in the organization to identify/assess major strengths and weaknesses of the HR department, using an approach much like the organizational mirror; (2) receive surveys and compile responses, sending them back to original participants for prioritization; (3) rank strengths and weaknesses of the department in order of importance; and (4) feed results of the audit back to key decision-makers for use in strategic planning for HR. Though powerful, the Delphi can be expensive to use because of the time needed for preparing surveys, circulating them, and assessing results.

Regardless of what approach is chosen for collecting data in an HR audit, don't lose sight of the purpose of the effort: identifying HR department or functional strengths and weaknesses. A conceptual model can be very helpful for this purpose. Such a model is illustrated in Figure 5-4.

Any audit is essentially a comparison between condition *(what is?)* and norm or criteria *(what should be?)*. Hence, for any item under investigation, auditors describe the present condition and compare it with an ideal or desired state. Issues for investigation in a comprehensive audit can include the purpose, goals, objectives, structure, rewards, policies, programs, and tasks of the HR department. In fact, any HR issue of importance to strategists, other members of the organization, or HRP practitioners is a potential item for investigation.

The first step for auditors is to describe the condition of the item investigated, addressing the stated purpose of the HR department, its structure, its practice areas, its present reward systems, and the status of group functioning within the department and between members of the department and others in the organization.

An audit with a different scope will, of course, be directed to similar items for investigation. For instance, in an audit of the training division, focus might be on its stated purpose, activities, structure, and results.

The next step is for auditors to develop authoritative criteria or norms relative to each item under investigation. Sources of criteria include opinions of senior managers, HRP practitioners in the organization, HR experts from out-

Figure 5-4: A Conceptual Model for Diagnosing HR Discrepancies

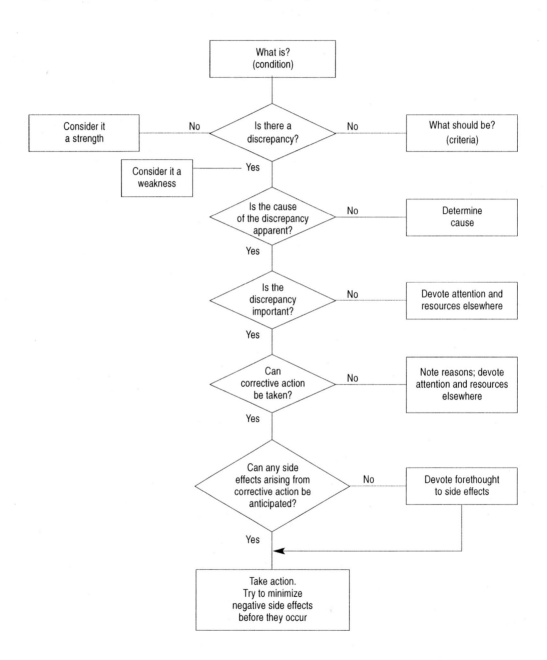

side the organization, HR experts from inside the organization, academicians, published theories, and data from government or industry sources. In short, *a criterion is any standard from a reliable source that suggests how the department should be functioning, and the state of affairs that should exist at present.*

It is not easy to find authoritative criteria. Experts vary in their opinions about what the criteria should be. Industry practices are not always clear, and it is difficult to obtain some information—especially from competitors. Though some managers might feel surveyed to death, ratios and measures do not exist for everything. Legal requirements are sometimes vague or contradictory. Information from MBO plans can be out of date or represent wishful thinking.

To complicate matters further, HR auditors have to decide whether criteria should represent *minimal acceptable performance* or *a true ideal state of affairs* of what is desirable.

Suppose, for instance, that 60 percent of competitors do *not* plan for the replacement of key executives. If HR auditors use minimal acceptable performance as the basis for criteria, then an organization that does not plan for executive replacement can still meet industry requirements. On the other hand, if an ideal state of affairs is used as the basis for criteria, then lack of an executive replacement plan is a discrepancy when compared with expert opinions on desirable practices.

Given these problems, how then are authoritative criteria established? The answer to this question depends on how much involvement in the audit is accorded to higher-level decision-makers in the organization and to those whose work is examined. Perhaps the best strategy is to give auditees an opportunity to review or even establish criteria before they are used in the HR audit. The reason is that auditees are often closer to events than outside auditors, and probably have a good sense of which criteria are fair. In addition, if people agree with the criteria ahead of time, results will be more readily accepted afterward. However, if an adversarial approach is adopted, then auditors themselves or top managers whose opinions are solicited become creators and arbiters of criteria.

Once criteria have been selected and existing conditions have been described, then auditors can collect meaningful data through the methods we have discussed. Each issue on the final audit plan is examined. Condition is compared with a corresponding criterion on each issue. Discrepancies between *what is* (condition) and *what should be* (criteria) are identified and recorded on a findings sheet. (See the example in Figure 5-5.) Auditors use the findings sheet and other information they have collected to prepare a final audit report. They rate significant negative discrepancies between conditions and criteria. Each negative discrepancy is considered a weakness of the HR department.

Although the flowchart in Figure 5-4 implies that all discrepancies are negative and, thus, are weaknesses, they do not always have to be. Indeed, it is possible to note instances in which conditions are *better* than criteria. Examples include cases when the HR department leads the industry, uses methods more advanced than reflected in published accounts, or far exceeds minimal requirements expressed through industry measures or national ratios. In such cases, discrepancies of this kind represent significant department strengths and should be recognized as such.

However, identifying negative discrepancies is the first step in finding solutions. The next step is to determine their causes—rarely easy to pinpoint. In fact, many factors can lead to a discrepancy: poor leadership, inappropriate structure, insufficient resources, or differing perceptions about desired results, to name just a few. Auditors need to determine cause as nearly as they can so that subsequent corrective actions will be directed at the source of problems, rather than at mere symptoms of them.

The significance of the discrepancy should also be examined. Not all problems, discrepancies, and departmental weaknesses are of equal value. Some demand prompt attention and command high priority for corrective action; some do not. Importance varies, depending on perspective. Consider these questions:

I   How much influence has the discrepancy *historically* exerted on the efficiency and effectiveness of the HR department and/or the organization?

I   How much influence is the discrepancy *presently* exerting on the HR department and/or the organization?

Figure 5-5: A Findings Sheet

Topic _____

Date _____

Auditor's initials _____

1. What is the condition?* (describe the present status)

2. What should be the condition? (describe criteria)

    (a) Identify source(s) of criteria.

    (b) Explain why the criteria are authoritative.

3. Is there a discrepancy between condition and criteria? If so, explain whether it is negative (an HR department weakness) or positive (an HR department strength).

4. (*For negative discrepancy only*) What is the cause of the discrepancy? (If more than one, explain.)

5. (*For negative discrepancy only*) What is the significance of the discrepancy?

    (a) Has the discrepancy been historically significant?

    (b) Is the discrepancy significant at present?

    (c) Is the discrepancy likely to become more significant at some future time? Why?

6. (*For negative discrepancy only*) What action should be taken to rectify the discrepancy?

7. (*For negative discrepancy only*) What negative side effects or consequences are likely to result from actions taken to rectify the discrepancy? How can they be anticipated beforehand and their negative effects minimized?

* The topic should be keyed to an objective or task on the Final Audit Plan.

I   How much influence, given strategic business plans, is the discrepancy likely to exert on the department *in the future* and/or on the organization?

For instance, lack of replacement planning for key executives might not adversely impact on the organization historically. But what happens if an airplane crashes, killing the CEO and his or her chief subordinates? A discrepancy of this kind has great *future* significance.

The last two steps in the model involve examining what corrective action will rectify a discrepancy and then anticipating what negative side effects are possible from that action. Simply stated, HR auditors should recommend what to do to improve operations of the auditee, regardless of where the auditee is assigned. It isn't enough to make a recommendation: You must anticipate results, pro and con, and suggest in advance how to minimize negative side effects that result from corrective action.

A simple example should help clarify what we mean: Suppose auditors uncover a discrepancy between the amount of management training offered by the organization and the amount offered by others in the industry. From interviews, they determine that the underlying cause stems from the perception of key managers that training is a waste of time, and there is not enough appropriate talent to develop the training. The discrepancy is significant, because it affects how well managers will keep up with new approaches, prepare for future advancement, and improve their present job performance. Auditors might want to recommend creation of a management-training program. However, by anticipating negative side effects in advance, they can see that such a program will not be successful until key managers first perceive the importance of this training. The auditors can recommend a program of education, either overt or covert, to convince senior managers of the importance of training prior to any action to establish a formal management training program.

Compiling Audit Results

The final results of an HR audit are compiled from findings-sheets and notes made during the data-collection process. They are presented, in writing or through oral presentation, to those who requested the audit. Other interested parties also receive information. It is a good idea to summarize HR department strengths and weaknesses in a manner such as that shown in Figure 5-6. A short, simple list can then be used later in planning for organization, auditee, and human resources generally.

In the next two chapters, we shall have more to say about using audit results. For now, suffice it to say that audits identify present strengths and weaknesses of the HR department, and help pinpoint fruitful areas for corrective action. They are essential for strategic HR planning, since they provide a sense of what is happening now. Having that sense of current strengths and weaknesses is essential to establishing future direction and thus future strategy for HR.

Figure 5-6: A Summary of HR Department Strengths and Weaknesses

Chief strengths of the HR Department (List in order of importance. The greatest perceived strength should be first):

1.

2.

3.

4.

5.

6.

7.

8.

9.

Chief weaknesses of the HR Department (Place the greatest perceived weakness first):

1.

2.

3.

4.

5.

Activity 5-1: Issues to Consider in a Stakeholder Analysis for an HR Audit

Directions: For each question listed below, provide an answer in the second column. Add more paper if necessary.

Questions   *Answers*

1. Who are the stakeholders? In other words, what groups of people depend on the HR department to meet their needs? List them below.

    a. _____

    b. _____

    c. _____

    d. _____

    e. _____

    f. _____

2. What does each group expect from the HR department, in the opinion of HRP practitioners?

    a. _____

    b. _____

    c. _____

    d. _____

    e. _____

    f. _____

3. What do HRP practitioners think about each group of stakeholders?

    a. _____

    b. _____

    c. _____

    d. _____

    e. _____

    f. _____

4. How accurate are HRP practitioners in their perceptions about stakeholders?

    a. _____

    b. _____

    c. _____

    d. _____

    e. _____

    f. _____

Activity 5-1: *(continued)*

5. What do stakeholders want to find out from the HR audit?

    a. _____

    b. _____

    c. _____

    d. _____

    e. _____

    f. _____

6. What do HRP practitioners hope to find out from an HR audit?

    a. _____

    b. _____

    c. _____

Activity 5-2: An Initial Diagnosis Worksheet for an HR Audit

Directions: Column 1 below lists issues and areas for possible review at the outset of an HR audit. Check in Column 2 those issues/areas warranting explanation, considering the tentative audit plan. In Column 3, list sources of information about these issues/areas.

Column 1 Issues/Areas for possible review	Column 2 Should information about this issue be collected? Yes (✓) No (✓)		Column 3 Where can this information be obtained?
1. The purpose of the HR department*	( )	( )	
2. Goals of the HR department	( )	( )	
3. Measurable objectives of the HR department	( )	( )	
4. Structure of the department			
a. Divisions shown on organizational charts	( )	( )	
b. Purpose of each division	( )	( )	
c. Goals of each division	( )	( )	
d. Measurable objectives of each division	( )	( )	
5. Activities of the department, including			
a. Services offered	( )	( )	
b. Types of problems addressed	( )	( )	
c. Types of problems not addressed	( )	( )	
d. Service delivery methods used	( )	( )	

* The same general issue or area can apply to a program or to the organization's handling of a special problem (e.g., turnover).

Activity 5-2: *(continued)*

	Column 1	Column 2	Column 3
	e. Service delivery methods that are possible but are not used	( ) ( )	
	f. Groups served by the department	( ) ( )	
	g. Groups *not* served by the department	( ) ( )	
6.	People of the department, including		
	a. Who the leaders are	( ) ( )	
	b. What the leaders value	( ) ( )	
	c. Previous back-ground (education/experience of leaders)	( ) ( )	
	d. Who the employees (nonsupervisors) are	( ) ( )	
	e. What employees value	( ) ( )	
	f. Previous backgrounds of employees	( ) ( )	
	g. Performance ratings of employees and supervisors	( ) ( )	
7.	Resources available		
	a. Is there sufficient money for achieving department goals/objectives?	( ) ( )	
	b. Is there sufficient time for achieving department goals/objectives?	( ) ( )	

Activity 5-2: *(continued)*

	Column 1	Column 2	Column 3
8.	Relationships of the department with		
	a. The environment outside the organization	( ) ( )	
	b. Specific groups inside the organization	( ) ( )	
9.	Relationships of groups within the department		
	a. How are relations between groups within the department?	( ) ( )	
	b. How are relations between individuals in the department?	( ) ( )	
10.	The history of the HR department		
	a. What events have had a major impact on it?	( ) ( )	
	b. What stories do those inside the HR department tell about it? On what issues do those stories focus?	( ) ( )	
11.	The strategy of the department		
	a. How is it trying to contribute to organizational objectives/plans?	( ) ( )	
	b. How is it trying to achieve its own plans?	( ) ( )	

Activity 5-2: *(continued)*

	Column 1	Column 2		Column 3
12.	Work flow: How does work			
	a. Flow in?	( )	( )	
	b. Flow out?	( )	( )	
13.	Differentiation:			
	a. How is work divided up?	( )	( )	
	b. How is work not divided up?	( )	( )	
14.	Integration:			
	a. How are people/ groups not coordinated?	( )	( )	
	b. When are people/ groups not coordinated?	( )	( )	
15.	Technology:			
	a. What equipment is used by the department?	( )	( )	
	b. What equipment could be used that is not?	( )	( )	
16.	Conflict: How are conflicting interests handled?	( )	( )	
17.	How is the HR department affecting the organization's			
	a. Financial position?	( )	( )	
	b. Marketing practices?	( )	( )	
	c. Production/service methods?	( )	( )	

Activity 5-2: *(continued)*

	Column 1	Column 2	Column 3
18.	Resource analysis: To what extent is there evidence that the HR department successfully		
	a. Innovates?	( ) ( )	
	b. Produces what it is supposed to?	( ) ( )	
	c. Markets what it is supposed to?	( ) ( )	
	d. Obtains necessary finances?	( ) ( )	
	e. Manages its operations?	( ) ( )	
19.	Program areas: What is the HR department doing in such traditional HR practice areas as		
	a. Recruitment?	( ) ( )	
	b. Selection?	( ) ( )	
	c. Training?	( ) ( )	
	d. Job analysis?	( ) ( )	
	e. Job design?	( ) ( )	
	f. Employee performance appraisal?	( ) ( )	
	g. HR planning?	( ) ( )	
	h. Career planning?	( ) ( )	
	i. Compensation?	( ) ( )	
	j. Benefits?	( ) ( )	
	k. Health and safety?	( ) ( )	
	l. Equal employment opportunity?	( ) ( )	
	m. Labor relations?	( ) ( )	

Activity 5-2: *(continued)*

	Column 1	Column 2		Column 3
	n. Organization development?	( )	( )	
	o. Employee assistance?	( )	( )	
	p. HR research?	( )	( )	
	q. HR information systems?	( )	( )	
20.	What additional issues warrant consideration?			
List them:				
		( )	( )	
		( )	( )	
		( )	( )	
		( )	( )	
		( )	( )	
	.	( )	( )	

Other Remarks

Activity 5-3: An Interview Guide for Assessing the Strengths and Weaknesses
of the HR Department

1. In your opinion, what is the chief strength of the HR department in
    a. contributing to achievement of organizational strategic plans?
    b. contributing to the achievement of your department's objectives? Operations?

2. In your opinion, what is the chief weakness of the HR department in
    a. contributing (or not contributing) to achievement of organizational strategic plans?
    b. contributing (or not contributing) to achievement of your department's objectives? Operations?

3. What has the HR department been doing exceptionally well?

4. What should the HR department be doing that it is not doing at present?

5. What has the HR department been doing rather poorly?

6. What should the HR department *not* do that it has been doing?

7. In what ways do you feel that the HR department could contribute most effectively to achievement of organizational plans?

8. In what ways do you feel that programs or activities of the HR department impede achievement of organizational plans?

Activity 5-4: An Interview Form to Collect Information about Critical Incidents Pertinent to HR Department Strengths and Weaknesses

Directions: The purpose of this interview is to elicit information about an important situation in which the respondent personally experienced either special help or hindrance from the HR department in the performance of the respondent's job responsibilities. Record notes from the interview on this form. Feel free to ask questions to follow up on remarks made by the respondents. After the interview, use your notes to write a memorandum about the interview. Be sure to provide your name, the respondent's name, the date of the interview, and its location. Once written, show the memorandum to the respondent. Ask for corrections (if needed), and have the respondent initial it to indicate that the memorandum accurately reflects the respondent's statements.

Think of an important situation when you requested help from the HR department and the assistance provided by that department was *especially useful.*

1. Briefly describe the situation or event.

2. When did it happen?

3. For what reason was this situation especially important for you or your department?

4. To what extent, if any, was the situation related to long-range (strategic) plans of the organization?

5. What were the consequences of this situation? In other words, what happened as a result of the HR department's assistance?

Think of an important situation when you requested help from the HR department and the assistance provided by that department was *not at all useful.*

6. Briefly describe the circumstances.

7. When did it happen?

8. For what reason was this situation important?

9. To what extent, if any, was the situation related to strategic plans of the organization?

10. What were the consequences of the situation?

Activity 5-5: Case Study

Directions: Read over the case that follows, and then answer the questions at the end. (This case is entirely fictitious.)

The XYZ Corporation is a small, independently owned company that sells and services bulldozers and other construction equipment in a major metropolitan area. It employs 308 full-time and 103 part-time employees in various capacities related to sales and service.

Recently, the top managers—consisting of the owner/chief executive, the corporate comptroller, the corporate treasurer, the corporate sales manager, the corporate service manager, and the corporate personnel manager—met for the purpose of devising a strategic plan. Until recently, economic conditions were quite unfavorable to the firm: Interest rates were high, prompting major construction firms to delay purchase of new equipment. However, prospects for the next three years appear to be favorable, because interest rates are dropping and construction demand had jumped to a record high.

In this corporation, the HR department is responsible for recruiting and hiring all employees except the highest-level executives. The recruitment-hiring goal of the HR department centers merely on replacing employees as their positions are vacated through turnover or promotion. In general, the HR manager tries to replace someone who leaves with someone whose education and experience is identical to that of the original employee. The HR manager does not think he/she is or should be responsible for comparing amount of work to existing numbers and skills of workers.

Questions

1. Assume that an HR department audit will be performed in the XYZ Corporation. Based on what you read in the case, how would you summarize the personnel manager's perception of the HR department's role, goals, and objectives in hiring and recruiting?

2. According to the case, what change in environmental conditions will probably have to be acted on by the organization? Why do you think so?

3. In what different ways can strengths and weaknesses of any HR department be analyzed?

4. In what ways do you think the strengths and weaknesses of the HR department in this case should be analyzed?

5. How can data about this department be collected?

6. Who do you think should carry out the audit in this case? Why?

7. To whom should audit results be reported? Why?

CHAPTER 6

THE HUMAN RESOURCES ENVIRONMENTAL SCANNER

What conditions, trends, or events are likely to confront the organization in the future? What pressure will they put on the work people do, the kind of people who are needed to do the work, and the kind of human resource activities that will be needed to help deal with present and future conditions? Answering these questions is the responsibility of the HR environmental scanner.

What Does the HR Environmental Scanner Do?

The HR environmental scanner (hereinafter referred to as *scanner*) identifies future trends inside and outside the organization; assesses the likely impact of those trends; and determines the *desired* impact of those trends, considering future initiatives and plans of the organization. In many respects, the role of scanner is related to the roles of work analyst, workforce analyst, and HR auditor in these ways: (1) *work analyst* (scanners try to predict the future of jobs, positions, and job families; in contrast, work analysts focus on them at present); (2) *workforce analyst* (scanners try to predict the kind of people needed to do work in the future; the workforce analyst, in contrast, focuses on people who are presently available to do the work); and (3) *HR auditor* (scanners focus on future pressures from outside or inside the organization exerted on the HR department and its activities; HR auditors, in contrast, assess present strengths and weaknesses of the department). As you can see, scanners focus on the future rather than on the past or present. The information they furnish is compared with data from work analysts, workforce analysts, and HR auditors in order to choose a strategic HR plan that determines the future direction of the HR function for the organization.

Why Is Environmental Scanning Important?

Environmental scanning activities of all kinds have commanded increased attention in recent years, and rightly so: An organization's effectiveness increases as strategists become more aware of the work environment. Second, the more information that strategists collect and consider in making decisions, the greater the effectiveness of organizational performance. Third, organizational success is highly correlated with the appropriate amount of environmental scanning. Fourth, the key issues or trends for consideration in the environment vary by industry type and by the state of the economy. (Generally, economic conditions, customer or market analysis, and competitor analysis tend to be key areas of concern.) Fifth, and finally, strategists rely heavily on verbal sources for environmental information, particularly personal and professional sources. They are rather skeptical of formal, highly quantitative approaches to environmental scanning. Environmental scanning is thus an area of great importance to organizational effectiveness.

Scanning is perhaps of equal value in human resources planning (HRP) activities, but it is highly intuitive—more of an art than a science. It is really a process of forming impressions about the future, and then acting on those impressions in an effort to lead the target and beat competitors to the punch.

How Is the Environmental Scanning Process Conducted?

In order to enact their role as scanners, HR planners should:

1. Identify important trends (factors) inside and outside the organization.
2. Assess the likely effects of those trends on the work, on the workforce, and on the HR department.

3. Determine how you want these trends to affect the work, the workforce, and the HR department.
4. Describe, in terms as concrete as possible, expected gaps between what will probably happen in the future and what should ideally happen in the future.

Figure 6-1 illustrates these steps in the environmental scanning process.

Identifying Future Trends

We use the term *environment* to describe *the world outside organizational boundaries*. Organizational strategic planners have long been aware of just how important it is to analyze the external competitive environment. What happens outside the organization affects its ability to prosper or even survive. Trends, events, and conditions in the environment influence: (1) *Inputs:* the products, raw materials, resources, and information used by the organization; (2) *Transformation processes:* work methods applied to inputs that convert them to outputs; and (3) *Outputs:* the products or services of the organization that result from transformation processes (they are offered to the surrounding environment; examples are finished products or specialized services).

Rarely can one organization change external trends or alter events. Regardless of size, no single organization can (for example) manipulate the international economy or change social norms. Decision-makers in an organization who recognize these trends are at an advantage.

Any event, trend, condition, or circumstance that causes change in the external environment can affect any two organizations in very different ways, depending on (1) *purpose* (What is their business? What consumers do they serve? How are they served?), (2) *goals and objectives* (What level of achievement are managers trying to obtain?), and (3) *strategies* (How are organizations pursuing their goals and objectives?). For example, the Gerber company—the well-known maker of baby food—is affected significantly by U.S. population trends. In fact, declining birth rates prompted strategists in that company to reconsider the purpose of their business. On the other hand, Xerox Corporation is rela-

Figure 6-1: A Simplified Model of the Environmental Scanning Process

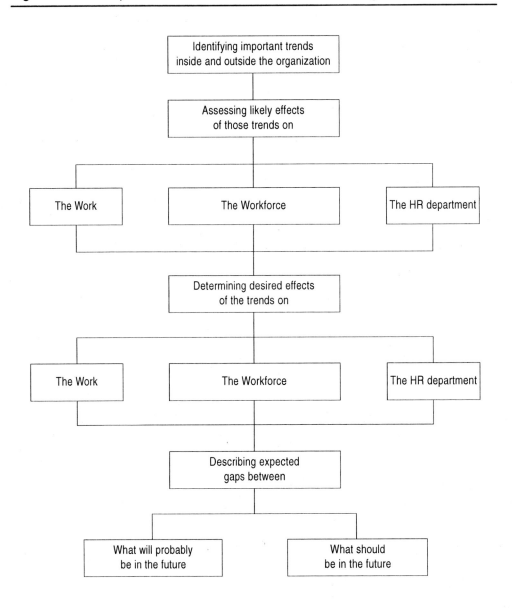

tively unaffected by birth rates by virtue of its business, but changes in technology will have a major impact.

Identifying the key trends affecting a business is a crucial step in planning. By taking that step, strategists place themselves in a position to anticipate and take advantage of matters in the surrounding world over which they have little or no control, rather than merely reacting to them and becoming victimized. They can thus direct their attention to preparing the organization for internal changes needed to cope with dynamically changing external environmental conditions.

Problems with Environmental Scanning

There is a paradox inherent in the rationale of scanning. As Davis (1983, pp. 160–161) once explained in a classic, and famous, quote:

> According to this paradigm which says you've got to know what you want to do before you know how to do it, the organization by definition has to come after the strategy. It can't come before it. Therefore, all organizations have got to lag behind the strategy. The best that they can do is catch up with the strategy.

Environmental scanning, when you come right down to it, is looking at the future. The paradox is that decision-makers rely on information about the past. An organization staffed in the past will not be able to position itself for the unpredictable future.

Perhaps the best that HR planners can hope to do is predict the *likelihood* of what will happen, and then help decision-makers try to *anticipate* it (Pastin, 1986). That is hard to do. Some future events can never be predicted, where others can only be predicted with reasonable probability. It will be difficult, in any case, to anticipate the full impact of future events on the organization and its people. It is worth the effort, however: Implementing organizational strategy takes time and requires human leadership and work skills needed to get from *here* (present) to *there* (future). HR scanning is important: The organization needs the right people at the right times and in the right numbers to implement its strategy. But who those people are, what they need to know and do, and when they need to be available cannot even be guessed unless decision-makers make some effort to predict what future environmental conditions will be like. Advance preparations are critical.

To state the case another way, the essence of HR planning—like any planning—is comparing existing conditions (i.e., what is) with *expected future conditions* (that is, what will probably be at some point in the future) or *desired future conditions* (that is, what should be at some future time). The result of such comparisons helps identify a *planning gap* or discrepancy between the way things are and the way they will probably be, *or* the way things are and the way they should be (see Figure 6-2).

Analyzing *what is* and *what will probably be* means little more than predicting the kind of future that will exist if no action is taken to change existing trends or deal with problems expected to come up. Consider, given present trends, what work members of the organization will do in the future. What kind of people will do that work? What kind of HR department activities will be offered?

In contrast, any analysis of *what is* and *what should be* involves extrapolation of strategic business plans into the future. Considering those plans, what kind of work should members of the organization do at a future time if their behaviors and results are to be consistent with strategic plans? Given the nature of that work, what skills and abilities should be possessed by those who do it? What should the HR department be doing? This estimate is normative, geared to desires and not necessarily to expectations.

Comparisons between *what is* and *what will probably be* are based on assumptions about the future. Considering the external environment, what will happen to jobs and people if managers do not deviate from business as usual? Comparisons between *what is* and *what should be in the future* are based on assumptions about an ideal or normative state. Comparisons between *what will probably be* and *what should be in the future* reveal a planning gap representing expected discrepancies arising in the future. Strategic HR planning is needed

Figure 6-2: Identifying a Strategic Gap in HR

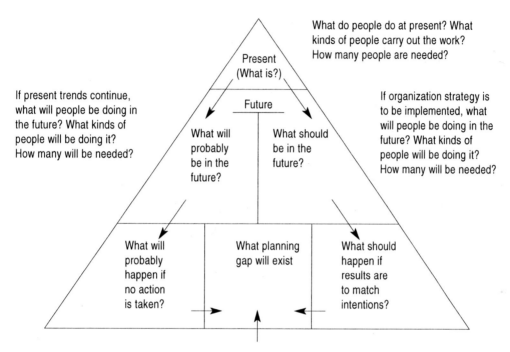

What do people do at present? What kinds of people carry out the work? How many people are needed?

Present (What is?)

Future

If present trends continue, what will people be doing in the future? What kinds of people will be doing it? How many will be needed?

What will probably be in the future?

What should be in the future?

If organization strategy is to be implemented, what will people be doing in the future? What kinds of people will be doing it? How many will be needed?

What will probably happen if no action is taken?

What planning gap will exist

What should happen if results are to match intentions?

When HR needs that are implicit in organization strategy are compared to projections of present trends into the future, what differences are evident?

to identify ways to narrow this gap between (1) *expectations* for jobs/people when no action is taken and (2) *desires* for jobs/people that match requirements implicit in organization plans.

Manipulating the Organization in Anticipation of Future HR Needs

To a great extent, the success of any organizational plan depends heavily on matching jobs and people with requirements created by environmental factors internal and external to the organization. To contribute to this success, scanners should

1. Compare what work will probably be done in the future (if there is no deviation from past practices in the HR area) and what work should be done if it is to match requirements implicit in strategic business plans. This comparison will reveal how much action is needed so that HR Grand Strategy can be selected.

2. Compare the kind of people who will be doing the work in the future (if no action is taken in the HR area) with who *should* be doing the work. You want their knowledge, skills, and abilities to match up to requirements implicit in strategic business plans.

3. Compare what the HR department will probably be doing in the future (if present activities continue) and what it should be doing if its practice areas match up to requirements implied by organizational plans.

The last of these comparisons is the basis for Strategic Human Resources (SHR) plans. It is intended to narrow any gaps between work and workforce requirements through HR department efforts. It is important to understand one key difference between environmental scanning for strategic business planning and HR planning: Business planners are able to focus their attention solely on conditions outside the firm. The whole point of strategizing is to anticipate how changes in the external world will threaten the company *or* provide opportunities worthy of attention. On the other hand, HR planners have at least two environments to think about: one *outside* the organization and one inside (Rothwell and Sredl, 2000). See Figure 6-3 for an illustration that helps clarify this point.

To state the point another way, notice from the arrows in Figure 6-3 that the HR subsystem is influenced *directly by the external environment* (events outside affect state-of-the-art work methods, types of people attracted for employment, and state-of-the-art practices of the HR department) and *indirectly by the external environment* (this means that external change is filtered through the

Figure 6-3: The Internal and External Environments

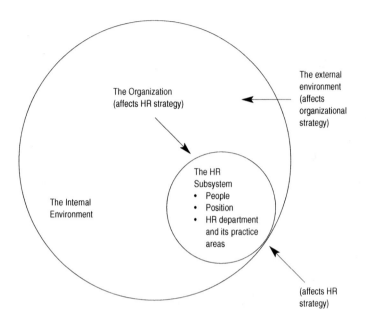

organization. Organizational purpose, goals, objectives, and strategies are, for example, affected by external conditions; they in turn affect what strategists *want* people to do, what kind of people they want to do it, and what they *expect* of the HR department to help achieve desired matches between actual and ideal).

External Factors

What trends or factors affect the organization and HR subsystem? They include:

1. *Economic factors:* What is the present status of the business cycle? How is it likely to change in the future?
2. *Technology factors:* How is the organization's work carried out? On what tools or work techniques does it especially depend? How are these tools and techniques likely to change in the future?

3. *Supplier factors:* What is the present cost/availability of raw materials? Energy? Capital? Labor? Information? How likely is it that cost and availability of these resources will change?

4. *Marketing/competitive factors:* What is the present status of competition in the industry? Is there the possibility that consumers can rely on substitute products or services? What is the present stage of the product life cycle? How are these conditions likely to change in the future?

5. *Government and legal factors:* What is the present status of laws, rules, and regulations pertaining to raw materials and supplies needed by the organization? What is the status of these laws relative to marketing practices and distribution methods? How are laws likely to change? How are government policies pertaining to mergers, acquisitions, and takeovers likely to change?

6. *Demographic factors:* What is the present status of the population? How will the population probably change in the future?

7. *Geographic factors:* Where are key suppliers and markets presently located? Where are they likely to be located in the future?

8. *Social factors:* What values and attitudes affect demand for products and services? How are those values and attitudes likely to change in the future?

Each external factor can influence the work people do, the skills they need to do it, and the appropriate HR department programs.

Numerous studies have examined the ways the external environment impacts the workplace and workforce, and thus HR planning and practice. For example, Kemske (1998) conducted a study that pinpointed 60 trends, with the most important over the next 10 years predicted to be (1) *increased workplace flexibility:* Collaborative work will become more common in a virtual office environment; (2) *global business:* Borderless business will require global workforce strategies; (3) *work and society:* People will increasingly adopt a philosophy of working to live, not living to work; (4) *workforce development:* Workers and employers alike will need to begin thinking of constant learning in a just-in-time format; (5) *definition of jobs:* Jobs get bigger and broader; and (6) *strategic role of HR:* HRP practitioners must become leaders, not just partners.

In another study, six key trends were identified to have the most likely impact on the future workforce and workplace over the next 10 years (Schechter, Rothwell, and McLane, 1996): (1) Changing technology, (2) Increasing globalization, (3) Continuing cost containment, (4) Increasing speed in market change, (5) The growing importance of knowledge capital, and (6) An increasing rate and magnitude of change. Information about such trends can be immensely helpful in shaping strategic HR plans and determining the competencies necessary for success in HR leadership in the future (Rothwell, Prescott, and Taylor, 1998).

Internal Factors

The HR subsystem is directly influenced by external factors, but also indirectly influenced through their effects on

1. *Structural factors:* What is the present distribution of work in the organization? What is it likely to be in the future?
2. *Leadership factors:* Who are the strategists? Who are they likely to be in the future? What issues are presently given high priority by strategists? What issues in the future are likely to be accorded high priority?
3. *Reward factors:* What behaviors and results are presently rewarded? What behaviors and results will probably be rewarded in the future?
4. *Process factors:* How are decisions presently made? What patterns of communication exist? How will future decisions probably be made? How will communication take place?

Each internal factor can influence work, the people needed to do it, and the initiatives of the HR department appropriate for facilitating adaptive change (see Figure 6-4).

Figure 6-4: Internal and External Factors Influencing the HR Subsystem

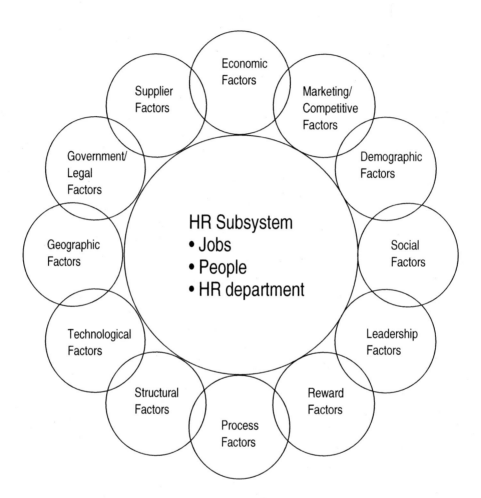

Assessing the Effects of Future Trends

How can we identify and evaluate the effects of future trends on jobs, people, and the HR department? The answer involves future-oriented work analysis, workforce analysis, and scanning. We will consider each of them.

Conducting Future-Oriented Work Analysis

Future-oriented work analysis describes what people will probably be doing in the future. It results in future-oriented job or position descriptions that sketch out probabilities of what might happen in the work as a result of trends in the external environment and within the organization. For every job, position, or job family, work analysis addresses this question: *What will probably be?*

Typically, future-oriented work analysis poses such questions as: (1) What will the title of the job probably be in the future? (2) What general purpose will the job probably serve relative to goals and objectives of the organization at some point in the future? (3) What job titles will probably report to job incumbents at a future time? (4) To what titles will incumbents probably report in the future? (5) What tasks will probably be performed by incumbents? (6) What duties and job responsibilities will probably exist in the future?

Scanners should also address such issues as: (1) What tasks or activities will probably occupy the most time for job incumbents in the future? (2) What tasks or activities will probably be most critical to successful performance in the future? (3) With what behaviors or results will tasks probably be associated in the future? and (4) What activities in the future will probably take longest for job incumbents to learn?

No standardized methods exist for conducting future-oriented work analysis. However, some methods used widely in futures research can be adapted: the critical incident process, the Delphi technique, nominal group technique, cross-impact analysis, scenarios, questionnaires, interviews, observations, and document reviews. Each has distinct advantages and disadvantages.

Critical Incident Process

This has been successfully applied to job analysis (Flanagan, 1954), training needs assessment (Johnson, 1983), and preparation of employee performance appraisals (McCormick, 1979a). It is frequently anecdotal and past-oriented. Critical incidents are solicited from many people. Each participant in the process is asked for only one narrative covering (1) a difficult *(critical)* situation faced by an incumbent in the past; (2) any specialized training that helped the job incumbent deal with the situation *(incident)* at the time it was encountered; (3) when or how long ago the situation took place; (4) what action was taken by the job incumbent to deal with the situation; (5) what outcomes or results were produced by the action; and (6) what incumbents should do in the future when facing similar situations. A job description, training, plan, or employee appraisal form is the final product.

The same approach can also be used, of course, to predict the probabilities of what will happen in the future. HR planners ask job incumbents and their superiors to predict, because of present trends, what behaviors or results will probably emerge as most critical to successful job performance at some future time. The results are then written as a job description.

A future-oriented critical incident approach is advantageous for developing information linked explicitly to behavior. It is disadvantageous in that the results are highly subjective and speculative. Data gathering is time consuming and costly.

The Delphi Technique

This approach is named after the famous oracle of ancient Greece who confounded those seeking wisdom with such ambiguous prognostications as "the Greeks the Romans will defeat." Adopted by the Rand Corporation in the 1950s as a means of forecasting, it has been widely applied to organizational strategic planning (Utterback, 1979), training needs assessment (Rath and Stoyanoff, 1983), and futures research generally (Linstone, 1978). It has also been applied specifically to HR (Gatewood and Gatewood, 1983). To use the Delphi in scanning, the HR planner: (1) selects a panel of "experts" consisting of job incumbents, their superiors, and (perhaps) top managers, (2) develops a questionnaire to solicit expert opinion about issues, trends, or job tasks potentially affecting a job or job family; (3) tests the wording of the questionnaire for clarity; (4) sends out questionnaires to the panel of respondents: (5) receives and analyzes the first round of responses from experts; (6) prepares a second round of questionnaires based on results of the first to seek agreement and solicit additional issues, trends, or job tasks; (7) sends out questionnaires; and (8) receives and analyzes results. This process is carried out until a consensus is reached, usually for about three or four rounds.

It is advisable to conduct two separate Delphi studies in future-oriented work analysis. One helps identify *what* problems, trends, or issues might influence jobs, positions, or job families in the future. A second helps identify how those problems, trends, or issues are likely to affect jobs, positions, or job families.

The advantages of the Delphi technique include its applicability to widely scattered groups and its tendency to remove the conformist mind-set of groupthink and minimize power struggles among group members. Disadvantages include its high cost, its tendency to pressure participants for responses regardless of quality, its sensitivity to recent events, and its potential for being manipulated by those so inclined.

Nominal Group Technique (NGT)

This approach has been successfully applied to many problems lending themselves to small-group decision-making (Martinko and Gepson, 1983). It is similar to the Delphi technique in many respects, except that participants meet face-to-face and evaluate ideas in front of each other, rather than responding to a survey. It takes its name from the tendency of group members to generate initial ideas individually, without discussion. Hence, groups exist in name only (that is, nominally).

When applying this approach, scanners:

1. Select participants with care. They include job incumbents, their superiors, or experts in the occupation. The important point is that participants in nominal group technique must be familiar with the job.
2. Ask participants meeting in a small group to list either trends that might change work methods or desired results of a job over time, or outcomes of a job at some future time.
3. Ask each participant to explain the first item on their list.
4. Record each item on a flipchart or blackboard in full view of other participants.

5. Continue sharing items from participant lists and recording them until all items are listed. (If an item is listed more than once, the group leader asks how many times it was listed. This number is then placed next to the item on the board.)

6. Ask participants to explain each item and its future relevance to the job, position, or job class. (This step is taken only upon completion of the list on the board.)

7. Ask participants, after their discussion, to weight each item based on importance or on some other quality (for example, the likelihood that an issue will have an impact on a job in the future). Typically, weighting is done on a scale of 1 to 10.

8. Compile results and use them as the basis for preparing a future-oriented job description.

As in the Delphi technique, we advise that you do two separate nominal group techniques: one to identify *what* issues or trends are likely to affect a job in the future, and another to identify *how* those issues or trends will affect the job.

Advantages of NGT include its orientation to concrete problems/issues, its structured approach to unprogrammed decision-making, and its reliance on the opinions of managers and job incumbents rather than on HR planners. Disadvantages include the time required to collect information and obtain results, the cost associated with the wages/salaries of participants, the difficulty of bringing together widely scattered participants for a meeting, the tendency for results to differ according to organizational level and placement of participants, the heavy reliance on writing skills of participants, the tendency of some participants to evaluate ideas before the appropriate time, and the difficulty of assigning rankings to issues/trends in an unknown and uncertain future.

Cross-Impact Analysis (CIA)

Like the Delphi technique, this approach was developed by the Rand Corporation. It is especially useful for judging the impact of one trend or issue on others. Typically, a cross-impact analysis used in future-oriented work analysis begins with two lists: one list of trends likely to affect the organization and its jobs, and a second list of likely results if trends have the impact they are expected to have. For each list, a probability is assigned to each trend or result. The two lists are prepared *before* the analysis begins, perhaps using results of a Delphi technique or nominal group technique.

To conduct a cross-impact analysis for work analysis, the scanner: (1) identifies what events are to be included (this step requires a prior study); (2) estimates the probability of *each* event; (3) estimates conditional probabilities of events; (4) identifies interactions to be determined by performing the analysis; (5) performs the analysis, itself, using a panel of experts; and (6) compiles results. Figure 6-5 illustrates a very simple matrix developed through cross-impact analysis.

This matrix indicates that if new production technology affecting the job class is introduced (event 1), it would have no effect on social trends favoring selection in the occupation; a substantial inhibiting effect on the likelihood that government regulation would be imposed on the occupation; and an even greater inhibiting effect on the likelihood of a recession affecting those already in the occupation. Other cells of the matrix reveal that most events would decrease the probability that the second event will occur. Only in one case is a positive value shown, suggesting that the first event increases the probability of the second.

The chief advantage of cross-impact-analysis is that it affords scanners an opportunity to consider interactive effects of one event on others. It has been

Figure 6-5: Linkage of Events in a Cross-Impact Analysis for Work Analysis

If this event occurs		The effect of the event would be . . .			
		1	2	3	4
1.	New production technology is introduced.		0	−6	−8
2.	Social trends favor a supply of trained people in the field.	0		0	−1
3.	Government legislation imposes strict licensing requirements.	−6	0		0
4.	A recession affects this segment of the labor market.	−1		−2	

advocated for supply and demand forecasting in HR planning. Of course, it does have major disadvantages. First, it is time consuming and costly. Second, it is complex and cannot be realistically used for more than a few events, trends, or issues.

Scenarios

A *scenario* is a brief narrative description of a possible future. Scenarios, widely used in strategic business planning and national defense planning, are holistic in their approach to the future, assessing events or issues in their full complexity.

There are several definitions of what a "scenario" is. It can be a description of a future situation or environment, a description of a trend or issue likely to have an impact in the future, or a record of actions taken by people in dealing with an issue, conflict, or problem. However, a scenario is usually understood to mean *a narrative describing a future situation.*

To prepare a scenario applicable to future-oriented work analysis, the scanner: (1) selects the job, position, or job family for examination; (2) determines how far into the future to go; (3) selects trends, issues, or problems likely to confront future job incumbents (trends, issues, or problems can be identified from results of previous Delphi, nominal group technique, or cross-impact-analysis studies; published forecasts of critical issues facing those in certain occupations can also be used); (4) makes assumptions about the nature of the trend or issue in the future (these assumptions are of major importance because they determine the nature of the scenario); (5) writes a scenario—or more than one—that describes a hypothetical future (the scenario describes a situation, a problem, an event, or a trend); (6) asks a panel of participants, selected for their knowledge of a job or occupation, to predict how job incumbents will probably react to time-bound events, developing trends in the environment, and problems or situations; and (7) prepares a job description based on responses provided by experts.

The chief advantage of a scenario is flexibility. It helps focus attention on the impact of many different issues on a job's future. Unfortunately, scenarios can also vary widely. They also bear little resemblance to actual events as they later unfold.

Scenario planning has been increasing in importance in recent years, due to the advantages afforded by online group-decision support materials. Even geographically scattered experts can be tapped for scenario generation using web-based software, some of which is free to use.

Questionnaires

Another way to conduct future-oriented work analysis is through written (paper-based or electronically-based) questionnaires completed by job incumbents and reviewed by their superiors. Questionnaires are used in traditional present-oriented work analysis to obtain detailed information about what job incumbents are doing at present and how much time they are devoting to various duties.

However, questionnaires can also be designed to ask job incumbents and/or their superiors about future work trends or expected future work outcomes. In fact, questionnaires can be geared to conditions not existing at present but only expected in the future.

The simplest way to approach this task is to change a standard work analysis survey from a present to a future orientation. For example, the scanner poses this question: "What activity, given present trends, will you expect to devote most time to in your job three years from now?" This question uncovers a job incumbent's expectations about the future.

The advantages of surveys:

- They can be used with large numbers of people.
- They are relatively inexpensive to administer.
- They are appropriate to use with people who are geographically scattered.
- They can yield results that are quantifiable and thus suitable for computerized analysis.
- Results tend to be limited to what respondents believe are the consequence of factors internal and external to the organization (in short,

they do not necessarily reveal important *underlying assumptions* about the cause of changes).

I Not everyone is knowledgeable enough about environmental factors to respond meaningfully to a survey.

I Many job incumbents, particularly those in highly structured jobs with little latitude for independent action, will not know what the future holds in store for their jobs or for them.

I Recent events, trends, and problems can distort perceptions about the future.

Interviews

An alternative to the questionnaire is the oral interview, conducted face-to-face, over the phone, or through videoconferencing technology. By using topics or questions prepared in advance, Scanners ask job incumbents or other knowledgeable people about trends in work flow, the industry or occupation, and other matters that will affect the job. Scanners then ask about likely consequences of those future trends on a job, position, or job class.

Interviews can be administered to individuals or groups. Focus groups, which are really group interviews, are probably more appropriate than individual interviews for exploring future trends: Groups tend to do better than individuals in identifying unstructured problems and solutions.

Interviews help pinpoint emerging trends. Indeed, they lend themselves to in-depth explorations in ways that surveys do not. However, interviews are also costly and time-consuming to administer. In most cases, data-gathering efforts are limited to only a few people because of the time and costs associated with travel to and from geographically scattered interview sites or the limitations to data gathering imposed by electronic means.

Observations

Another way to collect information about probable future work tasks is to simulate expected future work conditions and then observe what job incumbents do. While this sounds easy, it is not possible or practical in cases when future job behavior will be influenced by technological changes that have not yet occurred but that are expected or the job category does not easily lend itself to observation because activities are performed mentally (as in white-collar occupations). A disadvantage of observations is the cost or time needed to devise simulations often exceeds their value.

Observation is used in two ways in future-oriented work analysis. First, it can be used directly: Future job conditions and tools are painstakingly simulated. Employee behaviors and work results are then observed first-hand by HR scanners. Second, it can be used indirectly: Games or simulations are substituted for expected future job conditions. Employee behaviors and results are inferred by scanners from indirect observations.

Airplane simulators exemplify direct observation. Before the first new airplane rolls off an assembly line, pilots are exposed to the new craft through a cockpit simulator. Indirect observation is exemplified by an assessment center—a lengthy, structured process to evaluate individual behavior. Assessment centers use a series of exercises, tests, games, and work samples. Trained observers watch individual behavior and rate performance. Though most often used for jobs that presently exist, assessment centers can be designed for simulating expected future job conditions.

Future-oriented observation is a powerful approach. It anticipates job changes that might occur and helps assess the extent of those changes. Results are concrete, based on artificial experience in simulated future work conditions. In fact, job incumbents might even be motivated to prepare for impending change once they have experienced it first hand. Unfortunately, observation—especially the direct variety—is quite expensive. It can be very costly to simulate future working conditions or set up and manage an assessment center.

Document Reviews

Scanners need not rely solely on information supplied by job incumbents and/or their superiors. Instead, predictions about future work can be inferred from company documents intended for broad distribution; informal documents such as memos, letters, and reports; and professional literature pertinent to the occupation. By using this material to gauge projected job or occupational changes, scanners limit the focus of their analysis to assessing the causes of such changes and likely outcomes. They concern themselves with identifying trends, problems, events, or situations.

Content analysis is an inexpensive method for gathering information about work unobtrusively. It requires only time and effort by scanners. The key to the whole process is *category formation*—the development of a classification scheme for organizing information and using it to count the number of times certain key words appear. While scanners can develop such a scheme themselves, it will be more useful to form a panel of job incumbents and their superiors for this purpose. One reason to do so is that incumbents are more likely than HR planners to be familiar with issues of concern in their respective occupations. Another reason is that involvement of incumbents in the future-oriented work analysis process is likely to lead them to accept results more readily.

A major advantage of document reviews and content analysis is that they do not necessarily rely on information provided by job incumbents or superiors who might have reason to manipulate results. When work analysis of this kind is carried out with little involvement by job incumbents, there is less chance that incumbents will see and perhaps misinterpret predictions about what they will probably be doing. A major disadvantage is that results are not easily translated into job descriptions. In addition, the number of times that key words appear is not always the best indication of future importance. People sometimes communicate selectively, telling others only what they want to hear and not necessarily what is true or important.

Selecting a Means to Conduct Future-Oriented Work Analysis

The best approach to gathering future-oriented work information depends entirely on the priorities of those using the information. What *are* the priorities? Speed? Low cost? Accurate data? Building consensus among participants? Appropriateness for the job category being examined?

Naturally, each future-oriented work analysis method discussed so far has distinct advantages and disadvantages relative to these priorities. As Figure 6-6 illustrates:

1. Surveys or written questionnaires are the least costly method for collecting large amounts of information in the shortest period of time from the most people.
2. Interviews are costly and time-consuming to conduct. However, they do allow scanners to probe for information that is highly detailed.
3. Observations are very costly and time-consuming, but they can be quite revealing about future working conditions.
4. Document reviews are relatively inexpensive. They are fast to conduct but are not necessarily very accurate. What managers devote attention to is not necessarily indicative of what will probably come to pass.
5. Critical incidents are good for identifying possible future trends of importance. They are frequently past-oriented, however, and can be quite limited in what they cover.
6. The Delphi and nominal group techniques help build consensus about the future. These techniques are also costly and time consuming to conduct. When knowledgeable participants are selected with care, results can be reasonably accurate.
7. Cross-impact analysis is the best method for considering influences of one trend on others, but is often not appropriate for identifying trends in the first place.
8. Scenarios are very useful for training people to think strategically, to anticipate what should be done under possible future conditions. However, scenarios are not necessarily more accurate nor less expensive than other methods.

Verifying Results of Future-Oriented Work Analysis

Most approaches for verifying present-oriented work analysis results are also appropriate for verifying future-oriented results. They include (1) *using more*

Figure 6-6: Advantages and Disadvantages of Data-Collection Methods for Future-Oriented Work Analysis

Means of Gathering	Brief Summary of	Good for	Not Good for
Critical Incident	Ask people to identify situations likely to come up in the future and what should be done when they occur	I Anticipating key performance issues in the future	I Speed I Cost I Collecting much information
Delphi Technique	Ask people to identify future trends and/or future job tasks and how to deal with trends and/or prepare people for the new tasks	I Building consensus among participants I Accuracy	I Speed I Cost I Collecting much information from many people
Nominal Group Technique	Ask people to identify future trends and/or future job tasks/work outcomes; prioritize items	I Building consensus among participants I Accuracy	I Speed I Cost I Collecting much information from many people
Cross-Impact Analysis	Compare the impact of a trend/event on others; use results of a Delphi or nominal group technique	I Establishing priorities I Assessing interactions between trends	I Dealing with large amounts of information
Scenario	Assess how people should act under possible future conditions, using a brief narrative description	I Building consensus among participants I Training people in strategic thinking	I Speed I Cost
Questionnaire	Simply take a written survey used to collect present-oriented work information and revise it to reflect a future orientation	I Collecting large amount of information I Collecting data from many people I Speed I Holding down cost	I Accuracy; other methods are better I Follow up; futurist not necessarily sure who, where, what
Interview	Simply take an existing interview guide or schedule and revise it to reflect a future orientation	I Accuracy of perceptions; the futurists can follow up and gain more information I Relatively good for speed	I Dealing with diverse group of people I Holding down cost, especially when travel is required I Collecting much information from many people

Figure 6-6: *(continued)*

Means of Gathering	Brief Summary of	Good for	Not Good for
Observation	Observe a simulation, direct or indirect, of expected/ desired future working conditions, tools, and tasks	▪ Accuracy when job tasks lend themselves to observation	▪ Speed ▪ Cost ▪ Building consensus among participants ▪ Jobs that do not lend themselves easily to observation
Document Review	Examine documents to determine what issues seem to occupy the attention of managers; assume they will result in future action	▪ Avoiding manipulation of what people think or do simply by collecting data ▪ Speed ▪ Low cost	▪ Accuracy; document reviews reveal intentions, not necessarily what will be acted on

than one approach (compare information collected through more than one method); (2) *using more than one source of information* (check results by comparing responses of multiple sources or people); and (3) *using multiple raters* (check results by comparing perceptions of job incumbents, their superiors, and others whose opinions are appropriate to consider). While these verification methods help improve the accuracy of predictions, they will also increase the cost and the time needed to complete analysis.

Monitoring Factors Influencing Jobs

Future-oriented work analysis should be repeated whenever there is a major change in environmental conditions affecting the occupation, profession, or organization or whenever there is a major change within the organization. Examples include changes in organizational structure, leadership, policies, or reward systems. A change in organizational strategy—whether prompted by external environmental change or by new initiatives of leaders inside the organization—should also lead to review of how such change will or should influence job activities and outcomes.

One final note to bear in mind: All jobs in a job family should probably be analyzed at the same time. It makes little sense, after all, to consider one job in isolation.

Conducting Future-Oriented Workforce Analysis

Having completed future-oriented work analysis, scanners can then turn their attention to future-oriented workforce analysis. Traditional and present-oriented workforce analysis describes what kind of people should do the work. Similarly, future-oriented workforce analysis *predicts* which people should probably do the work. Armed with this information, scanners can compare the present to the projected and expected future of HR in the organization. To carry out future-oriented workforce analysis, scanners (1) infer from future-oriented job descriptions the education, experience, and personal characteristics that will probably be possessed by job incumbents at some future time; (2) consult with others in the organization in order to identify characteristics of employee performance that will probably be most important. The first step becomes the basis for future job specifications and person descriptions; the second is used in devising a succession planning system (Rothwell, 2000).

Future-Oriented Job Specifications

As we explained before, a job specification sketches the education, experience, and personal characteristics necessary to carry out duties set forth on a job description.

Future-oriented job specifications are closely related to "person descriptions," which describe the knowledge, skills, abilities, and attitudes needed to carry out each task on a job description. Job specifications differ from person descriptions only in detail. Both focus on what kind of person should do the work. Specifications are restricted, however, to very short summaries of education and experience. On the other hand, person descriptions are quite detailed. They are point-by-point revisions of corresponding job descriptions.

Why bother to go to the trouble of preparing a future-oriented person description or job specification? There is at least one good reason for doing so: they provide guidance for HR decision-making in changing environmental conditions. One problem with relying solely on present-oriented descriptions for making employee selections and deciding on training needs is that they are valid for a short time only. Individuals chosen for jobs today might not be the ones who are needed tomorrow.

Determining Characteristics of Employee Performance to Evaluate the Future

Appropriate yardsticks by which to evaluate employee performance do not remain static. Changes inside and outside an organization exert pressure on jobs and on people carrying them out. As a result, priorities change. Hence, some characteristics of employee performance will gradually assume greater importance than others. For example, individual initiative and entrepreneurship can have a relatively low priority in a heavily regulated industry but a much higher one as the industry undergoes deregulation.

During periods of environmental change, leaders are tempted to throw out an entire formal employee-appraisal system and start over with a new set of criteria yardsticks and perhaps a completely new set of procedures and forms. That temptation isn't limited only to periods of upheaval: Even in the best of times, some HR planners may hear a swelling chorus of complaints from managers that "a new appraisal system is needed." Pressure for change can also be created by various fads in appraisal methods, such as recent interest in multirater, full-circle assessment.

Anyone considering throwing out an entire appraisal system should think twice about it: continuity will be lost. It is impossible to track individual progress over time when different systems and performance criteria are used. Nor is it any easier to project performance needs into the future when criteria change.

One way to deal with this problem is to create two independent performance-appraisal systems. The first is present oriented; the other is future oriented. The future-oriented is called a "succession system" or an "executive review." Forms and procedures of such systems quite often resemble those used in employee appraisals, though perhaps only upper-level managers go through them. Of course, the same idea can be extended downward to all employees in an organization.

The criteria for future-oriented appraisals are generated through the same methods used in future-oriented work analysis. For example:

1. The *critical incident process* helps pinpoint which factors pertaining to employee performance will probably emerge as most important in the future.
2. Both the *Delphi and nominal group techniques* help determine what indicators of performance will probably become important for job incumbents in the future.
3. *Cross-impact analysis,* based on results from a prior Delphi or nominal group technique study, assesses possible relationships between performance measures expected to be important in the future.
4. *Scenarios* stimulate thought on performance criteria that will probably emerge as important.
5. *Questionnaires and interviews* of executives, job incumbents, experts in the field, or superiors of job incumbents help identify possible future-oriented performance criteria.
6. *Observations,* based on simulations of future job conditions, provide information about performance measures of likely future importance.
7. *Document reviews,* based on stated intentions of managers, are analyzed for content. The results are then grouped, by category into dimensions or traits.

In each case, it is possible to identify what kind of people will be needed at a future time and how their work performance will probably be judged.

Scanning for the HR Department

The HR department can match people and jobs over time. Indeed, each HR practice area is a tool for changing jobs and/or people in ways intended to anticipate organizational needs. However, these practice areas are themselves subject to changes wrought by environmental factors. For this reason, scanning for the HR department itself is necessary.

Methods of Scanning

The same methods used in scanning for jobs and people are also applicable to HR department scanning. They include surveys, interviews, observations, unobtrusive measures, critical incidents, the Delphi technique, the nominal group technique, and scenarios. Each can identify what trends will probably influence the HR department and its programs in the future and how those trends will probably affect the department.

Figure 6-7 illustrates a simple interview guide designed for departmental scanning.

Factors Considered in Departmental Scanning

The HR department is influenced by trends as well as factors internal and external to the organization, such as trends in (1) *managing HR departments* (What are state-of-the-art HR management methods? What are they likely to be in the future?), (2) *delivering HR department services* (What methods are used to offer HR programs? What methods are likely to be used in the future?), (3) *programming for HR department* (What kinds of services are presently offered by the department? What kinds are likely to be offered in the future?), and (4) *prioritizing departmental services* (What priority do the resource needs of the department presently command among competing interests in the organization? What priority will those needs command in the future?) In short, the HR field itself can be considered an environment of sorts. What is happening in it

Figure 6-7: An Interview Guide for HR Department Scanning

---

1. Over the next 3 to 5 years, how would you say that the HR department will probably be affected by each of the following situations:
    (a) Economic conditions?
    (b) Marketing/competitive conditions?
    (c) Suppliers?
    (d) Government/legal conditions?
    (e) Demographics?
    (f) Social change?
    (g) Geography?
    (h) Technology?
    (i) Leadership changes inside the organization?
    (j) Structure of the organization?
    (k) Processes (decision-making; communication) in the organization?
    (l) Reward systems of the organization?

2. *Which* factor inside or outside the HR department will probably exert the greatest influence on the department? Why?

3. *How* will the factor you described in question 2 affect the HR department?

4. If present trends in the HR department continue, what do you think its status will be within the organization in five years?

---

influences expectations about what the department will probably be doing or should be doing. To scan the HR field, HR planners rely on research about future directions in it or else conduct such research themselves. Trends affecting the field are regularly described in the professional literature.

Outcomes of the Departmental Scanning Process

The outcomes of departmental scanning depend on how scanning itself is carried out. If critical incidents or scenarios are used for scanning, then outcomes will be expressed in narratives, for example. However, it is possible to prepare structured questions that call for responses on a numbered scale. In those cases, outcomes will be expressed in quantitative terms.

No matter how results are expressed, scanners need to keep in mind that future-oriented results will be compared with present strengths and weaknesses of the HR department identified through HR audits. The comparison of present strengths/weaknesses to future trends/conditions is one basis for selecting a long-term strategy.

Determining Desired Effects of Environmental Factors

While future-oriented work analysis furnishes HR planners with information about what people will probably do, future-oriented *workforce* analysis provides information about what kind of people will probably do the work. HR department scanning helps identify and assess the probable influence on the department of factors inside and outside the organization. Each is fundamentally oriented to describing expectations for the future. Indeed, each addresses the basic question of what will probably be in the future. The assumption in each case is that present trends will continue without corrective action being taken or radical changes being made.

However, strategic plans for HR require more than a mere description of what will probably happen if no action is taken. To be useful for long-range planning, information is also needed about what *should happen* in the future. In other words, scanners try to envision jobs, people, and HR department activities at a future time so that they are consistent with strategic business plans. Figure 6-8 highlights the relationship between this question and others.

We have already described in this chapter how to conduct future-oriented work analysis, workforce analysis, and HR department scanning. Each is geared to simple identification of how factors inside or outside an organization will probably affect jobs, people, and the HR department in the future. In short, they address what will probably be.

In contrast, what we can call *strategic-oriented work analysis, strategic-oriented workforce analysis,* and *strategic-oriented HR department scanning* are similar to their *future-oriented* counterparts in many respects: Results of strategic-oriented work analysis are expressed as job descriptions. Results of strategic-oriented workforce analysis are expressed as job specifications, person descriptions, and employee appraisal methods. Results of strategic-oriented HR department scanning are often expressed as narratives. However, in each instance, results express what should be in the future if jobs, people, and the

Figure 6-8: Key Questions to Consider in Strategic Planning for HR

Present

What is?

What is the present status of
• Jobs (work)?
• People (workforce)?
• HR department?

Future
(How far)

Environment Factors

Strategy

What will probably be versus what should be the future status of
• Jobs?
• People?
• HR department?

What will probably be?

What should be?

Planning Gap
For SPHR

How can activities of the HR department
help narrow or eliminate the planning gap?

HR department exist in an ideal state supporting achievement of strategic business plans. The same methods used to develop future-oriented job descriptions, position descriptions, and HR department scans can also be used to develop the strategic-oriented analyses. The chief difference is that strategic-oriented analysis focuses on identifying an *ideal* state desired in the future, not the one most likely to occur if no action is taken.

Here is a comparison of future- and strategic-oriented documents:

1. Job descriptions will reveal a planning gap that can pinpoint development actions requiring change in the nature of jobs, positions, and entire job families in the future.

2. Job specifications will reveal a planning gap requiring change in education, experience, and personal qualities of job incumbents in the future.

3. Person descriptions will reveal a planning gap requiring change in the specific knowledge and skills of job incumbents in the future.

4. Employee performance appraisals will reveal a planning gap requiring change in employee performance criteria deemed important.

5. HR department scans will reveal a planning gap requiring change in practice areas of the HR department.

Activity 6-1: Future-Oriented Work Analysis

Purpose

This activity is intended to simulate one way of performing future-oriented work analysis.

Advance Preparation

1. Read (or reread) the pertinent section of this chapter.
2. Photocopy Activity 3-1 found in Chapter 3.
3. Change all verb tenses from present to future tense. (For example, the first question will begin: "How do you think you will perform special duties or use special skills that will be unlike those of others with your job title in two years?")

Group Size

Recommended for groups of three people.

Time Required

Approximately 115 minutes.

Materials Needed

1. Pen or pencil.
2. Photocopied "Position Questionnaire" revised as indicated above.

Special Seating Requirements

Movable chairs and tables are desirable but are not essential.

Activity 6-1: *(continued)*

Introduction

To plan for future HR needs of an organization, some methods are needed to project what job incumbents will probably be doing at some time in the future. There are limitations to this method: Not everyone will be able to predict with accuracy what they will be required to do in the future because not everyone is privy to all factors in the environment. It is at least one way to try to begin predicting future job duties.

Procedures

Step 1: 5 minutes

1. In each group of three people, one person should play the role of HR scanner, a second should play the role of a job incumbent, and a third should play the role of the job incumbent's immediate supervisor and should observe.
2. The scanner will interview the job incumbent (first), using the structured questionnaire/interview schedule. (If the exercise is conducted at a university, the job incumbent's present and expected future job will be that of student; if the exercise is conducted in a work setting, the job incumbent's position should be the same as in real life. If the person expects to be promoted or otherwise change jobs in two years, keep the focus on the present job and the respondent's opinions on how it will probably change *in two years.*)
3. The observer will take notes during the interview on how well the interviewer is able to elicit meaningful answers.
4. When the scanner has completed the interview with the job incumbent, the scanner will then interview the supervisor (played by the observer) by using questions provided on the last two pages of the structured questionnaire/interview schedule.

Step 2: 75 minutes

The scanner should conduct interviews with the job incumbent while the observer takes notes.

Step 3: 15 minutes

The scanner should conduct the interview with the job incumbent's supervisor (played by the observer).

Step 4: 20 minutes

Discussion.

Discussion Questions

1. Will observers from each group summarize their observations?
2. What common problems were apparent in conducting these interviews? What can be done to avoid these problems?
3. What can be done with the results of future-oriented work analysis?
4. How well do you think this work analysis would work for production employees? Clerical/secretarial workers? Managers? Technical personnel? Why the differences?
5. *(Optional)* Repeat the exercise with a focus on strategic-oriented work analysis. Change the "Position Questionnaire" items to reflect *what should be in the future,* rather than *what will probably be.* Then answer questions 1 to 4 (above) from the perspective of strategic-oriented work analysis.

Notes

CHAPTER 7

THE HUMAN RESOURCES FORECASTER

More often than not, human resource (HR) planners pay more attention to HR forecasting than to environmental scanning (London, Bassman, and Fernandez, 1990; Makridakis, 1990). Historically, literature on HR planning has emphasized forecasting and nearly ignored scanning. The difference between them is one of focus: Strategists and HR planners prefer to emphasize the influence of future trends on *the content* of jobs, the people doing those jobs, and the HR department's efforts over the *number* of jobs and the people doing them. Environmental scanning focuses on qualitative (content) changes over time; forecasting focuses on quantitative (numbers) over time. Some evidence does exist to suggest that HR planners are moving away from historical estimates of future HR needs and are beginning to think in terms of just-in-time approaches (Bartlett and Ghosal, 1998).

While we would argue that qualitative change is really far more important than quantitative change for planning purposes, we would be remiss to ignore an activity like forecasting that has been the center of so much attention among HR planners. This chapter will thus provide a brief overview of the HR Forecaster's role.

What Does the HR Forecaster Do?

The HR forecaster is responsible for estimating numbers of people and jobs needed by an organization to achieve its objectives and realize its plans over time in the most efficient and effective manner possible. In the simplest sense, HR needs are computed by subtracting HR supplies or numbers of people available from expected HR demands or numbers of people required to produce at a desired level.

To carry out the forecasting process, HR planners:

1. Classify *employees* into distinct and unambiguous categories, which include age, race, sex, length of tenure, and present position.

2. Classify *positions* into categories, which include (for example) educational preparation, experience required, or placement of the job in the organizational structure.

3. Equate historical relationships between output and staffing levels. For instance, how many people are needed to produce a specific number of goods? Offer a specific level of service?

4. Forecast demand by analyzing current HR requirements and projecting future HR requirements.

5. Forecast supply by analyzing current HR inventories and comparing expected internal and external availability of human resource supplies.

6. Forecast HR needs.

These steps are summarized in Figure 7-1.

What Are Some Models of Forecasting?

Forecasting can be looked at from more than just the perspective of the forecaster's role. In one classic and still-relevant treatment, Walker (1980) indicates that it consists of six steps. The first step is to assess the internal and external environment, either as part of strategic business planning efforts or as special stand-alone studies commissioned solely for human resources planning. The second step is to inventory available talent through examination of current employee appraisal information and succession plans. The third step is to forecast future labor supply based on attrition or turnover patterns, mobility or move-

Figure 7-1: A Simplified Model of the HR Forecasting Process

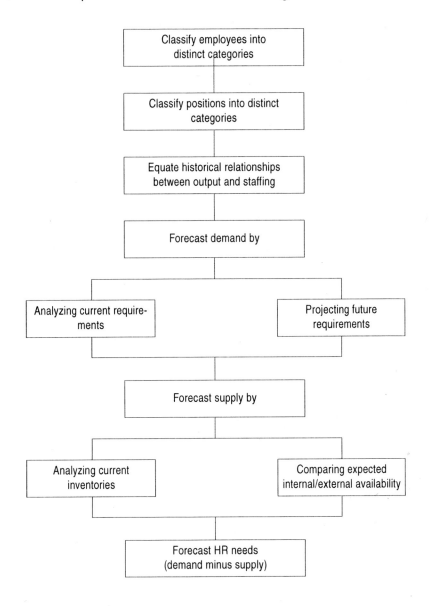

ment between job classes, skills utilization, and future assumptions. On the other side of the demand-supply equation, the fourth step consists of analyzing present HR requirements. Forecasters examine the number of present positions, the nature of the organization's structure, and the desired mix or pattern of occupations. The present is then projected into the future. Special attention is devoted to expected demand (what will probably be) and desired demand (what should be in the future). The final step is a comparison of supply and demand. This process indicates shortfalls where action will be necessary to bring together the number of people available and the number needed in the future. Action is taken through such HR practice areas as recruitment and training.

HR planners (1) assess labor demand by projecting requirements implied by organizational plans; (2) assess internal labor supply by examining turnover patterns and inventories of existing skills and people; (3) assess external labor supply expected in the future; (4) compare supply and demand; and (5) reconcile labor shortfalls in such categories as the number of people/positions, experience, abilities, and race/sex of employees.

External environmental issues as well as internal forecasting can be included in a model of human resources planning (HRP), which is thus based on making comparisons between short- and long-range labor supplies and demands. Demand is stimulated by external environmental, organizational, and workforce conditions. Supply is a function of internal and external availability.

These models are primarily quantitative, equating supply and demand to *numbers* of people or positions by category. People are viewed not so much as individuals with unique talents, strengths, and weaknesses but rather as members of classifiable groups, clustered for ease in quantifying attributes, patterns, and characteristics. This reflects the traditional quantitative bias of HR forecasting.

Steps One and Two: Classifying Employees and Positions

The first two steps in the forecasting model we propose involves classifying employees and positions into distinct categories. Depending on the purpose for which forecasting is conducted, it can be handled in several ways.

People are categorized by *age,* if the purpose of forecasting is to project expected numbers of retirements; by *race* and *sex,* if the purpose is to compare goals and results for diversity, equal employment opportunity, or affirmative action; by *tenure* or *seniority,* if the purpose is to predict turnover rates/promotion; by *educational level,* if the purpose is to narrow the pool of qualified candidates for transfers and promotions; and by *experience,* if the purpose is to assess bench strength or identify people with adequate preparation for transfers or promotions.

On the other hand, *positions* are categorized by *level,* if the purpose is to relate positions to decision-making authority; by *educational and training requirements,* if the purpose is to identify work or experience prerequisites, based on task differences that distinguish one position from others; by *employee type,* if the purpose is to classify positions according to designations provided by the U.S. Equal Employment Opportunity Commission and state government counterparts of that commission; by *location,* if the purpose is to identify positions by geography; and by *activity* or *function,* if the purpose is to identify positions by their location in organizational departments, divisions, and work groups.

Organization charts and budget documents are excellent starting points for establishing position categories. They show relationships between units and authorized staffing levels. They provide a snapshot of *what is*—present conditions. They can also serve as guides for dealing with *what will probably be,* or serve as projections into the future, taking into account assumptions and *what should be in the future,* or desired numbers of people/positions. Likewise, individualized career profiles provide a starting point for categorizing individuals, summarizing in a single place all the information pertinent to individual performance, education, career aspirations, and prior experience (Walker, 1980).

Decisions about what categories to use—and how many—depend solely on the purpose or aim of the HR forecast.

Step Three: Equating Staffing and Output

The key to forecasting is to determine some relationship between people and positions and organizational outputs. HR planners need to identify or devise a *predictor* or measure of revenues or outputs that relates numbers and types of people to goods or services produced. Predictors can be historic or past-oriented, based on projections into the future of relationships identified in the past; they can be judgmental or future-oriented, based on the expected influence on staffing of changes in such areas as technology, sales, and productivity. In any case, predictors must be *proportionate;* that is, changes in expected or required production levels must affect staffing levels and vice versa.

Unfortunately, it is not a simple matter to identify a predictor from past staffing/output relationships or to devise one based on judgments about the future. Research provides few clues about what predictors are being used, when they are appropriate or inappropriate, and when alternatives should be chosen.

Intuitive predictors are probably most common. Managers simply estimate how many and what kind of people they will need to achieve functional plans related to production, finance, and marketing, and to achieve output objectives established for their organizational units. Little attempt is made to pinpoint a precise mathematical variable or variables to serve as a predictor; rather, each manager simply relies on intuition. HR planners survey managers at each level and, in this way, arrive at forecasts of HR needs.

Of course, more sophisticated predictors can be identified from (1) *historical data* (from past staffing levels and output patterns, HR planners identify a productivity index; it is used, in turn, to estimate future staffing requirements resulting from expected or desired output levels); (2) the *total budget of the organization* (a ratio of workers to budget dollars is devised; as the budget increases, numbers of workers increase in proportion to it); (3) *numbers of units processed* (if the numbers of units expected to be processed increases, staffing is correspondingly increased); (4) *changes in productivity* (to the extent that outputs per worker are affected by identifiable trends, they can be used as predictors); and (5) *staffing cycles* (when staffing requirements vary by season or when the work itself is temporarily stepped up or slows down, it can be identified from past trends and then projected into the future).

Not one of these predictors sheds light on *what skills* should be possessed in what jobs. This important qualitative issue has been traditionally ignored by HR forecasters, though growing interest does exist in knowledge management and intellectual capital that examines these issues.

Step Four: Forecasting Demands

Forecasting demand is the process of estimating how many people will be needed in the future in various job categories, geographical locations, and organizational units. The process is based on applying the predictor identified or devised in the previous step. More art than science, *demand forecasting*—as it is sometimes called—is the driving force in HR planning. Estimates of supply are matched to it. Ward (1996) indicates that professional HR departments have, for the most part, devised well-established methods for addressing this issue, but that those methods are also the greatest source of dissatisfaction.

What Are Some Reasons for Demand Forecasting?

There are several good reasons to conduct demand forecasting. It can help to: (1) quantify the positions necessary for producing a given number of goods or offering a given amount of services in demand; (2) identify departments or work groups that can benefit from productivity improvement efforts; (3) determine what staff mix is desirable in the future (that is, numbers of people/positions of one class or occupational group relative to others); (4) assess appropriate staffing levels in different parts of the organization so as to hold down unnecessary costs; (5) prevent shortages of people where and when they are most needed; and (6) monitor compliance with equal employment opportunity goals. Demand forecasting thus helps control costs associated with human resources by ensuring that recruitment, management of HR, and promotions/transfers match organizational needs.

Causes of HR Demand

Demand for human resources stems from such causes as *changes in the external environment* (as economic, technological, social, demographic, and other external factors exert influence on work performed by the organization, labor demand is affected); organizational plans and *objectives* (How do strategists want the organization to perform? At what level of output do they plan to produce goods or offer services? Answers to those questions affect demand, especially when staffing is linked to output levels by means of a predictor); and *productivity levels* (How much is each worker producing? Labor demand remains constant or even decreases when each worker increases output). Each source of demand can be separately considered in the forecasting process.

Forecasting Methods

Few topics among HR planners have commanded as much attention as methods of forecasting. Indeed, it appears that writers on the subject place great faith in these tools of the HRP trade. Articles on forecasting outnumber those on almost any other topic in the HRP field.

Forecasting methods can be categorized as (1) quantitative/descriptive, (2) quantitative/normative, (3) qualitative/descriptive, or (4) qualitative/normative.

Quantitative/descriptive methods are most widely touted in the HRP literature. They focus on estimating how many people will be needed in the future in the various job categories. Their purpose is to describe *what will probably be*. Methods include summary statistics, moving averages, exponential smoothing, trend projections, regression models, and flow models. Each one is complicated.

Summary statistics is by far the simplest quantitative/descriptive method. Past personnel movements are tracked on the basis of movement (1) *into the organization* (What kind of people are being hired? How many will probably be hired?); (2) *through the organization* (How many people are moving to lateral positions? Higher-level ones? Lower-level ones?); (3) *out of the organization* (How much movement out of the organization occurs through turnover, through such means as voluntary resignations or retirements, as well as such involuntary means as firings and death). These statistics are used, in turn, to forecast future HR demand based on past movements. The method is quite appropriate when the organization's internal and external environments are relatively stable.

The *moving average,* as the name implies, literally averages data about HR demand from recent periods and simply projects them into the future. The actual number of people required over the past three, six, or twelve months is divided by the number of months in the forecast to compute a simple mean. That mean will vary slightly, depending on how much demand has fluctuated during the time included in the forecast.

Suppose we wish to forecast HR demand at month 10, using information on actual demand for 7 previous months and forecasted demand for 2 more. Assuming that a 3-month moving average is used as the basis of the forecast and that 85 people were needed in month 7, 102 were forecasted for month 8, and 110 were forecasted for month 9, then 99 people will be forecast for month 10. Yet if a five-month moving average is used, 106 people might be forecasted.

The chief advantage of the moving average method is its simplicity. Unfortunately, it also has serious disadvantages: (1) Months are weighed equally, when in fact they can differ greatly in significance, (2) seasonal or cyclical patterns are ignored, and (3) heavy reliance is placed on past rather than future data.

Exponential smoothing is a somewhat more sophisticated quantitative/descriptive method. The basic idea is simple enough. The forecast for the current period is added to an error term, computed by multiplying forecast error during the present period by a constant between one and zero. *Forecast error* is present demand less present forecast. Choice of a constant is judgmental, depending on the forecaster's awareness of management needs and the unique nature of the forecasting situation. In reality, exponential smoothing is a general term applied to a whole range of methods. It is more advantageous than moving averages because forecasters can vary weights associated with different time periods. It is disadvantageous for planning in that, like moving averages, its basis is the past rather than the future.

Trend projections are somewhat simpler. Forecasters plot past demand for HR on a graph. Numbers of people hired or requested are placed on one axis; time is placed on the other. Forecasters simply eyeball the data and plot a straight line from past to future. While not a method characterized by great accuracy, trend projections are easily explained to strategists and easily prepared by HR planners.

Regression models, similar to trend projections, are more mathematically precise. A line is fitted on a graph much like that in trend projection, except a mathematical regression formula is used to relate staffing and output variables. Multiple regression is similar except that more variables are included (Meehan and Ahmed, 1990).

Flow models are very frequently associated with HR forecasting. The simplest one is called a *Markov model.* Forecasters:

1. Determine the time that will be encompassed. This choice is, of course, based on the planning horizon desired, usually coinciding with the time horizon of strategic business plans. Shorter lengths of time are generally more accurate than longer ones.

2. Establish categories to which employees can be assigned. These categories, called *states,* must not overlap, but must take into account every possible category to which an individual can be assigned. The number of states must not be too large or too small.

3. Count annual "flows" or movements between states for several prior time periods. These states are defined as *absorbing* (gains or losses to the organization) or *nonabsorbing* (changes in position levels or employment status). Losses include death or disability, absence, resignations, and retirement; gains include hiring, rehiring, transfer, and movement by position level.

4. Estimate the probability of transitions from one state to another based on past trends. Demand is a function of replacing those who make a transition.

There are alternatives to the simple Markov model. One, called the *semi-Markov,* takes into account not just *state* but also *tenure of individuals in each state.* After all, likelihood of movement increases with tenure. Another method is called the *vacancy model,* which predicates probabilities of movement and numbers of vacancies. While the semi-Markov does the best job of estimating movement among those whose situations and tenures are similar, the vacancy model produces the best results for an organization.

Markov analysis is advantageous in that it makes sense to decision-makers. They can easily understand its underlying assumptions and are thus more likely to rely on the results. The disadvantages: past-oriented data might not be accurate in periods of dynamically wrenching change and accuracy in forecast about individuals is sacrificed to achieve accuracy across groups.

Unlike quantitative/descriptive demand forecasting methods, quantitative/normative ones optimize numbers of people and positions. Their purpose is thus to assess *what should be in the future, not what will probably be.* Specific methods include linear programming, goal programming, and assignment models.

Linear programming is the general title applicable to a whole range of techniques. It is appropriate to use when (1) managers seek a single, well-defined objective; (2) alternatives for action exist; (3) achievement of the objective is constrained by scarce resources; (4) objectives and constraints are expressed as mathematical functions ("linear inequalities"); and (5) a linear relationship exists between the objective and constraints on achieving it. This method helps determine HR demand equated with desired output. In other words, it assesses the *required* staffing level that matches *required* output levels.

Goal programming is a related method, pairing linear programming and Markov modeling. When constraints such as budget and promotion policies influence staffing and when the forecasting problem encompasses several time periods, the method is appropriate. It pinpoints attainable and optimal goals by comparing discrepancies between targets and forecasted results. It has been used in business firms and government organizations.

Assignment models match individuals to job vacancies. Their focus on individuals rather than groups distinguishes them from such other methods as linear and goal programming, Markov analysis, and regression or trend projections. Individuals are matched to positions on the basis of career aspirations or tenure in existing jobs, for example. The aim is to achieve great precision in examining use of talent and pinpointing shortages and surpluses.

The chief advantage of methods like linear programming, goal programming, and assignment models is that they establish norms or yardsticks for HR forecasts. They facilitate control of human resources, helping hold down costs. Unfortunately, they require sophisticated mathematics. The techniques are sometimes greeted with skepticism by managers who have trouble understanding the mathematics behind them.

Qualitative/descriptive forecasting methods constitute a third category of approaches to assessing HR demand. Like their quantitative/descriptive counterpart, they focus on *what is expected in the future,* not necessarily what is desired. Unlike their quantitative counterpart, however, they do not rely on mathematics. Specific methods include simple judgments by managers, the critical incident approach, the Delphi technique, the nominal group technique, and cross-impact analysis. These methods were described in Chapter 6, where we indicated that they identify *what* factors inside and outside an organization will influence jobs, people, and the HR department in the future, and predict *how* those factors will influence jobs, people, and the HR department. Without repeating lengthy descriptions of these methods, we shall simply note that they can be applied to HR forecasting as well as to environmental scanning. Each method is potentially useful for forecasting HR labor demand; each is directed at assessing *what will probably be.*

Qualitative/normative methods are directed at forecasting *what should be in the future.* They forecast according to the manager's desires in line with strategic business plans, not mere expectations. Numbers of people and positions are assessed without mathematics. Methods used in qualitative/descriptive forecasting are also used in qualitative/normative forecasting, though intent is different: to determine what ought to be, not just what will probably be. Hence, qualitative/normative forecasting can make use of the critical incident process, the Delphi technique, nominal group technique, cross-impact analysis, questionnaires, and interviews.

The state of the forecasting art is quite advanced. In short, the methods available—as we have seen—can be rather sophisticated, some relying on advanced mathematics that is easier to use with the appropriate software. While there are many mathematical methods available to conduct HRP, they are less often used in practice than they are touted in writings about HRP. Several reasons may account for this: (1) managers are sometimes skeptical of quantitative forecasts; (2) problems that confront organizations do change, rendering reliance on specific forecasting approaches inappropriate; and (3) not all HR planners possess appropriate skills to apply all forecasting methods.

Step Five: Forecasting Labor Supply

The fifth step in HR forecasting is analysis of the supply of workers—the numbers and the types of people expected to be available to meet demand. This worker supply can come from two places: *from the inside of the organization* (people can be promoted, demoted, transferred, or trained and developed to help meet future HR demand) and *from the outside of the organization* (people can be recruited from colleges, competitors, specialized training programs, and other sources to help meet future HR demand).

What Are Some Reasons for Supply Forecasting?

Fewer organizations estimate HR supplies than demand. One reason is that decision-makers tend to take for granted the existing workforce in the organization. In addition, some managers assume that employees are just "warm bodies" who can be easily moved or replaced at will. Old beliefs die hard, even at a time when (at this writing) most employers say that attracting and retaining talent is a key competitive challenge and a key constraint on organizational growth. HR planners still encounter managers who make this assumption, even when it is apparent that not just anybody can perform adequately in highly specialized positions requiring years of preparation.

Supply forecasting helps:

I   Quantify numbers of people and positions expected to be available in the future to help the organization realize its plans and meet its objectives

■ Identify how much productivity improvement is possible in areas of the organization that are thought to be able to benefit from such initiatives
■ Clarify likely staff mixes that will exist in the future
■ Assess existing staffing levels in different parts of the organization
■ Prevent shortages of people where and when they are most needed
■ Monitor expected future compliance with equal employment opportunity goals

Causes of Supply Shifts

Changes in HR supplies stem from:

1. *External factors.* For instance, internal supplies are influenced by economic conditions (as the economy heats up, turnover often increases; as the economy cools down, turnover decreases); technological conditions (automation can change the distribution of demand; it can mean reduction in supply like layoffs and creation of entirely new job categories); and governmental/legal conditions (changes in laws, regulations, and court rulings mean that some groups or employee categories are accorded specialized protection from layoff and are given specialized attention in hiring, training, and promotion).

2. *Internal factors.* Supplies in the organization are affected by job climate/morale (voluntary turnover increases when climate is poor, work group morale is low, and individuals experience job dissatisfaction) and structure (some organizational structures require more people than others).

3. *Workforce factors.* External HR supplies are affected by availability of talent from competitors; high schools, colleges, and universities; and different age groups. Smaller numbers of people in specific age categories mean that some HR supplies are less plentiful.

There are, of course, other reasons why worker supplies change. For example, as average individual job tenure or length of service increases, more people will be unavailable for the future. With longer job tenure, the probability of movement is greater. Turnover can also affect HR supply.

Supply Forecasting Methods

There are essentially two kinds of supply forecasting methods:

1. The quantitative, in which mathematical methods are used
2. The qualitative, in which nonmathematical and largely judgmental methods are used

Quantitative methods have most frequently been advocated by academic researchers. They trace historical movements between job categories and allow for loss resulting from turnover and retirement. A few methods are summarized briefly in Figure 7-2.

On the other hand, qualitative supply forecasting methods include staffing charts, replacement charts, succession charts, and kill inventories. They help clarify what future HR supplies will probably be available. They are not, like quantitative methods, based on mathematical calculations.

A *staffing chart* is prepared before or after an annual budget. Its time frame tends to be short-term—a year in most cases. This chart depicts numbers of people in each job category authorized for the year and numbers presently occupying those positions. Differences between those numbers reveal anticipated openings at some point, typically at the start of the budget period. The chart is a static representation that does not indicate whether openings will be filled from without. It is useful for identifying what head count should exist by the end of a budget period. Of course, it does little to establish targets for productivity improvement, because numbers of people/positions are not equated to output.

A *replacement chart* is a graphic depiction of who inside the organization is ready to assume a higher position. In simplistic terms, preparation of a chart is about the least that can be done to plan for the sudden loss of key executives. Replacement charts can also help plan for impending retirement of key execu-

Figure 7-2: Methods of Forecasting Supply

Method	Description	Advantages	Disadvantages
Actuarial Model	▪ Relates turnover to such factors as age, seniority	▪ Reflects past	▪ Might not be accurate in individual cases
Simulation	▪ Uses scenarios to test the effect of various personnel policies on movements	▪ Useful for considering alternative HR programs	▪ Accuracy varies
Probability Matrix	▪ Defines "states" in the organization—such as salary levels, performance ratings, etc. ▪ Identifies time period ▪ Identifies movements between "cells"	▪ Helps identify career patterns ▪ Helps perform turnover analysis	▪ Requires some mathematical sophistication ▪ Accuracy varies
First-Order Markov Model	▪ Multiplies number of people in each job category by the probability of movement between job/position categories. It assumes that current job/position category is the chief determinant of movement.	▪ Adequate for considering alternative effects of various HR strategies	▪ Not adequate for long-term forecasts (Stewman 1978) ▪ Requires mathematical sophistication
Semi-Markov Model	▪ Same as first-order Markov model, except that probability of movement is a dual function: (1) job/position category and (2) the individual's length of stay in the job class.	▪ More inclusive than a first-order Markov model	▪ Not very useful for considering alternative effects of various HR strategies ▪ Requires mathematical sophistication

tives or other employees. Unfortunately, they provide very limited information. As a result, managers in some organizations prefer more detailed *replacement summaries* that more completely describe replacement candidates, including information about their relative ages, educational backgrounds, and experiences.

Succession charts are more detailed and they are not limited to executives like replacement charts. Indeed, succession planning tends to be more long-term in focus and more developmental in thrust (Rothwell, 2000). Chief components of a succession planning program include:

I Candidate data, including performance appraisal information, career interests, and individual biographical information
I Position requirements, including expected organization structure, position descriptions, and career paths between positions, indicating what education and experience are needed to progress from one level to another
I An organized process for reviewing candidate data relative to position requirements over time
I Individual development plans such as training and education plans, developmental assignments, and testing methods
I Succession plans, including candidate summaries, indicating relative strengths/weaknesses for promotion, and position/succession summaries indicating what internal candidates are at what levels of preparedness for higher or alternative positions and how to overcome expected surpluses and shortfalls of supply for various positions (Rothwell, 2000b)

The culmination of a succession program is either a chart or series of succession summaries for most positions in the organization, except, perhaps, those like entry-level positions that are customarily filled through external recruitment. Companies vary in how they handle the succession-planning process.

Skill inventories are more comprehensive than replacement and succession charts. They provide very detailed information about everyone in the organization. Common data elements include employee name, work location, present position title, previous position titles, date of birth, date of hire, educational preparation, training completed, fluency in foreign language, career objectives, medical history, publications, professional licenses, hobbies, salary history, and potentially much more. The challenge is to decide what to include and what to exclude.

Forecasting External Labor Supply

It is much more difficult to forecast the supply of labor available outside than inside the organization. Several reasons account for this. First, no centralized, national projections of labor supplies exist. The U.S. Bureau of Labor Statistics provides some information of this type, though it is often too broad to be useful to individual employers. Second, few firms are large enough to justify the expense of devoting substantial effort to forecasting external supplies available nationally, regionally, and locally from colleges, universities, competitors, and other sources. Third, organizations differ in their unique requirements. It will not be enough to forecast general numbers, such as availability of accounting graduates in the United States. It might be more useful to narrow this forecast by focusing on those graduates possessing *several* characteristics desired by the firm. Of course, cross-matching of characteristics will mean that real supplies available dwindle quickly. There might be many accounting graduates in the United States each year, but there are substantially fewer who (for example) are minorities and who possess specialized experience in one industry. Fourth, and finally, labor availability differs by location. The distribution of the U.S. population is not even. There are, for example, more young workers in western than in northern states.

Very little information exists on how organizations estimate external labor supply. Perhaps few do. Some HR planners have proposed economic models to estimate labor supply. The prototypes of this approach were geared to determining, for purposes of equal employment opportunity, how many people in various sex and race categories could be attracted to employment with one firm. A more sophisticated approach is based on using scenarios of different economic and technological conditions.

There is just no simple way to go about forecasting external labor supply.

Step Seven: Forecasting HR Needs

The final step in HRP forecasting is a relatively simple one, as long as supply and demand are expressed in terms compatible enough to allow for comparison. In other words, if demand focuses on *numbers of people in job categories,* then supply forecasts must be expressed in similar terms.

One way to forecast needs is to graph expected demand and expected internal supply. The gap between them will have to be closed through:

1. *Recruitment and hiring.* This action will be affected by availability of external labor supply.

2. *Training.* This action will involve preparing people in some job categories to move into other categories in which HR demand is expected to increase.

3. *Promotions and transfers.* These actions typically follow training and involve actually moving people from one category to another.

4. *Job redesign.* The organization's allocation of work duties can be changed so as to alter need for more people. Job redesign usually implies enrichment—that is, loading a lower-level job category with responsibilities associated with a higher category. Another possibility is job enlargement, in which more of the same kind of tasks/duties are added to a job.

5. *Turnover reduction.* One way to increase available internal labor supply is to reduce the number of competent, experienced people who leave the organization. This strategy involves examining quality of work life issues such as job satisfaction, and employee intentions about leaving. It can also involve identifying existing or expected problems stemming from organizational policies on compensation/benefits, labor relations, and other issues.

6. *Increased productivity.* One way to change labor demand is to change the ratio between demand and staffing.

Overall, HR forecasting tends to focus more on quantitative than on qualitative issues. It has been the subject of much attention in HR planning literature, but there is still no foolproof method to handle it. The basis of most forecasting methods? Historic and past-oriented relationships between staffing levels and bottom-line measures of outputs and revenues. Even when some attempt is made to incorporate expectations about how the future will differ from the past, HR planners tend to preserve their heavy emphasis on past-oriented information. For this reason, environmental scanning is more valuable than quantitative forecasting for job incumbents, HRP practitioners, and managers in strategic planning for HR.

CHAPTER 8

THE HUMAN RESOURCES PLANNING FORMULATOR

Preceding chapters have treated single steps in the strategic planning for human resources (SPHR) process: work analysis, workforce analysis, HR department auditing, environmental scanning, and forecasting. In each case, the focus was on a single question or series of related questions: What work do people do? What kinds of people do it? What is the status of the human resource (HR) department? What factors and future trends will affect people, positions, and the HR department? How many people will probably be needed in the future? In this chapter, we turn to the process of bringing these questions together to select a single, long-term, and unified HR strategy to govern initiatives of the HR department. This step in SPHR is the responsibility of the HR planning formulator. HRP practitioners, as role incumbents acting in this capacity, direct their attention to this question: *What long-term HR strategy should be chosen?*

What Does the HR Planning Formulator Do?

It is pointless to analyze jobs, job incumbents, the HR department's present strengths and weaknesses, future trends outside and inside the organization that affect these matters, and numbers of people or positions needed if no use will be made of such information.

Few HR planning experts explain how to use this information to achieve a unifying direction for HR initiatives to help a business achieve its strategic goals and objectives. It is absolutely essential that a company take its vague impressions about HR needs and turn them into an action plan that will govern long-term HR initiatives. This neglected, critical phase is commonly called *HR programming*, the process of choosing the programs of the HR or the organization. Few firms make any attempt to choose a deliberate, integrated, and unified long-term HR strategy. The result is that human resources planning (HRP) provides little help in guiding long-term departmental or business decision-making. It is too often a fortunate accident, when it ought to be the result of planning when the right people are in the right places at the right times to support implementation of strategic business plans.

What is needed, then, is a deliberate effort to do these things:

1. Bring together, in one process, what decision-makers know about present and future jobs, people, and HR department practice areas as tools for changing jobs/people.
2. Identify alternative long-term HR grand strategies available.
3. Weigh pros and cons of each possible HR strategy.
4. Select the unified HR strategy most likely to succeed in the long term.

These steps encompass the HR planning formulation process and are the responsibility of the HR planning formulator (see Figure 8-1).

Bringing It Together: Conceptual Models for Strategic Planning for Human Resources

It is quite easy to fall into either one of two traps when you begin to take on the role of planning formulator: (1) You can get lost in the details of short-term personnel decisions about individuals, or (2) you can focus too much on long-term decisions about large numbers of people, strip them of their individual identities, and view them merely as representatives of a job category or department. The first problem is evident when, upon the loss of a key performer at any level,

Figure 8-1: A Simplified Model of the HR Formulation Process

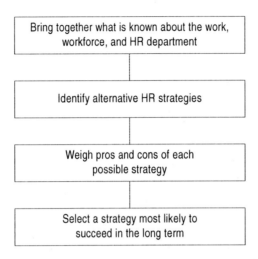

people madly scramble around to find a suitable replacement; the second is evident when people impassively rely on results of HR forecasters for abstract decision-making.

A conceptual model of strategic choice for HR can help avoid these two problems by furnishing a framework for decision-making and problem-solving. It brings together, in one place, what decision-makers know about present and future work, workers, and HR practices. In this respect, it is the first step in the HR planning formulation process.

Four-Factor Condition/Criteria Analysis

In earlier chapters, we provided pieces of this strategic choice model. Recall that analysts of work, workforce, and HR departments tend to compare existing conditions to norms or criteria of ideal conditions. Environmental scanners and forecasters, on the other hand, try to predict likely future conditions and future norms or criteria.

By writing these elements into a single conceptual model, we create a potentially powerful framework for HR strategic choice (Figure 8-2). Indeed, this model is useful for any decision-making situation when the search for a solution is likely to be highly subjective and creative. The reason is that it helps decision-makers think through what is happening now, what they want now, what could happen in the future, and what should happen in the future.

Figure 8-2: Four-Factor Condition/Criteria Analysis: A Model

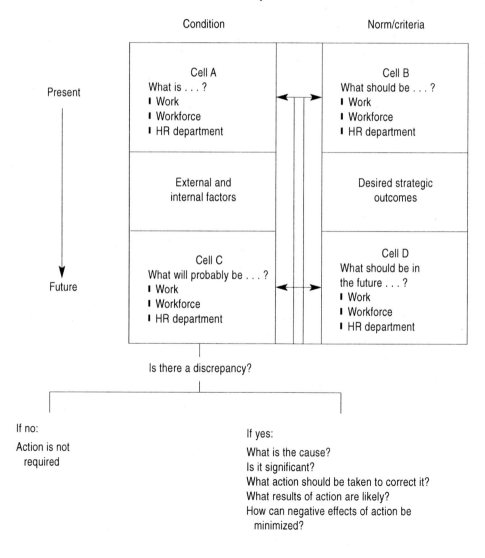

Condition   Norm/criteria

Present

Cell A
What is . . . ?
▪ Work
▪ Workforce
▪ HR department

Cell B
What should be . . . ?
▪ Work
▪ Workforce
▪ HR department

External and
internal factors

Desired strategic
outcomes

Future

Cell C
What will probably be . . . ?
▪ Work
▪ Workforce
▪ HR department

Cell D
What should be in
the future . . . ?
▪ Work
▪ Workforce
▪ HR department

Is there a discrepancy?

If no:
Action is not
    required

If yes:
What is the cause?
Is it significant?
What action should be taken to correct it?
What results of action are likely?
How can negative effects of action be
    minimized?

In this context, *what is* denotes present actual conditions or simple descriptions of them. For example: (1) *work analysis* centers on describing what people are presently doing in their jobs or positions; (2) *workforce analysis* centers on describing the education, experience, and personal characteristics possessed by members of the organization and by job or position incumbents; and (3) an *HR audit* centers on the present status of the HR department and its strengths and weaknesses. Typically, the intent of each investigation is to provide a snapshot of an organization's present jobs, people, and HR department. No value judgments are made about them.

What should be, on the other hand, denotes norms or criteria for judgment. They represent desired present conditions, what managers or other stakeholders want. Recall that job descriptions—products of traditional work analysis—are normative in that they set forth what job incumbents should be doing. The work analysis process itself is descriptive because its aim is to discover what people are doing. Job specifications and person descriptions, products of workforce analysis, are also normative. They list education, experience, skills, and personal characteristics that should be possessed by job incumbents. Criteria or norms used in an HR audit are derived from various sources: practitioners, managers, academic studies, benchmarking efforts, and state-of-the-art practices in the nation, industry, or HR field. They provide the basis for making value judgments by setting forth what is good, desirable, efficient, and otherwise beneficial to the organization and people in it.

What will probably be is a prediction of what the future will be like based on inferences about effects of trends inside and outside the organization on: (1) *jobs, positions, and job families* (What will future work be like if influential trends exert their expected effects?); (2) *people in the organization* (What will future job incumbents be like if influential trends exert their expected effects?); and (3) *the HR department* (What will probably be the status of the department if present trends exert their expected effects?).

The fundamental assumption is that, all other things being equal, internal and external trends will influence jobs, people, and the HR department. The intent is to project the impact of these trends to describe the likely future status of jobs, people, and the HR department if managers take no action to change the future.

What should be in the future is a product of imagination. It represents desired conditions in the future—the effects of strategic business plans on:

■ *Jobs, positions, and job families.* What will future jobs be like if work methods and results are consistent with organizational objectives and strategy?

■ *People in the jobs.* What kind of people should be carrying out work in the future, provided they possess education, experience, skills, and characteristics well matched to organizational strategy and job requirements?

■ *The HR department.* What should be the status of the HR department in the future if its practice areas support organizational strategy and take advantage of opportunities or avert threats posed by conditions in the internal and external environment?

From a vision of future conditions, strategists imagine what people should be doing, what kinds of people should be doing these things, and what HR department efforts need to be made to match people and organizational strategy. The results of this process are set forth in strategic-oriented job descriptions, job specifications, person descriptions, employee appraisals, and long-range planning documents for the HR department and its practice areas.

Strategic choice for HR begins by making comparisons between, for example, *what is* and *what should be.* Used in work analysis, this will reveal any gaps between what people are expected to do and what they actually do. In workforce analysis, the comparison can reveal an existing gap between desired and actual education, experience, or other characteristics. HR department audits can reveal gaps between what the department is presently doing and what it should be doing.

Comparing *what will probably be* and *what should be in the future* is difficult to do. It calls for considerable creativity, and the results will not always be reliable. It can reveal a gap or discrepancy between an *ideal* or *desired* future state that is implicit in strategic business plans and one that is quite probable if no action is taken to make HR changes in anticipation of desired requirements. A comparison between *what is* and *what will probably be* underscores the likely impact of trends and future events on jobs, people, and the HR department. A comparison between what should be *in the present* and what should be *in the future* underscores the difference between present desires of strategists versus their future desires implied in organizational plans. Discrepancies or gaps identified through these comparisons become the basis for assessing how well current long-term HR planning efforts support organizational strategy and determining present strengths/weaknesses and future opportunities/threats pertinent to human resources in the organization.

In this context, a *strength* is a distinctive feature of the organization's HR subsystem that gives it an advantage relative to either its present or expected future competition or its future needs, such as jobs, people, or the entire HR department. A *weakness* is the reverse, a competitive disadvantage or handicap in meeting future needs. An unfavorable or negative discrepancy between *what is* and *what should be* is a weakness; a favorable or positive discrepancy between them is a strength. A *threat* is a potential future negative discrepancy or gap between *what will probably be* and *what should be at that time;* an *opportunity* is a potential future positive discrepancy.

Positive discrepancies do not require corrective action, but strategists are well advised to take advantage of them. They represent *core HR competencies of the organization.* For example, an established training program could become the basis for marketing products to consumers as well as training employees. In the same way, a highly trained and motivated sales staff is a significant strength.

Negative discrepancies call for investigation and corrective action. As Figure 8-2 illustrates, they require HR planners to consider: (1) *cause* (What accounts for the discrepancy?); (2) *significance* (How important is the discrepancy at present? How important is it likely to become in the future?); (3) *action* (What should be done to correct the discrepancy?); (4) *likely results* (What outcomes—both positive and negative—are likely to result from corrective action? How can they be anticipated?); and (5) *minimizing negative results* (How can negative results stemming from corrective action be anticipated and their effects minimized *before* the corrective action is taken?). These steps are used to analyze any negative discrepancy and can be used at any level of the corporation as a whole, a strategic business unit, a function, a division, a work group, or an individual.

HR strategic planning usually focuses on broad and general discrepancies, rather than on individual cases. The basis of strategic choice for SPHR centers on analyzing and comparing cells in the model we have described. (See Activities 8-1, 8-2, and 8-3 at the end of the chapter.) This process helps surface key HR issues worthy of long-term attention.

Other Methods of Analysis

At least three other methods of analysis, in addition to four-factor condition/criteria analysis, can be used as conceptual tools to help develop HR Grand Strategy. These include WOTS-UP analysis, portfolio analysis, and the nine cell planning grid.

WOTS-UP Analysis

Another approach to bringing together what is known about work, workers, and the HR department is closely related to four-factor condition/criteria analysis. It is called WOTS-UP analysis. The first word of this acronym is based on the first letters of four words: *w*eaknesses, *o*pportunities, *t*hreats, and *s*trengths. It has been widely applied to strategic business planning.

WOTS-UP analysis is based on three key assumptions about the nature of effective strategy. The first assumption is that strategy identifies a distinctive competency that the firm is stronger in than most others in the industry. This is sometimes called a *core competency*. When applied to HR, it is called an HR core competency. The second assumption is that effective strategy should locate a niche, a situation for which the firm is well-suited. The third assumption is that effective strategy should match competence and niche. The whole point of WOTS-UP analysis is thus to find the best match that exists between trends and organizational capabilities.

The same approach can be applied to HR planning without substantial difficulty. Indeed, it has wide applicability and can also be used with individuals, work groups, departments, divisions, strategic business units, and an entire corporation. To apply the approach, HRP practitioners—by themselves or in conjunction with others—simply: (1) collect information about the work, workforce, and HR department at present; (2) identify trends that might exert increasing influence over time; (3) assess how those trends should affect the work, workforce, and the HR department; and (4) decide what constitutes present HR strengths/weaknesses and future HR opportunities/threats.

In this context, a threat is a condition in the environment unfavorable to the HR subsystem; an opportunity is a favorable condition; a strength is a unique advantage in the subsystem enjoyed by the firm; and a weakness is a unique disadvantage. To cite some examples, high turnover of key executives is a major *weakness;* high retention of the same group is a *strength;* possible automation can pose a *threat* to employee morale; high entry salaries paid by a firm can be a major *opportunity* for attracting talent.

A major problem in using WOTS-UP analysis is deciding the present position of the HR subsystem. Is the organization's *overall* HR status one of strength or weakness? Does the organization have to overcome major HR problems? By addressing these issues, WOTS-UP analysis helps clarify HR Grand Strategy.

Portfolio Analysis

A *portfolio* is a group of assets. In financial management, it consists of a group of stocks, bonds, and other securities. The basic idea is to spread the risk of investments across assets so that overall risk is reduced. Of course, spreading risk also means evening out any likely return on investments.

The notion of portfolio analysis has already been applied widely to corporate strategic planning. Each autonomous business unit, called a Strategic Business Unit (SBU) in a corporation, is viewed as a single asset. All SBUs, taken together, constitute a portfolio. Long-range planning is carried out from the perspective of financial management.

At least two forms of portfolio analysis exist. The first is called the *product/service life cycle*, the second, the *BCG growth/share matrix*. Though they have fancy names, they are based on simple ideas.

The Product/Service Life Cycle Approach to Portfolio Analysis

The product/service life cycle assumes that demand for a product or service varies by the length of time it has been on the market. There are four life-cycle stages.

1. The first stage is *introduction*. During this phase, the product or service is introduced to the market. The cost of doing business is high because productivity, in part a function of management and employee experience with the product or service, is low.
2. The second stage is *growth*. Demand for the product or service increases, while corresponding costs associated with meeting demand decline. Profits exceed losses.
3. The third stage is *maturity*. Managers and employees are experienced with the product or service. Productivity is at a peak. Profitability is best during this stage.
4. The fourth stage is *decline*. Competitors are attracted by market demand for the product or service. The firm that originally introduced it faces declining revenues as other firms begin meeting market demand with substitute products or services. The sheer number of competitors can drive out those that are least competitive or productive.

The appropriate strategy to select for an organization depends on the stage of the product/service life cycles with which the firm is faced, and the size and market power of the firm relative to its competitors.

The life cycle notion has been variously applied to organizations, training departments, and employees (Odiorne, 1984). For example, Odiorne classifies employees into four groups: (1) new hires who are in the introductory stage; (2) growth employees beyond apprenticeship who have between five and fifteen years of experience; (3) mature employees who have more than fifteen years of experience; and (4) pre-retirees who are in the final years just before retirement. By classifying employees into these groups, strategists can assess relative strengths and weaknesses of the workforce in the corporation, strategic business unit, division, department, or job class. A similar approach can be applied to jobs (Are they new occupations? Declining ones?) and to the HR department (How long have the same services been provided? How satisfied with these services are the stakeholders?).

The BCG Growth/Share Matrix Approach to Portfolio Analysis

The BCG growth/share matrix takes part of its name from the Boston Consulting Group (BCG). Like the product/service life cycle, it can be adapted to classifying human assets. It has been used extensively in strategic business planning and remains a widely used portfolio method.

Each business in a multidivisional corporation is plotted on a matrix (illustrated in Figure 8-3). The larger the circle on the matrix, the greater the revenue generated by the business as a percentage of total corporate earnings. One

Figure 8-3: A BCG Growth/Share Matrix

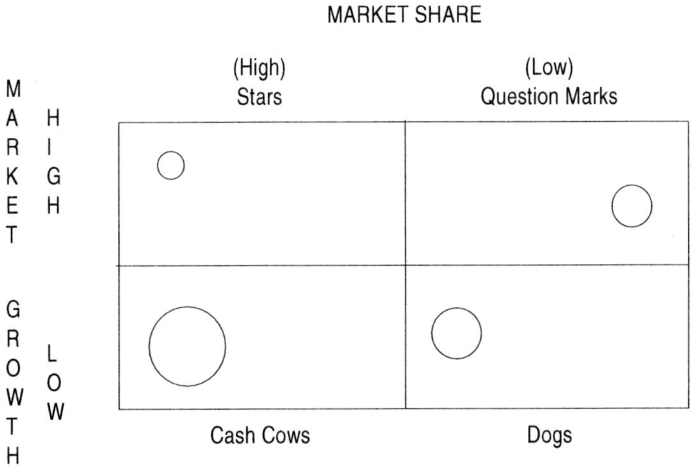

major benefit of this approach is that it allows decision-makers to see, at a glance, the relative quality and importance of each business to the corporation.

Odiorne (1984) suggests using the same basic approach to classify workers and, for that matter, jobs and the HR department. He divides employees into four categories: *workhorses, stars, deadwood,* and *problem employees.* This approach, though with some variations by firm, is widely used in succession planning (Rothwell, 2000b).

The matrix can also be applied to individuals, HR department practice areas, or job categories (Figure 8-4). For example, each HR practice area—recruitment, training, compensation, and employee assistance, for instance—is placed on a matrix relative to such criteria as value to corporate strategic objectives versus value to individuals. Any two factors are selected as criteria, depending on what HR planners or strategists want to examine. Likewise, individuals, job classes, or occupations are evaluated relative to their present or desired importance for organizational strategy, and their likely or desired future importance for strategy.

Figure 8-4: A Performance/Potential Matrix for Classifying Employees

PERFORMANCE

		HIGH	LOW
P O T E N T I A L	**H I G H**	Stars (Corresponds to "Star" companies)	Problem Employees (Corresponds to "Question mark" companies)
	L O W	Workhorses (Corresponds to "Cash Cow" companies)	Dead wood (Corresponds to "Dog" companies)

Nine Cell Planning Grid

General Electric adapted the BCG growth/share matrix for its own uses. This adaptation, used in strategic business planning, is called the *nine cell planning grid* or, more commonly, the *traffic signal grid*.

GE executives plot each of the corporation's businesses on such grid factors as business strengths and industry attractiveness. *Business strengths* consist of favorable market share, profitability, competitive position, technological status, market awareness, and people. *Industry attractiveness factors* consist of business size, market growth, competitors, and external environmental factors. The higher the business strengths and industry attractiveness, the more that expansion or a "green light" is indicated; conversely, the lower the business strengths and industry attractiveness, the more the sale or divestiture ("red light") is indicated. Medium strength and attractiveness factors suggest caution ("yellow light"). The planning grid is sometimes called the traffic signal grid because it helps decision- makers decide whether to stop, go, or use caution in making investment decisions.

The same approach can also be applied to HR strategic planning, albeit with different factors. *Strengths* have to do with the present importance of the job category to achieving corporate strategy, the present skills/unique competence of the workforce, or especially important HR department activities and programs. *External attractiveness* factors have to do with the anticipated future importance of the job category, the likely factors affecting workforce performance in the future, and the future advantages provided by HR practice areas when compared to industry practices. Separate grids are prepared for comparing strengths/external attractiveness of any one job category, segment of the workforce, or HR practice area. Alternatively, one overall grid is prepared for the organization.

Of course, any grid discussed in this section of the chapter is purely a matter of manager judgment, and so is the choice of factors to use for slotting jobs, people, and HR department practice areas on a grid. The purpose of any grid is to aid HR planning formulators and corporate strategists in decision-making.

The Range of HR Grand Strategies

As we explained, the starting point for HR planning formulation is some assessment of what HRP practitioners know about the present and future status of work, workers, and the HR department. Various conceptual models have been discussed that can aid practitioners. The process is highly creative and subjective, especially choices about *how* to examine jobs, people, and HR practice areas, and *what criteria to use* in doing so.

The results of this process are then compared to a topology of possible HR grand strategies so as to yield a range of choices for long-term action. Much like their strategic business planning counterparts, HR grand strategies provide the basis for long-term, strategic actions. HR Grand Strategy establishes the long-term direction of the HR department's practice areas so as to make it supportive of organizational objectives and plans. In this way, activities and outcomes of the HR department are vertically integrated with each other and horizontally integrated with the organization.

There are six major HR grand strategies, each encompassing several specific long-term directions for the HR department and its practice areas. They are:

1. *Growth.* This strategy involves any or all of the following: (1) adding tasks to existing jobs or increasing the number of jobs; (2) increasing education, experience, skill, and other characteristics to the existing workforce, or increasing numbers of "warm bodies"; and/or (3) expanding the range of programs and services offered by the HR department or numbers of people served by those programs/services.

2. *Retrenchment.* This strategy involves any or all of the following: (1) subtracting tasks from existing jobs, or subtracting—through layoffs, firings, transfers, attrition, and other means—the number of positions in the organization; (2) decreasing experience, skill, and other characteristics deemed necessary for satisfactory performance, or decreasing the number of people; and/or (3) decreasing the range

of programs/services offered by the HR department, or decreasing the number of people served by those programs.

3. *Diversification.* This strategy involves any or all of the following: (1) adding utterly new tasks to jobs or new job categories/duties to the organization; (2) adding people to the workforce possessing experience, skill, education, and other requirements that differ from traditional requirements; and/or (3) changing programs of the HR department and/or the groups it serves.

4. *Integration.* This strategy involves any or all of the following: (1) adding tasks to jobs, or new job categories to those otherwise found in the organization, that are deliberately related to activities of suppliers, competitors, or distributors; (2) deliberately adding people from suppliers, competitors, or distributors to the organization's workforce; and/or (3) establishing, through HR department activities, much closer ties to HR suppliers, competitors, or distributors. HR suppliers include colleges or industry-specific employment agencies; HR competitors can pool training and education; and HR distributors include firms historically receiving terminating staff members.

5. *Turnabout.* This strategy involves retrenchment followed by another strategy.

6. *Combination.* This strategy involves the simultaneous pursuit of two or more HR grand strategies in different parts of the organization at the same time.

These strategy options are summarized in Figure 8-5.

Any strategy can be chosen under any environmental condition. But some conditions warrant particular strategies more than others. For example, growth is appropriate when the external environment is generally favorable; diversification, when conditions favor a venture into a new business or new products/services more than expanding the size of the present business or adding new products or services; integration, when increasingly critical resources call for establishing special ties with suppliers, competitors, or distributors; turnabout, when a failing strategy must be reversed; and combination, when conditions warrant one strategy in one segment of the organization or one job class while a different strategy is applied in another segment or other job class.

Figure 8-5: A Summary of HR Grand Strategies

Strategy	Work	Workforce	HR Department
Growth	I Add tasks to existing jobs I Add jobs	I Add requirements or skills I Add "warm bodies"	I Expand range of programs/services offered I Expand number of people served
Retrenchment	I Subtract tasks from existing jobs I Subtract jobs or positions	I Decrease requirements for workers I Subtract "warm bodies"	I Decrease range of programs/services offered I Decrease number of people served
Diversification	I Add utterly new tasks to jobs I Add new job categories/duties	I Add utterly new types of people to carry out the work	I Change kinds of programs/services offered I Change groups served by programs/services
Integration	I Add new tasks to jobs that are explicitly related to supplier, competitor, or distributor activities I Add new job categories related to work of suppliers, distributors, or competitors	I Deliberately add people who have worked for suppliers, distributors, or competitors	I Establish, through HR department programs, much closer ties with HR suppliers, competitors, or distributors
Turnabout	I Use retrenchment strategy (above), followed by any other strategy	I Use retrenchment strategy (above), followed by any other strategy	I Use retrenchment strategy (above), followed by any other strategy
Combination	I Use two or more strategies in different parts of the organization at the same time	I Use two or more strategies in different parts of the organization at the same time	I Use two or more strategies in different parts of the organization at the same time

Weighing Strategic Alternatives

Which one of the six HR grand strategies is likely to result in desired outcomes over the long term? This question is addressed in the third step of HR planning formulation. Strategists and HRP practitioners compare each possible HR Grand Strategy to what they know about the status of the HR subsystem in the organization (Figure 8-5). Practitioners can then assess likely outcomes from each strategy and can weigh their respective advantages and disadvantages.

As logical as this sounds, strategists and HR planners rarely weigh alternatives. Why? There are several reasons. First, *changes in human resources are handled incrementally*. Each promotion, termination, and transfer is looked at as if only one person is affected. In reality, each individual change has long-term implications for the entire organization. This is particularly true at higher levels because of the importance of leadership in formulating and implementing strategic business plans. Second, *more than just a few managers are involved*. HR activities affect every part of the organization every day. It is hard to stand back and examine the "big picture," the pattern of tasks and jobs, people, and HR department practice areas. Third, *managers and HR planners lack means by which to assess alternative HR grand strategies*. Fourth, *some have never even considered the idea that the organization needs an HR Grand Strategy*. While these reasons might explain why no effort is usually made to think out alternative strategies for HRP in long-range terms, they are not adequate excuses for avoiding the process. Indeed, it is the responsibility of HR planners, if no one else, to accept a leadership role in establishing an integrated HR Grand Strategy (Rothwell, Prescott, and Taylor, 1998).

A simple process should suffice. HR planners and strategists need only: (1) list various HR Grand Strategy options, (2) predict their likely consequences over a given time horizon on positive and negative HR discrepancies or organizational strategy, and (3) rate each option according to its relative advantages and disadvantages.

Listing strategic options, the first step, is simple enough. HR planners should generate a list of what long-term HR grand strategies are possible. We have already summarized alternatives in Figure 8-4. However, more specific alternatives by job or employee category are possible in one organization.

Predicting consequences, the second step, is far more challenging. For each negative discrepancy identified in formulation, planners need to first assess how each potential HR Grand Strategy will help rectify the problem over time. If another conceptual model is used, such as portfolio analysis, then planners will need to consider how the proposed strategy will influence the future status of jobs, people, and the HR department.

Rating each option, the third step, is highly subjective. Planners simply weigh advantages and disadvantages of each possible HR Grand Strategy over time. In short, they must ask such questions as: How well will each one probably work out in terms of supporting strategic business plans? Improving morale? Contributing to achieving individual career goals and plans?

Approaches to Generating Alternatives

The same approaches useful in environmental scanning and HR forecasting can be adapted to generate a range of HR grand strategies. For instance:

1. *The Delphi technique.* Without meeting, strategists are surveyed about HR strategy preferences, likely outcomes, and desired outcomes.

2. *The nominal group technique.* In a meeting or other small group format, strategists generate their individual HR strategy preferences; discuss their assumptions about jobs, people, and the HR department; generate individual predictions about positive and negative consequences or advantages and disadvantages of HR grand strategies; discuss their assumptions about the predictions; and vote on an HR Grand Strategy and thereby reach consensus on action.

3. *Cross-impact analysis.* Using results generated by the Delphi or the nominal group technique, strategists estimate the probability of var-

ious consequences—such as increased turnover, for example—growing out of an HR Grand Strategy, assess interrelationships between consequences—that is, the chances that one action will create numerous reactions in the HR subsystem—and compile results.

4. *Scenario analysis.* Strategists are furnished with a narrative description of the organization as it exists at a future time. They are then asked for opinions about the likelihood that the future will come to pass; what kinds of jobs, people, and HR department practice area initiatives will be needed; and what HR Grand Strategy is likely to be most instrumental in creating the desired future.

5. *Questionnaires or interviews.* Strategists are asked about their HRP strategy preferences, likely outcomes, and relative value of each strategic alternative. A management committee then receives the results, and a strategy is chosen.

Each method has distinct advantages and disadvantages. In most cases, a combination of two or more is likely to produce more accurate predictions and lead to a better decision. The process of generating and evaluating alternatives is itself important, because the greater the strategists' involvement in decision-making, the greater the likelihood that they will be committed to the choice ultimately selected.

Who to Involve in the HR Planning Formulation Process

The people you include in the effort to establish and monitor an HR Grand Strategy depends, to a considerable extent, on the culture of the organization. In authoritarian or human relations cultures, it is perhaps best left to the senior HR executive, who will be held responsible for it in any case by the CEO and board of directors. In consultative and participative cultures, the senior personnel executive serves more as facilitator and coordinator than arbiter of strategy. For this reason, each major decision-maker inside and outside the HR department has a say in choice of HR Grand Strategy.

Timing of HR Planning Formulation

It is appropriate to consider or reconsider HR strategy when: (1) there is a change in the organization's Grand Strategy; (2) there is a major change in external environmental trends of internal organizational conditions, or in the field of HR management; or (3) there is a major change in the leadership, structure, or policies of the organization or the HR department itself. Each change can influence the purpose of the department and objectives that should guide strategy. All else being equal, departmental strategy should also be reviewed at least annually to chart progress.

The Relationship of HR Grand Strategy and Organizational Strategy

A natural question that arises at this point is this: Does HR Grand Strategy have to be the *same* as corporate or business strategy? On a theoretical level, the answer is *no*. The only requirement is that HR strategy should *support* that of the organization. However, any HR strategy can theoretically support any organizational strategy. Practically speaking, however, HRP practitioners often gear their efforts to reflect what the organization is doing. For instance, they will help cut or layoff staff during organizational retrenchment, or recruit new employees during organizational growth.

The real question to ask is this: What *is* the purpose of the HR department in HR Grand Strategy and/or in corporate strategy? When this question has been answered, it is much easier to see interrelationships between HR and organizational strategy. Figure 8-6 summarizes possible relationships between HR and organizational grand strategies.

Factors Complicating the Choice of an HR Grand Strategy

Decision-makers in recent years have become much more creative in their thinking about how to organize work. That has prompted some observers of the

Figure 8-6: The Relationship between Corporate Strategy and the Human Resource Grand Strategy

Human Resource Grand Strategies

Corporate Strategy	Growth	Retrenchment	Diversification	Integration	Turnabout	Combination
Growth	As the organization grows, ■ Tasks are added to existing jobs ■ New jobs are added ■ New requirements are established ■ More people are hired ■ HR department expands its services	As the organization grows, ■ Tasks are subtracted from existing jobs ■ Jobs are eliminated ■ Old requirements are subtracted ■ People are eliminated ■ HR department cuts back	As the organization grows, ■ Utterly new tasks are added ■ Utterly new jobs are added ■ Utterly new people are added ■ HR department changes what it does	As the organization grows, ■ Tasks, jobs, people, and HR department initiatives are explicitly tied to suppliers or distributors or competitors	As the organization grows, ■ HR retrenchment is followed by growth in a new way	As the organization grows, ■ The HR Grand Strategy is a combination one used in two or more different parts of the organization at the same time
Retrenchment	As the organization cuts back, ■ Tasks are added to existing jobs ■ New jobs are added ■ New requirements are established ■ More people are hired ■ HR department expands services	As the organization cuts back, ■ Tasks are subtracted from existing jobs ■ Jobs are eliminated ■ Old requirements are subtracted ■ People are eliminated ■ HR department cuts back	As the organization cuts back, ■ Utterly new tasks are added ■ Utterly new jobs are added ■ Utterly new people are added ■ HR department changes what it does	As the organization cuts back, ■ Tasks, jobs, people, and HR department initiatives are explicitly tied to suppliers or distributors or competitors	As the organization cuts back, ■ HR retrenchment is followed by growth in a new way	As the organization cuts back, ■ The HR Grand Strategy is a combination one used in two or more different parts of the organization at the same time

Figure 8-6: (continued)

Human Resource Grand Strategies

Corporate Strategy	Growth	Retrenchment	Diversification	Integration	Turnabout	Combination
Diversification	As the organization expands in new areas, ■ Tasks are added to existing jobs ■ New jobs are added ■ New requirements are established ■ More people are hired ■ HR department expands services	As the organization expands in new areas, ■ Tasks are subtracted from existing jobs ■ Jobs are eliminated ■ Old requirements are subtracted ■ People are eliminated ■ HR department cuts back	As the organization expands in new areas, ■ Utterly new tasks are added ■ Utterly new jobs are added ■ Utterly new people are added ■ HR department changes what it does	As the organization expands in new areas, ■ Tasks, jobs, people, and HR department initiatives are explicitly tied to suppliers or distributors or competitors	As the organization expands in new areas, ■ HR retrenchment is followed by growth in a new way	As the organization expands in new areas, ■ The HR Grand Strategy is a combination one used in two or more different parts of the organization at the same time
Integration	As the organization establishes closer ties with suppliers and distributors, ■ Tasks are added to existing jobs ■ New jobs are added ■ New requirements are established ■ More people are hired ■ HR department expands services	As the organization establishes closer ties with suppliers and distributors, ■ Tasks are subtracted from existing jobs ■ Jobs are eliminated ■ Old requirements are subtracted ■ People are eliminated ■ HR department cuts back	As the organization establishes closer ties with suppliers and distributors, ■ Utterly new tasks are added ■ Utterly new jobs are added ■ Utterly new people are added ■ HR department changes what it does	As the organization establishes closer ties with suppliers and distributors, ■ Tasks, jobs, people, and HR department initiatives are explicitly tied to suppliers or distributors or competitors	As the organization establishes closer ties with suppliers and distributors, ■ HR retrenchment is followed by growth in a new way	As the organization establishes closer ties with suppliers and distributors, ■ The HR grand strategy is a combination one used in two or more different parts of the organization at the same time

Figure 8-6: *(continued)*

Human Resource Grand Strategies

Corporate Strategy	Growth	Retrenchment	Diversification	Integration	Turnabout	Combination
Turnabout	Because a failing business is retrenched and grows in new ways, ■ Tasks are added to existing jobs ■ New jobs are added ■ New requirements are established ■ More people are hired ■ HR department expands services	Because a failing business is retrenched and grows in new ways, ■ Tasks are subtracted from existing jobs ■ Jobs are eliminated ■ Old requirements are subtracted ■ People are eliminated ■ HR department cuts back	Because a failing business is retrenched and grows in new ways, ■ Utterly new tasks are added ■ Utterly new jobs are added ■ Utterly new people are added ■ HR department changes what it does	Because a failing business is retrenched and grows in new ways, ■ Tasks, jobs, people, and HR department initiatives are explicitly tied to suppliers or distributors or competitors	Because a failing business is retrenched and grows in new ways, ■ HR retrenchment is followed by growth in a new way	Because a failing business is retrenched and grows in new ways, ■ The HR grand strategy is a combination one used in two or more different parts of the organization at the same time
Combination	Because different parts of the business pursue different strategies, ■ Tasks are added to existing jobs ■ New jobs are added ■ New requirements are established ■ More people are hired ■ HR department expands services	Because different parts of the business pursue different strategies, ■ Tasks are subtracted from existing jobs ■ Jobs are eliminated ■ Old requirements are subtracted ■ People are eliminated ■ HR department cuts back	Because different parts of the business pursue different strategies, ■ Utterly new tasks are added ■ Utterly new jobs are added ■ Utterly new people are added ■ HR department changes what it does	Because different parts of the business pursue different strategies, ■ Tasks, jobs, people, and HR department initiatives are explicitly tied to suppliers or distributors or competitors	Because different parts of the business pursue different strategies, ■ HR retrenchment is followed by growth in a new way	Because different parts of the business pursue different strategies, ■ The HR grand strategy is a combination one used in two or more different parts of the organization at the same time

contemporary business scene to bewail the death of the "job." While work never goes away, there are many ways that it can be accomplished. Gone are the days when changes in organizational strategy immediately translated into large-scale growth in so-called "permanent" positions or even widespread job cutbacks such as downsizing. Today's decision-makers think in broader terms than that, and HR planners need to take these issues into account.

There are, in short, many ways to answer this one simple question: How will the work be done? Answers are elusive. Rarely are they "all or nothing" propositions. Therefore, a key issue to consider in HR planning and in selecting HR Grand Stategy is how many and what types of workers will be affected by the various options for achieving work results, and in what locations.

Consider how much the organization will need to rely on:

I   Recruiting full-time workers from outside
I   Transferring full-time workers from inside
I   Using job-posting inside
I   Outsourcing all of the work
I   Outsourcing part of the work
I   Recruiting "permanent" part-time workers from outside
I   Recruiting workers on a flextime or "flex-place" arrangement
I   Using consultants
I   Using temporary and contingent workers on a daily basis
I   Using temps and contingent workers on a seasonal or work-cycle basis
I   Ceasing the work altogether
I   Reengineering the way the work process is accomplished and, in so doing, changing the type of staff and numbers of people needed.
I   Shifting some duties from one worker to another
I   Shifting some duties from one work unit or department to another
I   "Decruiting" workers (layoffs, early retirements, employee buyouts)
I   Shifting to virtual work, using telecommuters domestically or internationally

Of course, these and other strategies can be used throughout the organization or in only parts of the organization. As a consequence, the choice of HR Grand Stategy is complicated by a large number of alternatives by which to achieve the same results.

Selecting an HR Grand Strategy

The final step in HR planning formulation is selection of *one* HR Grand Strategy to guide the organization's efforts generally, and those of the HR department and its practice areas specifically. Strategic choice is quintessentially a creative decision-making process. It is affected by many factors. To enumerate a few:

1. *Acceptance by major stakeholders inside and outside the organization.*
   Will the HR strategy be acceptable to relevant groups outside the organization, to top managers, to middle managers, to first-line supervisors, to employees, to others? How well is it likely to be accepted by each group?
2. *Consistency with the strategic business plan.*
   Will the HR Grand Strategy be harmonious with organizational strategy? How much so? To what extent, if at all, are conflicting priorities likely to be evident?
3. *Value in taking advantage of positive discrepancies uncovered through four-factor condition/criteria analysis while correcting negative discrepancies.*
   Will the HR Grand Strategy build on organizational HR strengths? Will it help rectify weaknesses?
4. *Accuracy of assessment.*
   Is the HR strategy based on reasonably reliable assessments of current conditions? How reliable are those assessments?

5. *Appropriateness of comparisons.*

    Is the HR strategy based on accurate and appropriate norms for future conditions? These are often hard to estimate.

6. *Reasonableness.*

    Given prior HR strategy, to what extent is the contemplated one reasonable and realistic?

7. *Consistency with culture.*

    How much will the proposed HR strategy be consistent with prevailing beliefs, norms, and attitudes that govern behavior in the organization?

8. *Orientation to root causes of negative discrepancies and significant matters.*

    Will the proposed strategy help correct significant negative discrepancies? How much so?

By considering these questions in a structured way, HR planning formulators and organizational strategists can narrow down the range of choices and select one that they feel will take advantage of the present strengths and potential opportunities of the HR subsystem and avert present weaknesses in, and potential future threats to, the HR subsystem.

Activity 8-1: Worksheet for Summarizing, Using Four-Factor Condition/
Criteria Analysis

Directions: Use the worksheet below to summarize facts in and predictions about the organization's human resources. Begin with cell A. Describe the present status of a major job category, the people in it, and how the HR department is meeting their needs. Then complete cell B and the remainder of the worksheet. Use more paper if necessary.

CONDITION	NORM/CRITERIA

Cell A

What Is . . . ?

- Work
  _____
  _____

- Workforce
  _____
  _____
  _____

- HR Department
  _____
  _____
  _____

Cell B

What should be . . . ?

- Work
  _____
  _____

- Workforce
  _____
  _____
  _____

- HR Department
  _____
  _____
  _____

What major trends will affect work, workforce, and HR department? How will the effects be noticeable?

_____
_____
_____
_____
_____
_____
_____
_____

What is the organization's Strategic Plan?

_____
_____
_____
_____
_____
_____
_____
_____

PRESENT

Activity 8-1: *(continued)*

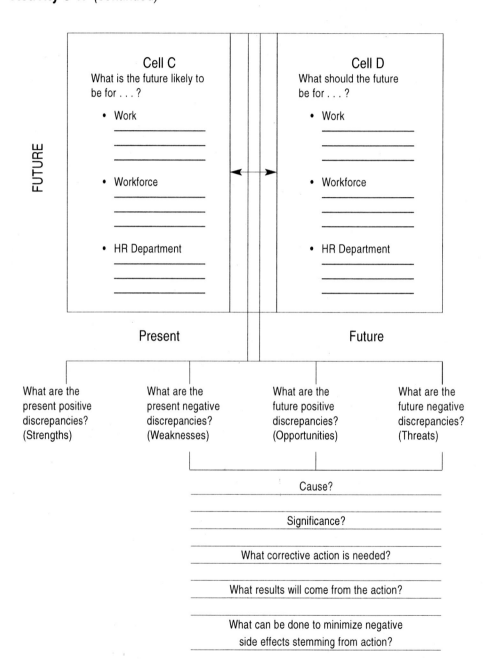

Activity 8-2: Worksheet for Four-Factor Condition/Criteria Analysis

Directions: This worksheet is similar to the worksheet shown in Activity 8-3. Briefly summarize an answer to each question and issue below.

Question	Issue		
	Status of job/work	*Status of workforce*	*Status of HR department*
What is?			
What should be?			
What will probably be in the future?			
What should be in the future?			
What should be the likely results of trends in internal/ external environment?			
What does "Organizational Strategy" imply?			

Discrepancies	*Cause(s)*	*Significance*	*Action*	*Results*	*Action to minimize negative results*
Negative-Present (Weaknesses)					
Negative-Future (Threats)					
	How can the strength/opportunity be taken advantage of?				
Positive-Present (Strengths)					
Positive-Future (Opportunities)					

Activity 8-3: A Worksheet Based on WOTS-UP Analysis

Directions: Use this worksheet to organize your thinking. Identify major HR strengths and weaknesses. Then identify major HR opportunities and threats. Summarize them below in abbreviated form and then distribute this sheet to other managers for comment.

What are our major HR strengths? List them.	What are our major HR weaknesses? List them.
What are our major HR opportunities? List them.	What are our major HR threats? List them.

Activity 8-4: A Worksheet for Classifying Jobs, People, and the HR Department

Directions: Use this worksheet to organize your thinking. Look at the chart below and then answer the questions. Use different colors for plotting jobs and people on the chart. Then connect the dots representing jobs and those representing people.

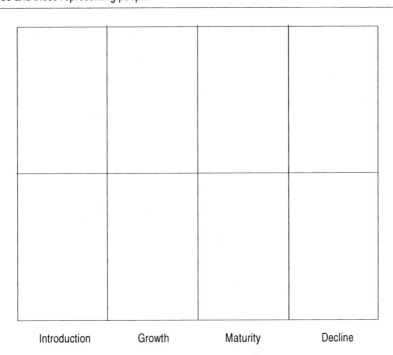

| Introduction | Growth | Maturity | Decline |

What jobs in the organization are in what stages? (Plot them on the chart.)

How many people in the organization are in what stages? (Plot them on the chart.)

What is the current stage of the HR department? (Plot it with a large red X on the chart.)

Adapted from Odiorne (1984, p. 61).

Activity 8-5: A Worksheet for Considering an HR Grand Strategy

Directions: Use this sheet to help you assess which strategy best meets the needs of your organization. Use a single sheet of paper for each strategy or substrategy, if you wish. Consider (1) How the strategy will work (describe it) and (2) What its relative advantages and disadvantages are (list them). Then (3) rate the strategy. Use the following scale: 1 = very disadvantageous, 2 = disadvantageous, 3 = neither advantageous nor disadvantageous; 4 = advantageous; and 5 = very advantageous. Summarize your results on this worksheet.

Strategy	Substrategy	How will the strategy work?	What will be the . . . ? Advantages	Disadvantages	Rate the Strategy Very Advantageous 5	4	3	Disadvantageous 2	Very Disadvantageous 1
Growth	A. Add task to jobs or add new jobs				5	4	3	2	1
	B. Add requirements/skills or new people				5	4	3	2	1
	C. Expand range of programs, services, or people served				5	4	3	2	1
Retrenchment	A. Subtract tasks from jobs or subtract jobs				5	4	3	2	1
	B. Subtract requirements or number of people				5	4	3	2	1
	C. Decrease range of programs/services or people served				5	4	3	2	1
Diversification	A. Add utterly new tasks to jobs or new job categories				5	4	3	2	1
	B. Add utterly new types of people to carry out work				5	4	3	2	1
	C. Change kinds of programs/services or people served by the HR department				5	4	3	2	1

Activity 8-5: *(continued)*

Strategy	Substrategy	How will the strategy work?	What will be the . . . ? Advantages	What will be the . . . ? Disadvantages	Rate the Strategy Very Advantageous 5	4	3	2	Very Disadvantageous 1
Integration	A. Add new tasks to jobs that are linked to suppliers, distributors, or competitors				5	4	3	2	1
	B. Add people who have worked for suppliers, distributors, or competitors				5	4	3	2	1
	C. Establish closer ties with HR suppliers, distributors, or competitors through HR department activities				5	4	3	2	1
Turnabout	A.1 Retrench the work				5	4	3	2	1
	A.2 Grow in a new way				5	4	3	2	1
	B.1 Retrench the workforce				5	4	3	2	1
	B.2 Grow in a new way				5	4	3	2	1
	C.1 Retrench the HR department				5	4	3	2	1
	C.2 Grow in a new way				5	4	3	2	1
Combination	Use two or more strategies in different parts of the organization at the same time; describe.				5	4	3	2	1

Activity 8-6: A Worksheet for Evaluating an HR Grand Strategy

Directions: Use this sheet to help you assess how well a proposed HR grand strategy is likely to work out. For each item listed in the left column, circle a corresponding number in the middle column using the following scale: 1 = very little, 2 = little; 3 = somewhat; 4 = much; 5 = very much.

To what extent is proposed HR grand strategy:	Very Little 1	2	3	4	Very Much 5	Remarks
1. Likely to be accepted by major						
a. Top management strategists	1	2	3	4	5	
b. Middle managers	1	2	3	4	5	
c. First-line supervisors	1	2	3	4	5	
d. Employees	1	2	3	4	5	
e. Others (organized labor, shareholders, consumers)						
Specify: _____	1	2	3	4	5	
_____	1	2	3	4	5	
2. Harmonious with organizational strategy	1	2	3	4	5	
3. Likely to help						
a. Take advantage of positive discrepancies (strengths/opportunities)	1	2	3	4	5	
b. Correct negative discrepancies (weaknesses/threats)	1	2	3	4	5	
4. Based on						
a. Accurate assessments of current conditions	1	2	3	4	5	
b. Appropriate criteria of present conditions	1	2	3	4	5	
c. Reasonable expectations about the future	1	2	3	4	5	
d. Reasonable inferences about criteria, considering organizational strategy	1	2	3	4	5	
5. Consistent with the culture of the organization	1	2	3	4	5	
6. Likely to help correct the cause(s) of negative discrepancies	1	2	3	4	5	
7. Geared to significant discrepancies	1	2	3	4	5	
8. Capable of being translated into action plans, such as						
a. Substrategies appropriate for program practice areas of HR	1	2	3	4	5	
b. Information that will help decision-makers in making and implementing strategic choices	1	2	3	4	5	

Activity 8-6: *(continued)*

To what extent is the proposed HR grand strategy:	Degree — Very Little 1	2	3	4	Very Much 5	Remarks
9. Likely to produce any major undesirable side effects						
a. In the short term	1	2	3	4	5	
b. In the long term	1	2	3	4	5	
10. Able to be modified so as to minimize the effects of undesirable consequences	1	2	3	4	5	
11. Realistic in terms of						
a. Money needed to implement it	1	2	3	4	5	
b. Staff needed to implement it	1	2	3	4	5	
c. Time needed	1	2	3	4	5	
12. Likely to be accepted by HRP practitioners	1	2	3	4	5	
13. Consistent with the skills/experience of HRP practitioners	1	2	3	4	5	
14. Consistent with other issues unique to the organization (list them):						
_____	1	2	3	4	5	
_____	1	2	3	4	5	
_____	1	2	3	4	5	
_____	1	2	3	4	5	
_____	1	2	3	4	5	
_____	1	2	3	4	5	
_____	1	2	3	4	5	

Activity 8-7: Case Study

Directions: Read through the case that follows, and then answer the questions at the end. (This case is entirely fictitious.)

The ABCD Company designs, manufactures, and markets video display terminals (VDTs) that are widely used in personal computers. The firm is 10 years old and has grown in that time from 5 people to 220.

Environmental trends in this industry suggest that for the next two to three years, there will not be significant growth in sales. The fastest growing segment of the industry has to do with teaching people how to operate their home computers.

The top executives of ABCD have decided to diversify into the field of training. To this end, they have purchased a chain of local stores that offer classroom-based group training on home computers.

The HR department of ABCD has coordinated what has been, until now, a growth strategy in human resources for the firm. Over the last two years, the major concern has simply been on recruiting talented individuals for the VDT business.

The president of ABCD will soon announce the purchase of LEARN-STORES, the name of the firm that was acquired. LEARN-STORES presently employs 60 instructors at the company's seven stores in the greater Chicago area. ABCD plans to sell shares to finance a nationwide expansion.

Questions

1. Based on the limited information provided in this case, explain why a reassessment of HR Grand Strategy should be carried out.

2. Given the business of LEARN-STORES, what human resource issues might be crucial to it but not so important to the ABCD Company? What impact could such differences have in the choice of an appropriate HR Grand Strategy? Why?

Activity 8-8: Case Study

Directions: Read through the case that follows, and then answer the questions at the end. (This case is entirely fictitious.)

The Michiana State University is a relatively small, liberal arts school supported by state funding. Approximately 6,000 students attend the school. It employs 75 full-time and 10 part-time professors of different ranks as well as a total of 60 custodians, cafeteria workers, and other civil servants.

The school is in the center of one of the fastest growing population centers in Michigan. For this reason, the school's strategic plan calls for growth over the next five years. The university is expected to expand to the point that 12,000 students will be served at the end of that five-year period. A majority of new students—about 4,000—are expected to enroll in business courses. The remaining 2,000 will enroll in all other disciplines. At present, 12 full-time and 6 part-time business professors serve 4,000 students. These professors teach full time (three classes/semester) and have no additional time at present to handle more students.

Questions
1. Divide the number of business students presently enrolled by the number of professors (*4,000* students-to-faculty ratio). Now divide the remaining students enrolled in the university by the number of professors available to serve them (students-to-faculty ratio). Discuss the implications of this difference in ratio on faculty members in the business program.
2. What criteria should be used for the *ideal* students-to-faculty ratio? Should it be the one in the business program, the one in the remainder of the university, or some other?
3. What is the discrepancy between the ratio of *what is* and the ratio of *what should be* regarding business students to faculty? Is it positive or negative? If negative,
    a. What is the cause? (How can you determine the cause?)
    b. What is the significance of the discrepancy?
    c. What action do you think should be taken? Why?
    d. What will be the likely results of the action? Are any side effects likely to be negative?
    e. How can negative side effects be anticipated?

CHAPTER 9

THE HUMAN RESOURCES INTEGRATOR

In Chapter 8, we described a variety of available HR grand strategies and how to go about assessing and selecting a Grand Strategy that will produce desirable long-term outcomes. We call this process *human resources planning (HRP)* formulation. However, once a human resources (HR) Grand Strategy is chosen, HRP practitioners have to consider how to translate the strategy into action. This step is called HR integration. It involves implementing an HR Grand Strategy, a responsibility that is associated with the role of HR integrator.

What Does the HR Integrator Do?

The HR integrator engineers change, bringing into reality what is only envisioned in an HR Grand Strategy. The importance of this role cannot be overstressed. Identifying what to do is important, but implementing change takes longer and requires constant monitoring. The integrator has to make some adjustments to the HR department and its practice areas so that they conform to HR Grand Strategy and serve as tools for changing people and jobs over time. You want the right people to be available at the right places and the right times to support strategic business plans.

How can you make that happen? To help implement HR Grand Strategy, the integrator: (1) develops long-term, intermediate-term, and short-term objectives for HR in the organization; (2) provides leadership not only to the HR department but to HR efforts of the entire organization; (3) makes sure that organizational rewards and controls are consistent with the Grand Strategy; (4) devises HR policies consistent with the HR Grand Strategy, coordinating practice areas within the HR department so that they contribute to achievement of the HR Grand Strategy; and (5) matches HR department structure to strategy and strategy to structure. These steps constitute a simplified model of the strategic planning for human resources (SPHR) integration process. This model is illustrated in Figure 9-1.

Figure 9-1: A Simplified Model of the HR Integration Process

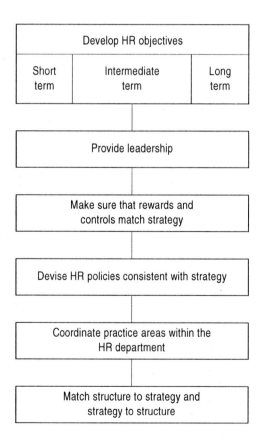

The integrator has many of the same interests and concerns as those carrying out other HR planning roles. *Developing objectives* is one of those shared concerns. The integrator is interested in this issue from the perspective of objectives used to foster coordination across practice areas over time. *Dealing with controls* is a concern shared by the integrator, the HR planning manager, and the evaluator. The integrator is interested in setting up controls to ensure coordination of effort during implementation. *Creating HR department structure* is a concern shared by the integrator and the HR planning manager. The integrator is interested in examining allocation of duties within the department prior to implementation of HR Grand Strategy. The manager is interested in structure as a device for helping to administer operational activities.

Many planning roles will overlap from time to time because the concerns are felt by several key individuals.

Developing HR Objectives

Objectives are relatively specific, concrete, and measurable indicators of overall corporate performance. They are tools for helping to clarify what to do and when to do it. Objectives guide implementation of HR Grand Strategy, and like different levels of planning (to which they correspond), they vary according to how much time they involve, what they focus on, how specific they are, and what they measure.

Strategic HR objectives are comprehensive in scope, they focus on what should be in the long-term future, they are stated in broad terms, and they are measurable by such indicators as value added and turnover averted. *Coordinative* HR objectives, narrower in scope, focus on what should be in the intermediate-term future. They are stated in terms related to HR practice areas and are measurable by dollars saved, changes in levels of productivity, and cost/benefit ratios. *Operational* HR objectives are narrowest in scope, focus on what should be at present, are stated in very specific terms, and are measurable in absolute terms (such as "a 15 percent reduction in turnover in one year").

Each type of objective corresponds to a level of planning; each level of planning preoccupies some managers more than others. Generally, strategic planning for HR is the chief concern of top-level managers, the highest ranking HR executive, and supervisors of special HR planning units. Coordinative planning for HR, on the other hand, is the concern of middle-level managers, the highest-ranking HR officials in such practice areas as training or compensation, and supervisors of special HR planning units. Operational planning for HR is the concern of lower-level managers, first-line supervisors, professionals in the HR department, and supervisors of special HR planning units. Each level of planning—and each corresponding type of objective—overlaps with others. Hence, there is an element of the comprehensive strategic plan for HR in *every* decision made, even those made daily by the lowest-level employees in the HR department.

Figure 9-2 illustrates levels of planning and their corresponding objectives.

Figure 9-2: Objectives and Levels of HR Planning

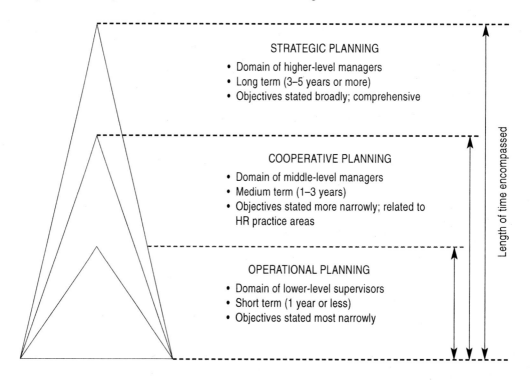

STRATEGIC PLANNING
- Domain of higher-level managers
- Long term (3–5 years or more)
- Objectives stated broadly; comprehensive

COOPERATIVE PLANNING
- Domain of middle-level managers
- Medium term (1–3 years)
- Objectives stated more narrowly; related to HR practice areas

OPERATIONAL PLANNING
- Domain of lower-level supervisors
- Short term (1 year or less)
- Objectives stated most narrowly

Length of time encompassed

In preparing HR objectives, a few guidelines might be helpful:

1. HRP practitioners—and HR planners in particular—should take initiative in helping establish objectives.
2. Strategic objectives should be identified first; coordinative objectives, second; and operational objectives, third. The process is top-down so that daily decisions are made within the framework of long-term initiatives.
3. Each objective should identify *what* should be accomplished; *when* it should be accomplished; how achievement is to be measured; and *who* is responsible for *what, when,* and *how.*
4. The way that objectives are prepared is perhaps as important as results. Consider: Is the process of objective setting likely to build commitment and consensus? Is some kind of follow up or HR control system in place to compare annual results to objectives? Will the process result in setting priorities among competing interests and produce benchmarks, standards, or indicators that are agreeable to most people or managers in the organization?

The whole negotiating process for HR objectives builds commitment to a coherent long-term plan across the organization. It also helps clarify, in concrete terms, who does what by when, so as to translate broad HR Grand Strategy into specific action. The process communicates to people at all levels precisely what the organization is trying to do and what its people needs are. Finally, objectives are very useful in planning HR budgets each year, allocating time to projects or programs, and devising HR policies.

Use Activity 9-1 at the end of the chapter to work through the HR objective-setting process.

Providing Leadership

Few people can dispute the importance of leadership. It is a crucial ingredient in implementing any plan and bringing about any change. Leaders galvanize support, mobilize resources, and engineer change. In the context of HR strategy, they develop HR objectives, make sure that reward systems and controls match strategy, devise HR policies, coordinate HR practice areas, and match HR department structure to strategy and strategy to structure. In implementing HR Grand Strategy, three roles are of fundamental importance: the chief executive, the top HR executive, and managers at all levels in the organization.

The Role of Chief Executive

The role of the CEO is important: He or she is the chief organizational strategist, instrumental in setting the tone for selecting and implementing the HR Grand Strategy. The CEO's role is symbolic, substantive, and political. It is *symbolic* in that the CEO's perceived commitment to HR strategy exerts a powerful influence on how others accept it. It is *substantive* in that the CEO has the power to assign managers to key positions. It is also one of the most difficult to use, since the "right" managers are not always available at the right times and in the right places to implement corporate or HR Grand Strategy. Finally, the CEO's role is *political* in that real commitment is likely to mean more money allocated to developing and implementing an HR strategy. Resource allocation is political to the extent that it represents success by the HR department as it competes with other parts of the organization for scarce funding and staffing to implement HR plans.

What should HR planners do to gain the support of the CEO for HR strategy formulation and implementation? Several approaches can be used: (1) *persuasion* (convince the CEO that the company needs an HR strategy or needs to begin implementing strategy once it is decided on); (2) *education* (without using the term "education," furnish the CEO with information about the need for establishing a long-term HR Grand Strategy and acting, over time, in a way consistent with it); (3) *lobbying* (convince those who are close confidantes of the CEO that the company needs an HR Grand Strategy and support to implement it, and ask them to discuss the matter with the CEO and among themselves); (4) *grassroots campaigning* (convince middle and lower-level managers that the company needs an HR Grand Strategy, and solicit their support in lobbying for it with their superiors); and (5) a *combination* of any two or more approaches noted.

The Role of the Top HR Executive

To be effective, the top HR executive must first have the support of the CEO and key managers and have the credibility necessary to function in the role of leader. CEOs generally want such take-charge leadership from their HR chiefs as well (Rothwell, Prescott, and Taylor, 1998). The career success of HRP practitioners depends on their ability to think strategically and to provide useful advice about HR Grand Strategy as a means of helping to engineer successful implementation of strategic business plans.

The Role of Managers at All Levels

Though the HR department is the major instrument by which to coordinate implementation of HR Grand Strategy, do not overlook the role of managers. Every manager should be held accountable for taking full advantage of the present skills of employees and for developing those skills in line with future organizational needs.

At the outset of implementing HR Grand Strategy, it is often worthwhile for the HR executive to assess relative commitment to any Grand Strategy by managers and to target initiatives so as to build support. The worksheet in Activity 9-2 (at the end of the chapter) will help explain how to do that.

Of course, it is not always possible to obtain the support of key managers. Some were 100 percent committed to prior HR strategies and cannot or will not change; some hold values that conflict with the actions that will have to be taken; some will not be able to translate broad HR strategy into specific actions, and some will view the whole exercise as pointless. For this reason, you might need to go beyond the simple issues listed in Activity 9-2, reassigning managers so that leadership matches the HR Grand Strategy. Of course, reassignment is only possible with full support of the chief executive, who is really the only one who can make such wholesale changes.

A *selective blend* is appropriate when the old strategy was effective but the new one calls for many changes. It takes advantage of the current executive's familiarity with people, events, and conditions, but also makes use of fresh insights and enthusiasm that outsiders can bring to the effort. The key question is: "To what extent do present managers possess values and skills needed to implement a new HR strategy?" If they do, they should be retained; if they do not, outsiders might have to be brought in.

A *stability strategy* should be pursued with respect to management assignments when past HR strategy has been effective and few changes are needed. In such cases, existing managers enjoy major advantages over replacements: They are already familiar with key people, jobs, and HR practices in the organization, and there is little need for people to change radically.

An *outsider* is appropriate when past HR strategy has been ineffective and many changes are needed. Outsiders are unhampered by prior decisions and interpersonal relationships. On the other hand, they are rightfully committed to bringing about a change, which led to their selection in the first place.

Finally, *reorientation of assignments* is appropriate when few changes are necessary to implement HR strategy and when past strategy has not worked out. In such circumstances, it might be enough just to encourage new approaches to old problems, perhaps with a few new people.

Each strategy for dealing with management assignments is thus more appropriate in some circumstances than in others. It is up to the CEO and the chief HR executive to assess how well members of the existing management team are suited to implementing HR Grand Strategy.

Matching Rewards and Controls to HR Strategy

How can behavior throughout an organization be controlled so that daily, weekly, monthly, yearly, and multi-yearly HR actions are consistent with long-term HR Grand Strategy? The question is a classic one. While there are no simple answers, there are two ways to bring behavior in line with strategic goals: rewards and controls.

Rewards and HR Strategy

One implication of short-term thinking is that there is little payoff for managers to groom their subordinates for meeting long-term organizational needs. As one manager quipped, "Why should I go out of my way to prepare my people for tomorrow, when I won't be around unless I do my job well today?"

Reward systems are powerful because they can influence behavior. They affect who is attracted to a job, who is motivated to perform, and who is or is not satisfied. Theories of motivation differ widely, yet almost everyone agrees that people are inclined to do what they are rewarded for doing. Reward systems can help or hinder implementation of HR Grand Strategy.

There are two kinds of rewards: (1) extrinsic (outside the individual who takes action), and (2) intrinsic (within and inseparable from the individual). Extrinsic rewards include salary, benefits, promotions, and awards. Intrinsic rewards include satisfaction with a job well done, or seeing how you helped develop others.

For any organizational reward system to be effective, it must exhibit five characteristics (Lawler, 1977):

1. *Importance.* People have to value the rewards. However, individuals differ in what they value and in how much they value it.
2. *Flexibility.* Because individuals differ in what they value, the range of rewards available must be broad enough to allow for choice among alternatives.
3. *Frequency.* The more often rewards are given, the greater their motivative force.
4. *Visibility.* People naturally want others to know when they have been singled out for exceptional performance or behavior. By awarding benefits with great fanfare, managers spur others to achievement.
5. *Cost.* There are limits to how much people can be rewarded. The greater the individual contribution or the greater the size of previous rewards, the greater the expectation that future rewards will be higher than past ones.

These factors are, of course, related to extrinsic rewards.

We can add six more factors associated with intrinsic rewards:

1. *Work that is interesting:* This is the most important factor. People want work that is interesting in itself.
2. *Potential for developing one's unique abilities:* People want to be able to become more of what they are capable of becoming. Work is a vehicle for self-actualization.
3. *Potential for seeing results:* People want to see the fruits of their labor. Observation of results is an important form of feedback on performance.
4. *Potential for applying one's present talents:* People want to be able to use their special abilities.
5. *Autonomy:* People enjoy exercising freedom when they approach a task. Work is a vehicle for expressing creativity.
6. *Problem-solving opportunity:* Generally, people prefer hard to simple problems so that the work is sufficiently challenging.

How, then, can rewards be geared to behavior that is consistent with implementing long-term HR Grand Strategy? While no simple answer exists, HR executives have to identify what will be rewarding for managers in the process of implementing HR Grand Strategy. They will then have to devise ways to capitalize on those rewards. The worksheet in Activity 9-3 at the end of the chapter should help you think through this process.

Management Control and HR Strategy

The simple aim of management control is to make sure that results conform to intentions. There are four steps in devising a management control: (1) deciding what behaviors or outcomes are desired, (2) establishing ways to measure behaviors or outcomes, (3) measuring what happens, and (4) allocating rewards based on achievement.

The first step is the basis for the entire process: What behavior and what outcomes are desired in order to implement HR Grand Strategy? Clearly, HR objectives should be helpful here in identifying what controls should exist; they can also suggest criteria for measuring how well strategy is being implemented.

Many different criteria can be used, so you will have to decide which ones to use, which ones to give priority to, and how you will handle conflicting criteria.

Measuring behavior or outcomes is usually handled through employee performance appraisals at all levels. Indeed, future-oriented employee appraisal, which is geared to long-term objectives rather than past performance, provides feedback to employees and managers about how well they are contributing to achievement of long-term plans. It also helps identify emerging problems and ways to deal with them, and pinpoints the need for specialized training and additional resources. In short, a future-oriented appraisal system is a powerful control device to make sure that HR objectives are being acted on.

If the focus is on results, a management-by-objectives system will probably be the most useful. Employees at all levels negotiate their own contributions to implementing HR Grand Strategy in their jobs. If the focus is on behavior or activity, a behaviorally anchored rating scale is devised for each job so that performance is compared to observable behaviors associated with implementing HR plans.

By tying allocation of rewards to results, HR managers create a powerful incentive for implementing HR Grand Strategy.

Devising HR Policies Consistent with Strategy

Policies are guidelines meant to guide thinking and acting in organizational settings. They indicate how managers should deal with routine events, situations, and problems so that what they do is consistent with the HR Grand Strategy. Organizations use policies to coordinate operations across functions and down the chain of command. HR departments use policies to guide diverse activities of HR practice areas and line managers.

A change in HR Grand Strategy typically requires a review of policies pertaining to career-management, recruitment, training, organization development, job design, employee assistance, labor relations, and compensation/benefits. In light of new HR Grand Strategy, decision-makers need to consider whether existing policies are consistent, practical, and cost-beneficial, and how much and how well they support achievement of desired HR objectives and provide guidance in important areas. Policies might need to be added, modified, or eliminated when they do not support implementation of HR Grand Strategy.

Any of the following questions can require new HR policies to support HR Grand Strategy:

1. Will adequate numbers of employees be available in the future?
2. Will the right kinds of people occupy each job category?
3. Will the HR department be capable of helping to change jobs and people over time in a way that facilitates achievement of strategic business plans?
4. On what basis will decisions be made about hiring? Training? Promoting? Transferring? Demoting? Terminating? Evaluating employee performance? Compensating? Changing job duties?
5. Will priority be given to training and developing people from the inside, or to recruiting people from the outside? Why?

Ideally, these questions should be considered during the strategic business planning process. After all, the answers affect organizational strategy itself. For HRP practitioners, crucial questions include the following:

1. What role does the HR department have, and what role should it have in acquiring the right numbers of employees to help meet organizational needs in the future and ensuring that jobs are designed appropriately, and that the right kinds of people are occupying each job category?
2. How can the HR department be prepared to play the role intended for it in the future?
3. How can HR divisions, departments, and work groups help achieve the HR Grand Strategy? Consider the roles to be played by those who focus on: Career planning, recruitment, training, organizational

development, job design, employee assistance, labor relations, and compensation and benefits.

How can activities within the HR department be coordinated so that they do not work at cross-purposes?

HRP practitioners should begin by collecting all existing policies, procedures, rules, and "standard operating procedures" having to do with major HR activities. Each should be examined in terms of (1) how well it has worked in the past, (2) how well it will probably work in the future, (3) what results are desired from the policy in the future, and (4) how the policy should be changed, if at all, so that it facilitates implementation of HR Grand Strategy.

There may be need for creation of utterly new policies. Consider the following questions: (1) How much time are managers now spending on the same HR problems? (2) What requests for assistance are most common for HRP practitioners? Are they receiving requests for help from operating managers on matters that should be handled routinely? (3) Given the organization's business strategy, are there likely to be new problems or issues coming up? For example, if retrenchment is selected as a strategy, does the organization have clear policies on layoffs, terminations, early retirement, part-time employees? (4) Are employees complaining that inequities are common within or between work groups? For example, one manager routinely grants vacation time whenever it is requested, while another denies it frequently on the basis of workload.

If answers to these questions produce a list of issues, then there is a good chance that a formal policy should be prepared to provide guidance. Written policies are usually preferable to unwritten ones because (1) they are more explicit, (2) they ensure consistent and equitable treatment, (3) they make information more certain of reaching users in the original form, (4) they look more official, (5) they make coordination across and down the organization more certain, and (6) they require careful forethought.

Coordinating HR Practice Areas

One major problem has accounted for more difficulty in implementing HR Grand Strategy than anything else: No attempt is made to coordinate HR practice areas.

The reasons for this lack of coordination include:

1. HR actions are taken in response to specific problems or issues. In other words, they tend to be reactive and crisis driven.
2. HR practice area specialists go their own ways without regard to what is happening in other practice areas.
3. HR objectives can actually conflict with each other.

A holistic approach is needed to choose HR Grand Strategy and then coordinate HR practice areas in line with it.

As a start in this direction, think of any HR practice area as *change-oriented.* They differ in the *focus* (Is a program intended to change individuals, groups, jobs, or some combination of them?), the *time frame* (Over what length of time is change to occur?), and *direction* (Is the intent to make a change that will restore a past condition or adapt to a future one?). Each HR practice area is an opportunity and a place to produce change in line with implementation of the HR Grand Strategy. Figure 9-3 briefly summarizes the focus, time frame, and direction of each HR practice area.

One way to coordinate separate HR practice areas is to begin with a strategic vision of what they should be like, and then work toward realization of that vision. Few theorists have attempted to provide a topology to guide the visioning process; among these who have made the attempt, Miles and Snow (1984) classify organizations into three types: defenders, prospectors, and analyzers. Their analysis is classic, and it is still relevant almost 20 years later.

Defenders have a narrow and stable product or service market. Firms of this kind focus on increasing efficiency. The appropriate HR Grand Strategy is "building," which means growth from within. Practice area strategies conform, more or less, to this overall direction: Recruitment is limited primarily to entry-level jobs, training programs (vehicles for movement on an upward career path)

Figure 9-3: The Time Frames, Change Orientation, and Focus of HR Practice Areas

HR Practice Area	Time Frame	Focus	Nature of Change
Career Planning	Primarily long-term	Individual	▪ For individuals: changes outlook of individuals so that they are more aware of opportunities and are motivated to reach their potential. ▪ For organization: changes outlook of managers through pressure, from bottom up, to specify requirements for promotions and transfers.
Recruitment	Both short-term and long-term	Job	▪ For individuals: changes affiliation of individuals; establishes initial expectations; begins socialization process ▪ For organization: changes composition of work force; brings in "new blood"
Training	Primarily short-term	Job	▪ For individuals: changes job-specific knowledge and skills; creates opportunity for productivity improvement ▪ For organization: changes organization by focusing attention on procedures or awakening in employees a desire for improvement
Organization Development	Primarily long-term	Groups and Organization	▪ For individuals: changes interactions between people; focuses on feelings and interpersonal relationships; improves teamwork ▪ For organization: changes modes of interaction between work groups; focuses on cooperation
Organization Job Design	Both short-term and long-term	Individuals/Groups and/or Organization	▪ For individuals: changes tasks in jobs or reporting relationships, thereby influencing skills/knowledge required and interpersonal relationships. ▪ For organization: redistributes work, thus affecting interaction between individuals and groups

Figure 9-3: *(continued)*

HR Practice Area	Time Frame	Focus	Nature of Change
Employee Assistance	Primarily short-term	Individual	■ For individuals: changes ability/skills for coping with personal and work-related problems ■ For organization: changes ability of organization to respond to individual problems which, though of a personal nature, can affect job performances
Labor Relations	Both short-term and long-term	Groups and Organization	■ For individuals: changes relationships between subordinates and superiors ■ For organization: creates a second authority structure with which individuals, groups, and organization must cope
Compensation/ Benefits	Primarily short-term	Individual	■ For individuals: changes motivation levels in the short-term for some people ■ For organization: changes cost of doing business, perhaps affecting profitability and competitiveness; affects ability to attract and retain needed talent

are extensive, and compensation programs are geared to maintaining equity within the organization.

Prospectors search for new opportunities such as new products, services, or markets. Firms of this kind focus on innovation. They are often industry leaders. The appropriate HR Grand Strategy is "acquiring," which means growth from outside. HR practice area strategies reflect it: Recruitment is common at all levels, training programs are few and far between, and compensation programs are geared heavily to competitiveness in the external labor market.

Analyzers function simultaneously in a relatively stable product market and in one that is more dynamic. Firms like this focus on rapid acceptance of new ideas and application of tried-and-true methods. The appropriate HR Grand Strategy is "allocating," which means helping integrate decisions appropriate for the two quite different kinds of environments confronting the organization.

HR practice-area strategies are mixed, geared to meeting the different recruitment, training, and compensation requirements for each of the two kinds of environments confronting the organization. There is no empirical support for this classification scheme—relatively little solid research has been done in this area—but it is a starting point for conceptualizing.

Few other writers have described how to coordinate HR practice areas or, for that matter, how to formulate and implement strategies unique to each of them. We suggest that this process is really little different from formulating and implementing organizational strategy or HR Grand Strategy. In other words, the manager in charge of each HR practice area:

1. Defines the purpose of the area (for example, the training department, the compensation/benefits department).
2. Appraises relative strengths and weaknesses of the department and its activities at present.
3. Scans the environment of the department or practice area inside and outside the organization for trends likely to affect future success.
4. Generates alternative strategies, each consistent with HR Grand Strategy (though not necessarily identical).
5. Selects a practice area strategy believed to be most conducive to success over time.
6. Implements strategy through practice area objectives, leadership, rewards, structure, and policy.
7. Evaluates practice area strategy by comparing results to intentions specified in objectives.

Each HR practice area is related to others. The challenge of implementing HR Grand Strategy is to devise a means of integrating them so that their unified impact is greater than the sum of their respective parts. At the same time, this integrated implementation must be coordinated with strategic business plans if HR practice areas are to complement initiatives of the organization.

HR objectives, leadership, rewards, controls, policies, and structure are tools for integrating HR practice areas and coordinating them with business strategy. It is also possible to weigh, in advance, the likely impact of each major new program or initiative in one practice area on other areas. Activity 9-4 at the end of the chapter provides a worksheet that can be useful for this purpose.

Note that the HR practice areas in Activity 9-4 are arranged in two columns to form a matrix. Any new program—for example, a new training course on supervision or a new employee assistance program for alcoholism—has the potential to influence all other practice areas. Simply write in the new initiative in the space indicated and then, moving down the vertical column appropriate to the area (e.g., training), brainstorm on possible effects exerted on other practice areas. Use your imagination. Skip the horizontal and vertical intersection of the same practice area.

When you have worked through an example or two using this worksheet, consider the following questions:

1. What is the probability that the new program will exert *considerable* influence on other practice areas? Are some areas more likely to be affected than others?
2. To what extent will these likely influences make implementing HR Grand Strategy *generally* easier? Harder? What makes you think so?
3. To what extent, if at all, can action be taken when implementing the new program to maximize beneficial effects? Minimize effects that are not beneficial?
4. What actions in other practice areas should be taken as the new program is being implemented?

Answers to these questions are worth thinking about during formulation of HR Grand Strategy because it is the *overall* impact of HR practice areas that is important. It is thus essential to consider not only the separate effects of each area but also their interactive effects.

Matching Structure to Strategy, and Strategy to Structure

A major concern in implementing any strategy is the way that the organization and its components are put together, the way work is allocated, and the decision-making authority delegated to managers at all levels. Obviously, implementation of any HR Grand Strategy depends in part on congruence between the strategic choice and:

1. *The values, attitudes, and beliefs of those charged with carrying it out.* Do they feel committed?
2. *The ability of managers to carry it out.* Do they possess necessary influence over results? Do they possess adequate resources? Do they have the skills?
3. *The selection of who does what.* Do managers have the ability to match people in a way that facilitates implementation?
4. *The selection of tasks in jobs.* Do managers have the ability to rearrange tasks and duties among units and individuals?

For many years, strategic theorists have wrangled over this question: What comes first, strategy or structure? Chandler (1962), the historian who wrote the first book about strategic planning, fired the first shot in this skirmish. He studied 70 firms over many years, and concluded that successful ones change their structure to match a new strategy. However, researchers who followed Chandler have found his conclusion problematic at best. Indeed, there might not be any correlation between success in the marketplace and "goodness of fit" between strategy and structure. It is more likely that, while existing structure constrains choice of radically new strategy, subsequent success depends on simultaneously matching environment conditions, structure, and strategy. Nearly any structure can work. What is not clear is what structure should be matched to what environment and what strategy.

There are five basic types of structure: (1) entrepreneurial, (2) functional, (3) divisional, (4) project, and (5) matrix. An entrepreneurial structure is least complex: All employees report to a single superior.

In a functional structure, tasks are divided up by specialty, such as finance, production or operations, marketing, and personnel/human resources. Managers are placed in charge of each specialty, and employees report to them. The managers, in turn, report to a chief executive.

In a divisional structure, tasks are divided up both by function and by some organizing device, such as product or service line, geographical region, or consumer type.

If the environment is unpredictable, project managers are added below divisional managers. These managers oversee each large-scale assignment from start to finish.

Even greater environmental uncertainty prompts the creation of a matrix structure, in which each project manager is elevated to the same status as a divisional manager. In a matrix organization, employees report both to a division and to a project supervisor.

Why is structure important for implementing HR Grand Strategy? There are four reasons: (1) choice of structure determines allocation of tasks to jobs and the grouping of jobs in departments, (2) structure affects leaders with whom HRP practitioners must deal, (3) organizational structure affects the status of the HR department, and (4) the way the organization is structured can—and should—affect HR department structure itself.

Of course, the way tasks are allocated to jobs and the way jobs are grouped together exert powerful influences on individual and group behavior. The tasks individuals perform can be satisfying or frustrating and well or poorly matched to their unique talents, and they will call for high or even low skill levels. The grouping of jobs can produce high or low levels of cohesiveness, innovation, communication, and supervisory control. While task and job grouping clearly affect what work is done and by whom—both of which are crucial in HRP—the trouble is "that in many instances organizational performance suffers because managers are unable by training or intellect to design a structure that guides the behavior of individuals and groups to achieve high levels of production, efficiency, satisfaction, adaptiveness, and development" (Gibson et al. 1985, p. 419).

HR planners can provide some help on issues of task and job grouping because they are perhaps best suited of any in an organization to study what works and what does not. After all, work analysts focus on what is done, workforce analysts focus on who does it, and environmental scanners focus on what changes are likely and even desirable.

The organization's structure also determines who makes HR decisions and how and what decisions are made. Unlike other departments in organizations, activities of the HR department cut across all others. Every manager shoulders part of the burden—and pleasure—of HR work. Without people, no organization can exist.

The relationship between the HR department and other parts of the organization varies. Typically, personnel practitioners provide advice to line managers as part of their staff responsibility, furnish specialized services to the line organization, devise HR policies (such as for hiring and firing) to guide activities usually handled by line managers, and exert functional control by making "binding" suggestions to line managers. These responsibilities can and do conflict. For instance, it is difficult to enjoy the rapport necessary for providing advice when HRP practitioners also monitor line management for compliance with government regulations and company rules.

The key to an effective relationship between HRP practitioners and line managers stems from common values, beliefs, and norms. However, potential for conflict clearly exists. Members of the HR department tend to be younger, better-educated, and more humanistically inclined than line managers. For these reasons, it is not always possible to build on common values, beliefs, and norms.

Organizational structure also affects the status of the HR department and its ability to contribute to organizational and HR strategy. Is the top HR executive included in strategic business planning efforts? Is he or she on the same level as the highest ranking line officers? It is unlikely that the HR department can contribute much to implementing business strategy if the answer to either question is no. To command authority, the HR executive must first have it delegated. That responsibility rests with the organization's preeminent strategist, the chief executive.

Much like an organization, the HR department can be structured according to five fundamental arrangements: (1) entrepreneurial, (2) functional, (3) divisional, (4) project, and (5) matrix. Simple arrangements (the first three types) are usually preferable to more complex ones unless the environment is so dynamic that a complex form is necessary.

In an entrepreneurial structure, one personnel or HR officer is in charge. He or she is a generalist who uses perhaps a few assistants and clerical support staff to do everything: recruiting, training, employee counseling, administering salaries and benefits, and much more. The organization is relatively small; the environment, typically stable.

In a functional structure—one of the most common—a unit or division exists for each HR practice area, or at least for each one with high priority associated with it. Hence, there is a separate division for wages and salaries, benefits, training, recruitment, labor relations, and organization development (Figure 9-4).

A functional structure is appropriate for a medium to large firm in a relatively stable industry. The choice of what divisions or units to create is, of course, the important one. High priority areas earmarked for action in HR Grand Strategy should clearly be reflected in HR department structure. One reason is

Figure 9-4: A Functional Structure for the HR Department

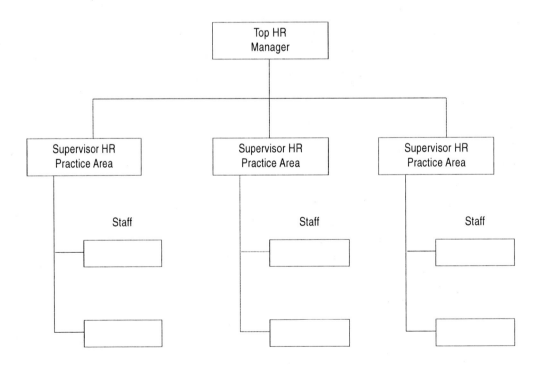

that by creating a unit with special responsibility, managers at higher levels institutionalize a way to devote time and attention to a priority. Another reason is that existence of a special unit sends signals throughout the organization that the area *is* a priority.

A divisional structure is typified by several separate HR departments, each placed in an autonomous or semi-autonomous part of the firm. This placement is intended to make the department more responsive to the unique needs of divisions, whether they are oriented to regions, special product lines, or special consumer groups. This is especially true if the organization is large or even multinational, and if it is confronting a complex, dynamic environment.

For divisional structures, a key question is this: To what extent are HR departments in each division accountable to corporate headquarters? Does the top HR official in each division report to line managers at the division level, or to the top corporate HR executive? What is the relationship of divisional HR departments to the corporate HR department?

One approach is to make each division's HR department completely autonomous, answering to the line manager in charge of the division. The advantage is that the department is thus more likely to serve the division exclusively; the disadvantage is that separate departments lose economies of scale that result when their separate efforts are pooled. A second approach is to make each department only an extension of a centralized, corporate-level HR department. In such cases, economies of scale and coordination are advantages; loss of responsiveness to any one division is a potential disadvantage. Figure 9-5 illustrates these structures.

There are variations. At the division level, the HR department can report both to the corporate HR executive and to the divisional manager. The result is likely to be conflicts between the two. An alternative is for the corporate-level HR department to provide highly specialized services that are carefully laid out so as not to overlap or conflict with those at the division level. There are significant advantages to this approach: corporate personnel practitioners serve as specialists and divisional practitioners as generalists.

Matrix and project structures for the HR function are perhaps most rare. There will be occasions when a single project is so large and runs for so long

Figure 9-5: Divisional Structures for the HR Department: Some Alternatives

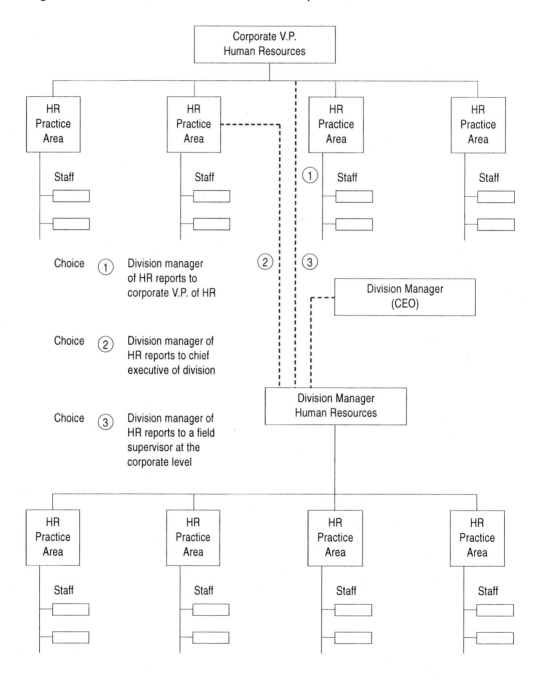

that it resembles a divisional structure. NASA's Apollo moon project and large scale U.S. Department of Defense contracts are examples. In such instances, an entire HR department can be structured around one project.

In thinking about a new structure for the HR department, consider

1. *The external environment.* Is there "goodness of fit" between the demands imposed from outside the organization, the HR Grand Strategy, and HR practice areas? Does the department's existing structure help or hinder responsiveness to outside job applicants? Customers? Governmental regulatory bodies?

2. *The internal environment.* Is there "goodness of fit" between demands imposed by line managers, the HR Grand Strategy, and HR practice areas? Does the department's existing structure help or hinder its responsiveness to line management needs or to employee needs?

3. *The HR Grand Strategy.* Does the structure of the HR department match up to priorities in HR strategy? For example, if recruitment of external talent is a priority, does a unit on external recruitment exist?

4. *The existing structure.* Does the department's structure help or hinder interaction between people?

5. *The purpose and objectives of the department.* How much does the department's structure reflect the time devoted to providing advice to line managers? Delivering specialized services to meet needs of company customers? Managers? Employees? Devising HR policies? Exerting functional control over line activities?

Use the worksheet in Activity 9-5 at the end of the chapter to do some brainstorming about the desirable structure for the HR department and to assess its present strengths and weaknesses.

Activity 9-1: A Worksheet for Developing HR Objectives

Directions: Use this worksheet to begin the process of converting a broad HR Grand Strategy into a blueprint for action. (Add more paper if necessary.) Be sure to consider initiatives on career planning, recruitment, training, and other HR practice areas.

STRATEGIC OBJECTIVES

What should be accomplished? (Desired Outcomes)	When should each outcome be achieved? (3–5 years or more)	How will achievement be measured?	Who is responsible?

COORDINATIVE OBJECTIVES

For each strategy objective listed above, prepare corresponding objectives for a shorter time frame (1–3 years or more).

OPERATIONAL OBJECTIVES

For each coordinative objective listed above, prepare corresponding objectives for a shorter time frame (less than 1 year).

Activity 9-2: A Worksheet for Assessing Management Support
for the HR Grand Strategy

Directions: Circle the appropriate level of degree and importance in columns 2 and 3 for each of the items listed in column 1 (items 1–4). Use the following scale: 1 = very little; 2 = little; 3 = neither little nor much; 4 = much; 5 = very much.

Column 1	*Column 2*					*Column 3*				
	Degree					*Importance*				
	Very much				*Very little*	*Very much*				*Very little*
To what extent do managers in the organization	*5*	*4*	*3*	*2*	*1*	*5*	*4*	*3*	*2*	*1*
1. Already know key people involved in										
a. Strategic business planning?	5	4	3	2	1	5	4	3	2	1
b. Strategic HR planning?	5	4	3	2	1	5	4	3	2	1
2. Already understand										
a. Strategic business plans?	5	4	3	2	1	5	4	3	2	1
b. Strategic HR plans?	5	4	3	2	1	5	4	3	2	1
3. Favor implementation of HR Grand Strategy because of										
a. Their values?	5	4	3	2	1	5	4	3	2	1
b. Organizational culture?	5	4	3	2	1	5	4	3	2	1
c. Previous experience?	5	4	3	2	1	5	4	3	2	1
4. Feel bound by										
a. Their past decisions?	5	4	3	2	1	5	4	3	2	1
b. Past HR strategy?	5	4	3	2	1	5	4	3	2	1
c. Short-term pressures/concerns?	5	4	3	2	1	5	4	3	2	1

5. Are there any key managers whose support is crucial? If so, list them:

6. Which of the managers, listed in question 5, are unlikely to support HR Grand Strategy at present?

7. What accounts for the possible opposition of each manager listed in question 6?

8. How can the concerns of each manager be overcome (persuasion, participation, success in other parts of the organization)?

9. What should be done to overcome opposition?

Activity 9-3: A Worksheet for Matching Rewards to the HR Grand Strategy

Directions: For each characteristic described in columns 1 and 2 below, answer the questions in columns 3, 4, and 5. Use this worksheet to do some brainstorming to identify what incentives presently exist for managers to develop employees (column 3), what incentives need to exist in the future in order to facilitate implementation of HR Grand Strategy (column 4), and how incentives can be created for developing employees in line with HR Grand Strategy (column 5).

Reward system characteristics	Meaning of each characteristic	What incentives for managers now exist in this area for developing employees?	What incentives for managers need to exist in the future in this area in order to encourage development of employees in line with HR strategy?	What can be done to narrow gaps existing between columns 3 and 4?
Column 1	Column 2	Column 3	Column 4	Column 5
Importance	The value of a reward to an individual			
Flexibility	The choice of what to use as a reward			
Frequency	How often rewards are given			
Visibility	How much attention is given to the act of rewarding			
Cost	The value of a reward in dollar terms			
Interesting work	The interest that grows from the work itself			
Potential for developing one's abilities	The desire to become more of what one is capable of becoming			

Activity 9-3: *(continued)*

Column 1	Column 2	Column 3	Column 4	Column 5
Potential for seeing results	The desire to see the fruits of one's labors			
Potential for applying one's present talents	The desire to use the talents one is aware of			
Autonomy	The freedom to exercise creativity			
Problem-solving opportunity	The desire for challenge in one's work			

Activity 9-4: A Worksheet for Assessing the Influence of a New Program Initiative in One HR Practice Area on Other Areas

Directions: Describe the contemplated new initiative. Then, working down the vertical column of the HR practice area from which the initiative stems, brainstorm likely effects on other HR practice areas. Skip the intersection of vertical columns and horizontal rows (e.g., training-training intersection). If you wish, add more HR practice areas such as employee performance appraisal, health and safety, or security or other practice areas that are associated with HR in your organization.

What is the new program initiative? Describe it.
From which of these HR practice areas does the initiative stem?

HR practice area that is influenced/ HR practice area expecting influence →	Career planning	Recruitment	Training	Organization development	Job design	Employee assistance	Labor relations	Compensation benefits
Career planning								
Recruitment								
Training								
Organization development								
Job design								
Employee assistance								
Labor relations								
Compensation benefits								

Activity 9-5: A Worksheet on HR Department Structure

The External Environment

1. Is there "goodness of fit" at present between demands imposed from outside the organization, the HR Grand Strategy, and HR practice areas?
    a. If so, why?
    b. If not, why?

2. What can be done by way of changing HR department structure to improve "goodness of fit" in the future?

3. Do you think that the HR department's present structure makes it more responsive to those outside the organization?
    a. If so, why?
    b. If not, why?

4. What can be done by way of changing HR department structure to improve "goodness of fit" in the future?

The Internal Environment

5. Is there "goodness of fit" at present between demands imposed by line managers, the HR grand strategy, and HR practice areas?
    a. If so, why?
    b. If not, why?

6. What can be done, by way of changing HR department structure, to improve "goodness of fit" in the future?

7. Does the HR department's present structure help or hinder its responsiveness to those inside the organization?
    a. If so, why?
    b. If not, why?

8. What can be done, by way of changing HR department structure, to improve "goodness of fit" in the future?

The HR Grand Strategy

9. Does the present structure of the HR department match up to priorities in the HR Grand Strategy?
    a. If so, why?
    b. If not, why?

10. What can be done, by way of changing HR department structure, to improve its match to priorities in HR Grand Strategy?

Components of the HR Department

11. Is the present structure of the HR department conducive to interaction between its parts?
    a. If so, why?
    b. If not, why?

Activity 9-5: *(continued)*

12. What can be done by way of changing HR department structure to improve interaction between parts?

Role and Objectives of the HR Department

13. Does the HR department's present structure reflect the amount of time devoted to
    a. Providing advice to line managers?
    b. Delivering specialized services to meet needs of company customers, managers, employees?
    c. Devising HR policies?
    d. Exerting functional control over line management activities?

14. What can be done, by way of changing HR department structure, to improve the amount of time devoted to
    a. Providing advice to managers
    b. Delivering specialized services to meet needs of company customers, managers, employees?
    c. Devising HR policies?
    d. Exerting functional control over line-management activities?

Activity 9-6: Case Study

Directions: Read through the case that follows, and then answer the questions at the end. (This case is entirely fictitious.)

The AVCO Insurance Company is a very small, highly specialized firm. It offers only one kind of insurance: malpractice coverage for physicians. The firm is over 50 years old and caters to a highly select clientele. It charges the highest rates but offers the best coverage in the business.

Demand for an AVCO policy is very high. However, the firm chooses its policyholders with great care. To be approved, the applicant must have been in practice for at least 10 years and must have avoided any malpractice claim (true or false) during that time. Once an applicant becomes a policyholder, the firm is quite aggressive in defending him or her if a lawsuit is later filed.

Insiders in the insurance industry know that AVCO settles out of court less often and has the best score-card for winning lawsuits of any company in its field.

Much of the company's success is attributable to the people who work for AVCO. The company employs a mere 70 people, excluding agents who sell policies. The firm is structured along functional lines: There is a sales division (with only 6 people), a policy and claims division (with 22 people), a legal division (with 8 people), a finance and billing division (with 28 people), and a personnel division (with 3 people). The chief executive, his secretary, and his top assistant bring the total to 70.

AVCO has long pursued a business strategy best called "stable growth." The managers are highly averse to risk, preferring instead to concentrate on the market they know best: physician malpractice insurance. Though they could no doubt seize most of their market if they wished to do so—malpractice insurance is being dropped by many large companies—they want to concentrate on doing what they do well. They do not believe that the company can handle growth that is too rapid. Nor are they concerned about being the biggest or even the most profitable in their market; rather, they want to offer the *highest* quality to the *safest* clientele.

Activity 9-6: *(continued)*

The company's strategy for human resources reflects that of the firm itself. The managers prefer to hire only the most experienced in their field. They want to minimize training costs, but are willing to pay better than the going rate. The company is not unionized.

The HR department consists of one manager (a 60-year-old who has had 40 years with the company), her assistant (a 50-year-old with a Ph.D. in organizational behavior and 20 years in the industry), and a secretary. The HR manager enjoys the confidence of the company president and participates in strategic business planning. The HR Grand Strategy reflects that of the company: It is one of stable growth. The highest priorities are recruiting top-flight talent and keeping salary rates above those of its competitors.

Questions

1. How can top managers in AVCO establish
   a. Strategic objectives for recruitment?
   b. Strategic objectives for compensation/benefits?

2. In what ways can the HR manager exercise leadership in implementing HR Grand Strategy?

3. How much support for this HR Grand Strategy would you guess exists among managers in the firm? Why do you think so?

4. How can control be exercised over this HR Grand Strategy?

5. What policies for HR should
   a. Be reviewed?
   b. Be created?

6. What impact, would you guess, will the firm's heavy emphasis on recruiting experienced talent and paying above-competitive-rates exert on appropriate initiatives in such HR practice areas as
   a. Career Planning?
   b. Training?
   c. Organization Development?
   d. Job Design?
   e. Employee Assistance Programs?
   For each one, explain why you believe this influence is likely.

7. How do you think the HR department
   a. Should contribute to implementing HR Grand Strategy? Why?
   b. Should be structured?

8. What changes, if any, do you feel will be necessary in the HR department if it is to assume a major role in implementing a new HR Grand Strategy?

CHAPTER 10

CAREER PLANNING AND MANAGEMENT

What is the role of career planning and management in implementing HR Grand Strategy? What is the traditional approach to career planning, and what is the traditional approach to career-management? What are some problems with traditional approaches? How can career issues be addressed strategically? This chapter, the first to focus on one HR practice area, answers these questions. In doing so, it begins to show how one HR practice area can be integrated with HR Grand Strategy.

The Role of Career Planning and Management in Implementing HR Grand Strategy

It is difficult to overestimate the importance of career planning and management in implementing human resources (HR) Grand Strategy. While the authors of this book have emphasized HR planning from the standpoint of the organization, it is important to realize that *no HR plan will be successful unless it takes into account individual career goals and aspirations.* Employees at present are increasingly career-oriented, preferring self-allegiance over organizational loyalty. One survey revealed that 51 percent of respondents would prefer to be running their own businesses rather than working as employees for others, a fact that shows some dissatisfaction with traditional employment opportunities (Alderman, 1995). At the same time, career resources have become more widely available to individuals than ever before, with more than 11,000 web sites devoted to career-related issues (Koonce, 1997). Indeed, many excellent resources for career planning are available on the web. Just to list a sample, see:

- http://www.careerplanit.com/
- http://content.monster.com/
- http://www.jobweb.com/catapult/career_info.htm
- http://careerpathsonline.com/intro/default.htm
- http://careerplanning.miningco.com/careers/careerplanning/
- http://www.careercc.com/

Job hunting and career changing have never been easier, with such online sources (Abernathy, 2000). That ease of job hunting, coupled with the increasing importance of retaining key talent, has resulted in many organizations attempting to reinvent career-management programs (see, for instance, Hirsh, 2000). Career programs are also important as part of an overall succession strategy for an organization (Rothwell, 2000b).

Career planning is an individual's lifelong process of establishing personal career objectives and acting in a manner intended to bring them about. *Career management* is the process of deciding what work opportunities to accept or reject, depending on their perceived value in helping achieve career objectives. It includes not only decisions made by an individual but also those made about the individual by managers and others who control what work opportunities can be made available. *Career development* is the process of improving an individual's abilities in anticipation of future opportunities for achieving career objectives. Finally, and perhaps most importantly, a *career* consists of the organized structure and sequence of patterns in an individual's work life.

Career planning is a continuous process. Individuals are not satisfied solely by the job-specific feedback on performance they receive through the performance appraisal process. They also want information that is more long-term.

For organizations, career-management must be a continuous process in the same way that career planning is for individuals. Promotion and job transfer systems nurture talented employees, motivating and developing them at the same time. Unless managers use these systems in some coherent and unified way, the most promising people will leave.

Career management has enormous implications for an organization's future. It influences:

1. The willingness of people to allow themselves to be recruited, promoted, or transferred.
2. An individual's readiness to learn in training. Indeed, motivation to learn will be influenced by an individual's perception that instructional outcomes contribute to achieving career objectives.
3. The willingness of members in a work group to interact. Is there competition for desired duties? Promotion? These issues can have a bearing on organization development efforts.
4. Job design considerations, especially when there is broad latitude in how to go about doing the work. Individuals personalize their jobs, adapting what they do to their abilities.
5. Employee assistance programs. Many organizations offer formal career planning programs for their employees, and they are becoming more popular.
6. Union agreements. Young employees in union settings are not always so eager to accept seniority rather than performance as a basis for promotion.
7. Compensation and benefits. To the extent that employees are not allowed the kind of advancement they would like to see, managers might need to broaden salary ranges to show that they value increasing proficiency in a job over extended periods. In fact, skill-based salary systems are becoming more popular. They compensate on the basis of what people know.

Career-management efforts are one way to ensure that employees are being offered opportunities to develop themselves while, at the same time, the organization is creating a pool of internal talent for managers to choose from for promotions, transfers, and strategic changes.

The Traditional Approach to Career Planning

Career planning is the sole responsibility of the individual, but career-management is a responsibility shared by the individual and by the organization. Individuals decide *what* they want to do. Managers, in an organizational context, decide *what opportunities to offer* and *what development activities are necessary prerequisites to qualify for them.*

Many theories of career planning have been proposed. Each is descriptive more than normative. In other words, theories tend to describe assumptions underlying career decision-making more than directing individuals in how to go about the process.

Economists were among the first to advance a coherent career-planning theory. They argue that people choose careers and decide on occupations in a highly rational way intended to maximize their *utility,* a complex term that encompasses both extrinsic (money) and intrinsic (personal happiness) rewards.

Psychologists of a Freudian persuasion, on the other hand, believe that career choice is only partly rational: It stems from the need for instinctual ratification, which stems from early-childhood experiences. A career is a lifelong psycho-play intended to restore the stability of childhood to the unconscious.

Sociologists stress the influence of the family. Children learn to think of occupations and careers based on observation of family role models. The effects of early socialization are felt for life.

However, developmental theory is undoubtedly the most popular way to explain career planning. It is based on the views of psychologist Erick Erickson (1959, 1968). He advanced the notion that individuals progress through distinctive *life stages,* each of which is characterized by an issue leading to a central life crisis. In order to mature, individuals must resolve the life crisis at each stage. Developmental theorists differ from Freudian theorists in their belief that people are not so much affected by the distant past (i.e., childhood) as by the immediacy of a current life stage.

Donald Super (1957, 1980) was the first to translate Erikson's ideas into a scheme directly applicable to career planning. He asserted that individuals pass through five career stages: growth, exploration, establishment, maintenance, and decline.

Other theorists have accepted the basic idea of career stages from Super and Erikson, but have proposed alternative ways of conceptualizing these stages. In a classic treatment, Dalton et al. (1977) expressed the belief that individuals pass through such stages as apprenticeship, self-dependence, mentor, and senior manager. In another classic treatment, Levinson et al. (1978) believe career stages depend on cycling and recycling experiences. They propose six such stages. In a third classic treatment, Edgar Schein (1978) offered a somewhat different, though related, view of development. He based his ideas on the *career anchor*, which serves to organize experience and measure success and self-perception. It is (1) broader than traditional notions of job values or motivation, (2) a product of discoveries made through work experiences, (3) only possible to identify after several years of work, (4) a result of interaction between abilities and values, and (5) a source of stability in the midst of continuing personal and occupational growth. Schein noted five anchors: autonomy, creativity, competence, security, and advancement. One anchor emerges as predominant for each individual, serving as a guiding force in career planning.

For Schein, individuals progress through predictable career stages within an organizational setting. As they are being socialized into the organizational culture, they undergo a series of tests by the organization. At the same time, they are also testing themselves. The results yield information of value in establishing career anchors.

Of what value is career planning theory? First, it helps individuals understand themselves. Second, it helps supervisors and HR planners understand how people think about career matters. With this information, individuals and managers are in a better position to plan accordingly.

The Traditional Approach to Career Management

From the standpoint of organizational decision-makers, career-management efforts serve several purposes. They (1) improve morale by giving employees information about opportunities available in the organization; (2) encourage employees to establish and work toward achieving career objectives; (3) motivate employees to seek out career-development opportunities, like training, education, and developmental job assignments; and (4) provide the organization with a means to trace relationships between jobs, and then identify candidates for recruitment to or advancement toward other jobs.

There is a very close relationship between organizational career management and HR planning. It is seen most clearly in the area of forecasting needed talent. Career management helps assess available supplies of internal talent and influences initiatives in other HR practice areas.

The Organizational Career-Management Process

Think of the organizational career-management process as one in which managers and HR planners:

1. Identify or describe common, historical career patterns in the organization.
2. Identify potential career patterns.
3. Establish formal and informal programs to help individuals achieve their career objectives while helping the organization develop talent for future needs.

Describing Career Paths

One starting point in any career-management program is to describe actual career paths in an organization. What *are* common entry points to job classes? How common is change from one job class to another? What kind of people are most likely to make these changes? Answers to these and related questions are immensely useful in planning career programs and initiatives in other HR practice areas.

Of course, most Americans still believe fervently in the Horatio Alger myth that a poor boy or girl, through sheer hard work and ambition, can rise from rags to riches. Recruitment and career-planning literature frequently builds on this myth, stressing opportunities available in an organization for those who perform well. To be sure, such success stories do exist. The trend toward policies favoring "promotion from within" adds to these expectations.

However, employees and managers are not always fully aware of career patterns common in their own organizations. Every organization is characterized by an identifiable pattern affecting career mobility. In some settings, they are highly evolved and are influenced by HR forecasts, selection methods, and career policy; in other cases, they are much less evolved.

One starting point for devising a coherent career policy, then, is to first identify entry points to the organization, job classes, divisions, departments, or work groups, and then to identify common career patterns recently (over the last 3 to 5 years) and over the long term (over the last 25 to 30 years) and causes of career imbalances (changes in organizational size, restructuring of jobs, labor market pressures, and inequalities/problems in age distribution, etc.). This process can be handled through quantitative methods by which employees are reduced to numbers in predefined categories or through qualitative methods like case studies in which stories about individuals are used to illustrate common career movements and possible causes for them.

To identify career patterns—perhaps the key step in the whole process—HR planners should:

1. Collect information on the actual work activities of incumbents in entry job "portals."
2. Assess what kinds of skills and knowledge have historically led to success in the entry job and contributed to promotion (or other movement).
3. Identify common movement patterns and causes of movement.
4. Verify by checking with employees and supervisors, predicting future movements, and assessing reliability of predictions.

Realistic career counseling for individuals begins with this information. At the same time, career-management programs sponsored by the organization can be based on actual experiences of people in the past.

Identifying Potential Career Patterns

The very nature of career management implies that there is more to a career program than merely describing past experiences. Decision-makers have a responsibility to chart desirable future career paths. There are at least three ways to go about this process: the traditional approach, the career path approach, and the lattice/network approach.

The *traditional approach* is probably most common. Employees and managers simply look at the chain of command in each organizational unit. Career progress is equated with upward mobility. People begin at the lowest level and work upward. This approach, however, is too restrictive for some.

A second way is called the *career path approach*. Every job in an organization is analyzed in detail for similarities in work methods and/or work results. The basic assumption is that jobs can be grouped around these underlying similarities. Individuals can move into altogether different job classes as long as similarities exist in activities or results.

Traditional work analysis is the basis for career paths. In fact, it involves little more than describing *what should happen* as people increase their job skills or gain seniority. They should be given increasing responsibility over time—unless, of course, they choose to forego that responsibility or they face real barriers to mobility.

A third way to establish relationships between jobs is called the *lattice approach*. Individuals are capable of moving into *any* other position over time. HR planners develop a matrix that describes what skills and what levels of skill proficiency are required to perform satisfactorily in every job. From this information, planners then develop a comprehensive directory to help individuals chart a course for career movement in almost any direction.

Establishing Career-Management Programs

On the basis of analysis of historical and potential career patterns, HR planners establish career-management programs and encourage informal activities that contribute to individual career development. Examples of such activities include mentoring, employee appraisal, career instruction workshops, and professional career counseling.

Mentoring can be organizationally sponsored or individually initiated. A mentor is an adviser. Research has demonstrated that successful executives were sponsored on the way up the ladder of success by at least one mentor, and sometimes several. They, in turn, serve others in the same capacity. A mentoring relationship is a mutually satisfying experience. The "sponsor" enjoys seeing his or her "charge" succeed much as teachers do when their pupils learn. At the same time, the "charge" gains much, too: protection from political forces, and useful information from someone who has the status to obtain it.

Formal mentoring programs are more rare than informal mentoring relationships that arise through the initiative of one seeking sponsorship. Yet formal programs do exist. One example is a *peer mentoring program* for newcomers. An experienced employee helps orient and socialize a new hire. Another example is a specialized type of *management-development program*. A senior executive guides a junior one, providing career advice of all kinds.

Employee appraisal, like mentoring, can be formal or informal. The purpose of appraisal is twofold: to evaluate how well individuals have been doing and to advise them about the future.

In one sense, supervisors are appraising people all the time. Feedback on daily activities is a form of appraisal, albeit informal. The feedback a supervisor gives a subordinate about daily task performance is an important element in shaping behavior and, indeed, in helping to coach employees for future performance.

In a more formal way, the annual performance review is a good opportunity for supervisor and subordinate to discuss the future. It is a chance for the supervisor to describe existing career paths in the company and provide detailed advice to an employee about how to pursue promotion and increased responsibility. If career paths in the firm are blocked or constrained by sluggish organizational performance or other problems, the supervisor also has the responsibility to alert the employee to opportunities existing outside the firm.

At the same time, the appraisal interview is also a chance for the subordinate to clarify his or her career aspirations and acquire information about opportunities consistent with them.

Though appraisal interviews furnish the *chance* for developmental discussions, significant evidence exists to show that they are not used in this way. In fact, employees generally misperceive their own potential, and supervisors themselves are not much more informed. Indeed, supervisors sometimes avoid discussions about "potential" because they do not wish to raise expectations (they might actually want superior performers to remain where they are). Thus, employee appraisal is *a possible* tool to inform people about careers, but it is not always used.

Career instruction is another way to inform employees about career paths in the firm. Instruction is offered through (1) general self-study material; (2) organization-specific self-study material; (3) group workshops and training courses; and (4) organization-specific workshops and training courses (Rothwell and Sredl, 2000).

General self-study material can be (1) programmed or web-based instruction, (2) course materials in a book, (3) textbooks and articles on career management, or (4) videotape presentations. The format does not involve use of a "live" instructor: Employees simply read about the theory of career planning and management. No attempt is made to suggest how this information can be used in one organizational setting, nor to describe possible or desirable career paths. People are simply given material about careers; applying what they learn is up to them.

Organization-specific, self-study material is in the same kind of format—programmed instruction, videotapes, and looseleaf courses—but is, as the name implies, geared to career paths in *one* setting. Employees are given workbooks based on job analysis and career ladders or matrices. Going through this material and establishing career objectives and developmental action plans is left up to them, however. No promises are made; rather, employees are simply informed that individual preparation, evidenced through training and off-the-job education, is considered in promotions and other personnel decisions. It is not the sole criterion for these decisions, however.

Group workshops and training courses resemble their self-study counterparts. Employees are helped to explore their occupational interests and values, and to set their own career objectives in these settings. The focus is on career management and planning theory rather than on actual career matters in one organization.

Organization-specific workshops, like their self-study counterparts, are geared to career paths and opportunities in one organization. While approaches vary, they include:

1. *The pure workshop.* Course participants go through a career workbook in a small group, sharing and testing their ideas with the help of peers and a group facilitator.
2. *The lecture/discussion.* Course participants are told about career opportunities in the firm, work through tailor-made exercises on the subject, and ask career-related questions.
3. *The forum.* Four or five supervisors participate in a panel discussion about career opportunities in the firm and respond to questions from the audience.

A course can be the starting point for a full-scale organization development intervention intended to create a climate that is open to career-related discussions. After all, a course will tend to evoke interest in the subject. Supervisors at all levels will suddenly find themselves faced with answering their subordinate's probing questions on career paths and career issues.

A professional career-counseling program is a fourth way that the organization's decision-makers can see to it that individuals receive career information. Relatively few organizations, however, employ full-time professional career counselors. More often than not, they are hired on a short-term basis. During widespread staff cutbacks and plant closings, professional counselors and outplacement programs can help employees find new jobs. Such efforts have met with some success.

Problems with Traditional Approaches to Career Planning and Management

Theories of career planning help describe individual decision-making and highlight issues of concern during each lifecycle stage. They do furnish a theoretical framework for counselors faced with facilitating individual career decisions and for individuals who need to do some soul searching. However, they do not provide concrete guidance to individuals. The focus of most career theory is on describing why people choose what they do, not on *how* to make good decisions.

Career-management programs sponsored by employers are usually geared to historical or past career patterns or those theoretically possible by virtue of similarities in present job activities or outcomes. Traditional programs make no attempt to predict how career patterns will probably change in the future or how jobs should change if they are to be consistent with strategic business plans. As a result, individual career development and planning is often based on out-dated information. Employees find themselves preparing for knowledge and skills needed only now, not at a future time. What is needed, then, is a more future-oriented approach to career planning and management.

Strategic Career Planning

Instead of devoting so much attention to explaining or describing why people decide on the careers they do, individuals and career counselors probably need to devote more attention to strategic career planning. Using this framework, individuals focus on such issues as:

1. Who am I? Where am I going?
2. What are my present personal strengths and weaknesses?
3. What conditions inside and outside the organization—as well as occupation—will create future opportunities or pose future threats for me in my occupation or job?

4. What choices for long-term career strategy are available to me?

5. Which choice is likely to do the best job of maximizing my present strengths and future opportunities while, at the same time, minimizing my present weaknesses and future threats?

6. How can my long-term career strategy be implemented? In particular, what skills will I need over time? What is the role of family and personal life in my career?

7. How can the relative success of my career strategy be evaluated? When should it be evaluated?

By considering these questions, individuals can establish long-term direction in their careers (Rothwell 1984).

Clarifying Individual Identity: Step 1

For an individual, a starting point for career planning is the process of clarifying individual identity: (1) Who am I? (2) What are my interests and values? and (3) What do I want to do? By considering these questions and reconsidering them at critical times, the individual develops an idealized self and gradually works toward realization of it.

The role of the career counselor is to help people by administering tests that provide feedback to them about their interests and skills. Many vocational tests are available. Tests help people clarify *career identity,* their sense of who they are now or who they can be occupationally.

Self-help books serve much the same purpose and are widely available.

Assessing Career Strengths and Weaknesses: Step 2

The second step in strategic career planning is assessment of strengths and weaknesses. A *strength* is any competitive advantage in the labor market, whether internal or external. The internal labor market is inside the organization or occupation; the external labor market is outside the organization or occupation. A *weakness* is any competitive disadvantage of the individual in the labor market.

Strengths include (1) education that is well-matched to the typical requirements of an occupation or job, (2) experience that is well-matched to requirements of an occupation or job, (3) personal characteristics and interests associated
with a job, (4) acquaintances in the occupation or acquaintances who have
friends in the occupation, (5) active sponsorship by someone in the occupation
or a specific firm, and/or (6) specialized training beyond formal education. In
short, whatever gives an individual a competitive edge in career matters is a
strength; whatever gives others the "edge" is an individual's weakness.

Of course, strengths and weaknesses are also *contextual,* arising from the
particular labor market in which one chooses to compete. For example, having
someone with a Ph.D. in electrical engineering is only a strength when the position is in electrical engineering or one closely allied to it, when the job requires
the expertise associated with a doctorate, and when that level of achievement
is relatively uncommon. The same amount of education can actually be a weakness if an individual tries to switch out of the field into another that is totally
unrelated (for example, teaching French literature) or when he/she seeks a job
that does not require a Ph.D. and is only one of many people holding the same
degree. While appropriate education is perhaps the single most important competitive strength, it is not as important as it once was.

The worksheet in Activity 10-1 at the end of the chapter can be used by individuals in assessing their relative career strengths and weaknesses at present.

Scanning the Environment: Step 3

Environmental scanning is the third step in strategic business planning. It is
the process of identifying conditions outside the organization that can affect
it. Typically, these conditions are beyond the direct control of strategists. The
best they can hope to do is take advantage of conditions or avoid threats created by them.

The basic concept of environmental scanning is applicable to career planning and management. However, individuals in any occupation face *four* related
environments: (1) the environment inside the organization and occupation, (2)
the environment inside the organization but outside the occupation, (3) the

environment outside the organization but inside the occupation, and (4) the environment outside the organization and occupation. Figure 10-1 depicts these environments.

What happens inside and outside organizations and occupations will exert considerable influence on job incumbents, creating career opportunities and threats. For any individual, however, several questions must be asked for purposes of career planning:

1. What changes will occur, over time, in the organizational environment? The occupational environment?
2. How will those changes affect the occupation inside the organization? The organization generally? The occupation outside the organization? The occupation generally?

As in organizational strategic planning, important factors to scan include (1) economic conditions, (2) technological conditions, (3) social conditions,

Figure 10-1: The Four Environments Faced by Individuals in Career Planning and Management

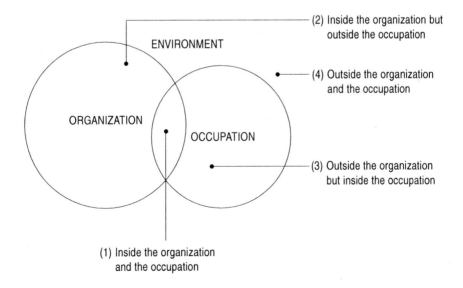

(4) geographical conditions, (5) governmental and legal conditions, (6) market conditions, and (7) supplier conditions. Each exerts influence on the organization and/or on an occupation and thereby creates career opportunities or threats for individuals.

A simple example will illustrate. An entry-level accountant in a relatively small domestic steel firm faces several opportunities and threats. The influence of economic conditions on a firm of this kind, which faces uphill competition against foreign manufacturers, will probably increase the value of the accountant's services within the firm, even though the firm might be struggling for survival. At the same time, other firms employing accountants might be willing to pay more, and other occupations within the firm might be more lucrative and attractive to this individual. Hence, this person faces numerous opportunities inside and outside the firm and occupation.

Of course, other factors—unique to one organizational setting—are also worth scanning. For example:

1. *Leadership:* What occupations seem to be most valued by the organization's leaders? Will the leadership change? What influence might such a change exert on opportunities within the firm?
2. *Structure:* To whom do members of an occupation report? Obviously, reporting relationships influence potential for advancement. A Ph.D. in engineering who reports to an M.B.A. might have to get a business degree to advance *within* the firm. Is a change in structure likely? What influence might such a change exert on requirements for advancement?
3. *Policy:* Do policies create demand for the services of an occupation? (Suppose nobody can be fired without review of the case by the industrial relations department. To the extent that firings are common, demand for members of this occupation—and their relative importance to the firm—will increase.) Is a change in policy likely? If so, who benefits?
4. *Reward Systems:* On what basis are people rewarded? Is it easier for some occupations to receive rewards than for others? If rewards are allocated on the basis of profitability, what problem does that pose

for staff groups viewed as "expense centers"? Is a change in reward systems likely?

By considering these issues, an individual can begin to identify opportunities and threats posed by each environment. Of course, there are always constraints on complete freedom of choice. Some individuals are forced to forego other opportunities because of their family situation, or persuaded by genuine dedication to a firm or absorbing interest in one occupation.

Use the worksheet in Activity 10-2 at the end of the chapter to brainstorm about likely threats and opportunities inside and outside the organization and occupation.

Identifying the Range of Career Strategies: Step 4

The fourth step in strategic business planning is to compare organizational strengths/weaknesses and external conditions, and generate alternative strategies. To put it another way, strategists consider this question: Given present organizational strengths and weaknesses and likely future conditions, what alternative action plans are possible?

The same basic concept is applicable to career management and planning, though with a few changes. Career strategies include:

1. *Growth* in the occupation or the organization, meaning simply doing more of what one has been doing.
2. *Retrenchment:* This translates to mean "cutting back to weather a storm of unfavorable conditions." It is rarely effective as a long-term career strategy, but might be useful in anticipation of retirement, during a search for another employer, or during preparation for entry to another occupation.
3. *Diversification:* Branch out to an utterly new and more promising occupation, job, or employer.
4. *Integration:* Make a move to a related occupation, job, or employer.
5. *Turnabout:* Retrench and select another strategy.

6. *Combination:* Pursue one strategy in a present job or occupation while simultaneously pursuing a second strategy by preparing for a completely new job or occupation.

See Figure 10-2 for a more complete summary of each career strategy in the context of four different environments.

Generally speaking, two ways exist to generate alternative career strategies. Individuals can

1. *Build from strengths.* How can the most benefit be derived by an individual from his or her occupational or personal strengths, given expected conditions?
2. *Build from opportunities.* How can the individual take advantage of future changes that are likely? Brainstorming is one place to start. The individual describes what he or she will do to implement each long-term career strategy. (See the worksheet in Activity 10-3 at the end of this chapter.) The individual then tries to assess how successful the strategy is likely to work out.

Selecting a Long-Term Career Strategy: Step 5

The fifth step in strategic business planning is to select a long-term Grand Strategy to govern initiatives of an entire corporation. This Grand Strategy commands the highest priority and is the basis for coordinating autonomous or semiautonomous businesses. Though selection is intended to maximize advantages and minimize disadvantages of a firm in competition with others, actual choice of *how* to do so is heavily influenced by (1) what strategists value, (2) power struggles inside and outside the organization, (3) past strategies, (4) time pressures, and (5) the relative changeableness of the external environment.

The same basic concepts can be applied to career management and planning. Individuals consider career strategy in light of

1. Their own values and preferences.
2. Values and preferences of such "significant others" as peers, family, and mentors.

Figure 10-2: A Summary of Career Strategies as They Relate to Different Environments

Career Strategy	Inside Organization and Occupation	Inside Organization but Outside Occupation	Outside Organization but Inside Occupation	Outside Organization and Occupation
Growth	▪ Build present skills ▪ Build expertise in the occupation ▪ Prepare for more responsibility ▪ Learn to supervise others	▪ Enter new occupation ▪ Build skills in a new occupation	▪ Move to a different organization but in same job	▪ Build existing skills/ knowledge for use in unrelated occupation and different type of organization
Retrenchment	▪ Move to a lower level job in the same occupation and in the same organization	▪ Move into a lower level job in a different occupation in the same organization	▪ Move into a lower level job in a different organization	▪ Cut back on work ▪ Seek satisfaction through avocations and hobbies ▪ Prepare for new occupation
Diversification	▪ Branch out into a more promising area within one's present occupation (increase emphasis on a new area of work)	▪ Branch out into a more promising line of work in the organization (one with major differences from past occupation)	▪ Make a move into an organization with more promise, but remain in the same occupation	▪ Branch out into a more promising occupation in an organization with more promising long-term prospects than present employer

Figure 10-2: *(continued)*

Career Strategy	Inside Organization and Occupation	Inside Organization but Outside Occupation	Outside Organization but Inside Occupation	Outside Organization and Occupation
Integration	▪ Branch out into a more promising area within one's present job (but an area of work like what has been done in the past)	▪ Branch out into a related line of work in the same organization	▪ Make a move into a new organization that is related to the present employer (supplier, distributor, wholesaler, retailer)	▪ Branch out into a related occupation in an organization somehow related (supplier, distributor, wholesaler, retailer) to present employer
Turnabout	▪ Retrench (slow down on activities/outputs) ▪ Follow retrenchment with a new strategy: growth, diversification, integration, or combination	▪ Retrench (move out of organization) ▪ Use a new strategy: growth, diversification, integration, or combination	▪ Retrench (move out of occupation) ▪ Use a new strategy: growth, diversification, integration, or combination	▪ Build new skills (perhaps return to school) for entry into an entirely new line of work. Grow in the new occupation.
Combination	▪ Apply two or more strategies at once: one to organizational status, another to occupational status	▪ Apply two or more strategies at once	▪ Apply two or more strategies at once	▪ Apply two or more strategies at once

3. Past career strategies and choices (for example, education, experience acquired).
4. Time pressures involved in making choices.
5. Relative predictability of expected opportunities and threats posed by change.

Each individual has to make these determinations for himself or herself.

Implementing Career Strategy: Step 6

The sixth step in strategic business planning is implementation, the translation of a broad long-term plan into specific action steps. If there is a single area of major importance in planning, it is this one: Without successful implementation, no plan will *ever* be effective. Unfortunately, implementation is often the weakest link in the strategy-making process.

Organizational planners typically view the following steps of extreme importance during implementation: (1) establishing objectives to guide and coordinate parts of the organization in line with the strategy that has been chosen; (2) reviewing existing policies—and creating new ones—as needed; (3) selecting leaders at every level whose abilities, skills, and attitudes match the strategy; (4) rewarding employee and management performance in line with strategy; and (5) examining organizational structure to make sure that it is adequate to sustain implementation of strategy.

Individuals can apply the same basic ideas to their own career-planning efforts. For example, they can (1) establish career objectives to measure their achievements over time, (2) consider personal policies about dealings with others, (3) cultivate skills and knowledge or seek education and training in line with their aspirations, (4) reward themselves for noteworthy personal achievement, and (5) re-examine the time allocation to tasks in their jobs, occupations, and personal life. While the ability to change is not always easy, it makes as much sense to believe that career strategy can be a driving force in the life of an ambitious individual as strategy can be for an organization.

The worksheet provided in Activity 10-4 at the end of the chapter is a starting point for considering implementation of career strategy.

Evaluating Career Strategy

The final step in strategic business planning is evaluation, the process of considering how well results match objectives. It takes place at three points: after an "experiment" or a test, periodically, and after a long period.

Evaluation is as applicable to career planning and management as it is to business planning. Individuals can:

1. Try out a new job, a new occupation, or a new employer on a trial basis. This constitutes a risk—especially if one is unsuccessful—but it is less risky than to completely "leap" into a new environment, job, or occupation. Sometimes testing is simply not possible, but internships can serve the same purpose.

2. Assess progress on career objectives at periodic intervals. Is the salary measuring up to what was desired? Is professional or occupational growth adequate?

3. Examine one's entire career and preparation for it. Is there anything the individual would do differently? If so, why? What lessons, learned in the past, can be used to advantage in the future? What lessons can be passed on to younger people?

Evaluation is a monitoring device and a means to recognize the need for a change in career strategy. Like evaluation of business plans, it is only useful when individuals *want* to evaluate their career strategy and are willing *to act* on deficiencies they find.

There are, of course, many yardsticks for measuring how well career plans have worked. They include: (1) *consistency with values and interests* (How well has the career strategy been attuned to the individual's needs, interests, and values?) (2) *consistency with organizational demands* (How well has the career strategy helped the individual realize his or her potential in the organization?)

(3) *consistency with occupational demands* (How well has the career strategy helped the individual realize his or her potential in the occupation?) (4) *consistency with environmental demands* (How well has the career strategy helped the individual to seize opportunities presented by the environment? Avoid problems or threats posed by the environment?) (5) *appropriateness, given the resources available* (To what extent has the career strategy been appropriate, given the time that is available to the individual? The money available to the individual?) (6) *acceptability of risk* (To what extent has the career strategy fit preferences of significant others, including peers? Family members? Mentors?) (7) *appropriateness of time horizon* (How well has the career strategy matched up to individual goals over time?) and (8) *workability* (How well has the career strategy satisfied individual career objectives?) These questions can never be answered with complete certainty, since successful career strategy is not within the total control of an individual. These questions can, however, help identify the need for further planning and future *acting* on career issues.

Use Activity 10-5 at the end of the chapter as a starting point for evaluating career planning.

Strategic Career Management

There are three steps involved in strategic career management: (1) identify likely career patterns in the organization's future, (2) identify desired career patterns, and (3) establish formal and informal programs to help individuals achieve their career objectives while helping the organization develop talent for future needs. These steps are not different from those in more traditional approaches; rather, the emphasis is shifted from a past or present to a future orientation. Of course, individuals must also accept increasing responsibility for their careers, since organizational decision-makers can no longer guarantee stability at a time when downsizing, mergers, acquisitions, takeovers, and other workplace changes alter the business landscape at an increasing pace (Altman, 1998).

Identifying Likely Career Patterns

The results of future-oriented work analysis can be aggregated in order to make some predictions about how relationships between jobs will probably change as a result of conditions inside and outside the organization.

One place to begin this process is with a prediction about what factor is likely to emerge as *most crucial* to organizational survival and success. During inflationary periods in the economy, the finance/accounting function emerges as one such factor. During times of social upheaval and changing consumer preferences, the marketing/competitive function emerges as a key factor. When rapid adaptation to technological change in service delivery or product manufacture spells the difference between organizational survival and extinction, production/operations emerges as a key.

Typically, choice of a chief executive depends heavily on this key factor. Indeed, the CEO's background provides important clues about what factors are considered most important. External pressures—like those exerted by inflationary economic conditions or rapid technological change—will prompt choice of a leader who can deal with the major problem confronting the organization. Naturally, CEOs tend to value what they know about. As a consequence, the functions that receive attention from the CEO are most often those that command visibility and obtain resources.

Hence, the CEO's background is likely to provide some important indications about the direction of career patterns in the firm. There is no empirical support for this theory, and predicting crucial factors is fraught with uncertainty, but it is one way to try to predict how career patterns are likely to shift over time.

Another way is to form a standing committee of people from different levels, occupations, and locations in the firm. Serving much like a "focus group" for marketing purposes, committee members participate in Delphi panels and nominal group technique meetings for purposes of forecasting directions in career patterns. The results are, in turn, fed into other HR practice areas for planning initiatives.

Identifying Desired Career Patterns

It is not enough to predict where career patterns are *probably* headed; rather, managers also need to identify where they *should be* headed in view of organizational Grand Strategy.

One way to identify desired career patterns is to use the organization's strategic plan as a starting point to revise job descriptions from a past or present emphasis to one that clarifies what people should be doing in the future if their work is to be consistent with business strategy. Strategic job descriptions are then translated into "person descriptions" that specify knowledge, skills, and attitudes that individuals will need to carry out duties outlined on job descriptions. Finally, these descriptions are then applied to the traditional career-ladder or lattice/network approaches to create new, more desirable relationships between jobs. The result of this process represents what is desirable over time, not necessarily what exists at present or is expected. To bring about such career relationships, managers have to establish incentives and programs to encourage individuals to prepare accordingly.

Establishing Programs

As in traditional career-management efforts sponsored by an organization, a strategic effort can make use of mentoring, employee appraisals, career workshops, and professional career counseling. Rarely is one sufficient. More typically, two or more should be used to supplement each other.

Though mentors serve many functions, they can advise their youthful charges on how to prepare for the future. In this sense, they help individuals acquire skills in anticipation of the time when they are needed.

Employee appraisals can be reoriented to the future such that individuals are counseled during performance reviews more on what they should prepare to do than on what they have done. However, appraisals rarely provide sufficient or detailed enough information for good career planning. They should therefore be paired with other efforts.

Career workshops designed for individual or for group presentation can be geared either to (1) introduce people to general career planning in line with the strategic model or (2) guide people in establishing plans based on information made available about likely or desired future career patterns in the organization. A simple outline of the first kind of workshop is illustrated in Figure 10-3.

Finally, professional career-planning counselors can (1) help individuals clarify identity, identify trends, and assess strengths and weaknesses and (2) teach supervisors how to serve as mentors and how to function as career counselors themselves.

Figure 10-3: A Sample Outline for a Career-Planning Workshop

I.   Introduction
   a. Course Purpose
   b. Course Objectives

II.   Individual Values and Interests
   a. Nature of Values and Interests
   b. Importance of Values and Interests in Career Planning
   c. Assessing Individual Values and Interests

III.   Individual Strengths and Weaknesses
   a. Defining Strengths and Weaknesses
   b. Importance of Advice from Others

IV.   Scanning the Environment
   a. What is the Career "Environment"?
   b. How is the Environment "Scanned"?
   c. Why "Scan"?
   d. Exercise

V.   Identifying and Choosing Career Strategies
   a. What is a Career Strategy?
   b. Why Set Strategy?
   c. How is Strategy Selected?

VI.   Implementing Career Strategy
   a. Establishing an Action Plan
   b. Coordinating Efforts

VII.   Conclusion: Where Do I Go from Here?

Strategic career management efforts are likely to become increasingly necessary as decision-makers think through, in long-range terms, what skills, knowledge, and attitudes will probably be needed in the future in order to achieve long-term objectives and implement strategic business plans in a successful way. At the same time, individuals will find that the pervasiveness and rapidity of change—regardless of occupation or organizational affiliation—will necessitate their own strategic career planning.

Activity 10-1: A Worksheet for Assessing Career Strengths and Weaknesses

Directions: Use this worksheet to do some brainstorming about your career strengths and weaknesses. In column 1, list position tasks of a job you seek in 3–5 years. (It can be the next higher job in your organization *or* one you create.) In column 2, convert each task from column 1 into what you have to be able to know or do to perform the task. In column 3, rate how well prepared you are at present in each skill area in column 2. A rating of 1 or 2 is a career weakness; a rating of 4 or 5 is a strength. If possible, ask another person to give you advice on your strengths and weaknesses after you complete this worksheet.

Column 1	Column 2	Column 3						
		To what extent does the individual's present qualities match skills required?						
Position tasks	Skills required	Education	Experience	Personal characteristics	Acquaintances	Sponsors	Training	
		very little ... very much	very little ... very much	very little ... very much	very little ... very much	very little ... very much	very little ... very much	
		1 2 3 4 5	1 2 3 4 5	1 2 3 4 5	1 2 3 4 5	1 2 3 4 5	1 2 3 4 5	
		1 2 3 4 5						
		1 2 3 4 5						
		1 2 3 4 5						
		1 2 3 4 5						
		1 2 3 4 5						
		1 2 3 4 5						
		1 2 3 4 5						
		1 2 3 4 5						

Activity 10-2: A Worksheet for Scanning the Career Environment

Directions: Use this worksheet to begin the process of scanning environments pertinent to your career. (Choose whatever time horizon you wish.) Answer the first question by moving across the rows below. One is designated "the organizational environment"; the other, "the occupational environment." Under each column, describe *what* change you believe will probably occur as a result of a major change in each category.

For instance, the job of training director will probably be influenced most, in terms of the organizational environment and technology—by the widespread introduction of computers in the workplace. List that under "technological conditions." At the same time, the introduction of computer-based and computer-managed instruction will probably affect the *occupation* heavily. Then answer the second question by describing (briefly) *how* the change will probably affect you.

1. What change will probably occur, over time, in the...

As a result of changes in:

	Economic conditions	Technological conditions	Social conditions	Geographical conditions	Government/ legal conditions	Market conditions	Supplier conditions	Organizational leadership	Organizational structure	Organizational policy	Organizational rewards
Organizational environment											
Occupational environment											

2. How will changes probably affect . . . ?

	Economic conditions	Technological conditions	Social conditions	Geographical conditions	Government/ legal conditions	Market conditions	Supplier conditions	Organizational leadership	Organizational structure	Organizational policy	Organizational rewards
Occupation inside the organization											
Organization (generally)											
Occupation outside the organization											
Occupation (generally)											

Activity 10-3: A Worksheet for Identifying the Range of Career Strategies

Directions: Use this worksheet to do some brainstorming about *possible* career strategies available to you (over a time horizon of your choice). Working from your present situation, identify what each possible career strategy means for *you*. (Refer to Figure 10-2 to get a *general* idea of each choice, and then restate it in terms directly related to you. For instance, growth in column 2 means seeking promotion into the next higher job in your present occupation and with your present employer.)

Column 1	Column 2	Column 3	Column 4	Column 5
Career strategy	*Inside organization and occupation*	*Inside organization but outside occupation*	*Outside organization but inside occupation*	*Outside organization and occupation*
Growth				
Retrenchment				
Diversification				
Integration				
Turnabout				
Combination				

Activity 10-4: A Worksheet for Implementing an Individual Career Strategy

Directions: Use this worksheet to begin the process of establishing action plans to implement your individual career strategy. In column 1, set forth career objectives first. (Start with long-term objectives.) Begin by making the objectives *measurable,* addressing these questions: *What* is to be done? *By when? How well?* Then move across the sheet from column 1 and, in each column, consider personal policies, skills, rewards, and time allocations (or real-locations) required to achieve the objective.

Column 1	*Column 2*	*Column 3*	*Column 4*	*Column 5*
What objectives can the individual establish for implementing career strategy . . . ?	*What personal policies for dealing with others need to be reviewed, modified, or created . . . ?*	*What knowledge and skills are needed to realize career objectives . . . ?*	*What rewards for achievement will the individual establish . . . ?*	*What structure (that is, allocation of time) should the individual consider . . .?*
Long Term (3–5 years)				
Intermediate Term (1–3 years)				
Short Term (up to 1 year)				

Activity 10-5: A Checklist for Evaluating a Career Strategy

Directions: Use this checklist to do some soul-searching. (There are no right or wrong answers.) For each question in the left column below, *circle* a corresponding number in the right column. Use the results of this exercise to decide whether you need to reassess—and perhaps change—your career strategy.

To what extent has my career strategy	Very much			Neutral			Very little
1. Been in tune with my individual							
a. Needs?	7	6	5	4	3	2	1
b. Interests?	7	6	5	4	3	2	1
c. Values?	7	6	5	4	3	2	1
2. Been in line with my potential in an organizational setting?	7	6	5	4	3	2	1
3. Been in line with my potential in my occupation?	7	6	5	4	3	2	1
4. Been successful in							
a. Helping me seize opportunities posed by the external environment?	7	6	5	4	3	2	1
b. Helping me avoid problems posed by the external environment?	7	6	5	4	3	2	1
5. Been appropriate for me, given							
a. Time available?	7	6	5	4	3	2	1
b. Money available?	7	6	5	4	3	2	1
6. Fit the preferences of significant others, including							
a. Peers?	7	6	5	4	3	2	1
b. Family members?	7	6	5	4	3	2	1
c. Mentors?	7	6	5	4	3	2	1
7. Included time goals?	7	6	5	4	3	2	1
8. Satisfied my career objectives?	7	6	5	4	3	2	1

CHAPTER 11

RECRUITMENT AND SELECTION

What is the role of Recruitment and Selection in implementing HR Grand Strategy? What is the traditional approach to Recruitment and Selection? What are some problems with the traditional approach? How can Recruitment and Selection be addressed strategically? This chapter, the second to focus on a single HR practice area, answers these questions. In doing so, it begins to show how Recruitment and Selection can be integrated with HR Grand Strategy.

The Role of Recruitment and Selection in Implementing HR Grand Strategy

Organizational strategy implies the need for particular kinds of work to be done and particular kinds of people to do it. Human Resources (HR) Grand Strategy specifies what kinds and how many people are needed to realize organizational strategy. One way to acquire that talent is by searching outside the organization or outside the unit in which the work is to be done. *Recruitment* consists of activities intended to identify sources of talent to meet organizational needs, and then to attract the right numbers and types of people for the right jobs at the right time and in the right places. *Selection* is the process of searching for and then identifying an appropriate match between the individual, the job, the work group, and organization. Recruitment and Selection are thus separate but related efforts.

Consider for a moment the influence of Recruitment and Selection on other HR practice areas. The kind of people who are recruited and selected will determine training and other programs. (1) Their knowledge, skills, and abilities upon entry will influence how much training they need. (2) Their self-concept and career objectives will influence what career planning and management programs are appropriate. (3) Their attitudes and interpersonal skills will influence what organizational development efforts need to be made in order to improve work-group relations. (4) Their individual values and abilities will influence job design (the reason is that people will try to personalize their jobs, reshaping work requirements to fit their skills and perhaps even their interests). (5) Their individual abilities to deal with job-induced stress and personal problems can affect their need for the Employee Assistance Program. (6) Their perceptions about labor unions can influence potential for unionization. (7) Their individual desires and expectations can influence appropriate compensation needed to reward, retain, and motivate them.

Recruitment has become the focus of widespread attention in recent years. With record low levels of unemployment and record high levels of turnover (averaging 14% nationally in 2000), some organizations and some regions have had to become innovative in their approaches to attracting and retaining talent (Harrington, 2000).

When the organization's corporate and HR Grand Strategy calls for growth, recruitment is a major tool for obtaining increasing numbers of appropriately qualified people in a relatively short time. *Decruitment*—that is, *outplacement*—is sometimes used when HR Grand Strategy calls for retrenchment or turnabout. Recruitment of different kinds of people might be the most important issue when the organization plans to move into new and potentially more profitable businesses or seeks closer associations with suppliers, competitors, or distributors. The reason is that new talents will be needed to manage new businesses or deal with concerns of suppliers and other organizations.

The Traditional Approach to Recruitment and Selection

The Recruitment/Selection Process

Think of the Recruitment and Selection process as one in which:

1. Sources of appropriate talent are identified.
2. Continuous recruitment efforts are established for critically needed talents.
3. Specific requirements are established for vacancies as they come open.
4. Individuals are recruited for vacancies as they occur.
5. Individuals are initially screened.
6. Employment tests are used to assess relative strengths and weaknesses of job applicants.
7. Interviews are conducted with promising candidates.
8. A background-check of a promising applicant is carried out.
9. An offer is extended to a promising applicant.
10. Orientation and placement begins.

These steps are illustrated in Figure 11-1.

Identifying Sources of Appropriate Talent

There are two chief sources of talent: talent that is external to the organization, and talent that is internal to the organization but external to the job or work group. The first is called the *external labor market*; the second is called the *internal labor market*.

The difference between internal and external sources is similar to a *make-or-buy decision in purchasing*. The decision-maker must first answer this question: Should we buy what we need from outside, or make it inside?

The same question applies to recruitment: Should we look for needed skills from outside the organization, or locate skilled people and perhaps nurture them over time from within?

Figure 11-1: The Recruitment/Selection Process

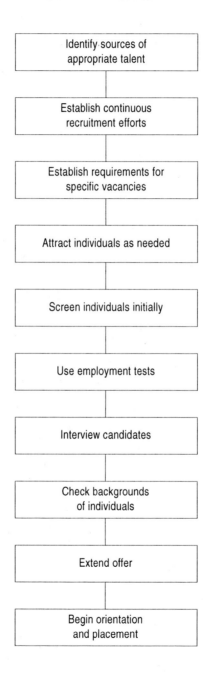

Generally, recruitment is not—as some managers tend to think of it—a one-shot effort undertaken only when vacancies exist. It takes time to locate and establish ties with external sources. For some specialties—nuclear physics, for instance—only a few sources for recruitment exist at all.

External sources of talent include: colleges and universities; professional societies; labor unions; federal and state employment agencies; government-sponsored training programs; private employment agencies; competitors; referrals from employees; people who walk in the employer's personnel office without an appointment; people who answer advertisements by the employer; and referrals to managers from acquaintances. Of course, some sources are likely to be more appropriate than others in specific cases. In recent years, the Internet and World Wide Web have proven to be an important and growing source for recruitment: At present, there are some 1 million résumés and 1.2 million job listings online. Some 5,800 firms conduct recruiting online, and there are presently 3,512 recruiting sites. Annual increases in web-based recruitment are expected to average 150 percent (*Staffing Industry Report,* 1997).

Internal sources of talent can be identified through comprehensive HR inventories for matching people and jobs: seniority systems, job postings, and referrals by employees or supervisors.

Establishing Continuous Recruitment Efforts

As we noted earlier, HR managers are often tempted to put off recruitment until the organization has immediate vacancies that need to be filled. Crisis-oriented recruitment like this is unwise.

A professionally operated recruitment program functions year round, both at times when people are not needed and times when massive hiring is anticipated.

Why go to this trouble? There are several advantages to continuous recruitment: (1) The organization will be more likely to remain on the mailing lists of appropriate groups, such as college placement offices, employment agencies, and professional organizations. (2) It will know which people to deal with at placement firms and college offices. (3) It will be easier to obtain hard-to-come-by space at recruitment fairs, college placement offices, and other locations.

(4) It will be able to more effectively influence the design of college programs and other sources of critically needed talent so that "raw material" (people) more closely approximate specific organizational needs. In short, there are major advantages to keeping the company's image in front of people who come in contact with individuals possessing skills that might be needed by the organization.

There are other advantages to continuous recruitment. First, the organization's recruiters can see to it that information about the firm is available at frequently visited locations. For example, placement files containing recruitment literature, job descriptions, and other data about the firm, such as annual reports and videotapes about company occupations, can be established at local universities. Second, by keeping company HR needs in view of the public, the recruiter can create a large applicant pool from which to gather likely candidates as vacancies occur.

Of course, continuous recruitment should be directed inside as well as outside an organization.

One way is by doing a comprehensive HR inventory. Every job in the organization is reduced to its essential requirements: education, experience, and even tasks or work outcomes. Each employee is described in similar terms: education and experience possessed, task capabilities, and career objectives. When an opening occurs, the two data sets (one of jobs; one of people) are compared in order to identify prospective in-house recruits. Walker (1980) describes the same approach in more detail. A second way is through a seniority system. Whenever a job is vacant, those people at the next-lower job level are scrutinized. Unless there are good reasons to select some other candidate, the person with the longest job tenure is given the promotion.

Job posting is a third way to recruit in-house. The aim is to increase employee awareness about specific job openings. Historically, posting has been limited to lower-level jobs, but the trend is to post even for professional jobs. Notices of job openings are advertised on company bulletin boards, in company newsletters, and through special handouts displayed in cafeterias, next to restrooms, and in other prominent locations. It is up to employees to apply for openings in much the same way as external applicants.

Referrals by employees and supervisors is a fourth way to recruit. One advantage of referral is that the applicant already has support from someone inside the organization: Someone who has a stake in the applicant's subsequent job success. Unfortunately, the disadvantage of referral is that applicants tend to resemble those already employed in the organization and might pose problems regarding equal employment opportunity/affirmative action (EEO/AA) goals when the labor force is already predominantly, say, white and male.

Establishing Specific Requirements

Two positions that share the same job description and specification are rarely identical. The secretary to the company president and the secretary to the training director might share the same job title, but they are likely only to be equivalent —not the same.

This is why you need to identify which tasks are to be performed in a position and how much time it takes to do them. With this information, recruiters will be able to identify candidates with skills demanded by the opening. One way to handle this process is to ask the supervisor to describe the exact nature of duties critical to successful performance in the position. Another way is to ask the same question of the departing job incumbent. A detailed position analysis is performed upon the departure of an incumbent to identify (1) specific tasks that he or she performs, (2) how much time is devoted to them, (3) how critical the tasks are to successful performance, and (4) how long it will take for a person possessing necessary background skills to learn them. Position analysis is probably most critical for professional and managerial jobs in which there is broad latitude for action, but it is also important to do one when you are recruiting people for secretarial or even production jobs.

Attracting Individuals

Organizations use many different methods to attract applicants. Executives frequently perceive some methods to be more successful than others: newspaper advertising, walk-ins, employee referrals, private employment agencies, and search firms.

Probably the most common tactic in attracting individuals is the "sell" approach. The basic idea is to:

I   Stress only the positive features of the organization or job.
I   Distort other features to make the job or organization appear even more appealing.
I   Conceal negative features of the organization or job.

The traditional philosophy is based on a desire to obtain a favorable selection ratio, because it leads to large applicant pools requiring much processing, which in turn makes the HR department look like it is performing effectively.

There are other reasons as well. Decision-makers focus on matching applicant abilities to job requirements, rather than individual needs to organizational culture and climate. They stress job performance over individual satisfaction, and hope to maintain greater control over who enters the organization, thereby reducing the risk of making poor selection decisions.

A more realistic approach is to accurately describe the organization, work group, and job, positively as well as negatively. Recruitment will then be a more cost-effective job because people will not have unrealistic expectations of the company or the demands of the position. They will also simply fit in better. A note of caution: It would not be wise to strictly control entry, in view of government policy mandating equal employment opportunity and Affirmative Action.

We must emphasize, however, that the process of attracting applicants is constrained by the organization's perceived business and public image. People tend to apply to firms that are consistent with their own self-concept. For example, the Central Intelligence Agency might need HR experts or accountants as much as any other organization, but people with those skills will probably be more difficult to recruit unless they also see themselves as "spies." Hence, public image can sometimes stymie or complicate recruitment efforts.

Of course, applicants attracted from within an organization might not face these problems, or at least face them to the same degree as outsiders. Internal applicants probably have some idea about the nature of a job before they apply.

They will be familiar with the organization's corporate culture, if not the unique *microculture* within a specific work group. Unfortunately, these qualities that make for low social friction during job orientation might not be appropriate when there is need to change work methods dramatically. Someone from the outside might be a better choice for the fresh insights and skills he or she can bring to bear on work issues.

Screening Individuals

Once applicants are attracted to apply, they must follow a series of screening steps intended to narrow the field of available candidates. The most common approach to screening is the *multiple hurdles process*. It takes its name from the numerous hurdles erected to "winnow the wheat from the chaff." An alternative method is the "compensatory process," in which applicant's strengths in some areas are seen as a way to counterbalance weaknesses in other areas.

Screening usually begins with the written application form. Job applicants complete a written or online form that asks for information about themselves. The simplest forms are a page or two in length and ask for data about prior employment, education, specialized licenses, and proficiency in foreign languages. Forms are useful for structuring information and obtaining facts that might not be included on a résumé.

The *Biographical Information Blank* is a specialized application, typically containing both hard or factual and soft or attitudinal questions. Measures of job success, previously identified, are compared to answers on the application. A high score indicates a greater likelihood of subsequent job success.

The *Weighted Application Blank* is somewhat similar. Job incumbents in the organization are divided into categories based on performance. The characteristics of people in each category are then analyzed to identify commonalities. When a job applicant completes the form, his or her characteristics are compared to those of job incumbents. Applicants with higher scores are admitted to subsequent stages of the selection process; those who score much less are sent polite letters in which they are told that other people are more suited for the vacancy.

In lower-skill jobs, a "knock-out" interview precedes the ritual of filling out an application. Job applicants are asked two or three key questions and are only encouraged to complete an application if their answers are acceptable.

Using Employment Tests

One of the most traditionally controversial issues in the HR field is the use of employment tests. They are controversial because a substantial—even over-whelming—body of case law and governmental regulation governs their use. Most notable among these is the *Uniform Guidelines on Employee Selection Procedures.* However, some authorities believe that only 5 percent of job inter-viewers do well in pinpointing the best applicants, compared to a higher per-centage identified through testing (Solomon, 1997; also see, for instance, *http://www.uniformguidelines.com/uniformguidelines.html* or *http://www.dot.gov/ ost/docr/ 29CFR54.HTM*).

There are four kinds of employment tests: physical, ability, personality, and skill and achievement. *Physical tests* focus on the applicant's health and phys-iological status; *ability tests* focus on the applicant's general intelligence and verbal, mathematical, and performance abilities; *personality tests* focus on self-descriptions; and *skill and achievement tests* focus on job samples or multiple-choice tests about the work.

Physical tests have emerged as one of the most controversial of all pre-employ-ment tests. Early ones were little more than physical exams, carried out to ensure that the employer would not subsequently be held legally liable for a new employee's pre-existing illnesses. Today they are that, and more. A national epi-demic of drug use has prompted employers to undertake widespread drug test-ing. Advanced medical technology can even be used to determine whether an individual is genetically prone to illness, perhaps sensitive to specific chemicals or other hazards in the workplace. Finally, employer fears of theft as well as fears of inflated or bogus credentials have prompted use of so-called *honesty tests*.

Ability tests measure intelligence in its various forms. They have been shown to be useful predictors of success during the initial training period, but can be misleading and ineffective when it comes to predicting future job performance.

Common examples of such tests include the Wechsler Adult Intelligence Scale and the General Aptitude Test Battery.

Personality tests are very controversial. They measure descriptions of self and use this information to draw conclusions about the applicant or compare the applicant to other groups about whom a pool of data exists (usually job incumbents). Examples include the Thematic Apperception Test (TAT), consisting of ambiguous pictures and various sentence-completion tests. Skilled psychologists are usually needed for the crucial task of interpreting test results. Some employers administer the Myers-Briggs Type Inventory (MBTI) or some alternative personality measure assessment comparable to it as a form of pre-employment test in order to assess how well an individual might fit into an existing work group.

Skill and achievement tests are less controversial, and if they are designed properly, job applicants will most likely think they are fair. They are usually based on the job's tasks or on exercises related to such tasks. For example, an applicant for training director might be asked to supply samples of lesson plans prepared for training courses he or she has previously delivered, or else asked to prepare such a plan from information supplied by the prospective employer. Assessment centers, described in Chapter 10 as tools for employee performance appraisal, use management games and/or exercises requiring applicants to demonstrate skills associated with the job an individual has applied for.

Conducting Interviews

Once an applicant has received a passing score on an employment test, he or she is usually asked to take part in a series of interviews. The selection interview remains the single most popular tool for making staffing decisions, even though frequent and serious questions have been raised about its validity and reliability. Of course, validity refers to the *appropriateness* of a given measurement technique; reliability refers to its *consistency over time.*

There are two kinds of selection interviews, just as there are two kinds of research interviews: structured and unstructured. Structured employment interviews rely on a list of predetermined questions, posed to all candidates in precisely the same way. The unstructured employment interview is much more freewheeling, based on interviewer preferences and on specific matters pertaining to the applicant's qualifications.

The interview, often the single most important step in the selection process, can be conducted by any of these people:

I   An HR representative
I   The person to whom the job incumbent will report
I   The supervisor to whom the job incumbent will report
I   Peers of the prospective incumbent
I   Subordinates of the prospective incumbent
I   A committee consisting of any or all of the above

Generally, research suggests that the structured interview has greater interrater reliability than the unstructured, and that the group interview is more valid and reliable than an interview conducted by an individual.

Under the *Uniform Guidelines for Employee Selection Procedures,* the federal document governing employment testing, the employment interview is considered a selection test. It is thus subject to all requirements with which more formal tests must comply. Research does suggest that the interview is subject to bias in that people who resemble the interviewer are more likely to be viewed favorably. Decisions about the acceptability of applicants are made rapidly, often in the first three or four minutes (Webster, 1964 and 1982).

Checking Applicant Background

Most firms take some step, following the interview, to verify education, experience, and other qualifications claimed by applicants. This precaution is critical: Some applicants, perhaps as much as 25 percent of them, inflate their credentials in some way. Popular areas of exaggeration include previous salary, work duties, and college degrees.

Numerous well-publicized cases of impostors heighten employer interest in verifying credentials. In one well-publicized case, an employee of a highly respected U.S. newspaper was awarded a Pulitzer Prize in journalism. It was later discovered that she not only did not earn the college degree she claimed to have, but even worse, the "actual case" she wrote about in her award-winning journalistic exposé was made up. Other examples exist: the college professors who claim numerous degrees from schools they never attended, the medical doctors who perform surgery with no medical degree or training, etc.

While it is relatively easy to verify facts about credentials such as academic degrees, it is not so easy to verify an applicant's previous work duties. Many firms verify information by phone, though some are reluctant to do so in light of employee privacy laws and concerns over the handling of information they collect. Another way to verify applicant background is by letter, though some former employers will not respond or will do so only in a very guarded fashion. In checking background, a prospective employer is likely to receive the most useful and accurate information from the applicant's previous supervisor, rather than from impersonal or low-level HR staff.

Extending an Offer

Assuming that the employer is satisfied with a job applicant and wants to hire the person, the next step is to extend an offer. This step can be handled immediately or at the end of the interview, or can be delayed until after the applicant's background has been checked. As a practical matter, some employers might decide to change their minds at this point and either leave a job open until a better candidate comes along or restructure the job or even an entire department. They can even hold off and opt for some staffing alternative, such as outsourcing the work, relying on a part-time or contingent worker, using a consultant or a telecommuter, or using job-sharing, in which two persons hold the same job at the same time and each works only part-time.

Extending an offer is not a matter to be taken lightly. It represents a contractual agreement between job applicant and employer, initiated by the employer. Matters are not resolved simply because decision-makers in the organization have made up their minds about who to choose. The question is this: What does the applicant want? Is he or she even available? Will he or she accept the offer, or will subsequent negotiation be necessary?

In the United States, high-level executives often formalize their agreements in written contracts that stipulate exact conditions of employment, salary, and other matters. These agreements are only rarely used with lower-level employees, such as when special commitments are necessary. Some countries have laws requiring written employment agreements to protect the worker, employer, or both, and in some countries, it is simply customary.

Placing and Orienting Employees

The final step in Recruitment and Selection is twofold: (1) Place the employee in the job and (2) orient him or her to the company, work group, and job. This step, too often overlooked, is crucial for retaining newcomers whose recruitment and hiring were often performed at great expense.

Successful orientation involves two key components: (1) *socialization,* the process of initiating an individual into the corporate culture or "the way things are done here," and (2) *personalization,* the process of adjusting job duties and results to fit the unique talents of the individual. Newcomers entering a work group find themselves confronted by an existing social structure, one possessing its own rules of behavior. *Work rules,* the regulations governing conduct in the organization, are often easiest to learn. But *social norms,* the agreed-upon ways of interacting between people, are more difficult to master and can be more important. Newcomers must fit in if they are to survive in the organization and be successful. If the job calls for the exercise of creativity and allows for individual latitude in decision-making, then personalization is also important. It is relatively easy for newcomers to learn what *results* are expected, but it is sometimes not so easy learning how to achieve according to the work rules and social norms of the organization.

Some firms help employees learn about the company through *formal orientation,* a kind of training program that describes the company and benefits or rules of special interest to newcomers. These orientations can be supplemented by *peer mentoring programs,* in which experienced and culturally savvy co-workers introduce the newcomers to others and, more than that, facilitate their acceptance.

When there is a serious discrepancy between expectations raised during the recruitment process and actual job conditions, employees suffer *reality shock*. It is likely to be most pronounced upon transition from school to the first job. Its effects—increased likelihood of turnover, for one—can be mitigated by realistic recruitment from the outset. To state the case bluntly, prospective workers must be told the truth about the job and organization during the recruitment process if they are to avoid reality shock once selected (Saks, 1994).

Problems with the Traditional Approach to Recruitment and Selection

The problem with traditional Recruitment and Selection methods is that they are past- or present-oriented, like most HR practice areas. Recruiters identify sources of talent from habit. If this habit persists long enough, you have an *old boy network* where only people with common affiliations or degrees from certain schools are sought.

Recruitment from within is often touted as a way to improve morale and serve as a means of developing internal talent, but it also tends to strengthen the status quo. People who have been socialized according to one set of norms are likely to present barriers to precisely the kind of change needed to implement strategic business plans, especially when the plans are radically different from previous strategy. When they are simply promoted or moved to another job, their roles change as a result; the negative consequence is that many beliefs are carried up the chain of command, where they serve as barriers to change rather than catalysts to progress.

The use of past-oriented job descriptions is even more insidious than inbreeding and resistance to change that results from promotion-from-within policies and repeated recruitment from the same source. The traditional practice is to use job descriptions to create corresponding person-descriptions, which are then used as guides for locating, attracting, and selecting necessary skills. The focus is usually exclusive: It is on the vacancy at hand. Yet such an approach ignores changes that are desired or that are likely in the job context, and ignores an individual's long-term potential promotability to higher-level jobs.

Unfortunately, hiring people on the basis of *past or present needs* is not likely to facilitate implementation of strategic business plans. There is some evidence that organizational decision-makers do consider individual-strategy matches when recruiting high-level executive talent. However, lower-level talent, especially at entry, does not seem to be handled in the same way. More often than not, managers persist in thinking of warm bodies to fill boxes on organization charts, rather than in choosing people who may ultimately command the chart itself as top-level executives. We should not be surprised that it is the successful firms in each industry that are more likely to take a long-range view of recruitment and people planning at all levels. Unsuccessful firms are held back by their notions of "past practice."

Strategic Recruitment and Selection

To re-orient recruitment to a strategic emphasis, HR specialists have to:

1. Reconsider the purpose of the recruitment function in the context of the HR department, HR strategy, and organizational strategy. What is it at present? What should it be in the future, considering HR Grand Strategy?

2. What are the present strengths and weaknesses of the organization's recruitment efforts? Can present strengths be built on? Can present weaknesses be rectified?

3. What trends in the external and internal environments are likely to affect the recruitment/selection function? How much will economic conditions make it easier to recruit certain kinds of talent in the future? How will economic trends affect future labor supply outside the organization? Inside the organization? How much will technological change influence the kinds of talent needed? The appropriate sources to look for that talent? Methods of selecting/screening prospective employees? How much will market conditions in the

industry influence labor supply? Demand? Will entry or exit of major competitors in the labor market affect what talent is available? If so, how? How much will governmental and legal conditions affect recruitment/selection? Will new laws restrict use of polygraphs, genetic testing, and drug testing? If so, how? What are the trends in case law pertaining to employee selection? How much will geographical movement of organizations affect the process of attracting critically needed talent? How much will social changes affect public views about employer recruitment/selection methods? How will those changes affect state-of-the-art practices?

4. What range of Recruitment and Selection strategies are available?

5. What choice of Recruitment and Selection strategy is appropriate, considering HR Grand Strategy? Initiatives in other HR practice areas?

6. How is a new recruitment strategy implemented? Consider: What skills will be needed by recruiters? Managers? What rewards can be given to those who act in a manner consistent with new recruitment strategy? What structure is appropriate for recruitment? Should it be a full-fledged unit of the HR department? Part of the duties of another unit, such as training? What policies need to be formulated in the organization to facilitate implementation of strategic recruitment?

7. What criteria should be used to evaluate recruitment?

One place to start re-orienting recruitment to a strategic emphasis is with the steps in the recruiting process itself.

First, recruiters have to locate new sources of talent to match strategy requirements. By using results of future and strategic-oriented job analysis and HR forecasts, recruiters have to identify suppliers that can meet future—not just present—HR needs. Where is it that people are likely to be trained and to gain experience in a way that will match future organizational requirements? In addition, HR information systems that contain data about internal labor supplies have to be modified so that people can isolate and use the information that relates to future needs.

Second, it is more important than ever to establish long-term ties with external sources of labor supply: colleges, universities, professional associations, employment agencies, and others. Instead of relying on available supplies, recruiters have to become more aggressive in locating people with talent likely to be needed in the future and manipulating the external environment, to the extent possible, so as to create supplies of needed talent. Recruiters should lobby universities to change curricula and can speak to students so as to motivate them to build their skills to anticipate future requirement.

Third, recruiters have to reconsider the basis of selection efforts. Instead of focusing narrowly on present or past needs in one job, recruiters have to broaden the focus to include consideration of future job changes and individual potential.

Fourth, recruiters have to be more innovative in the approaches they use to attract applicants. There may have to be more intensive use of specialized employment firms, those concentrated on single occupations. College recruitment activities need to go beyond emphasizing the first job in an area related to a college major—such as marketing or even personnel and industrial relations—to describe career opportunities available *beyond* the first job. At the same time, they should be careful to avoid building unrealistic expectations about speed of advancement or the ease with which major career changes can be made.

Fifth, screening methods, employment tests, and interviews need to be reexamined carefully to minimize or at least counterbalance their tendency to focus on past-oriented information about job success. Interviewers should be trained to look for individuals who are likely to be successful in the kind of environment expected in the future and in the kind of organization desired at that time. One method is to conduct future-oriented selection-interview training, where managers learn to rate qualities associated with strategic job descriptions. Another method is to devise future-oriented assessment centers and then use them to judge talent.

While extending offers and checking backgrounds are not steps that particularly lend themselves to a future orientation, placement practices can. From the date of hire, new employees can be trained about the strategic direction of the organization and about what will be expected of them at each step over time.

It is quite important during Recruitment and Selection to emphasize to applicants the difference between *present* job requirements and skill needs and *expected* or *desired future* job requirements and skill needs. Armed with this information, candidates can see not only how they *presently* fit in but also how they can fit into the organization's strategies *in the future*.

Finally, recruiters need to see to it—to the extent that they can—that employee performance-appraisal systems support behavior consistent with future organizational needs. It is pointless to recruit for future needs if no consideration is given to rewarding and reinforcing behavior consistent with meeting those needs over time.

CHAPTER 12

TRAINING

What is Training? What is the traditional approach to it? What are some problems with the traditional approach? How can training be addressed strategically? This chapter, the third to focus on a single HR practice area, answers these questions. In doing so, it begins to show how recruitment and selection can be integrated with HR Grand Strategy.

What Is Training?

Training consists of organized learning activities capable of improving individual performance through changes in knowledge, skills, or attitudes. In a broad sense, it includes experiences intended to meet essential job requirements, update skills, prepare people for career movement of any kind, rectify knowledge or skill deficiencies, and evoke new insights or even create new knowledge. It is thus an important tool for changing individuals by giving them new knowledge and skills. However, training is not usually effective as a means of changing groups of people, since it is rarely possible to train enough people at one time to influence the existing work environment.

Of course, at the same time that training is growing more important due to a dynamic workplace that requires almost continuous upgrading, organizations are beginning to emphasize the importance of learning (Banfield, 1997). Learning is what the individual does; training is what the organization does. They can and should go together.

The Role of Training in Implementing HR Grand Strategy

Training has several possible roles in the implementation of HR Grand Strategy.

First, it is a way to create a supply of talent within the organization. Through structured but flexible long-term learning plans or individual development plans (Dubois and Rothwell, 2000), individuals are prepared for promotion, transfer, or even substantive change in existing jobs. In short, training creates a pool of qualified applicants in the right numbers and with the right skills for higher-level jobs inside an organization—especially when paired with job rotations and individual learning activities.

Second, training can be an important and useful tool for equipping individuals with the knowledge, skills, and attitudes they need to implement organizational strategy. In this sense, it is a short-term instrument for change, geared to existing jobs and problems faced in implementing an existing strategy. Training of this kind is geared to helping managers and workers see and even experience why changes stemming from strategic objectives are necessary. The issues discussed in such training sessions are current and are perhaps controversial. Exercises are designed around real problems so that when the training program is over, the solutions are of practical value on the job.

Third, training can help an organization that is moving toward implementation of a new strategy in a changing environment. As a consequence of pressures inside and outside an organization, individuals face new problems and forces for change. These pressures call for new skills from job holders and can change expectations about desirable job performance. While anticipating future change is no simple matter and is fraught with problems (not the least of which is inaccurate prediction), training can serve as a medium for simulating artificial experience to anticipate future events. One benefit of this approach is that it helps people understand what knowledge and skills they might need in the future, thereby motivating them to learn to meet future rather than past needs.

Fourth, training is a potential tool for giving individuals the skills they need to think strategically. One implication of a rapidly changing environment is that everybody must think strategically, especially when decision-making is highly decentralized. Successful implementation of long-term organizational strategy is not the sole responsibility of top managers, though formulation might be. What employees and managers do on a daily basis can and does affect successful implementation of strategy through actions taken with customers, suppliers, distributors, and other such stakeholders of the organization.

Training can serve any or all of these purposes. Hence, it is a powerful tool of great potential value in the implementation of HR Grand Strategy.

Training conducted by an organization has enormous implications for the future.

1. Training is a potential alternative to recruitment, and vice versa. Needed skills can be acquired from outside through recruitment, or cultivated from inside through training.
2. Training can be integrated with the selection process so that an employee's learning time on a new job is reduced. The result: increased efficiency.
3. Training can admittedly increase the risk of turnover, especially when it builds skills transferable from one job to jobs in other organizations.
4. Training is a vehicle for career progress that can help move people in a way that is consistent with their career plans and/or the career management programs of the organization.
5. Training tends to build expectations for change, and thereby helps foster new attitudes. It thus influences organization development efforts and can be used as a tool in such efforts.
6. Training builds skills, and can thus influence—and be influenced by—job redesign initiatives that might depend on the range of skills possessed by job incumbents.
7. Training can convey information about how to deal with personal problems. It thus serves to change the behavior of supervisors when they encounter "problem employees." In this way, training can influence employee assistance programs.

8.   Training can increase individual productivity by giving employees skills they did not have before. Such productivity improvement efforts are generally opposed by unions unless they are accompanied by corresponding increases in pay and job security. On the other hand, unions typically support upgrading skills so that people stay current and occupationally mobile.

9.   Training can create the expectation for increasing compensation and benefits as employees improve their productivity and knowledge.

When the organization's corporate and HR grand strategies call for growth in the present business or diversification into utterly new businesses, training is an appropriate tool for building new skills among people already employed by the organization. During retrenchment efforts such as downsizing, smartsizing, or rightsizing, training is useful in helping employees obtain new jobs in the same or in different occupations.

The Traditional Approach to Training

The Training Process

Think of the training process as one in which HRP practitioners rely on the instructional systems design model to:

1.   Analyze performance problems.
2.   Identify employee training needs.
3.   Devise instructional objectives.
4.   Prepare test items based on objectives.
5.   Select or design instructional content or subject matter based on objectives and test items.
6.   Choose delivery methods in line with subject matter and with resource constraints.
7.   Offer instruction.
8.   Evaluate transfer of training back to the job.

These steps are illustrated in Figure 12-1 (Rothwell and Kazanas 1998).

Figure 12-1: The Training Process

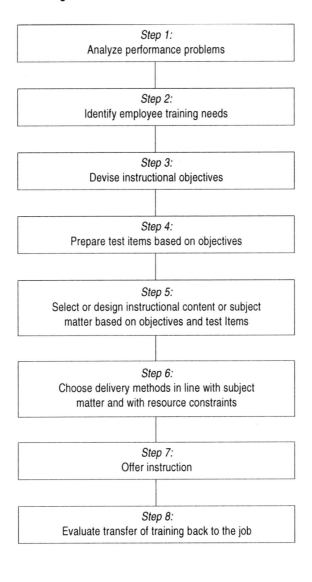

Analyzing Performance Problems

Performance analysis is sometimes called *front-end analysis,* and the terms are usually regarded as synonymous. Performance analysis pinpoints the causes of job performance problems. It was first thoughtfully articulated by Gilbert (1967). Gilbert defined a deficiency as *skill mastery* minus initial *skill repertory.* Two types of deficiencies are possible: *Skill deficiency,* which is appropriately addressed through training, and *execution deficiency,* arising from inadequate feedback about performance, punishment for good performance, problems of motivation, and interruptions preventing performance.

Training is only an appropriate solution when skill deficiency is the cause of a problem. It merely furnishes individuals with skills they need to perform. Training is not appropriate to deal with execution deficiency and thus cannot solve problems stemming from such causes as unclear work contexts, mental/physical disability, or lack of feedback. In those cases, other corrective measures have to be taken, and they must usually be taken by the organization's management.

Performance analysis is increasingly considered to be the foundation for human performance improvement (Rothwell, 2000a; Rothwell, Hohne, and King, 2000). The causes of human performance problems are systematically examined and solutions, called *interventions,* are matched to causes. To do that, HRP practitioners (or others) should pose the following questions when they confront any human performance problem (Rothwell, 1996): (1) What is happening? (2) What should be happening? (3) What is the difference between what is happening and what should be happening? (4) How important is that difference? (5) What is the likely cause (or likely causes) of that difference?

Identifying Needs

Needs should only be systematically identified when the cause of a performance problem is lack of knowledge, skill, or appropriate attitude. Otherwise, management action in an area other than training is probably what is needed (Rothwell, 1996; Rothwell, Hohne, and King, 2000).

Training is based on *needs,* defined as gaps or discrepancies between an ideal and an optimal state. They are different from *wants* and *interests,* which are consciously desired and arise from within the person. Needs, on the other hand, arise from the job, from a comparison between desired and actual work methods, or between desired and actual work results (Rothwell and Sredl, 2000).

Training needs assessment is the process of discovering precisely what gaps exist between what people know, do, or feel and what they should know, do, or feel in order to perform competently. The oldest writing about training needs assessment suggested that training needs should be synthesized from three sources: *organizational analysis, work analysis, and individual analysis* (McGehee and Thayer, 1961).

In the broad *organizational analysis*, trainers compare what the organization is doing and what it should be doing. Trainers focus attention on organizational objectives, skills, inventories, organizational climate, and indices of efficiency, including costs for labor, materials, and distribution.

The second source is *work analysis.* Somewhat more narrow than organizational analysis, work analysis compares what the job requires to what the job incumbent can do. Trainers identify individual skill deficiency, the gap between what people *need* to perform and what they can presently do. Such deficiencies are measured by comparing job results to work standards, job descriptions to employee skills, and perceptions of job requirements to those actually demonstrated on the job.

The third source is *individual analysis.* Most narrow of all, individual analysis is centered on a person doing the job. Does he or she know *what to do? How to do it? The minimal acceptable level of performance?* Attention focuses on comparisons between *what should be at present* and *what is actually happening* as measured by employee performance appraisals, tests, and attitude surveys. The results of organizational, work, and individual analysis are synthesized; that is, they are compared, checked, and double-checked.

Some training needs are predictable. They require repetitive programs offered on a regular schedule. Orientation is one such program. All new employees lack knowledge of an organization's unique ways of doing things—its work rules and methods, for example. As a consequence, an orientation program is designed to help meet this predictable need for all newcomers.

Other needs are short term. Suppose the company purchases a new machine. Workers who will labor on that machine, perhaps one with which they have never before come into contact, need training. When a new word processor is purchased, for instance, everybody who will use it has a training need. Training of this kind might only have to be repeated when people leave and new people replace them.

A *training curriculum* is geared to long-term needs (Rothwell and Sredl, 2000). It consists of a series of organized learning experiences over time for those in a job. It is implemented through planned classroom experiences and planned work experiences, such as developmental job assignments. A training program, on the other hand, is comparable to a single and sometimes one-shot learning event. A program can be part of a curriculum intended to meet predictable long-term needs or be a one-shot offering to meet a short-term need.

Preparing Instructional Objectives

An instructional objective describes the results or outcomes sought from instruction. There are three parts to any objective: (1) *performance*—what learners will be capable of doing after the instructional experience is completed; (2) *conditions*—what context and what tools will be necessary for performance to occur; and (3) *criterion*—how well the performance will be exhibited. In some cases, a condition need not be specified when no special tools are required.

An instructional objective is the link between needs and results. As Figure 12-2 illustrates, objectives help identify what instruction to offer so as to meet a need and thereby close a performance gap. There are two ways to categorize objectives: by type and by scope.

There are three types of objectives: *cognitive objectives,* which have to do with knowledge and information; *affective objectives,* which have to do with feelings and beliefs; and *psychomotor objectives,* which have to do with the ability to manipulate objects. Most training in organizational settings is heavily cognitive.

Figure 12-2: The Role of Instructional Objectives

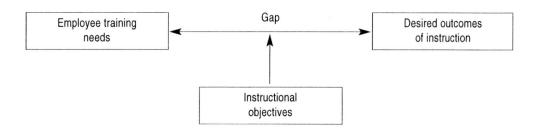

There are two ways to think of the scope of objectives: (1) *terminal,* which are behaviors exhibited *at the end* of instruction, and (2) *enabling,* which are behaviors that contribute to mastery of terminal objectives. They are typically capable of being exhibited *at the end of parts of instruction,* components of a larger instructional experience. Terminal objectives express what learners will be able to do upon completion of a course or program. They are most frequently the center of a trainer's attention.

Preparing Test Items

To demonstrate that learners have mastered behaviors that a training program has been designed to teach, trainers prepare test items corresponding to each instructional objective. In this way, subsequent instructional content or subject matter is clearly focused on results and linked to measures of achievement like test items.

Broadly speaking, tests for training are categorized into two types: *norm referenced,* in which achievement is assessed relative to other learners, and *criterion referenced,* in which achievement is assessed relative to individual success in mastering instructional objectives. In short, norm-referenced tests compare each learner to others, while criterion-referenced tests compare a learner's progress to pre-established measures.

Another way to think about tests is on the kinds of behaviors or skills they measure. There are four types, all criterion-referenced: (1) *An entry test* measures how well the learner has mastered instructional prerequisites. One prerequisite to instruction might be simple reading ability. But how well do learners read? (2) A *pretest* measures the learner's present knowledge or level of skill relative to outcomes sought through instruction. If a learner achieves a score of 100 percent on a pretest, he or she does not need instruction. (3) A *post-test* measures what the learner knows or can do following instruction. It indicates how well the learner is able to perform, and thus serves as a quality control check on the instruction and the learner. (4) An *embedded test* is carried out during instruction to assess how well the learner is progressing toward achievement of terminal objectives. An easy way to distinguish between these tests is by placement: entry and pretests occur before instruction, embedded tests occur during it, and post-tests occur after it.

There are essentially five formats for tests used in training: (1) *paper-and-pencil tests,* in which learners tackle all-too-familiar multiple choice, true-false, and fill-in-the-blank test items; (2) *oral objective tests,* in which learners are asked to respond orally rather than in writing (the format of items resembles those in paper-and-pencil tests); (3) *ratings tests,* in which learners respond with a numerical or adjectival score; (4) *essay tests,* in which learners write a composition to answer a question; and (5) *performance tests,* in which learners perform a task or exhibit a behavior. The choice of which format to use depends on what objectives are being tested: cognitive objectives lend themselves to paper-and-pencil tests, oral objective tests, and essay tests; affective objectives lend themselves to ratings or essays; and psychomotor objectives lend themselves to performance tests.

To prepare a test, the trainer must do the following (Rothwell and Sredl, 2000):

1. List all objectives, terminal objectives and enabling objectives.
2. Identify the purpose of the test. Is it to be an entry test, a pretest, an embedded test, or a post-test?
3. Decide what kind of test to use. Should it be paper and pencil, oral objective, rating, essay, or performance?
4. Establish standards for test performance. They can be expressed as

a percentage of items correct in paper/pencil and rating tests, or as absolute scores in other tests.

5. Test the test yourself to make sure that items are not ambiguous and that the test matches the instruction offered and the instructional objectives on which the test items are based, and to make sure it can be scored.

Selecting or Designing Instructional Content

The decision of *what to teach*—that is, the selection or design of instructional content—is based on test items and instructional objectives. In this process, it is important to consider whether the content should be (1) located from existing sources, such as textbooks, other training courses, and/or published articles, (2) tailor-made for the purpose at hand, or (3) prepared from some combination of externally available and internally developed content. In many cases, the choice depends on instructor preferences and on relative costs and benefits associated with each method.

Despite the wide variety of media available, the traditional lecture remains a popular delivery method. When it is used, instructional content is prepared through lesson and unit plans. A *lesson plan* describes the objectives for one lesson. It usually includes the subject matter to be mastered by the learner and the means of measuring learner achievement. A *unit* is a group of related lessons. Many different lesson plan formats have been suggested. While choice of format depends on instructor preferences and the policy of the training department, the basic idea is to plan learning experiences. In this way, each objective is adequately covered. If instruction is offered in a format other than lecture, content is prepared in a way that will (of course) be appropriate for the delivery method.

Choosing Delivery Methods

The decision of *how to teach* is closely related to *what to teach*. In fact, these two questions comprise the quintessential issues in training design. Like content, choice of delivery method depends to some extent on instructor preferences. Yet much research has been done in this area. It is clear that some delivery methods are more appropriate than others for particular kinds of learning. Figure 12-3 lists some common delivery methods, briefly describing them and their relative advantages and disadvantages.

In recent years, technology-based and technology-assisted delivery methods have revolutionized the training field. Some call this approach *e-learning*. Managers and workers alike are anxious to find multimedia-based training solutions. However, e-learning is impersonal, and it does not tap into the individual's needs for social interaction or capitalize on the value of group instruction where new ideas can be more easily formulated. For this reason, although the e-learning revolution is most likely to continue, a balance between e-learning and classroom learning is probably necessary (Farrell, 2000).

Offering Instruction

Training can be offered on-the-job by the supervisor, off-the-job by in-house trainers, and off-the-job and outside of the organization.

On-the-job training is the most difficult to recognize because it is usually informal and is rarely distinguishable from regular work activities. Seldom is it preceded by formal needs assessment or preparation of instructional objectives. Instead, people receive instruction and feedback on performance while working (Rothwell and Kazanas, 1994). If it is organized, supervisors show them what to do, explain what they demonstrated, demonstrate it again and observe while employees demonstrate, coach employees on what they do wrong and praise them for what they do right, let them do the job but continue to monitor them, and then gradually leave them alone. Some organizations have moved to in-house worker certification tied to on-the-job training (OJT). Such an effort usually involves analyzing competence, training, testing, communication about performance, recertification as working conditions and job requirements change, and rewards for results (Robertson, 1999).

Training is probably most commonly associated with formal instruction rather than OJT, however. There are over 200,000 full-time trainers in the United

Figure 12-3: Training Delivery Methods and Strategies

Method	Description	Appropriate for
Lecture	▪ A structured presentation, usually lasting an hour or longer	▪ Group presentations ▪ Orienting employees to policies, introducing topics, providing information
Tutorial	▪ A one-on-one, structured instructional experience	▪ Individualized presentation ▪ On-the-job training ▪ Building skills, demonstrating how to use equipment
Case Study	▪ A narrative description of a situation, real or fictitious, prepared for instructional purposes, usually written	▪ Stimulating discussion, especially in a small group setting ▪ Identifying problems in realistic situations ▪ Weighing alternative solutions
Critical Incident	▪ A very short narrative description of a problem situation, usually only a sentence or paragraph in length	▪ The same purposes as case study
Role Play	▪ Trainees are assigned parts to play in a dramatized version of a case study or problem situation	▪ Groups of two or more ▪ Dealing with instruction about interpersonal situations
Game	▪ A ritualized representation of a job duty	▪ Group instruction ▪ Especially useful for developing cooperation or assessing leadership in a team setting
Simulation	▪ An extended role play or game	▪ Same purposes as game
Buzz Groups	▪ A small group of people assembled to identify a problem or problems and consider and select alternative solutions	▪ Use with case study, critical incident ▪ Taking advantage of the ability of small groups to deal with unstructured problems more effectively than individuals
Panel Discussion	▪ A structured or unstructured presentation on a topic, problem, or issue by a group of from three to ten people to a larger group	▪ Stimulating insight ▪ Posing problems ▪ Clarifying issues/problems
Computer-Based Instruction	▪ The use of a computer, usually a microcomputer, to present instruction	▪ Communicating information very efficiently (but not necessarily cheaply)
Videotape	▪ The use of a televised presentation to provide instruction, often in a form that mixes instruction with entertainment	▪ Demonstrating effective interpersonal skills ▪ Conveying information in an interesting (but not necessarily cheap) manner

States, and expenditures in this area rival those for all government-sponsored education combined. This kind of training is more formally structured, though research suggests that even in large corporate training departments, needs-assessment methods are rarely carried out with the kind of rigor espoused in most texts.

Finally, colleges and universities as well as many training consulting firms offer off-site training and education. They are useful for learning about state-of-the-art practices in the occupation or field.

The advantage of on-the-job training is that it is highly applied: There is no boundary between who instructs and who supervises. One disadvantage is that supervisors frequently have trouble structuring learning experiences. Another disadvantage is that some learners tend not to ask questions because they don't want to appear dense. Off-the-job training is expensive in terms of the time it takes away from productive labor, but it is cost-effective for large groups of people sharing similar needs. In addition, it can be more professionally structured; there is also a separation between the trainer who provides instruction and the supervisor who subsequently judges the adequacy of individual job performance.

Transferring Learning Back to the Job

When off-the-job training is successfully applied on the job by an employee, then trainers say that the learning was "transferred." Of course, the whole point of off-the-job training is usually to give employees the knowledge and skills they need to perform effectively. That is often easier said than done. Staff trainers who conduct the training are not the employee's supervisors and are rarely aware of conditions on the job that prevent transfer of learning. These conditions are called "barriers" to transfer.

What are some common barriers? They include

1. *The individual (learner).* If learners do not see value in applying new skills, believe that there won't be rewards for doing so, or do

not value the rewards, then there won't be a transfer of learning from the classroom to the job. In short, lack of motivation impedes application.

2. *The job.* If individuals have little or no latitude to change what they do because job tasks are tightly controlled, then training can never be applied unless the job itself is changed first.

3. *The supervisor.* If a learner's superior disapproves of instruction, then there is little likelihood that new behaviors will be exhibited. Supervisors exert powerful influence over behaviors of subordinates because they control rewards and punishments.

4. *The work group.* If a trainee returns to co-workers only to find new ideas greeted skeptically or disapprovingly, then there won't be a successful transfer of learning. People will not risk social ostracism or put up with the jeering contempt of their peers for very long. They will conform to behaviors that are acceptable.

Of course, the reverse of this principle is also true. The likelihood of successful transfer increases as people see how they benefit from applying what they learn, believe that application of new knowledge or skill will be rewarded, and value the rewards associated with application. Transfer also takes place when people can decide to apply the skill or knowledge on the job and are encouraged by supervisors and co-workers. Generally, the greater the similarity between the job and the training, the greater the likelihood that individuals will successfully transfer skills from one to the other.

Problems with the Traditional Approach to Training

Training is only appropriate for dealing with problems created by gaps between what people can or should do *at present* and what they should do *in the future*.

However, trainers do not do a good job anticipating future job conditions that will probably confront people. What will be the future work context? What will individuals be like in the future? What will worker behavior be like? Work results? Feedback about results? These questions are typically ignored. The result is that training intended to equip learners for dealing with an uncertain future is based on *past* performance problems; *past* data about organizations, jobs, and individuals; and *past* competencies. In short, the training needs assessment process typically ignores the future.

Strategic Training

To re-orient training to a strategic approach consistent with HR Grand Strategy, those responsible for training programs have to become thoroughly familiar with the organization's strategic plans and HR plans. They need to search for answers to classic questions similar to those posed by the strategic planning model:

1. What is the purpose of the training program and the training department?
2. How well have existing training programs been working? How well has the training department been working?
3. What conditions inside and outside the organization, jobs, and individuals will create or affect future training needs? Future training programs? The training department?
4. What long-term strategies can be used by the training department in an effort to meet future needs? Deal with present strengths/weaknesses versus future opportunities/threats facing training programs? Deal with present strengths/weaknesses versus future opportunities/threats facing the training department?
5. What strategy for training is likely to be most successful?
6. How can subsequent results of strategy be evaluated?

The purpose of strategically oriented training is to anticipate performance problems before they occur and build individual competencies required to implement organizational strategy. The problem is that individuals are only motivated to learn when they first recognize the necessity for it. Such recognition usually stems from experience, a consequence of *past*, not *future*, events.

To motivate learners to anticipate the future, then, you might have to simulate the experience under future conditions.

How are traditional steps in training re-oriented to reflect an emphasis on the future? This question has generated substantial interest among trainers. There is no one answer; rather, there are several answers.

Re-orienting the Traditional Steps in Training

One place to start in re-orienting training to a strategic emphasis is with steps in the training process.

First, trainers should anticipate rather than merely react to instructional needs. Training Needs Assessment, for example, will continue to rely on a synthesis of organizational, work, and individual analyses. However, the *nature* of each analysis is different from that used in the traditional method. Trainers first compare present conditions to present criteria. Second, they forecast future conditions resulting from the influence of external trends on the organization, jobs, and individuals. Third, they envision what the organization, job, and individuals should be like in the future. Fourth, they compare expected future conditions to future criteria.

Of course, the same approach is used in formulating HR Grand Strategy. The difference is that in formulating training strategy, the scope of analysis is much narrower. It is restricted to individual knowledge and skill deficiency only.

Beyond a simple re-orientation of needs assessment from a past-to-future emphasis, trainers have to reconsider the instructional objectives they derive from needs assessment. One way is to distinguish between levels of instructional objectives. Of course, objectives are intended to guide instructional design and delivery so that instruction will rectify performance deficiencies stemming from lack of knowledge or skill. Good objectives (1) describe what learners will be able to do after the instructional experience is over; (2) furnish a measurable criterion of *how well* learners will be able to perform, and (3) describe under what conditions or with what tools or other resources the learners will be able to perform.

More than one writer has criticized traditional instructional objectives on the grounds that they are far too restrictive and short-term. Indeed, more than one critic suggests viewing objectives along a continuum from short- to long-term.

Trainers should also distinguish between levels of tests in much the same way as levels of objectives. In other words, trainers need to focus more attention on testing how well training is being applied back on the job.

At least two ways exist to assess instruction in this manner. One way is to focus on future-oriented employee appraisals as a vehicle for following up on the job impact of training over time. Of course, training is not the single reason accounting for adaptation to job change over time, but its examination through appraisal is better than nothing. A second way is for trainers to go out to the job setting and observe learners. In this way, they can test for application in the actual job context and identify barriers that prevent application.

As the next step in re-orienting the training process to a strategic emphasis, trainers can select or design content to provide learners with the knowledge and skills they need for the future. Training has traditionally been a short-term change strategy. It can be used to evoke new insights and ideas and thereby increase how well the work is done. But more often than not, it is used to increase efficiency (how quickly work is done) by making sure that people conduct their work in line with organizational policies and management expectations. In fact, this kind of training in work methods and work procedures is one of the most common subjects for in-house instruction.

While there will always be some need for training that is conducted to ensure consistency in application of policies and work methods, that should not be its sole purpose. In fact, training can facilitate implementation of organizational strategy by furnishing people with the knowledge and skills they need to gear their work activities and outcomes to those envisioned in strategic business plans, and furnishing people with the skills they need to *think* strategically. At the same time, training is a tool for implementing HR Grand Strategy by creating, inside the organization, a pool of applicants to meet future labor needs.

Once future-oriented instructional objectives and test items are written, it should be relatively easy to identify instructional content that will lead to desired results. Trainers select such content from available sources—textbooks or other training packages, for example—or can prepare it specifically for learners.

As a next step in re-orienting the training process to a strategic emphasis, trainers select instructional delivery methods appropriate for the teaming experience. How can instruction be delivered in an appropriate way? Traditionally, trainers have answered this question by considering such issues as the relative costs associated with different methods, compatibility with instructional objectives, the type of learners, the type of instructors, and the availability of space and time. Though some delivery methods are more appropriate than others for certain types of training, lecture remains the single most popular one.

Two matters are particularly important in choosing delivery methods for future-oriented training: learner experience and small-group decision-making.

In traditional and highly *directive* training, learner experience is generally not very important. In cases such as newcomer orientation or preparation for promotion, trainers cannot rely on learner experience because (quite simply) they do not have any. The instructor's role is in fact to "present distilled experience." A refinement of this approach is to present distilled experience and then give trainees an opportunity to practice newly acquired skills.

In traditional but *nondirective* training, learner experience is quite important. The instructor becomes the "group facilitator," helping learners share insights. The training event provides an experience that is greater than the sum of previous individual experiences.

In strategic or future-oriented training, learner experience is *simulated* artificially during instruction. The designer's responsibility is to create exercises like role play, case studies, and scenarios that resemble situations learners *might* encounter if conditions forecast in the future affect the organization as expected. The aim of such training is to simulate future conditions, giving learners an opportunity—however artificial—to gain experience *before* they confront real conditions. Following the exercises, learners discuss the discoveries they made and how they can be applied at work, and establish learning plans to build the skills they expect to need in the future.

Small-group decision-making is important in future-oriented training. Many future-oriented exercises are handled in a small-group format. Learners share their experience together the way teams often do in grappling with real problems in the work setting. Another reason for using small groups is that they generally do a better job than individuals in dealing with unprogrammed or unusual decisions and situations. Future-oriented training exercises are precisely that. Individuals thus gain experience in dealing with others when confronted with such unusual problems.

The final step in re-orienting the training process to a future orientation is to transfer the learning. In traditional training, the issue of transfer (as we have said) is peripheral to the instructional task. In other words, trainers worry about it as an issue *after* instruction.

In future-oriented training, however, the transfer of learning is a concern that permeates the entire instructional process. It is considered:

1. *During needs assessment.* Trainers identify conditions that impede performance, even those not caused by individual knowledge or skill deficiencies. They are taken into account during instructional planning.
2. *During preparation of objectives and tests.* Although barriers to application are not always capable of being influenced by learners, those that are can be identified and addressed during instruction.
3. *During instructional delivery.* Trainers deal with individual strategies for influencing barriers to transfer on the job.
4. *Following instruction.* Trainers follow up with learners to see how the future unfolds in the present. How accurate were predictions of the future? How helpful was the training experience for anticipating it? They also follow up to see how the learner handles barriers to application.

Through strategic training, learners are thus able to anticipate the future and prepare for it. Alternative models other than the traditional instructional system design (ISD) model might have to be used as the foundation for strategic training (Rothwell, 1999a).

CHAPTER 13

ORGANIZATION DEVELOPMENT

Organization Development (OD) is an approach to group change that relies on the participation of those who are influenced by the change. In a classic definition, French and Bell defined Organization Development as:

> . . . a top-management-supported, long-range effort to improve an organization's problem-solving and renewal processes, particularly through a more effective and collaborative diagnosis and management of organization culture—with special emphasis on formal work team, temporary team, and intergroup culture—with the assistance of a consultant-facilitator and the use of the theory and technology of applied behavioral science, including action research (French and Bell, 1984, p. 17).

In the broadest sense, then, Organization Development is about changing organizational culture and about long-term change. It typically focuses on a group or an entire organization rather than on one person. This group-orientation distinguishes OD from individually focused change efforts like training. The introduction of comprehensive human resources planning (HRP) in a firm that has never before used it is, in one sense, an OD *intervention* or change effort.

The Role of OD in Implementing HR Grand Strategy

To understand the role of OD in implementing HR Grand Strategy, you must first understand the importance of culture in strategy and the nature of organizational change.

Culture

This abstract concept nearly defies simple definition. On a simplistic level, however, it usually means the pattern of shared beliefs and behaviors common to individuals in one social setting or context. When everybody in an organization shares certain common values, a *dominant culture* is said to exist. Variations of these values, resulting from differences in role perspectives and placement in organizational structure, create *subcultures* or *microcultures*.

Culture originates from two sources. The first source of culture is the entrepreneur who founded the firm, since that person usually stamps the organization with his or her personal business philosophy from the outset. This philosophy leads to assumptions about the organization's purpose, competitive position, and way of dealing with customers or constituents. The second source of culture is the firm's experience in dealing with its competitive environment. As the organization functions, its members learn from experience. While individuals come and go, the organization—as an institution—survives. Recollections of prior events and their impact on the firm also survive, preserved in an *institutional memory* embodied in the memories of the longest-tenure organizational members (who are sometimes called the "software" of institutional memory) and in formal and informal policies, procedures, job descriptions, and management rules (sometimes called the "hardware" of institutional memory). These formative influences on culture are subsequently kept alive by the beliefs of top managers, by people recruited and selected for entry, by the way that newcomers are socialized, by stories told in the organization about the founder and other people as object lessons in appropriate behavior, by rituals that institutionalize the importance of an event (for example, retirement, promotion, completion of a probationary period), and by the language of specialized terms unique to those in an organization, work group, or occupation that increase their cohesiveness.

Culture and Strategy

Before an organizational Grand Strategy can be implemented, changes usually need to be made in people, policies, rewards, and structure: The culture of the organization will not be the same after strategic implementation. OD is an important means by which to bring about those necessary changes.

But what is the relationship between culture and strategy? That question warrants some attention.

In a classic and still-relevant description, Pearce and Robinson (1985) use a four-box matrix to illustrate how to manage the strategy-culture relationship. They labeled one side of the grid "potential compatibility of changes with existing culture," and they labeled dimensions "high" and "low." The other side of the grid was labeled "changes in key organizational factors that are necessary to implement the new strategy," and the dimensions were labeled "many" and "few." All changes to strategy can thus be assessed for their impact on culture.

Cell 1 of Pearce and Robinson's matrix represents many changes with high compatibility to the existing culture. Four basic considerations have to be emphasized:

1. Change has to be linked explicitly to the organization's purpose.
2. Existing personnel have to be used to make changes so as to preserve continuity.
3. Any change in rewards has to be consistent with the existing reward system.
4. Attention should be centered on potentially disruptive change, with care taken to minimize the extent of that disruption.

Cell 2 of Pearce and Robinson's matrix represents few changes with high compatibility to existing culture. Two key issues have to be considered: How can this situation help magnify and reinforce existing beliefs and ways of handling matters? How can time be used to remove roadblocks to change?

Cell 3 of Pearce and Robinson's matrix represents few changes with low compatibility to existing culture. The best idea in this situation is to manage around the culture by using task forces, external consultants, and other means to avoid direct cultural conflict.

Cell 4 of Pearce and Robinson's matrix represents the worst situation: Many changes are needed but are incompatible with existing culture. The first step is to consider whether such drastic change is necessary. If it is, then the CEO should take a visible lead in each change. Top management, training, and orientation programs might need to be changed, and reward systems will have to be altered. Desired behavior will have to be made clear and concrete, and there must be real congruity between stated and real priorities. Other advice:

- Create "slack" to prevent overloading people and systems.
- Insulate parts of the organization in which major and disruptive change has to occur as much as possible.
- Make clear what action has to occur and when.
- Communicate about the need for change, and monitor change to make sure events are progressing as desired.

The Nature of Broad-Scale Change

According to such open systems theorists as Katz and Kahn (1978), any organization exists in *dynamic homeostatis,* meaning that it preserves stability in the midst of change.

One way to conceptualize what we mean by "broad-scale" is to look at the classic but still relevant idea of force fields (Lewin, 1948 and 1951): Any organization is pressured to change by forces from outside and inside. That which impels change is a *driving force.* At the same time, there is resistance to any change. It is called *restraining force.* To implement change, you must strengthen a driving force or weaken a restraining force.

Driving forces include (1) threats to the survival of the organization, such as economic or competitive pressures; (2) opportunities to "win big" by changing the way the organization conducts transactions with consumers, suppliers, distributors, or other important groups; and (3) changes in leadership, policies, rewards, or reporting relationships. On the other hand, major restraining forces include organizational culture and perceptions of individuals about outcomes of change. In general, people are cautious about change, especially when they are uncertain about how the change will impact them, their concerns, and their priorities.

When it comes to broad-scale change, weakening restraining forces (see Figure 13-1) is usually preferable to that of strengthening the driving forces. The reason is that any increase in the strength of a driving force is usually accompanied by a corresponding increase in the strength of a restraining force. Consequently, reducing the strength of a restraining force is likely to produce greater readiness for change.

Figure 13-1: Driving and Restraining Forces

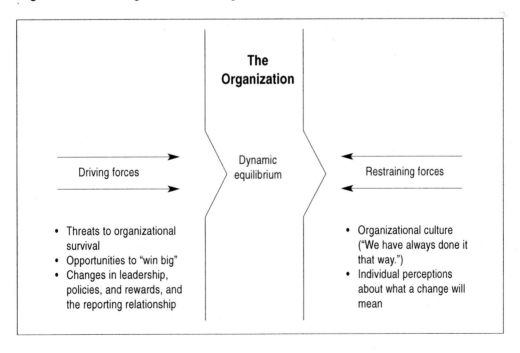

Organization Development is a strategy for reducing the strength of restraining forces. It is an approach to change that had its origins in the 1940s and 1950s. OD has been experiencing a rebirth of attention in recent years (Edmonstone, 1995), and as of this writing is one of the most sought-after HR specialties (Kiser, 1999), sparked in part by the introduction of new technology, which created upheaval in social relationships within organizations. Perhaps the greatest example is the implementation of Enterprise Resource Planning (ERP) Systems that integrate a firm's software in a single program because the human side of the organization is too often downplayed or ignored by the technologists who are usually charged with leading the organizational transition from many functionally specific software programs to one integrated program. Changes of this kind might require, for instance, a so-called *sociotechnical systems* intervention in which human social issues are given due deference when changes are made in the technology that people use to do the work. OD can also be helpful in knowledge management, energizing staff creativity in ways that technological innovations sometimes cannot (Cross and Baird, 2000).

OD and Other HR Practice Areas

OD can influence other HR practice areas, and those areas will also shape OD. First, OD is a potential tool for dealing with how people are socialized into an organization, a work group, and a job. In this sense it influences transmission of cultural beliefs and affects recruitment and selection. Second, OD is a potential tool for influencing the learning needs that people identify—thus affecting training. Third, OD can help individuals plan their careers and help managers implement career-management programs. Fourth, OD is a tool for helping individuals deal with changes in organizational or work group structure, and changes in work methods/procedures. Fifth, OD influences the climate of the work group; co-workers are more supportive of each other. In this sense, OD influences the help individuals receive when they face personal problems. Consequently, OD influences employee assistance programs. Sixth, OD can improve negotiation and conflict-resolution techniques, and thus affect labor relations. Seventh, OD serves as a tool to help formulate and implement compensation/benefit programs that take advantage of group incentives.

From an organizational standpoint, then, OD is one way to go about changing culture; strategic business plans and HR plans can thus be implemented more easily and more successfully.

The Traditional Approach to Organization Development

The Action Research Process

Think of an OD *intervention* (change effort) as synonymous with the action research process. The stages in an intervention or action research process include (1) problem recognition, (2) preliminary focusing, (3) data collection, (4) feedback of data and preliminary diagnosis, (5) action planning, (6) action, and (7) re-examination of the problem. These steps are illustrated in Figure 13-2.

Organizational Development theorists differ in how they label these steps. They all agree, however, that OD—like action research—is continuous, long term, and based on a process of cycling-in data about problems, feeding them back to interested people, and helping people establish plans for solving problems. Organizational Development is also a relatively structured approach.

Problem Recognition

Before any OD effort can begin, some person or some group must *want* to change, detect a problem, or feel one exists. Most mainstream OD theory rests on this key assumption. In other words, crisis is usually the motivator for change efforts. Of course, definitions of "crisis" vary. That which constitutes a crisis for a field supervisor may not be the same as a crisis for a top manager.

Most OD practitioners weigh the views of top managers—the "dominant coalition," those holding the reins of power—as most important. When members of this coalition feel that a problem exists, OD often is used to introduce broad-scale change.

Figure 13-2: Steps in Action Research in OD Interventions

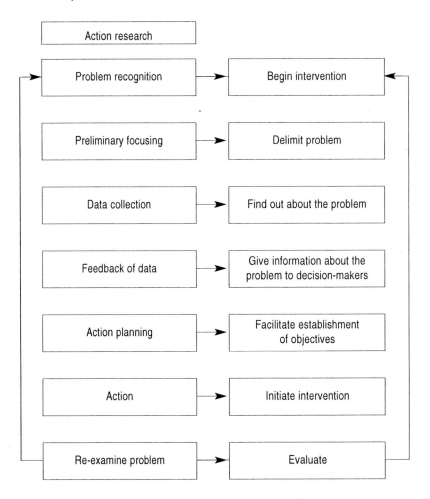

Sources of problems vary. For example, pressures from outside an organization can create an impetus for change. Competitors introduce refinements to products or services that call for a firm to respond. The tools or technology used in manufacturing might change, creating a need for new investments and training so that workers can use the technology. Economic conditions unfavorable to the organization can prompt layoffs that demoralize workers, and favorable conditions can lead to growth that strains resources.

Similarly, pressures come from within. A new chief executive might want to introduce a new strategy for the organization; a new marketing vice president might want to change the firm's traditional pricing policies; a new vice president for human resources might want to offer new types of training. Similarly, changes in the organization's structure give some groups more contact with key external stakeholders while denying contact to other groups.

Nor are these matters the only ones that can prompt desires for change. Lippitt, Lancseth, and Mossop (1985) list others in their classic treatment of this topic: increasing organizational complexity; organizational mission and goal miscoordination; competition between units or departments; and differences in values between older and younger people, to mention just a few.

Any of these problems can lead to awareness of a significant gap between what the organization is and what it should be. It is recognition of this gap by those whose opinions matter that generally provides initial impetus for an OD effort.

Preliminary Focusing

Managers are constantly bombarded with problems, but the causes are not always apparent. This is why practitioners want to find out as much about the problem as possible at the beginning of an OD effort. Perhaps the best starting point is with the persons or group who first noticed it: What do they believe the problem is? How do they describe it? What led up to it? What consequences has it had? What condition *should* exist? How far from desired conditions are actual conditions?

Armed with answers to these questions as a starting point, OD practitioners can then focus on *what* they will look at and *what* data-collection methods are appropriate for studying the general problem.

Data Collection

After the general problem has been identified, OD practitioners then consider how to collect information about it. Four methods used in collecting work and workforce information can also be used for OD data collection. They include written surveys, interviews, observation, and unobtrusive measures. Depending on the problem and the time available, practitioners can tailor-make surveys and other instruments for specific uses, or purchase and use off-the-shelf instruments.

Generally speaking, most OD practitioners prefer as much staff participation as possible because it usually leads to commitment. In other words, the process of collecting data builds expectations for change and thereby intensifies pressures favoring it.

However, broad-based participation in data collection is not always possible: Sometimes decision-makers need information quickly, or the organization is too large or geographically diffused to get everyone involved. In such cases, limit participation to what is practical, given the time, resources, and specific situation.

Feedback and Preliminary Diagnosis

Feedback is simply the process of presenting results of data collection to those who recognized the problem or those who have the power to mobilize resources to take corrective action. The key requirement of useful feedback is that it should galvanize support in favor of change and action. Many failures in OD have resulted from poorly conceived, mistimed, or poorly handled feedback.

Two issues are of key concern in the feedback stage: (1) What is presented (content)? and (2) How is it presented (process)?

The chief question by which to evaluate results of a data-collection effort is this: *So what?* In other words, no feedback will be successfully presented unless it addresses key concerns of the audience. Suppose, for example, that results of an attitude survey demonstrate that many production workers experience low job satisfaction and deeply resent what they believe is personal favoritism. Managers reviewing this information have the right to ask: What does that mean? Of course, this example is an easy one: Conditions like those described suggest an organization ripe for unionization and perhaps high turnover, high absenteeism, and incidents of sabotage.

How the results are presented is of at least equal importance. A written report without a meeting is not likely to galvanize support for change. Some people will simply skim a report; others will not read it at all. Those who do read it might be aware of the results but are reluctant to push for unified action. For this reason, a group meeting of the managers is the ideal. A meeting makes everyone in the group aware of key results and forces a discussion about results to take place. In addition, group pressure will probably favor action.

Who should make the diagnosis? Beer (1980) contrasts two approaches: client-centered and consultant-centered. Generally, the client-centered approach means that members of the organization—and particularly members of the dominant coalition—take on the burden of filtering results of data collection to determine the exact nature of problems and changes needed. It is particularly appropriate, Beer believes, when those receiving feedback are themselves targets for change and when the problem has to do with behavior and attitudes. The consultant-centered approach means that the consultant interprets results and makes a diagnosis, much like a doctor treating an illness. It is appropriate when the people receiving feedback are the principal targets for change and when the problem has to do with structure, policies, and rewards.

Action Planning

What should be done about the problem identified? How should a solution be implemented? These two questions are the focus of action planning. These questions have to do with setting objectives, deciding on an intervention, and determining how to intervene.

There are three ways to carry out action planning: (1) through unilateral action, (2) through delegated action, and (3) through shared action. On this change continuum, *unilateral action* involves action planning by managers only. They simply review alternatives, select one, and then act by issuing orders. They replace key people and change reporting relationships or span of control to what they think is more in line with what will facilitate long-term change. *Delegated action,* which is on the other end of the change continuum, involves negotiations between superiors and subordinates during action planning.

Carrying out action, however, is left in the hands of subordinates once agreement is reached. *Shared action* is a middle ground in which superiors and subordinates negotiate on a change before, during, and after taking action.

Different methods of action planning are appropriate for each approach. In unilateral action, the CEO or the top managers as a group decide what to do. Meetings are held to brainstorm on solutions to a problem, establish objectives, and create an action plan. In delegated action, two methods are appropriate:

1. *Discussion meetings:* Managers and their subordinates meet. In each work group, the manager states the problem but does not suggest a solution; rather, he or she solicits ideas on what action to take.
2. *T-group meetings:* In a relatively unstructured setting, managers and subordinates begin the change effort. There is a heavy focus on interpersonal and intragroup relationships and feelings.

In contrast, *shared action* relies on:

1. *Group decision-making:* Subordinates are encouraged to identify solutions and help establish action plans.
2. *Group problem-solving:* Managers and their subordinates at each level in the organization meet to go over results of data feedback, identify problems, brainstorm on action plans leading to improvement, and determine what action to take.

To succeed, any action plan must clarify (1) who is to take what actions, (2) what the deadlines are, (3) how performance will be measured, and (4) what rewards will result from taking desired action. In addition, some means must be established to monitor action as it is taken so that actions in line with change can be distinguished from mere routine.

The role of the change agent varies during action planning, depending on the method selected for dealing with the problem. In unilateral action, the change agent facilitates interaction of top managers, guides them through a process of projecting what results are likely to come from the change effort, and helps them establish concrete plans. In delegated action, the change agent facilitates interaction of work groups. The same role, on a continuing basis, is appropriate for shared action.

Action

This phase of an OD effort involves actual implementation of an intervention. Interventions vary by scope and focus. In this context, *scope* refers to how much of the organization is to be changed. *Focus,* on the other hand, refers to what will be changed.

Generally speaking, the scope of an intervention can be (1) the entire organization, (2) one or more functions (such as marketing, production/operations, human resources, or finance), (3) one or more divisions (by geographical area, industry, product line, or consumer type), (4) one or more projects, (5) one or more work groups within a function or division, or (6) one or more individuals. However, most writers assert that OD is *an organization-wide* change effort. Hence, the traditional scope is comprehensive, encompassing the entire organization.

Focus also varies. Common interventions include

1. *Team building.* The focus is on setting priorities, analyzing roles of team members in the work process, examining how team members interact, and examining interpersonal relationships. The intent is to change how members of a work group get along.
2. *Sensitivity training.* The focus of this sometimes controversial intervention is on the individual. Its intent is to increase individual awareness of self and others in interpersonal relations. The starting point is a meeting without an agenda, held away from the work site. Group members examine self and group processes in a supportive environment. Although such efforts do lead to increased self-awareness, there is some doubt whether such training affects performance when participants return to their jobs.
3. *Process consultation.* The focus of this intervention is on increasing awareness of how the organization's members interact. The intent

is to change how individuals think of themselves, others, and the groups with which they come in contact. As a simple example, a process consultant might attend a meeting as observer and then give feedback about individual and group behavior.

4. *Survey feedback.* The focus of this intervention is on the entire organization. An attitude survey is used to collect information from all parts of the organization. Then data are fed back through interlocking conferences: first to the top managers, and then to the immediate reports of each manager, from the top down. At each level, the manager and his or her subordinates identify problems and establish action plans to solve them. It is a powerful approach when properly used.

Many other interventions have been described in the literature, and a few are summarized in Figure 13-3.

OD interventions are typically long term, are directed at solving a particular problem, and are structured around steps in the action research model. They can be used to

- Point out contradictions between actual conditions in the organization and desired conditions
- Describe existing behaviors and the causes of them
- Critique existing methods and search for better ones
- Examine personal assumptions about other people
- Examine interactions between individuals in one group or competition and conflicts between groups
- Project probable results of different courses of action
- Examine the historical background of problems that have emerged in the organization
- Direct attention to the outcomes of structure and reporting relationships
- Examine organizational or group "culture"

In the broadest sense, HR practice area initiatives—an organized recruitment program, a training program, changes in compensation/benefits, to name

Figure 13-3: A Summary of OD Interventions

Intervention	Target for Change	Useful for Dealing with	Activities
T-Group	Individual	I Dysfunctional social norms I Education for new knowledge and skills	I Uses short lectures and discussions in conjunction with agenda-less meetings
Grid OD	Individual (can also focus on organization)	I Increasing communication I Improving inter-personal relationships I Education for new knowledge and skills	I Relies on six basic steps: (1) analysis of managerial styles on a grid (2) development of interpersonal relations within work groups (3) development of relationships, cooperative in nature, between work groups (4) preparation of plans (5) implementation of plans (6) critique (evaluation) of plans
Third-party peace-making	Work groups	I Increasing communication I Resolving conflicts I Improving morale	I Helps two people to identify issues or problems and deal with each other more effectively
Role analysis	Individuals (or people in small groups)	I Individual sense of duties/ responsibilities I Appropriate behavior of the individual in a work setting	I The OD practitioner helps people discuss the purpose of the role, determine prescribed and discretionary components, and examine linkages with other roles
Organiza-tional mirror	Departments or work groups	I Feedback I Increased communication	I The OD practitioner collects information/ perceptions about one department or division from others and feeds it back to stimulate change

a few—can be viewed as OD interventions. However, today's OD practitioners are well-advised to focus their primary attention on such issues as building community, establishing social contracts between employer and employee, building trust, addressing culture clashes in organizations, directing attention to employability issues for workers, and indicating how corporate power is and should be used (Burke, 1997).

Re-Examination of the Problem

Since OD is usually a tool for responding to a perceived problem, it makes sense that sometimes it will be worthwhile to examine how well OD has contributed to solutions. This step is really the same as evaluation.

Evaluating OD is a controversial issue because OD specialists frequently differ from line managers in defining success. Line managers typically value economic contributions; OD practitioners, on the other hand, tend to be more interested in such elusive matters as "group climate," "participative management," "feeling over facts," and "interpersonal trust." There is a real difference in perspective: Line managers want to see hard data such as dollar increases, while OD practitioners want to see soft "data" such as results on attitude surveys.

One way to solve this problem is to establish joint committees of line managers and OD practitioners to make sure that methods of evaluation are built into an OD intervention at the start and that the results of evaluation will respond to information needs of both line managers and OD specialists. In this way, evaluative information will be available in times of subsequent economic crisis, when hard-eyed and bottom-line-oriented managers are tempted to push for reductions in funding of OD efforts.

Finally, evaluation serves as a new starting point or "renewal system" for reinvigorating a change effort after it has been going on for some time. In this way, it generates new interest in the issue that the OD intervention was initially undertaken to solve.

Problems with the Traditional Approach to Organization Development

Organization Development has been criticized on several counts. First, its advocates promise more than they have delivered. Second, it has been called a tool to manipulate workers in line with top management desires and whims. Third, some claim that it is heavily value-laden in ways that are inappropriate in some organizational cultures. Yet it is not on these counts that OD is most weak.

Recall from earlier in the chapter that the starting point of any OD intervention is problem recognition. The idea is simple enough: *An OD intervention is only initiated when somebody expresses a desire for change.* Beer (1980) indicates that only a crisis leads to such a desire. In short, a problem must not only *exist* but must also be *felt* or *experienced* before a large-scale change effort will be undertaken. As a consequence, organization design tends to be a "fix-it" strategy chosen during the aftermath of a crisis.

This line of thinking is passé. A crisis has to happen before people are ready for change, but surely OD can also be a tool for dealing with conditions that led up to the crisis in the first place. Organizational Development clearly has the potential for being re-oriented to the future.

In recent years, however, a new model to guide the change process has been emerging. Its advantage is that it is crisis-oriented. Called *appreciative inquiry,* it begins not with a problem but with what energizes and excites people most about the work they do and the organization of which they are part; it does not begin with a problem.

Strategic OD

It is important to distinguish between a strategic planning intervention and organization design in implementing organizational and HR Grand Strategy. In the first instance, OD is built into the very fabric of *formulating* strategy; in the second, OD is used to help *implement* strategy.

In organizations in which strategic planning has never before been used, its introduction is a broad-scale change in its own right. Smaller firms carry out the strategy formulation process through team meetings of top managers. Even in larger firms that have corporate planning departments, meetings are also important for communicating information, deliberating on new ideas, making decisions, and arriving at consensus.

In any meeting, how people interact or fail to interact is a function of task demands, resources, and group processes. OD practitioners, serving as process consultants, can facilitate *how* people interact in planning meetings. By doing so, it can be argued, they help deal with such key issues as: (1) how the group organizes itself to deal with the task; (2) how the group members arrive at decisions; (3) how group members interact with each other; and (4) how members plan for action.

In short, then, strategy formulation calls for effective teamwork, especially when top managers function together in the strategy-making process. A team-building effort, either preceding strategy or taking place through process consultation during planning meetings, can be a useful way to facilitate team interaction.

On the other hand, OD can also be helpful in implementing strategy. Researchers have found that managers at levels below top management have significant influence on strategic choice and implementation. More specifically, lower-level managers

1. Filter perceptions about strategy through their own lenses, so to speak, which are in turn affected by their roles and the objectives of the units/departments that they head.
2. Offer ideas and propose projects that they *believe* are acceptable to their supervisors, and do not propose projects—regardless of merit— that they think superiors will not approve of.
3. Screen ideas extensively before allowing them to reach top managers.
4. Propose projects that minimize personal risk.
5. Become so committed to courses of action in which they have personal stakes that they will tend to commit more resources even when results are negative.

These research findings suggest that there is potential to use OD to (1) increase commonality of interests, (2) reduce provincialism and role-bound behavior in favor of increased team work, (3) reduce hesitancy in proposing new ideas, (4) create common grounds for action, and (5) improve coordination of organizational members during implementation. Perhaps the last one mentioned is most important.

How can OD be used during strategy formulation and implementation? One approach is through survey feedback. The OD practitioner can:

1. Gather preliminary information from top managers about (1) organizational purpose, objectives, and goals; (2) areas representing potential strengths and weaknesses; and (3) areas representing potential trends affecting the organization over time.
2. Prepare a questionnaire to collect data about these issues.
3. Survey those inside the organization about their perceptions on point 1 above. Stakeholders outside the organization might also be surveyed.
4. Feed results of the survey back to decision-makers in "interlocking conferences."
5. Facilitate action planning meetings at different levels in the organization to establish ways of dealing with the issues uncovered.
6. Prepare results of these meetings into a single planning document.
7. Monitor progress on the organizational plan.

This approach is just one of several possibilities for formulating and implementing an organizational strategic plan. A similar approach could be used to conduct HR planning or prepare long-term employee development plans.

As a tool for dealing with long-term change, OD thus has continuing applicability for use in strategic business planning.

CHAPTER 14

JOB REDESIGN

This chapter focuses attention on another HR practice area: Job Redesign. This practice area—which is also sometimes called *work redesign*—has been the focus of considerable attention among employers as they struggle to find more productive and cost-competitive ways to achieve the same or better results than ever before. It is this dual focus on productivity improvement and cost reduction that has placed Job Redesign center-stage in process-improvement efforts and creative staffing strategies. Job Redesign has also figured prominently under the label *job restructuring* as a means by which employers can comply with the Americans with Disabilities Act, which requires employers to make *reasonable accommodation* for workers with disabilities so long as it does not pose an *undue hardship* on business operations.

But what is Job Redesign? What is its role in implementing HR Grand Strategy? What is the relationship between organizational design theory and Job Redesign? What is the traditional approach to Job Redesign, and what are some problems with it? How can Job Redesign be made more strategic in its emphasis? This chapter answers these important questions and, by doing so, sheds new light on the topic of Job Redesign.

What Is Job Redesign?

In a very simple sense, *job design* means the ways that decision-makers choose to organize work responsibilities, duties, activities, and tasks. *Job Redesign* thus involves changing work responsibilities, duties, activities, and tasks. It is another human resources (HR) practice area that can be used to implement HR Grand Strategy. It is closely associated with *organizational design,* the allocation of work responsibilities within an organization, and *organizational redesign,* the process of reallocating or reorganizing work responsibilities.

Organizations have been experimenting widely with job or work redesign over the last decade in an effort to overcome bureaucratic notions about jobs, improve worker satisfaction, enhance productivity, improve coordination and communication in organizations, improve the climate with organized labor, and other reasons (Baytos, 1995; Bohlander and Campbell, 1993; McCann and Buckner, 1994). Many organizations have experimented with teams or self-directed workteams—a form of Job Redesign (Cordery, 1995).

The Role of Job Redesign in Implementing HR Grand Strategy

The way an individual's job is structured and placed in an organization exerts tremendous influence on perceptions, performance, future preparation, and even mental health. Indeed, job design influences just about every area of HR: the people recruited and selected; the training appropriate for helping individuals learn how to perform the work; the career plans that are realistic, given experience acquired in a job; the Organization Development initiatives appropriate for improving individual-job match, interaction of job incumbents with the other members of the work group, and the interaction of job incumbents with those outside the work group; employee assistance programs, particularly those that help individuals cope with pressure stemming from the job itself; labor relations negotiations because union officials are rarely in favor of combining unrelated tasks in one job; and compensation and benefit programs, since the tasks people perform are weighted for importance and are often used as a basis for preparing wage and salary schedules.

The process of designing and redesigning jobs is at the heart of human resources planning: The job, perhaps more than anything else, is where the individual and the organization interface the most.

Organization and Job Design

The basis for job design theory is organization theory, which can be classified broadly into three strains of thought: the classical, the behavioral, and the situational.

Classical theory was expounded in early writings of Max Weber and Henri Fayol. For the classicist, any organization achieves efficiency through its division of labor. Managers identify the overall purpose of the organization. They then divide this overall purpose into jobs, each rationally related to the whole. Jobs are, in turn, grouped to create work groups, divisions, and departments. Finally, each group is assigned a supervisor, who is responsible for overseeing the work of subordinates and reporting the results to his or her own superior.

Behavioral theory is quite different. Unlike the classicist, the behavioralist is much less interested in allocating specific tasks to specific jobs, making sure that the authority matches the position, and then trying to attain higher efficiency through specialization of labor. Behavioralists prefer simple organizational structure, decentralized decision-making, and informal departmentalization. In an organic structure, subordinates feel free to discuss their performance problems with superiors and have a positive view of the organization. They participate in decision-making and communicate with those whose views are needed to solve immediate problems. These characteristics are in stark contrast to conditions in a traditional organization, where subordinates are guarded and negative about the organization, do not feel sufficient trust to communicate openly with those of higher status, and are not permitted to participate in decision-making.

Situational theory differs from both classical and behavioral theories. Advocates stress the influence of the external environment on the allocation of responsibilities and tasks within the organization, work groups, and jobs. Allocating responsibilities and tasks means creating a structure. Appropriate structures differ according to technology, markets, production, research, and information.

Traditional Approaches to Job Redesign

The Job Redesign Process

Think of traditional Job Redesign as a process in which the HR planner

1. Establishes a goal or purpose for redesign efforts.
2. Devises a performance model.
3. Analyzes existing jobs.
4. Changes a job or jobs, or a work group.
5. Implements changes.
6. Monitors the results of change.

These steps are summarized in Figure 14-1.

Figure 14-1: The Job Redesign Process

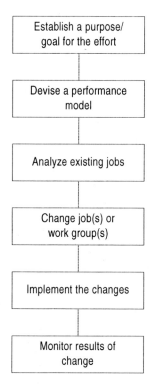

It is important to understand that work results can be achieved in a myriad of ways. Often, the only real limitations are creative ones, rather than legal mandates such as employment laws: People simply do not see the many creative ways by which the same results can be achieved. Recall from Chapter 8 that decision-makers have many choices they can make about how to organize work: recruiting full-time workers from outside the organization; transferring full-time workers from inside the organization; outsourcing all of the work; outsourcing part of the work; recruiting "permanent" part-time workers from outside the organization; recruiting workers on a flextime or flexplace arrangement; using consultants; using temporary and contingent workers on a daily basis; using temporary and contingent workers on a seasonal or work-cycle basis; calling a halt to doing the work altogether; reengineering the way the work process is accomplished and, in so doing, changing the number and type of staff needed to do it; shifting some duties from one worker to another; shifting some duties from one work unit or department to another; and shifting to virtual work, using telecommuters domestically or internationally to carry out the work. Each choice—and there are others as well—represents a form of Job Redesign and also impacts the organization's HR and staffing requirements. These solutions are used in countless organizations, but they require a willingness on the part of a company's leadership to go beyond what has been done before.

The Goal or Purpose of Job Redesign

Job Redesign efforts are undertaken to make three kinds of improvements: to improve the efficiency and effectiveness of work activities; to match more closely individual and job tasks more closely, or to a work group; and to improve the quality of work life and individual job satisfaction.

The first job design efforts took place at the beginning of the 20th century. Seminal figures in modern management, such as Frederick Taylor and Frank and Lillian Gilbreth, set about trying to increase *efficiency,* defined simply as the ratio of outputs to inputs. At that time the focus was on the activities of individual workers. Taylor and the Gilbreths analyzed jobs through *work measure-*

ment, the examination of physical movement relative to time. They then reconstructed those movements to find "the one best way" to carry out tasks with the greatest efficiency. Little thought was devoted to worker satisfaction and needs: Taylor believed that those needs would be met if wages were increased for increased work output.

The Hawthorne experiments, carried out at the Hawthorne, Illinois, plant of Western Electric in the late 1920s and early 1930s, resulted in attention being paid to the needs of employees. Key findings of the Hawthorne research suggested that: (1) work output is more related to how workers are treated than to physical surroundings; (2) people are more easily influenced by peers than by superiors; (3) individuals acquire and maintain their sense of identity through relationships with others and particularly with co-workers; and (4) leaders should devote at least as much attention to the social requirements of employees as to work requirements. The Hawthorne experiments focused on *effectiveness:* how much a job meets the needs of the job incumbent.

Researchers are now focusing more on improving the match between individual needs/desires/expectations and job tasks, work group relations, and organizational culture. The timing is right: Employee downsizing and increased demands on productivity have placed a great deal of stress on workers. These improvements are working: Many managers cling to the hope that humanizing the workplace and improving worker satisfaction in general will improve performance. The relationship between satisfaction and performance is difficult to establish, however, in part because "satisfaction" and "performance" are such broad, multi-faceted concepts, but also because clearly improved worker satisfaction reduces absenteeism and turnover. Innovations such as self-directed work teams and quality-improvement efforts help instill pride in the work people do. Improving worker morale achieves many organizational objectives.

Devising a Model of Performance

If we are to redesign jobs, we need to conceptualize what can be redesigned; Performance models simplify the whole process of conceptualizing key job design issues.

Many such performance models have been proposed over the years. Most of them include at least the following components or related features:

1. *The organization.* What is its purpose? Policies and procedures? Structure or allocation of work duties? Culture (unspoken rules and beliefs)?
2. *The work group.* What is its size and degree of cohesiveness?
3. *The individual.* What are his or her knowledge, skills, attitudes, expectations, and aspirations?
4. *The job.* What is its situation? (How clear are conditions requiring performance?) What are the task requirements? (What actions or behaviors are supposed to occur?) What will be the consequences? (To what extent does performance lead to desired outcomes?)
5. *The supervisor.* To what extent does the supervisor provide feedback on performance and reward performance?

These components are illustrated in Figure 14-2. Job Redesign occurs through changes in any or all of these components.

Analyzing Existing Jobs

One starting point for Job Redesign is work analysis. Because traditional work analysis is usually limited simply to the tasks performed, it is probably not comprehensive enough for most Job Redesign efforts. The focus must be on work in the total context of a performance model like that shown in Figure 14-2 because, unlike work analysis, Job Redesign must examine not only *what people do* but also *how they feel about what they do.*

Various tools for Job Redesign have been devised. Perhaps the best known is the Job Diagnostic Survey (JDS) of Hackman and Oldham (1980). It is not copyrighted and can thus be readily used by practitioners. More recent information about job diagnostic surveys in an international setting can be found in Edwards (1999).

Figure 14-2: Components in a Simplified Model of Performance

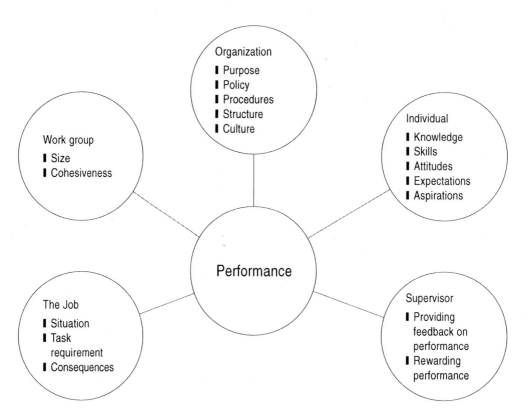

The Job Diagnostic Survey is based on a performance model of its own. According to Hackman and Oldham (1980), jobs should be examined relative to

1. *Skill variety.* How much does a job require the exercise of different skills?
2. *Task identity.* How much does a job call for completion of an identifiable piece of work associated with the job incumbent?
3. *Task significance.* How much do job activities or outcomes influence the lives or the work of other people?
4. *Task autonomy.* How free is the incumbent to exercise creativity in performing the work?

5. *Feedback.* To what extent does the job incumbent receive frequent and clear information about job performance through the process of carrying out the work?

The first three characteristics—variety, identity, and significance—lead to meaningful work. Jobs with autonomy give workers a sense of responsibility. Jobs that yield feedback give incumbents a means to evaluate their own performance and take corrective action as needed. In a research study reported by At-Twaijri (1995), the Job Diagnostic Survey was used to assess the most motivating factors in a Saudi Arabian industrial setting. The researcher concluded that a job's motivational potential can be attributed to five key issues: skill variety, task richness, task significance, autonomy, and feedback from the job.

The relative importance of these characteristics differs by individuals. Some people have stronger needs for some than for others. Individuals with higher growth needs are most likely to benefit from the psychological states resulting from job enrichment.

The real differences depend on individual perceptions more than on an objective criteria of "enriched jobs." Individuals are the best judges of what is or is not satisfying, motivating, and desirable in what they do. To find out what they want, don't spend unnecessary time devising an elaborate approach such as a comprehensive attitude survey. Just ask.

Changing a Job or a Work Group

Changing any component of the performance model shown in Figure 14-2 will assist in Job Redesign, but traditional approaches make it their focus by task grouping, meeting the needs of individual job incumbents, and meeting demands imposed by the organization and its surrounding environment.

Job design and redesign by task grouping takes the most time. Frederick Taylor, an advocate, suggested that managers should first segment each job into discrete activities, each with a beginning and an ending (which he called *tasks*). Second, they should analyze how workers perform the tasks by studying body movements and time needed to complete them. Third, they should examine alternative and more efficient ways of carrying out the tasks. Fourth and finally, they should train workers to perform tasks in the most efficient ways, discovered through observation of the most experienced, highest performing workers (called *exemplars*). This approach to job design stresses that to achieve efficiency, jobs should be highly specialized or simplified. Managers devote their attention to studying how observable work activities or processes are carried out. Recent efforts to simplify work or to improve work processes tend to bear strong resemblances to Taylor's traditionalist views.

From this description, it is easy to see that advocates of task grouping emphasize the arrangement of work activities and efficiency in carrying out those activities. Major elements for examination include (1) *task range,* meaning the number of tasks carried out in a job; (2) *task depth,* the amount of discretion exercised by the individual; (3) *time span,* the amount of time it takes to carry out an activity or the time needed to determine whether the task was properly performed; (4) *task relationships,* the relative dependence of one task on another in the same job or the dependence of one job holder on work outcomes of another; (5) *task efficiency,* the speed with which an activity is performed; and (6) *task effectiveness,* how well the activity is performed. Taylor emphasized high task efficiency and narrow task range, depth, and time span. Of course, his studies focused on production workers in industrial settings. Their jobs tend to center on observable tasks. The tasks lend themselves to relatively easy segmentation.

In the 1970s and 1980s, advocates of task grouping directed their attention to several specific approaches to job design: *job enlargement, job enrichment,* and *work flow rearrangement.*

Job enlargement involves adding more of the same kinds of tasks to an existing job (see Figure 14-3). The idea is that productivity can be increased when fewer people do more. At the same time, advocates argue that doing more of the same kinds of tasks adds variety to the work. A very simple example of job enlargement is giving a secretary reports and letters and memos to type.

Job enrichment involves adding a task or series of tasks that require more knowledge, technical expertise, responsibility, or other characteristics *not* otherwise typical of a job generally (see Figure 14-4). In other words, it is a qualitative rather than quantitative change in duties. Advocates argue that it leads to individual development, since it prepares job incumbents to handle duties more typical of higher-level jobs, like those normally performed by superiors. At the same time, it is argued, enrichment increases employee motivation because it is intrinsically satisfying to be given more responsibility and more demanding, challenging work. An example of job enrichment is giving a secretary responsibility for typing, proofreading, and distributing a report without insisting on having a superior review it.

Work flow rearrangement is not necessarily distinct from job enlargement or job enrichment, though it can be. Some jobs are dependent on others. On an assembly line or in document processing, for example, what one worker does is dependent on what others do. Job tasks are thus interrelated, with outcomes of one job flowing into a second and those in turn flowing into a third (see Figure

Figure 14-3: Job Enlargement: Add More of the Same Kinds of Tasks

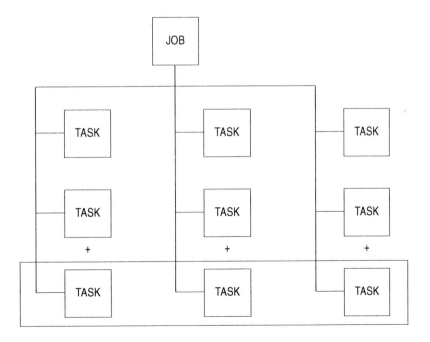

Figure 14-4: Job Enrichment: Add More Tasks of a Higher Level

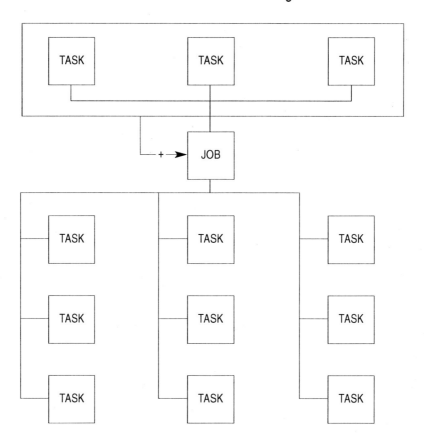

14-5). One way to redesign a job, then, is to rearrange which jobs perform which tasks in the chain. It is thus possible to pull tasks into one job permanently or push tasks from the second job into a third. A very simple example is switching the task of gluing boxes from the laborer at the end of an assembly line to the last person prior to the laborer. Another option, of course, is to automate gluing. Many other options exist as well (Hupp, 1995).

Two other approaches to Job Redesign are related to work flow rearrangement. One is job rotation. The other is work modeling.

In *job rotation*, people move into jobs with new tasks. The duration of a job rotation is usually several months. Advocates of this method argue that it devel-

Figure 14-5: Work Flow Rearrangement: Rotate Tasks

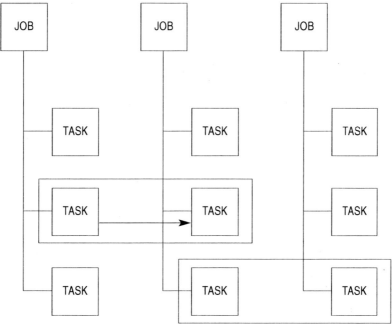

ops individuals, increases their appreciation for the roles of others, and improves flexibility in assigning employees to jobs. In addition, it motivates people by adding variety to the work. Job rotation is usually thought of as a lateral or horizontal move to a position of similar task difficulty, though the tasks themselves might be different. Temporary promotions can be handled in a similar way.

In *work modeling,* people are also moved, just as in job rotation. However, the duration is much more brief, usually lasting only a few hours. It can be used quite effectively to add variety to otherwise tedious tasks in boring, repetitive jobs. An example is to switch positions periodically on an assembly line.

Behavioral theorists approach the issue of job design from a different standpoint. They are less interested in *structuring* job tasks, an issue that preoccupies classicists; rather, they are more interested in what people *feel* about what they do. Individuals differ in (1) what kinds of tasks they find intrinsically rewarding, (2) career objectives and thus the tasks that contribute to meeting those objectives, and (3) the importance associated with task outcomes and the rewards associated with outcomes.

Finally, contingency theory suggests that appropriate job design is a function of matching individual needs and aspirations, work group norms and values, organizational goals/requirements, and present and predicted environmental conditions.

Other approaches to Job Redesign are worth mentioning. They include autonomous work groups, job sharing, staff leaseback arrangements, changes in work scheduling, and supervisory training.

Autonomous work groups, more frequently called *teams* or even *self-directed teams,* extend the principles of job enrichment to an entire work group. Each group is given a goal to achieve and considerable freedom in how to pursue it. Supervisors do not even need to be needed. Group members themselves establish production schedules, working hours, and rest breaks; they also select new members, evaluate present ones, and initiate discharge of unsatisfactory performers.

Job sharing exists when two employees, usually each a part-timer, share a single job. They can choose to divide up work duties. Perhaps a more common arrangement is for one person to work mornings and the other afternoons, or to alternate days on and off the job. It creates a flexible arrangement for two people who might otherwise not be free to work at all. Some organizations prefer such job-sharing arrangements because part-time employees are not entitled to full benefits, hence representing a cost savings. The disadvantage is that dealing with two people in place of one creates unique problems of supervision, because directions might have to be repeated.

Staff leaseback arrangements are quite rare, but they do offer an alternative that some organizations may find useful to explore. The basic idea is to sell the rights to the organization's workforce—or some portion of it—to a third party, which then conducts all hiring, training, and disciplining, and performs other HR duties. The firm pays a fee to the third party to "lease" the workforce. Employees are then paid by the third party rather than by the firm.

Changes in work scheduling have to do with increasing the individual's flexibility in scheduling working hours. Each employee decides when the work day ends and when it begins, at least within limits. Typically, everyone is scheduled to be present during a certain core period, but individuals are free to select starting and ending times outside of that. For example, suppose the core is from 10 a.m. to 4 p.m. Some will choose to start at 9:00 and leave at 5:00; others will choose to start at 8:00 and leave at 4:00 and so on. Research evidence suggests that flextime leads to improved employee job satisfaction. Managers might find it difficult to organize activities outside the core period, however.

Finally, *supervisory training* is another way to redesign jobs. In most organizations, supervisors have some leeway in how much authority they can delegate to subordinates. This is particularly true in white-collar settings. When decision-making is relatively decentralized and thus left up to subordinates, each individual is given an opportunity to assume greater responsibility and develop greater capability in self-management. Responsibility can be an intrinsic motivator in its own right, because each person participates more in matters affecting him or her. Supervisors are trained to decentralize decision-making, giving employees the chance to assume greater responsibility and to provide regular feedback on performance. Each approach—increasing decision-making responsibility and increasing feedback—can be used to redesign jobs, thereby enriching them. There is a cost, however: Subordinates are bound to make some mistakes that could have been averted by a more skilled superior. Hence, the tradeoff is between long-term development of subordinates through decentralized decision-making and short-term efficiency and effectiveness in daily operations.

Implementing Job Redesign

Obviously, the way that Job Redesign is implemented will largely determine how successful it is.

One approach to use is coercion. The manager simply announces the change to the startled employee or work group and then uses threats and discipline to enforce compliance. Resistance to the change will probably be quite pronounced at the outset and perhaps for some time afterward. Employees will no doubt express growing resentment about the change in the job, but also about the supervisor. Turnover, absenteeism, and even sabotage are possible consequences. The advantage to using coercion, however, is that changes can be made quickly.

A second approach is *bribery*. The manger uses the same tactics as in coercion, except that monetary or other rewards are substituted for punishment and discipline to enforce compliance. Resistance is likely to be just as great as when coercion is used. Members of the work group might undercut desired change by ridiculing or ostracizing those who pursue rewards. Change will take place slowly, if at all. The advantage of bribery, however, is that hard feelings will not be as pronounced as when coercion is used.

A third approach is *persuasion*. The manager sets out to convince an individual of benefits that can result from going along with Job Redesign. If those benefits are perceived to be capable of attainment and are valued by the individual, rapid change is possible. The advantage of this approach is that it is not likely to create ill will; the disadvantage is that chances for success are relatively uncertain, depending on the individuals.

A fourth approach is *educational*. The manager teaches employees how to do their jobs differently, and then leaves the application of the training to individuals. The advantages of this approach are that ill will is less likely, but there is greater likelihood that the job incumbent will know precisely what is expected. The disadvantage is that change might be slow in coming, especially if it is constrained by contrary work-group norms or by lack of individual motivation.

Job Redesign can really be looked at as a form of OD intervention in that it takes time and requires that an entire work group change as well as individuals.

Monitoring the Results

The final step in any Job Redesign effort—whether the focus of change is on one person or an entire group—is evaluation. In one sense, evaluation involves little more than finding out whether the desired purpose was accomplished. How much, for example, did the redesign effort improve (1) efficiency; (2) effectiveness; (3) the match between job incumbent and tasks, responsibilities, and duties; (4) the match between individual and work groups, and between the individual and the organization; and (5) individual satisfaction and quality of work life? More important from the perspective of the HR planner, how well did redesign efforts facilitate successful implementation of HR Grand Strategy and strategic business plans?

One way to evaluate redesign efforts is to repeat analysis and diagnosis of jobs. In this way, it is possible to compare measures or perceptions before and after change. Other approaches to evaluation are more broad-based and can include employee attitude surveys, interviews of job incumbents, structured observation of duties, and secondary measures such as output, scrap rates, and turnover.

Problems with the Traditional Approach to Job Redesign

The usual starting point for traditional Job Redesign efforts is to analyze present conditions, rather than how conditions *are likely to change* or *should change* over time. As a consequence, most redesign efforts are focused on present performance and individual perceptions. Job Redesign is intended to restore equilibrium between the individual and the job that exists only at present, but job conditions might be different when environmental and organizational changes are made. What is needed, then, is a more future-oriented approach.

Strategic Job Redesign

In strategic Job Redesign, the focus is on anticipating conditions likely to arise in the job and making adjustments to the design to facilitate implementation of long-term business strategy. In this way, Job Redesign can be used in implementing HR Grand Strategy. The center of attention is on the long-term development of people over time, so that the right people are in the right places and possess the right skills at the right times.

It all sounds quite easy to do. It is not. Yet clearly it is intuitively appealing to anticipate problems before they arise, rather than merely waiting to take action when they come up.

The Strategic Job Redesign Process

Think of strategic Job Redesign as a process that, in form at least, is quite similar to its traditional and thus present-oriented counterpart. The HR planner

1. Establishes a goal or purpose for the redesign effort.
2. Devises a performance model.
3. Analyzes existing jobs, changes likely to occur in existing jobs over time, and desired job conditions in the future.
4. Redesigns jobs in anticipation of future needs and conditions.
5. Implements changes.
6. Monitors the results of the change.

The Purpose of the Redesign Effort

From a strategic standpoint, the purpose of Job Redesign is to facilitate implementation of HR Grand Strategy. The goal is to redesign jobs so that they match future conditions and help create an internal pool of talent in the organization, which should be prepared to deal with those conditions.

Devising a Model of Performance

To consider employee performance strategically, HR planners need to (1) identify key features of job performance, such as the condition of the organization, work group, individual, job, and supervisor; (2) forecast likely changes over time in these conditions; (3) decide on what conditions are desired (i.e., what strategists would like to see in the future by way of conditions in the organization, work group, individual, and job); (4) compare what is to what should be, and what will probably be to what should be in the future; and (5) consider action plans to anticipate future changes. This model, unlike its traditional counterpart, adds the element of forecasting. It is directed toward solving anticipated performance problems in the future, rather than in the present.

Analyzing Jobs

For strategic Job Redesign, HR planners need to devote more than the usual amount of attention to

1. Diagnosing *total* job context. In other words, the focus needs to be on more than what is customary in traditional work analysis. Each part of the performance model described in the previous section should be assessed relative to the job. The same performance model can be used to predict external influences on an entire work group or department.
2. Forecasting likely and desired change in the internal and external environment.
3. Comparing *what is* to *what should be* and *what will probably be* to *what should be in the future.*

These steps are illustrated in Figure 14-6.

The first step, diagnosing the total job context, is exactly the same as the corresponding step in traditional job diagnosis described earlier in the chapter. By using a survey like the Job Diagnostic Survey, the HR planner assesses *present* employee satisfaction and productivity. This step helps furnish data about *what is*. An advantage of using the Job Diagnostic Survey is that since it has been used previously in many organizations, corresponding criteria representing "what should be" are available. Managers in any organization can always establish their own desired benchmarks, instead.

The second step, forecasting, is what distinguishes strategic from traditional job design. Its aim is to (1) identify what trends inside and outside the organization are likely to influence jobs or work groups, (2) assess the nature of changes that will probably occur, and (3) clarify desired changes in line with organizational and HR plans and strategies. One way to go about this is for HR planners to collect information about changes expected outside the organization and then ask job incumbents, through surveys or interviews or other methods, to predict the likely job impact of each trend. At the same time, strategic busi-

Figure 14-6: Steps in Strategic Job Redesign

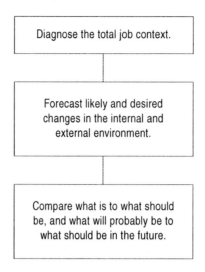

ness plans are separately assessed as potential and desirable influences on work groups and jobs. HR planners then compare results in order to identify gaps or discrepancies for action.

Changing a Job or a Work Group

Job Redesign, as a strategy for closing gaps between *what is* and *what should be in the future,* is a tool for facilitating implementation of organizational and HR Grand Strategy. Traditional methods such as task grouping, job enrichment, and job enlargement can be used, but their selection is based on *how much* HR planners believe they will contribute to achieving successful implementation. In this key respect, then, their use differs from the traditional approach in which Job Redesign is a means to increase efficiency, effectiveness, employee satisfaction, or individual-job match.

Implementing Job Redesign

As in traditional Job Redesign, implementation of strategic Job Redesign can be carried out through coercion, bribery, persuasion, or education. The last of these—education—is probably most appropriate. The reason is that strategic Job Redesign is really a form of organization development intervention that coincides with strategy implementation. Different Job Redesign efforts take place in different work units or job classes over time so as to re-orient jobs in ways that will anticipate and avert future problems before they come up.

Monitoring Results

The final step in strategic Job Redesign is to monitor results. Since the purpose of any strategic redesign effort is to facilitate successful implementation of business and HR strategy, the best way to monitor results is to periodically review how well it has served that end. Each redesign effort—that is, every single job that has been changed—will have to be evaluated separately. In this process, HR planners can solicit information on such issues as the following ones:

1. How much, if at all, has Job Redesign helped anticipate problems before they have come up? Describe a success story when the right person was available in the right place at the right time.
2. How much has Job Redesign failed to anticipate problems before they have come up? What do you feel accounted for the failure? What should have happened?

How important was the failure? What can be done in the future so that the same problem will not be repeated? What negative side effects, if any, do you foresee if your recommendation for action is accepted? What can be done, from the outset, to eliminate or minimize negative side effects?

Though evaluative data of this kind will be highly subjective and anecdotal, it will furnish a starting point for reassessing job design in light of strategic business plans and HR Grand Strategy.

CHAPTER 15

EMPLOYEE ASSISTANCE PROGRAMS

Employee Assistance Programs (EAPs) are organized efforts to help workers with a range of individual problems. Common problems include alcoholism, drug abuse, gambling, theft, sabotage, family difficulties, personal problems, mental illness, violence in the workplace, and stress. Estimates of the extent of employee problems vary.

But these estimates share one ingredient in that they are all shocking. Murray and Lopez (1996) express the impact of illness in terms of "disability-adjusted life year," a measure that describes years of life that are lost due to premature death and years of severe disability. They indicate the causes and incidence globally for 1990, the most recent year for which reports exist, as follows: all cardio-vascular conditions (18.6%), all mental illness (15.4%), all malignant diseases (cancer) (15.0%), all respiratory conditions (4.8%), all alcohol use (4.7%), all infectious and parasitic diseases (2.8%), and all drug use (1.5%).

Consider just a few facts that provide a backdrop for Employee Assistance Programs:

I   The American Council on Alcoholism (ACA) estimates that upwards of 20 million people throughout the United States (an estimated 10 percent of the population) have a serious problem with alcohol. A problem drinker impacts the lives of six other people. (*http://www. aca-usa.org/*).

I   The Center for Substance Abuse Prevention (CSAP) estimates that
    employed drug abusers cost their employers about twice as much
    in medical and worker compensation claims as their drug-free co-
    workers. Monthly drug use rates in 1992 among workers dropped
    to 7 percent from nearly 17 percent in 1985.

I   The Lewin Group for the National Institute on Drug Abuse and the
    National Institute on Alcohol Abuse and Alcoholism estimated that
    the total economic cost of alcohol and drug abuse in 1992 to be
    $245.7 billion, $97.7 billion due to drug abuse. This estimate includes
    substance abuse treatment and prevention and other healthcare costs,
    costs associated with reduced job productivity or lost earnings, and
    costs to society such as crime and social welfare. The study also
    determined that these costs are borne primarily by state, county, and
    local governments (46 percent), followed by those who abuse drugs
    and members of their households (44 percent). The 1992 cost esti-
    mate has increased 50 percent over the cost estimate from 1985 data.
    This increase is attributed largely to the epidemic of heavy cocaine
    use, the HIV epidemic, an eightfold increase in state and federal
    incarcerations for drug offenses, and a threefold increase in crimes
    attributed to drugs. More than half of the estimated costs of drug
    abuse were associated with drug-related crime. These costs included
    lost productivity of victims and incarcerated perpetrators of drug-
    related crime (20.4 percent); lost legitimate production due to drug-
    related crime careers (19.7 percent); and other costs of drug-related
    crime, including federal drug traffic control, property damage, and
    police, legal, and corrections services (18.4 percent). Most of the
    remaining costs resulted from premature deaths (14.9 percent), lost
    productivity due to drug-related illness (14.5 percent), and health-
    care expenditures (10.2 percent).

I   According to the National Domestic Violence Hotline, there are an
    estimated 960,000 incidents of violence against a current or former
    spouse, boyfriend, or girlfriend per year and 4 million women who
    are physically abused by their husbands or live-in partners per year.

While women are less likely than men to be victims of violent crimes overall, women are 5 to 8 times more likely than men to be victimized by an intimate partner.

I Mental disorders collectively account for more than 15 percent of of disease in the U.S. from *all* causes, slightly more than all forms of cancer (Murray and Lopez, 1996).

The Role of Employee Assistance Programs in Implementing HR Grand Strategy

Individuals make productive employees only when they are willing and able to perform their work and contribute to the work of others. Yet they are not always able to do so. People are not just cogs in vast organizational machines; rather, they experience problems on and off the job that impede their performance just as much as any lack of individual knowledge or any structural deficiency in job design. Behavioral problems, when they exist, can deprive an individual of happiness, earnings, promotions, and even continued employment. On the other hand, these problems can cost an organization in more subtle, yet just as damaging, ways.

Employee Assistance Programs (EAPs) are organized attempts to cope with behavior problems.

1. They influence recruitment and selection by increasing the pool of fully productive employees for promotion and retention.
2. They influence training by reducing the extent to which employees with behavior problems pose special challenges to carrying out organized instruction.
3. They influence career planning and management by improving career prospects of individuals and increasing the pool of fully productive employees available for promotion, transfer, and job enrichment.
4. They influence organization development by removing the strain placed on work groups by individuals with behavior problems.

5. They influence job design by (1) pinpointing characteristics of jobs that may produce stress and thereby induce behavior problems and (2) creating the need to rethink allocation of work duties while individuals undergo prolonged—or, for that matter, temporary—treatment.

6. They influence labor relations by establishing an area of common agreement between management and organized labor.

7. They influence compensation and benefits in that some EAPs—such as financial or legal assistance programs—are really benefits that would otherwise have to be paid for by individual employees.

Behavior problems represent a major and often hidden cost of doing business that influences the level of employee performance, individual work satisfaction and group morale, and the present use and future development of staff. Employee Assistance Programs can accomplish many objectives, and any comprehensive strategic plan for human resources (HR) should factor them in.

The Traditional Approach to Employee Assistance Programs

The Employee Assistance Process

Any Employee Assistance Program (EAP) consists of steps in which a supervisor or a co-worker:

1. Observes and monitors employee performance.
2. Detects the existence of a performance problem.
3. Gathers information about the problem to ascertain its cause and importance.
4. Determines that the problem is caused (or exacerbated) by individual behavior.
5. Determines that the problem is important enough to warrant action.
6. Plans a discussion with the employee.
7. Discusses the problem with the employee.

8. Outlines what the employee is responsible for doing, what results are expected, what the employee is presently doing, and what results are presently being achieved.

9. Points out the performance discrepancy—the gap between what should be and what is.

10. Considers, with the employee, what action steps can be taken to close the performance gap.

11. Helps the employee make a commitment to change, establish a plan for improvement and methods of monitoring results, and seek outside professional help if necessary.

12. Follows the employee's progress. If improvement occurs, the employee is praised for it; if no improvement occurs, the employee is disciplined.

These steps are illustrated in Figure 15-1.

Steps 1 and 2: Observing Performance and Identifying a Problem

Employee assistance begins by first identifying a problem that interferes with job performance or individual happiness, either directly or indirectly.

What are some indicators that a problem exists? Problems with personal appearance or personal hygiene; a dramatic or unusual increase in the number of personal phone calls made or received; fights with co-workers; unusual change, typically for the worse, in job performance; avoidance of others (peers, superiors, or even friends); and tardiness and absenteeism resulting from illness. These are just a few warning signs of possible trouble.

Of course, efforts to prevent workplace violence—itself a symptom of other problems—are useful in their own right. After all, a problem like homicide is now the second most-common cause of death in U.S. workplaces (Stieber, 1999). Some organizations are giving training to supervisors and workers on how to handle workplace violence and are trying to identify any proclivity toward violence during the screening process (Zinno, 1995).

Figure 15-1: The Employee Assistance Process

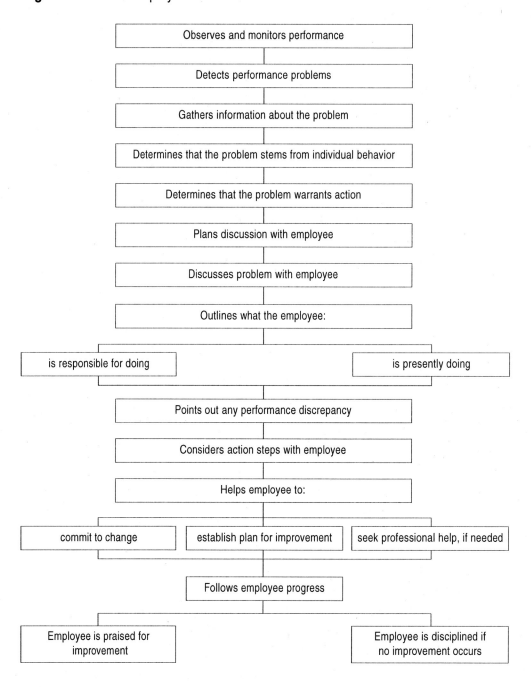

How does a supervisor confirm that these signs indicate the existence of a personal problem? Methods include

1. *Direct observation of the problem.* A sure sign is when the individual is observed drinking excessively or gambling, whether on or off the job.
2. *Observation of specific behaviors associated with a problem.* Does the individual stagger around, reeking of liquor? Is someone seen taking pills?
3. *Observation of excessive or unusual emotion.* Is an employee caught crying or laughing inappropriately? Sending outrageous e-mails? Having problems with anger?
4. *Observation of symptoms.* Is there a sudden, dramatic change in individual performance? Is the individual fighting with others? Acting aggressively, perhaps in an uncharacteristic way?
5. *Rumors.* Though rumors are not always accurate, they are sometimes worth checking out, especially when they can be supported with other evidence indicative of a personal problem.

These categories represent a hierarchy of evidence for detecting the need for employee assistance. The first is obviously most overt; the fifth, least so.

Who should identify a problem? The answer is simple: Anyone who notices. Personal problems can be identified by those inside the work setting (peers or teammates, superiors, or subordinates, etc.) or those outside it (family members, friends, or acquaintances).

However, a key point is this: No individual is ready for employee assistance until he or she recognizes that there is a problem and expresses willingness to do something about it. Acceptance that help is needed is an essential first step in any solution and any self-improvement effort. For example, the alcoholic who refuses to acknowledge that he/she has a problem cannot be successfully helped until he/she admits it. Nor can the gambler, the thief, or the potential suicide. For that matter, no employee performance problem can be effectively addressed as long as the person exhibiting it or experiencing it refuses to confront the problem. (The same can be said for organizational problems. No such problem can be solved until management and workers first acknowledge that it exists.)

For this reason, then, it is important to discuss the problem with the employee. This responsibility is not one that supervisors relish. Some argue that it is not the supervisor's responsibility to deal with personal issues in the workplace. Others counter that any behavior that impedes employee performance is rightly a matter for supervisory concern and action.

Steps 3, 4, and 5: Gathering Information, Determining Cause, and Assessing Significance

What is the employee's problem? What caused it? How important is it? Addressing these questions are the next steps in the employee assistance process.

Frequently, a supervisor notices the symptoms before encountering the problem itself. A few symptoms were described earlier. The question is: Is the problem behavior isolated, or is it only a symptom of something else? If the answer is not immediately apparent, most supervisors know that the truth will eventually become apparent. There are always a few people who create problems; what you want to be on the alert for is a *pattern* of problem behavior.

Detecting a pattern of behavior takes time. Unfortunately, in many cases, the key to successful treatment depends on *early* recognition of a problem and prompt referral to skilled professionals. Early recognition of a problem with drugs or alcohol is not always easy, however, especially for a supervisor who rarely comes in direct personal contact with subordinates.

Supervisors can deal with this problem by closely monitoring their work groups. Ask questions. Express concern. Take an interest in what people say about their home life. Don't be obvious, but do think of it as one way of taking the pulse of the work group and the individuals.

Another way to detect problems early is to encourage subordinates to talk openly about their problems or those of co-workers about whom they are concerned. Stress that *anything,* including family matters, is fair game for discussion.

As the supervisor expresses willingness to listen, detecting problem behavior becomes easier. Training in recognizing problems and counseling are additional skills that will help supervisors gather information and determine what kind of help (informal or professional) is needed and when.

Steps 6, 7, 8, and 9: Planning and Carrying Out a Discussion

There are three ways to conduct a counseling interview: (1) the tell-and-sell approach, (2) the tell-and-listen approach, and (3) the problem-solving approach. The first is highly directive, the second is nondirective, and the third is interactive.

In the *tell and sell approach,* the supervisor describes the performance problem, sketches what he or she knows about it, and suggests a specific course of action. The purpose of such an interview—a "positive confrontation"—is to persuade the employee that a problem exists and then to clarify what the supervisor thinks should be done about it. This approach is useful for shaking individuals out of complacency, but it should be exercised with care: It can provoke defensiveness and serve just the opposite purpose for which it was intended.

In the *tell and listen approach,* the supervisor describes a problem from his or her perspective and then listens carefully to employee explanations and comments about it. The purpose is to solicit information and gather facts. This approach is appropriate when good rapport already exists between supervisor and subordinate.

In the *problem-solving approach,* the focus is on direct mutual communication. The supervisor interacts with the employee on two levels at once: content and feeling. On the content level, the supervisor focuses on the performance problem; on the feeling level, he or she tunes in to the subtleties of the employee's emotions, whether expressed vocally or through body language. The interview opens a dialogue on an issue or problem, conveys concern, and explores solutions.

Planning a counseling interview is critical. The supervisor should begin with a clear purpose, have facts about the employee's job requirements and actual performance close at hand, and be prepared with questions. Figure 15-2 provides some pointers. Undoubtedly, training in counseling skills can improve the abilities of supervisors to conduct such interviews and help them recognize problems and tones when a referral to a trained psychologist or other healthcare professional might be appropriate.

Peer counseling, which is usually informal, can help some troubled persons as much as supervisory counseling. Professional psychologists often question the wisdom of letting untrained people deal with those experiencing a personal problem, but sometimes all that is really needed is a good listener. Many lonely people only lack a support group consisting of family and friends; the influence of peers or a work group on behavior or the individual performance is powerful for good or ill. The recent widespread adoption of work teams in organizations promotes such interpersonal closeness, essential at a time when the influence of families, religious institutions, and other traditional support networks is decreasing.

Figure 15-2: Pointers for Planning and Conducting a Counseling Interview with a Problem Employee

---

I Hold the meeting in private.

I Minimize potential for interruptions (e.g., phone calls, drop-in visitors).

I Begin with small talk to set the employee at ease.

I Make clear early on in the discussion that the focus is on the employee, but the interview is not for disciplining.

I Describe what is known about the employee's long-term performance over the past few years (if possible).

I Give praise if it is due.

I Describe performance requirements for the employee's job (What should be?).

I Describe the employee's recent performance (What is?).

I Pinpoint gaps between requirements and realities.

I Stress the importance of the gap and its consequences.

I Explain what the cause appears to be.

I Suggest action; listen to employee response; help deal with the problem.

Steps 10 and 11: Planning and Carrying Out Action

Once it is apparent that an employee has a personal problem that affects work performance, the question is this: What should be done about it? If the supervisor is satisfied that the problem stems from the person rather than from inadequate feedback, interdependency of work tasks, poor control over work outcomes, or other matters that the individual can rarely influence, the next question is this: Is the problem primarily limited to the work environment, or is it only part of a larger problem affecting the individual?

For problems limited to individual work performance alone, one approach to planning and carrying out corrective action is *performance contracting*. A performance contract is an agreement between the employee and the supervisor, perhaps formalized in writing. To solve a specific problem, such as tardiness, a *limited contract* might be all that is necessary. Employee and manager negotiate what the problem is, what standard of performance is expected (for example, no tardiness is acceptable, but even with good excuses it cannot exceed two instances per month), how performance will be measured, how often performance reviews will take place, and what the consequences of poor performance will be. This approach can lead to definite improvement in behavior. If it does not, then the employee can either be disciplined or referred to professional help, depending on the nature of the problem.

Professional counseling is appropriate if the problem stems from an individual's personal difficulties. Most personal problems can be handled without professional counselors, however. In fact, professional counseling is only appropriate for about 10 percent of all troubled employees.

Two types of professional counseling arrangements are possible: counseling conducted by trained psychologists employed by the organization, and counseling conducted by an outside group on contract with the organization.

Let us describe briefly a few specific kinds of Employee Assistance Programs.

Alcoholism programs are perhaps the most common. The history of EAPs goes back to the efforts of two companies: In 1914, Ford Motor Company established a department for employees' personal affairs. Three years later, Macy's department stores set up counseling programs for their employees. It was not until the 1940s that interest in such programs began to grow. At that time, alcoholism was a pervasive problem, as it is today. The earliest alcoholism programs were staffed by recovered alcoholics, usually working out of company medical departments.

There is little doubt that companies need to do something about this problem. Between 8 and 10 percent of the entire U.S. labor force suffers from alcohol abuse. About 45 percent of alcoholics found in organizations can be found in the ranks of professionals and managers, about 30 percent are manual workers, and 25 percent are in white-collar jobs.

The detection of an alcoholic's problem in the work setting usually rests with the superior. Early detection makes it easier to deal with the problem, but detection is often delayed because (1) the individual's performance may actually improve at the start; (2) the supervisor wants to avoid involvement and may have been a past drinking partner; (3) alcoholics are often very likable people, making it all the more difficult to approach them (in some cases supervisors will actually help them conceal the problem); and (4) other employees may help conceal the problem, too, either because they like the drinker or because they see a chance for some personal gain resulting from the alcoholic's plight. An individual's chances of recovering can be improved substantially when supervisors are trained in how to recognize early stages of alcoholism and know when to refer individuals to professionals for treatment.

The usual thrust of alcoholism programs is to retain the problem employee while forcing him or her, on pain of dismissal, to seek treatment. To prevent legal hassles, it might be necessary to have alcoholics and other problem employees sign a "last chance agreement" prior to treatment. Typically, professionals work under contract to the company, and employees are referred to them.

Drug abuse programs are quite common, prompted by changes in the law. Drug abuse, perhaps even more than alcoholism, is a national scandal. It has reached epidemic proportions. Perhaps as many as one in eighteen employees sells drugs.

There are several ways to offer treatment: (1) an *intensive day program,* usually lasting about a month; (2) an *outpatient program,* usually lasting for some time but set in weekly counseling sessions; or (3) an *evening program,* operated by company-employed professionals. The more obvious and severe the problem, the more often intensive day programs are recommended.

Emotional wellness programs address other personal problems. One study cited by McClellan (1985) indicated that 18.7 percent of U.S. adults suffered from an emotional problem during *one* six-month period. Two-thirds of those experiencing problems were troubled by simple phobias or by a traumatic event, such as the death of a spouse, divorce, separation, or imprisonment of a child. The remaining one-third experienced alcohol or other problems.

Counseling programs that deal with emotional problems can be short-term or long-term. They can be informally handled by supervisors or peers, company-sponsored and held in-house, or company-contracted and held off-site.

There is no doubt that most serious personal problems are recognized in the work place. Supervisors and peers show varying amounts of sensitivity when a colleague is suffering. Most people are willing to be understanding, at least in the short term.

Long-term problems that persist longer than several weeks should be referred to professionals. Most in-house and company-sponsored efforts geared to treatment last under one year. More complex problems usually have to be handled at the employee's expense. Companies also offer family/marital counseling, financial counseling, legal assistance, and retirement programs for employees. Some organizations have made counseling assistance available online, which has the advantage of permitting initial anonymity. These have been dramatically successful (Starner, 2000).

Retirement programs are informational in nature. A company representative meets with pre-retirees in a setting that resembles a training course. Pension benefits, insurance, and Social Security are discussed. In some cases, the program presenter also deals with emotional preparation for retirement and with career opportunities inside and outside the company that are available to retirees. (Such programs are likely to be increasingly important as a majority of the U.S. workforce, the so-called Baby-Boom generation, nears retirement.)

Financial counseling and legal assistance programs are for individuals facing an immediate problem: a divorce, a child-custody case, or financial difficulties severe enough to result in an order to garnish the employee's wage. First, the immediate problem is handled. Subsequent counseling, of limited duration, focuses on detecting and remedying the underlying causes or consequences of that problem.

Marital counseling is usually handled by trained counselors and psychologists. Such programs are often contracted-for externally. Couples attend numerous sessions in individual or group settings. Among problems addressed by such counseling is the serious matter of domestic abuse, a situation that is probably apparent to co-workers and supervisors.

Evaluating EAPs

How does a manager decide whether or not their firm ought to sponsor an Employee Assistance Program? Which kinds of EAPs should be offered? What criteria can be used to judge the potential value of an EAP?

Most large firms will probably find it cost beneficial to implement a broad-based EAP program. EAPs can reduce absenteeism and increase the productivity of individuals otherwise not working up to potential. EAPs can also help hold down spiraling healthcare and worker compensation expenses or claims. Many issues of interest to HRP practitioners can in fact be addressed through EAPs.

To determine which or how many programs to offer, HRP practitioners can survey employees and/or supervisors to estimate the incidence of problems noticed in the organization and then interview randomly selected people at different levels in the organizational hierarchy or people at different worksites about the kinds of programs they would like to see. People are often reluctant to admit the need for such programs, so survey and interview results might be incorrectly skewed toward *not* dealing with such problems. Before offering any specific EAP, it might be wise to consider whether it meets criteria for success. Training and information dissemination directed at executives and supervisors can over time increase the chances for program success.

After a program has been operating for a time, HRP practitioners should evaluate how well it has been working (Cohen, 1998). Though such evaluation is only rarely done, the information that does exist indicates that success can be dramatic. If the organization conducts regular climate or attitude surveys, either on paper or online, decision-makers can use that method as one way to evaluate employee perceptions of the usefulness of such programs. Follow-up phone calls, interviews, or written evaluations can also produce insights and information useful in evaluating a specific program.

Problems with the Traditional Approach to Employee Assistance Programs

There are two major problems with EAPs. The first problem is that they constitute a potential liability for the organization (Capron, 1998). Such programs are the target of litigation under the Americans with Disabilities Act, employee privacy laws, and religious discrimination. The second major problem with most EAPs is that they tend to be *crisis* driven. In short, individuals have to experience a problem before they are given assistance or referred for help. The result is, of course, loss of otherwise productive work time, not to mention hidden costs in employee morale. What most programs need then, is a greater emphasis on anticipating problems and heading them off before they occur.

Strategic EAPs

There are several ways to anticipate employee problems and deal with them before they occur. One is to set up a *wellness program*. A second way is to place a greater emphasis on *risk screening* during recruitment and selection. A third is to develop a more strategic EAP.

Wellness Programs

Rather than focusing on diagnosis and support during illness, the traditional emphasis of Employee Assistance Programs and of medical science, wellness programs are preventive in nature. To a significant extent, many illnesses are either self-inflicted or stem in part from stress-related behavior. To cite some examples: Smoking causes lung cancer and emphysema; excessive consumption of fats and low consumption of fiber contribute to colon cancer; and lack of exercise has been linked to heart disease.

An ideal wellness program has five components (Naditch, 1985):

1. *Assessment.* The purpose of assessment is to determine which wellness programs will have the most impact and what kinds of programs are most cost-beneficial in preventing costly illness. This step is carried out initially, and repeated periodically, through employee and management surveys and interviews.

2. *Risk review.* Employees undergo physical exams. The results are used to complete a specially designed appraisal of each individual's risk of death. Information is compiled both about behavior and about current physical status. This information is confidential but is provided to each person.

3. *Courses.* A comprehensive wellness program includes a variety of courses on smoking cessation, stress and weight reduction, healthy eating, and occupational safety; they are offered in the classroom or through individualized study, and increasingly through computerized instruction.

4. *Organization development.* Wellness courses directed at individuals should be accompanied by or supplemented with organizational development efforts intended to transform the organization into a place where individual health is promoted as a goal in its own right. Through team efforts resembling quality circles, employees identify health problems or improvement opportunities and propose specific changes to management. Many organizations have even installed comprehensive wellness or fitness centers where individuals exercise, focus on weight loss, and receive group training or individualized counseling.

5. *Evaluation.* The entire effort is evaluated periodically through follow-up medical examinations and surveys to assess employee/man-

agement perceptions about the effectiveness of the program and differences between aggregate data about individual risks before and after the program begins.

Clearly, a wellness program is strategic in nature because it is based on a risk review, which is more or less the same as a forecast of individual health problems. Wellness programs are geared to anticipating and preventing problems *before* they arise.

Risk Screening

Another way to anticipate problems is to conduct risk-screening of job candidates. You will be able to detect and screen out people who show signs of high risk before you hire or promote them to stressful positions.

Clearly, risk screening during the hiring process leads the organization into murky legal waters. Evaluating job applicants on the basis of a current medical condition is a well-accepted practice, but assessing the potential for future problems (or even the genetic inclination toward specific diseases) might open you up to lawsuits. For this reason, review any such screening plans with company legal staff *before* implementation. Important note of caution: *genetic testing* is particularly controversial.

Risks other than physiological ones can also be assessed, but they, too, open up possibilities of litigation unless they are carefully examined for this potential in advance. For example, employers who might want to request a credit investigation on applicants must be careful that such investigations are conducted in compliance with the Fair Credit Reporting Act of 1971 as enacted and subsequently amended. Illnesses must be considered, too, in light of pertinent equal rights laws that prohibit discrimination on the basis of race or sex. While risk screening is one way to reduce the need for Employee Assistance Programs, only specific problems can safely be assessed in light of current law.

Strategic Emphasis on the Employee Assistance Program

Strategically emphasizing EAPs means, first and foremost, focusing on prevention rather than on detecting, and then dealing with problem employees. Wellness programs are a key part of any strategic EAP, as is prevention of such non-health problems as those having to do with personal finances, marriage, family matters, and legal difficulties.

There are many advantages to taking a preventive approach. It reduces employee suffering, regardless of cause. It heads off problems before they disrupt morale or create lost production time in an entire work group. Finally, a preventive approach is consistent with the trend toward holistic management.

The components of a strategic EAP program include

1. *Policy.* What issues pertaining to employee health do decision-makers address? How much does policy outline the purpose/goals of EAPs? Responsibilities of management, labor unions, supervisors, and individuals?
2. *Individual stress forecasting.* What problems for individuals seem likely to come up in the future?
3. *Work-context stress forecasting.* What problems seem likely to be induced from the future work context?
4. *Program planning.* How can policy be enacted in light of expected problems likely to affect individuals and jobs in the organization?
5. *Action.* What do individuals need to do to head off risks? How can supervisors help in early problem detection?
6. *Evaluation.* How useful is the current EAP? What problems might it prevent in the future?

A clear policy on employee assistance represents a starting point for subsequent action. In formulating policy, HR planners must first assess the business philosophy. How willing do decision-makers appear to be to adopt a holistic management view? How willing are they to deal with individual performance problems when they are caused by personal problems in areas of health, family, personal finance, and/or other matters outside the immediate work setting? On the other hand, how willing are they to support employee assistance when a problem is caused by poor work design or working conditions, or lousy group relations or supervision? By asking these questions in a structured way through surveys and interviews, HR planners can draft an employee assistance policy that can be reviewed and subsequently supported, perhaps after modification, by management and organized labor.

What separates the strategic approach from the traditional approach? The focus on forecasting *future needs*. What kinds of employee assistance needs are likely to emerge? How should the organization and its members prepare to deal with them in advance? Some matters are easier to forecast than others (drug abuse, for example, is already at a crisis level and is expected to get worse). Other matters are not so easy to predict. How will stress-induced illness or its effects be increased as a consequence of future changes in the job, work group or organization? A merger, for example, can dramatically affect the need for an EAP, yet such a dramatic change is not always common knowledge, nor is it always desirable.

Individual stress forecasting refers to forecasting individual problems. Each employee completes a stress profile once a year that records major life events or crises, such as divorce, childbirth, or marriage (confronted or expected). A separate profile is completed about existing or impending job changes. The two scores are then aggregated to assess the individual's susceptibility to stress-induced illness. The final score identifies those at particular risk who should receive periodical counseling.

Work-context stress forecasting is the second kind of forecasting. It relies on people who, functioning as a team, forecast the likelihood of increasing stress created by changing conditions in the work setting. Each team recommends action to management. The focus, of course, is on the work environment rather than on individuals. A major impetus for this forecasting is an increase in stress-related disability claims and the growing stress levels in many U.S. organizations.

Program planning for EAP initiatives stems from a combination of policy, which clarifies what problems should be addressed, and forecasting, which clarifies what problems *will probably come up*. Program plans (1) identify what kind of programs will be offered, (2) specify how the programs will be offered, (3) clarify what resources—time, money, staff, and contractual assistance—will be needed and when they will be needed, and (4) establish measurable objectives against which to assess *future* progress.

The sixth step in a strategic EAP program is to implement the program. This involves (1) setting up ways to compile data about individuals, (2) training supervisors about the scope and intent of EAPs, (3) communicating to employees about EAPs, (4) establishing a team (or teams) of people to conduct work-context stress forecasting, (5) finalizing program plans, and (6) implementing EAPs.

Finally, evaluation is carried out periodically to compare program objectives to program results. This information is, in turn, used to evaluate how well the Employee Assistance Program has contributed to implementation of HR Grand Strategy.

CHAPTER 16

LABOR RELATIONS

Labor relations refers to the continuous relationship between a union representing the collective interest of workers and the organization's management. This relationship focuses primarily on union and management rights, a written contract, and the interpretation of the written contract. Traditionally, labor relations has been viewed by many HRP practitioners as the study of negotiation under highly contentious conditions, though recent research indicates that the labor relations climate is becoming dramatically more or dramatically less contentious, based on the firm (Cutcher-Gershenfeld, 1996a). Labor union influence in the United States has been on the decline for 40 years, and attitudes have changed regarding the relative value of unionization (Cutcher-Gershenfeld, 1998; Fuller, 1998; Harper, 1994).

The specialized terms used in labor relations as a specialty area in HR include

- *Collective bargaining.* The process of negotiation between a labor union and an employer.
- *Grievance.* Any dispute between a union member and management.
- *Arbitration.* The process of submitting a grievance for resolution by an independent and presumably neutral third party who is not employed by the firm in which the grievance is filed.

- *Mediation.* The process of using a third party to help settle labor contract negotiations between a union and a company.
- *Unfair labor practice.* The use by a company or union of tactics prohibited by law.
- *Strike.* The suspension of work by a union. An authorized strike is one organized by the union. An unauthorized strike is called a *wildcat* or a *walkout.*
- *Lockout.* The reverse of a labor strike. When managers deliberately prevent people from working because of unresolved labor problems, it is called a *lockout.*
- *Trade* or *industry unions.* The earliest unions consisted of people engaged in a trade. Examples of tradespeople include carpenters, plumbers, electricians, and bricklayers. These unions still exist, usually dominating a geographical area. Industry unions consist of organized labor in particular industries. Some examples of industry unions are the United Auto Workers, the Teamsters, and the American Federation of State, County, and Municipal Employees.
- *Bargaining unit.* The smallest group of workers who can bargain collectively.

The research and published writing on labor relations has been largely done by Americans, but labor relations is also important in international settings (Cutcher-Gershenfeld, 1996b). Of particular interest is labor relations practice in rapidly developing or highly productive international settings (Wang, 1995). Multinational corporations are particularly attuned to organized labor practices globally, and some experts have predicted pressure for the advent of multinational labor unions to challenge multinational organizations (Rothwell, Prescott, and Taylor, 1998). Such pressure is increased by the growing ease of communicating globally through such means as the World Wide Web.

The Role of Labor Relations in Implementing HR Grand Strategy

Clearly, unionized firms must function in ways different from those that are nonunion. More specifically, the presence or absence of a labor union will affect

1. *Recruitment and selection.* Unionized firms have higher wages and salaries than their nonunion counterparts, thus making it easier to hire and retain qualified employees.
2. *Training.* Generally, unionized firms enjoy the luxury of investing in training that is more generalized and less job-specific than nonunion firms because employees are not in competition for promotion.
3. *Career planning and management.* Unionized firms bring stability to the issue of promotion through systems frequently based on seniority. They also transfer and promote more frequently than nonunionized ones.
4. *Organization development.* Unionized firms are characterized by higher levels of employee dissatisfaction, an issue that can be addressed through organization development. Areas covered by the collective bargaining agreement tend to be particular sources of dissatisfaction. It appears that some employee dissatisfaction is necessary for a union to survive.
5. *Job redesign.* In unionized settings, people are very interested in personnel matters. Unions battle for more jobs, so they generally oppose job redesign efforts that increase individual or group productivity without also providing guarantees of job security. In fact, some unions favor make-work policies, such as arbitrary limits on output or the use of otherwise unnecessary labor. Unions resist attempts to increase individual workload without commensurate pay increases.
6. *Employee assistance programs (EAPs).* In adversarial union-management environments, distrust of EAPs is pronounced. Employees fear that information about their health or personal habits will be used against them.

7. *Compensation/benefit programs.* Labor costs and employee wages/salaries are important issues that must be covered in any collective bargaining agreement. Fringe benefits are frequently prized by unions and are sought even when wage concessions are necessary.

It is quite apparent that the presence of a union changes the HR practices of any organization. Whether a union limits management's flexibility in dealing with HR Grand Strategy, however, is debatable: It depends on what strategy the organization wishes to pursue.

The Traditional Approach to Labor Relations Programs

Reasons for Unionization

One 20th century version of a quote by Thomas Jefferson goes like this: "Managers get the kind of union they best deserve." Unionization is often a consequence of management behavior. When employees are dissatisfied, they are more open to unionization. Research indicates that employers who believe that their industries should pay lower wages in order to remain competitive seem to face the most difficult labor relations climate (Birecree, 1997). And some evidence exists that there are broader wage differentials between unionized and nonunionized workers in the United States than in European firms (Kahn, 1998).

What are some *causes* of employee dissatisfaction that give rise to unionization? They vary. Examples include

1. *Inequitable treatment on wages, salaries, and/or benefits.* When employees feel that others in the organization or in the same geographical area are receiving higher wages and/or better benefits for comparable work, they are motivated to reduce this feeling of inequity. Collective bargaining is one way to do so.

2. *Treatment in recruitment and promotion practices.* When employees feel that poorly qualified people are hired or promoted, they are offended by the perceived injustice.

3. *Unfair treatment.* When people are disciplined or dismissed for trivial matters, or when managers are perceived to be applying rules capriciously, then employees are motivated to restore consistency.

4. *Working conditions are not acceptable.* When employees feel that working conditions are unsafe or are unjustifiably severe, they might want to force improvements.

The key terms are *feelings* and *inequity.* Unionization is one of several *group* reactions to perceived unfairness in the workplace.

Individuals vary in their reasons for supporting unionization. Generally, they are more inclined to unionize when they desire influence over decisions affecting them and see no other route to gaining that influence; when they believe a union will improve conditions; or when a small, hardcore group of disaffected workers takes the lead, organizing a drive for union membership.

The Organizing Campaign

The starting point for any unionization effort is an organizing campaign. Employee activists contact a representative of a union, or paid union organizers seek out activist employees. When union officials believe there is a good chance of organizing workers, they will help start an organizing campaign.

The first step is to collect signatures on authorization cards. If cards are signed by more than half of an organization's employees, then the union can ask employer representatives for voluntary recognition. The union then files with the National Labor Relations Board (NLRB), the federal agency that deals with union-management agreements, as the "exclusive" bargaining agent. On the other hand, if fewer than half but more than 30 percent of employees sign authorization cards or if the employer refuses to grant voluntary recognition after more than half the workers sign cards, then the union submits to the NLRB a petition to hold an election.

The NLRB investigates this petition. If it meets requirements, a worker election is scheduled. Prior to that election, organizers try to increase worker support for unionization. Managers try to decrease support. If more than half the employees vote in favor of union representation, then the employer is forced to recognize it as bargaining agent. If fewer than half the employees vote for the union, then a new organizing campaign can begin only after completion of a one-year waiting period.

Managers are prohibited by law from punishing labor activists during an organizing campaign, unless that punishment is in accordance with pre-existing policies and work rules of the company. In short, managers cannot fire or discipline employees simply because they are union activists. Nor can managers take sudden, favorable action, such as raising wage rates. Such actions are called *unfair labor practices*. They can result in costly and drawn-out lawsuits.

However, managers can still try to influence workers to vote against union representation. The HR department usually takes the lead role in collecting unfavorable information about the union, particularly about any unattractive experiences in other organizations. Examples include trends in union dues, strikes, and other facts that shed unfavorable light on the union. The HR department provides this information to first-line supervisors, who represent the company to most front-line employees. The way those supervisors deal with the information determines in large part whether employees will try to unionize to begin with, and whether an organizing campaign is ultimately successful.

Of course, while managers work to decrease union support, company activists and union organizers point to unfavorable features about the company's record of dealing with employee concerns.

The reverse of an organizing campaign is called *union decertification*—an effort to throw out an existing union. Union decertification efforts have been increasing since 1950, and more and more are successful, though workers in unionized firms are sometimes unaware of it as an option (Meeker, 1999). Union vulnerability to decertification has increased, a trend that is in line with the membership decline experienced by unions throughout the United States. The reasons for this trend are many: more foreign competition by cheaper labor; fewer blue-collar workers with historical penchants for unionization and more white-collar workers who have historically resisted unionizing efforts; increasing public disenchantment with lengthy strikes; increasing numbers of women in the labor force (a group that has never favored unionizing); and an increasing willingness on the part of employers to move to smaller, less centralized locations in geographical areas where unions have never been strong.

Traditional Components of a Labor Relations Program

The starting point for any labor relations program is a contractual agreement between the union and the employer.

The Labor-Management Relations Act requires that issues like wages, conditions of employment, and hours of work must be negotiated. In short, they are mandatory *contract issues.* Other concerns include job security, union security, management rights, and length of the labor agreement.

Wages and salaries are not the only issues considered in negotiations between management and labor: Union members are also interested in preserving equity—they want to be paid at least as well as others in the firm or the geographical area. Managers are of course interested in keeping the company's labor costs as low as possible so that the firm can compete successfully (and they can keep their jobs).

Several matters are of key concern in wage, salary, and benefit negotiations. One is the *ability to pay,* the relative profitability or financial status of the organization. The better its position, the more likely that union members will ask for wage concessions, and the more tenaciously they will cling to their demands. Another matter is *pay equity,* the belief that wages in the organization are as good or better than in other organizations. Of course, wages and regular work hours are not the only issues of concern: Others include what the hours will be, how overtime will be scheduled, when it will be scheduled, and what indirect compensation or fringe benefits employees will receive.

Job security is another matter for negotiation. Who will be laid off in the event of production cutbacks? How will people be selected for layoff? Typically, unions favor job security based on seniority: Employees should be laid off on the basis of who has been with the company the least amount of time. The longer the employee's tenure, the less chance he or she will be subject to layoff. Managers, on the other hand, wish to reserve the right to decide who will be laid off on the basis of individual job performance.

Union security is the ability of the union to strengthen its status. Union negotiators would like company representatives to agree that all new employees will have to become union members. If they cannot win this concession, *agency status* is nearly as good. In the latter instance, new employees are not forced to join the union, but are required to pay the equivalent of union dues if they benefit from concessions won in collective-bargaining agreements.

Management rights are similar in some respects to union security; they have to do with specifying what kinds of decisions managers are free to make without union approval, sanction, or awareness. Company negotiators vary in their opinions on this matter. Some believe it is important to spell out management rights so as to make them clear; others contend that this practice is unwise in that it is unduly restrictive, tending to limit otherwise unlimited rights.

The length of the labor agreement is a final matter of major concern. Generally, company representatives prefer longer contractual agreements because of the stability they provide. Most contracts cover two or three years.

The process of labor negotiation begins when union officials meet to agree on a package of requests while managers separately agree on an offer to make. Each side has priorities—some issues that are deemed more important than others. During negotiations, one side is usually willing to concede on one matter in order to obtain agreement on a more important issue. If negotiations are successful, union members vote to ratify a new contract and a work stoppage is averted.

Negotiations are considered unsuccessful when labor and management cannot reach agreement on a contract. When it becomes apparent that negotiations are headed toward an *impasse*—a point at which further talks are fruitless until one side yields—union members begin to build a strike fund. At the same time, managers increase production so that excess inventory will be available in the event of a work stoppage. Typically, neither union nor management wants a strike. However, it is a tool of last resort when there is an impasse.

Lengthy strikes might ultimately result in the need for a third-party mediator who can bring union and management together to facilitate the process of reaching an agreement. The Federal Mediation and Conciliation Service (FMCS) is one source for mediators who collect facts and establish committees to deal with the toughest issues. Some state governments also provide mediators to help break deadlocks when they exist, or avert them when they are anticipated.

As soon as an agreement is reached, contract administration begins—the day-to-day process of abiding by the contractual arrangement. Indeed, it occupies the attention of company supervisors, employees, labor relations specialists, and union stewards. Union stewards are the lowest-level of union representation. They are typically selected from employee ranks, are paid out of union dues, and are the first ones approached when employees dispute a supervisor's order.

Contract administration is necessary because labor agreements are, like most legal documents, rather general in what they cover and are open to differing interpretations. As Figure 16-1 illustrates, individual cases such as who is assigned to what job or tasks (as well as on what basis that decision is made) lend themselves to disagreements between company and union representatives.

Figure 16-1: The Role of Interpretation in Contract Administration

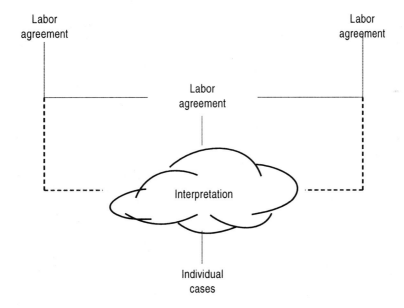

If no initial agreement is reached about the problem, the employee files a grievance. It is usually done first verbally and then in writing. The supervisor receives it, reviews its merits in light of his or her understanding of the labor agreement, and then decides to accept or reject the argument. If the first-line supervisor rejects the grievance and the employee is still dissatisfied, it is transmitted to the next level of management. The company's labor relations specialists become actively involved at this point and might in some cases overrule the supervisor. If the employee remains dissatisfied with the decision made at this level and if the union chooses to "push" the matter, a third-party arbitrator will probably be asked to decide. When both management and labor agree in advance to accept the arbitrator's decision without further dispute, the process is called *binding arbitration*. It will take some time to select an arbitrator whose prior positions in other cases show an inclination to decide an issue of this kind one way or the other.

The grievance process, as described in the previous paragraph, appears to be quite rational, with minimal potential for political jockeying and power plays. Nothing could be further from the truth! In reality, the grievance process represents continuous collective bargaining between management and labor. Union leaders will flood formal channels with grievances, serious and frivolous. They can use the grievance process as a tool to try to gain back-door concessions that were not granted in the original labor agreement. Nor are they or their management counterparts above "trading" agreements so that a favorable decision on one grievance is exchanged for a favorable decision on another.

Grievances are a small but highly significant part of the contract administration process. About 80 percent of all grievances are resolved at the lowest level (between and among employee, supervisor, and steward), and another 19 percent are resolved at the next level. Only one grievance in a hundred reaches arbitration, but that "one" is important, because it represents a genuine area of disagreement that might surface again in future contract negotiations. In one study of arbitration practices in Ontario, Canada, 54 interviews with union and management officials actively engaged in negotiations revealed that most officials surveyed viewed arbitration either in a neutral or a negative way—more of a face-saving tactic than an especially effective tool for collective bargaining (Rose 1996).

Problems with the Traditional Approach to Labor Relations

The traditional management approach to labor relations is best summarized as "keep the rascals out." Two ways of avoiding unionization are typically used: a genuine human *resources* philosophy, and a human *relations* philosophy. In the first approach, company managers provide benefits and programs otherwise sought by unions because they genuinely believe the employees deserve them. The second approach is used solely to avoid unions.

When union avoidance efforts fail or are unsuccessful, managers have several options in response to a union:

1. *Hostility.* Management tries to "break" the union.
2. *Controlled conflict.* Management tries to limit union influence.
3. *Tolerance.* Management accepts the reality of the union and shows a willingness to engage in collective bargaining.
4. *Acceptance.* Management and labor actually work together on some issues.
5. *Cronyism.* Management and union officials work together to their benefit and to the detriment of employees.

These options represent a continuum. Tolerance probably represents the most common approach found today, even though many firms do work toward union decertification.

Present conditions in the labor market favor union concessions. The influence of unions in all but public sector settings is waning in light of a host of unfavorable factors: increasing numbers of women, white-collar workers, and the highly educated in the labor force (all groups that have resisted unionizing); decreasing public support for unions; decreasing demand for products associated with industries known for unions; and increasing foreign competition.

Traynor (1997) pointed out a qualitative shift in collective bargaining practice since 1981 when President Ronald Reagan fired and replaced striking members of the Professional Air Traffic Controllers Organization (PATCO). Before that time, labor relations could have been characterized as "soft": Persuasion was the traditional tactic used by management in dealing with organized labor.

Labor relations are now characterized as "hard": Coercion and the threat of unemployment are more often used.

Though it seems like heresy to say so, unions bring distinct advantages. First, they keep managers alert to employee needs and concerns. Second, they provide a structure for negotiations between employees and employer, a process that occurs with or without a union. Of course, without a union, negotiations are between individuals and the firm. Third, they provide an additional authority structure outside management that can contribute to improved communication between employer and employees.

The traditional approach to labor relations is inadequate because it tends to mean (1) avoiding unionizing drives in spite of some potential advantages to be gained by the company, (2) bargaining on some issues of employee concern, and (3) dealing with past or present issues rather than with those likely to emerge, over time, as more important. What is needed is a more strategically oriented approach.

Strategic Labor Relations

Strategic labor relations can be viewed in at least three contexts: (1) avoidance of unionization, (2) use of unions in organizational and HR planning, and (3) elimination of a union presence. Each warrants consideration.

Avoidance of Unionization

How can managers deal strategically with the issue of union avoidance? The answer is this: They must establish some kind of union avoidance program in advance of the first organizing campaign, and keep it going. Such a program should include (1) a decision about objectives, (2) regular assessment of conditions favoring unionization, (3) forecasting future trends that can encourage those conditions, (4) choice of nonunion strategy, and (5) implementation of the program.

The first step is to make a decision about objectives. What is it that managers want? *Why* do they wish to avoid unionization? One decision is to co-opt union organizing efforts. The aim in this case is to identify and solve problems that, if left unresolved, would give a union an opportunity to organize by taking advantage of employee dissatisfaction. Another decision is to draw boundaries, conceding some territory or job classes to unions and establishing a policy of defending others at all costs. A third decision is to reject the concept of union avoidance and to invite a union in on terms initially dictated by the company.

Assuming that the company's managers wish to avoid unions completely, the second step in an avoidance program is to periodically assess conditions that favor unionization:

- To what extent do employees view the company and supervisors as fair and even-handed? Unwilling to engage in favoritism? Competent to deal with employee and work problems?
- To what extent do employees feel that their jobs are relatively secure?
- To what extent do employees feel that people who are promoted deserve the promotion because of hard work?
- To what extent do employees view the HR department as competent in dealing with problems posed by working conditions? Supervisory practices? Problem employees?
- To what extent do employees think that compensation is equitable inside the organization? Outside? Benefits are commensurate with employee needs? With practices of other employers in the area?
- To what extent do employees believe that managers in the company listen—and act on—employee complaints? Care about employee concerns? Are willing to rectify problems?

These questions can be researched by using employee attitude surveys, interviews, and even quality circles. Problems in specific work groups can be targeted for action before they get out of hand.

The third step is to forecast. Managers must try to predict changes that are likely to come about over a particular time period in the organization, work group, or jobs, and then anticipate the probable effects of these changes on individual perceptions. In short, forecasting provides an early warning system about conditions that encourage unionization so that these conditions can be anticipated and their effects minimized or avoided.

The fourth step is to choose a non-union strategy. Through what means do managers wish to pursue their efforts? One choice is to co-opt the union by increasing wages and implementing new personnel policies to improve benefits, opportunities for promotion, and other issues that are the traditional focus of union organizers. A second choice is to increase efforts to communicate with employees through formal and informal meetings, company publications, bulletin boards, and other media. A third choice is to train supervisors on how to improve their communication and interpersonal skills, and to report conditions likely to produce significant employee discontent. A fourth choice is to do research on unions that might try to organize workers, collect any unfavorable information about them, and communicate the information to workers before the first sign of an organizing drive. Of course, these choices are not mutually exclusive. They can be and have been used in tandem.

The fifth and final step is to implement the strategy. Somebody in the organization must be given responsibility and authority to act. Typically, the personnel manager is a good choice. He or she should not only be familiar with applicable labor laws, but should be capable of keeping the union avoidance program going.

Use of Unions in Organizational and HR Planning

Some managers will consider it heresy to suggest that there are instances when unionization is actually beneficial for implementing organizational and HR plans. However, the presence of a union merely limits unilateral management action and arbitrary decision-making. A union might, in fact, tend to restore relative stability to a labor scene otherwise marred by personal favoritism and other destabilizing conditions.

The real choice to consider is this: What are the relative priorities of managers, based on the HR Grand Strategy, that the organization is to pursue?

In some cases, unions actually provide a competitive *advantage* of sorts. They are not always a disadvantage, as press accounts make them appear. For instance, in public-sector settings, elected officials often encourage unionizing in order to increase their appeal to certain portions of the electorate. In private-sector settings, some firms wish to have the union label so as to make their relations more cordial with skilled trades and other potential *consumer* groups with influential voices in the marketplace.

To a great extent, the successful use of unions in organizational and HR planning is a function of the contract negotiation process and contract administration.

Contract negotiations occur at regular intervals, usually every two or three years. As a consequence, there is a periodic cycle that lends itself to management deliberation on HR planning issues. With this information available, negotiators are in a better position to use *integrative bargaining*, in which the company concedes on some matters of importance to the union in return for union concessions on matters of strategic import to the firm. An important tool in this process is an employee communication program that helps workers understand company strategy, competition, and key strengths and weaknesses in the marketplace. As a consequence, workers will be more amenable to concessions of particular importance to a firm, especially in light of what happens to workers when the firm is a competitive failure. No union wins when a company goes bankrupt, shuts down a plant, or relocates overseas.

Contract administration is at least of equal importance. Strategic goals must be converted to action. It is in the contract-administration process that HR Grand Strategy, in a union setting, is implemented. Hence, the union must be made an active partner in all aspects of personnel decision-making on the shop floor.

Eliminating the Union

The decision to pursue decertification is a strategic one in its own right. It is not a decision to be taken lightly: An active management effort to decertify a union will (predictably) create severe short-term tension. Managers should thus be certain, before they start, that long-term benefits will outweigh short-term consequences.

When should decertification be sought? Of course, there is no one simple answer to this question. The real issue is whether the union has become a competitive liability that so constrains management decision-making as to pose a threat to company survival. It is rare that conditions will become this severe. But when they do or when they appear to be headed in that direction, decertification is one route to pursue. Others include filing for bankruptcy or simply relocating. The latter choices, to put it metaphorically, kill the patient in order to cure the disease. If a firm's managers can increase employee dissatisfaction about the union and take advantage of it, it is more likely that decertification will occur. Strategies include (1) making the union appear inept or ineffective, (2) communicating about prolonged strikes and other unpopular actions backed by the union in other settings, (3) taking advantage of factional bickering among union leaders to gain a favorable company image with employees, and (4) hiring specialized, experienced consultants in union decertification.

The choice of what labor relations strategy to pursue really depends on what managers want and to what extent they are willing to trade short-term advantages and disadvantages for long-term ones.

CHAPTER 17

COMPENSATION AND BENEFITS

Compensation refers to any monetary return or nonmonetary service received as a consequence of employment. There are two kinds: *direct compensation,* which is cash payment for work performed, and *indirect compensation,* which includes insurance and other non-cash payments. *Benefits* are a form of indirect compensation. *Total compensation* is defined as a combination of direct and indirect compensation (Pauly, 1996). Of course, total compensation is only a subset of a *reward system,* consisting of extrinsic (pay and benefit) as well as intrinsic personal satisfaction motivators designed to encourage individual, group, and organizational performance.

Reward systems, compensation, and benefits have been getting most of the attention. Decision-makers are trying to tailor rewards and compensation to the needs of individuals and their organizations, and to connect them with results or learning. These leaders want rewards and benefits to be more consistent with the needs of the so-called Generation X, more practical, more effective in attracting and retaining high-potential talent, more suitable to global requirements, more competitive with the reward and compensation practices of other firms, more innovative, more equitable in overcoming real or perceived gender pay differences, and more equitable when worker compensation is compared to executive compensation. Quite a laundry list! (For more information, see these sources: Atkinson, 2000; Brown, 1999; Bursch and Van

Strander, 1999; Case, 1996; Chen, 1999; Dolmat-Connell, 1994; Emde, 1997; Hays, 1999; Kalantari, 1995; Kerr, 1999; Laabs, 1998; Lawler, 2000; Logan, 2000; Luthans and Stajkovic, 1999; Petrone, 1999; Rabin, 1994; Reynolds, 2000; Robertson, 1999; and Sperling, 1998.)

Key Terms in Compensation and Benefits

Several important terms are used by HR specialists when discussing compensation and benefits, a technical area of HR that requires unique competencies of HRP practitioners (Shenenberg and Smith, 1999). These terms include

1. *Pay structure.* This term refers to rates paid to people in different job classes in an organization.
2. *Equity.* This term means "comparability."
3. *Job evaluation.* The process of determining the relative value of jobs.
4. *Job analysis.* A process that must precede job evaluation. Its focus is on identifying what people do and what they should do.

HRP practitioners in small organizations are keenly aware of sources on the web where information about compensation and benefit information can be found (Hansen, 1997). Among others, important web sites for compensation and benefit practice include the following:

▪ The World at Work (*http://www.acaonline.org/*)
▪ The American Management Association (*http://www.amanet.org*)
▪ Cornell University School of Industrial and Labor Relations (*http://www.ilr.cornell.edu*)
▪ Cornell University/Human Resources (*http://workindex.com*)
▪ Society for Human Resource Management (*http://www.shrm.org*)

Immensely helpful information can also be found at *http://hrvillage.com/* and at *http://www.gneil.com/index.cfm?sessionid=Sab2us2-934*

The Role of Compensation/Benefits in Implementing HR Grand Strategy

Pay and benefit programs unquestionably influence

1. *Recruitment and selection.* Generally, the greater the compensation levels and fringe benefits of an organization, the easier it is for the firm to attract talent, and retain and develop talent for greater (or different) responsibilities.

2. *Training.* Generally, employees prefer to be compensated when they undergo training. Training adds value to an employee; the company is investing in that person, and their pay reflects the desire to preserve that investment.

3. *Organization development.* Compensation and benefit programs can help or hinder long-term organizational change. People favor change when they are rewarded for undergoing it.

4. *Career planning and management.* Compensation practices can give employees reason to plan their careers and act in accordance with those plans. It is a fundamental tenet of organizational behavior that people will do that which they are rewarded for doing. However, individuals differ in how much they value extrinsic (money) rewards and in how much reward they seek.

5. *Job redesign.* Compensation and benefit practices can influence the relative willingness of people to experiment with and accept changes in their job duties and responsibilities. The danger of job enrichment is that employees will demand more "enriched" pay to correspond to "enriched" jobs. This will offset any gains from increased productivity or cost-reduction efforts.

6. *Employee assistance programs (EAPs).* Some people consider EAPs to be employee benefits. Are the costs associated with these programs subtracted from a larger pool of benefits, or are EAPs instituted *in addition* to other benefits?

7. *Labor relations.* Compensation/benefit issues remain a major focus of negotiations. A company's approach to labor relations might well

be examined by looking solely at how the employer responds to wage demands. Generally, unionized firms have higher salaries and wages than their nonunion counterparts.

The Traditional Approach to Compensation/Benefit Programs

The Compensation Process

Think of any compensation program as a series of continuous steps. In concert with managers in the organization, HRP practitioners:

1. Determine relative priorities of the compensation program. In other words, what primary purpose is it intended to serve?
2. Evaluate jobs inside the organization.
3. Evaluate pay rates prevailing outside the organization.
4. Establish a pay structure—or several of them—in line with compensation priorities and internal/external rates.
5. Place jobs in the pay structure(s).
6. Administer the compensation program, making judgments about individual progression through salary/wage ranges.
7. Evaluate benefits outside the organization.
8. Establish and administer the benefit program.

These steps are illustrated in Figure 17-1.

Purposes of a Total Compensation Program

The purpose of a total compensation program seems simple enough: paying people what they are worth. The trouble is that there are different views about "worth." For example, some leaders relate total compensation to *the external labor market:* Are compensation rates in line with what other employers are paying for similar jobs? Or *the internal labor market:* Are compensation rates adequately separated between jobs? Others relate compensation to *group pro-*

Figure 17-1: The Compensation Process

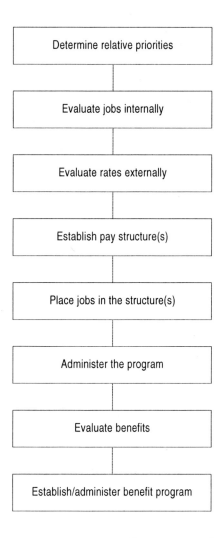

ductivity (Are work group incentives sufficient to induce people to work as teams at the highest levels of productivity?). Still others relate it to *individual productivity* (Are incentives adequate to induce individuals to achieve the highest productivity possible?) or *the training period* (Are rates adequate to encourage people to undertake lengthy training in preparation for an occupation or job?), or even *social equity* (Are rates comparable between races and sexes?).

Compensation doesn't just involve issues of worth. Decision-makers in the organization might ask whether the compensation program is *cost efficient* (How well do pay practices preserve assets of the organization?) or *administratively efficient* (How easy is a compensation program to administer?).

Each of these issues is someone's purpose for a compensation program. The question is, *What do strategists value most?* Emphasizing external labor market rates makes it easier for the organization to compete for people, though higher labor costs can price the organization's products off the market. Emphasizing the internal labor market serves as an inducement for individuals to seek transfer or promotion if rates are greater in jobs more important to the organization. Emphasizing pay-for-performance induces people to produce at the highest possible rate at present, but can also lead to neglect of long-term development without immediate performance benefits. Emphasizing social equity addresses the concerns of those who have historically been discriminated against, but perhaps at the expense of others who are performing well. Finally, cost efficiency preserves company assets, but short-term savings resulting from layoffs are often traded for long-term development because those who are laid off might not return.

There is no simple answer to these questions. The key issues are these: What does management value? Why? Once the answers to these questions are available, it will be easier to set relative priorities.

Evaluating Jobs Inside the Organization

The starting point for most compensation programs is *job evaluation,* defined earlier as the process of determining the relative value of jobs. Its purpose is to classify and prioritize jobs relative to pay within an organization.

It is important to understand that job analysis is the basis for job evaluation and must come first. That just makes sense: We have to know what we want done and what kind of people we want to do it before we know what to pay them. Moreover, the duties associated with a job title in one organization are not necessarily the same duties associated with the title in another organization.

There are eight ways to conduct job evaluation. They are (1) job ranking, (2) job grading, (3) job point method, (4) job factor comparison, (5) job guide-chart method, (6) time span of discretion, (7) job maturity curves, and (8) job guideline method (Burgess, 1984). We shall briefly describe these approaches.

Job ranking is the simplest method. It is appropriate in small organizations in which there are few jobs. Managers and/or HRP practitioners review job descriptions and then rank jobs from least to most important. Unfortunately, subjective rankings of this kind do not necessarily take into account degrees of importance. For instance, the company's vice president for marketing might actually be one hundred times more important to organizational survival than the job of company messenger. Yet when ranked, the V.P. is ranked #15 and the messenger is ranked #1.

Job grading is sometimes called the "classification method." It is somewhat more sophisticated than ranking, though not much so. The job is judged as a whole. Used widely in the public sector, job grading involves three basic steps: First, establish standardized descriptions of work based on complexity, prior training required, learning time, or some other characteristic. These descriptions are arranged in a hierarchy from simple to complex. Second, examine job descriptions and specifications. Third, place each job in a classification grade based on the standardized description that it most nearly matches. Unlike ranking in which jobs are compared to each other, job classification is thus based on comparing jobs to predetermined criteria. Classification grades are then equated with salary/wage rates.

The *job point method* is one of the most popular approaches in the private sector. Unlike ranking and grading, each job is broken down into parts. HRP practitioners and a committee of managers from the organization

1. Identify factors common to a broad range of jobs. Factors include responsibility, effort, working conditions, education, experience, difficulty, scope, and results required. They should be selected in line with unique needs of the organization and common factors associated with such different levels as unskilled and skilled labor, technical employees, professionals, supervisors, and managers.

2.   Identify subfactors. Within each factor, we identify subfactors. For instance, "responsibility" is broken down into such categories (subfactors) as "responsibility for people" and "responsibility for assets."

3.   Identify rankings for each factor. There are degrees within each factor. For instance, "responsibility" is ranked according to four, five, seven, or ten levels of degree (amount).

4.   Decide on points for subfactors. Allocate points, subjectively determined, to subfactors.

5.   Decide on points for levels. Follow the same procedure as in step 4.

6.   Determine the relative value of jobs.

7.   Rank jobs by points.

In this method, wages are based on points.

The *job factor comparison* resembles the point method in many ways. Though less commonly used than the point method, it involves (1) identifying critical factors (this step, handled by HRP practitioners and line managers, is conducted in the same way as in the point method); (2) selecting "key" jobs common to the organization (they serve as benchmarks—fixed points—against which other jobs are examined); (3) allocating wages to portions of each key job's duties or factors (the greater the importance of a factor to a job, the higher the wage rate assigned to the factor in that job); (4) comparing key jobs by factors, also called "factor comparison" (a chart is devised, representing the wage rate of each key job as a function of some factor; usually one job is a starting point for the process so that the hourly wage is broken down into portions under each factor, and other key jobs are then ranked in comparison to it); and (5) assigning all jobs in the organization (each job is ranked by its worth to the organization).

Though job factor comparison is relatively reliable, its complexity makes it less popular than other methods.

The *job guide-chart method* of evaluation has been popularized by the Hay Group, a well-known consulting firm. It is perhaps the single most widely used method and relies on three factors: (1) know-how, encompassing all skills needed to perform a job and consisting of practical procedures, ability to integrate functions such as planning and organizing, and ability to deal with other people; (2) problem-solving, defined as the process of examining problems and arriving at conclusions, and then including the setting or environment in which problem solving is necessary and the nature of the problems encountered; and (3) accountability, defined as how much the job is held responsible for actions and results; it includes the ability to act without authorization, the influence on results of action, and the influence of the general dollar value of results. The basic idea in using this approach is to reduce each job to its point value relative to factors described above.

The *time span of discretion* method is nontraditional. Its central assumption is that the importance of a job can be measured by time that elapses between initial assignment to a task and final review by a superior. Generally, a job that is closely supervised—such as a secretary or a production laborer—has a narrow span of discretion, perhaps extending only to a few hours. In contrast, the review of a chief executive's job performance can take several years and will not be appropriate before that.

The classic time-span method, the creation of Elliot Jaques (1964 and 1972), does not use job descriptions. Instead, Jaques advocates close questioning of superiors to determine the maximum time that a subordinate will be given before the superior wants to look over the employee's work. Jobs are ranked by importance according to those that have the longest time spans.

Maturity curves and the time-span approach both use time as a measure. Maturity curves can be used in various ways. A common way is to plot on a graph the salary of an occupational group (such as engineers) relative to years of experience on the job, or even to plot years in the workforce and years in the organization in order to construct a specialized salary scale. Maturity curves are more commonly used for professional and technical jobs than for other job categories.

Finally, the *job guideline method* is another nontraditional method. A wage survey is conducted, using key jobs in the organization as a starting point. A pay schedule is separately prepared. Then jobs are placed in the pay grades based on market rates.

Each approach to job evaluation has distinct advantages and disadvantages. The ranking method is the easiest (but the least sophisticated). Job grading, nearly as easy as ranking, is more appropriate for larger organizations, but does not adequately show distinctions concerning the importance of jobs. The point method is simple enough for workers to understand, but it can be very expensive to use. The job factor comparison method is reasonably valid and reliable, yet it is also more complicated than the point method. The guide-chart method shares the advantages and disadvantages of factor comparison. The time span of discretion is intuitively appealing, though data can be costly to gather. Maturity curves, though useful for ensuring external equity with those in the same profession or occupation, do little to ensure internal equity between professional-technical jobs and other kinds. The job guideline method has the same advantages and disadvantages as maturity curves.

Evaluating Pay Rates Outside the Organization

Job evaluation is only the first step in a total compensation program. A second step is to evaluate pay rates outside the organization to determine prevailing rates in the external labor market.

Several methods are commonly used for this purpose. You can use results of surveys conducted by the organization, other organizations, or professional societies. Larger companies have enough money and time to conduct their own tailor-made surveys to precisely meet their needs. Smaller companies tend to rely on firms that specialize in conducting salary surveys and selling results.

Smaller firms can go to an array of sources for salary/wage information. Professional associations, industry groups, consulting firms, and the U.S. government all compile data. Use it with care: There usually are differences in job duties across organizations.

Conducting a survey to meet the special requirements of one organization is usually expensive, especially if a large sample is used. The steps in carrying out such a survey are similar to those in any survey study: (1) Identify what information is needed, (2) write questions to obtain that information, (3) select a sample of representative people or groups, (4) mail out the survey or make telephone calls, (5) analyze results, and (6) present results to relevant decision-makers.

Establishing and Updating Pay Structure

Not all organizations choose to develop pay ranges or classes. In unionized settings, the same flat rate is sometimes paid to everyone with the same title; sales personnel are paid on commission, usually a percentage of goods sold. One pay structure will not always be appropriate: Different employee categories have different needs, in fact, and different ways of handling them.

In most cases, wage structures are devised by plotting on a scattergram the dollar rates of existing salaries on one axis, and plotting point values on the other. A straight line is drawn through dots representing existing rates. Other lines are drawn at percentages above and below that first midpoint line.

The pay structure is periodically updated in light of changing market conditions inside and outside the organization. Within the last 10 years, organizations have experimented with so-called "broadbanding." O'Neil (1993) defines *broadbanding* as "the use of job clusters or tiers of positions into bands for the purpose of managing career growth and administering pay. Such bands are being implemented as an alternative to traditional salary grade structures. In a compensation sense, banding collapses the number of salary ranges within a traditional salary structure into a few broadbands. A broadband is a single, large salary range spanning the pay opportunity formerly covered by several separate salary ranges. A broadband structure classifies jobs into a few wide bands, rather than many narrowly defined salary ranges." Broadbanding is just one of many recent efforts by organizations to increase the flexibility of compensation practice. Another is pay for knowledge or pay for skills, in which workers are compensated more for what they learn than for what they do (Dantico, 1994).

Placing Jobs in the Pay Structure

Most large organizations have several pay structures, one for each employee category: executive, managerial, supervisory, professional, technical, clerical, and skill/unskilled labor.

Placement of any job in a pay structure is an expression of the value of the job and its relative importance to an organization. For this reason, placement in pay structure will vary across organizations: A training director in one firm might be placed quite high, in another, very low. The process of placement is usually made somewhat more objective when points are allocated to the job, or when a management committee decides on placement. It is still a subjective system, despite the use of points.

Administering the Compensation Program

How do individuals progress through their respective pay structures? There are two methods: pay-for-performance and automatic increases.

Without doubt, pay-for-performance is the most popular so-called "merit pay." Unfortunately, many pay-for-performance systems are not real: They do not explicitly link individual output or activities to compensation, and the rate of compensation does not increase when output does.

Why not? Supervisors are part of the problem:

I Some supervisors simply do not like to "take the heat" associated with varying individual pay based on output.
I Supervisors in two departments rarely rate the same output in the same way, or reward accordingly.
I Individuals whose superior performances are not noticed by superiors can grow frustrated.

Despite these things, many firms continue to strive for such a system because its bottom-line emphasis is ideologically appealing.

More often than not, firms rely on an automatic-increase system, even when their managers call it "pay-for-performance." Under such systems, individuals are moved through pay ranges based on their longevity. Hence, the value of pay as a motivator is lost because differences between good and poor performance are slight.

Evaluating Benefits

Employee fringe benefits are of two kinds: intrinsic and extrinsic. The first is associated with pleasant work and good surroundings. The second is most commonly thought of in connection with benefits. As defined earlier in the chapter, benefits are really a form of pay, though they are more often a function of membership in the organization than of work performed. Many kinds of extrinsic benefits exist: employer health insurance, retirement plans, paid nonworking time, educational and training reimbursement, employee assistance programs, stock options, and many more.

What is the purpose of employee benefits? A better question focuses on *purposes*. From an employer's standpoint, they (1) reduce or eliminate employer liability in the event of job-related accidents and illnesses, (2) reduce potential for labor unrest, and (3) serve as tools for reducing turnover, absenteeism, and scrap rates. In fact, extrinsic benefits provide employees with "safety nets" in the event of all kinds of problems.

Employer benefit policies vary substantially. They reflect management philosophies. In some cases, there is a deliberate attempt to use benefits to head off unionizing efforts. In other cases, managers seem to be emphasizing *something* in particular: protection against accident and illness, employee-educational efforts, or problems stemming from troublesome employees. In fact, there should be an overall purpose of some kind underlying the administration of benefits.

One tool to use in the process is a benefits survey, conducted either as part of a salary survey or separate from it. Benefits surveys determine prevailing trends in the marketplace; they provide the information that organizational decision-makers need to decide whether to offer benefits that are more liberal, less liberal, or only comparable to those offered by similar firms. Specific issues to consider in such surveys include employee health coverage, pensions, and vacation and sick time.

Implementing and Monitoring the Compensation/ Benefits Program

Implementing the compensation and benefits program is nearly as important as the process of evaluating jobs and establishing pay structure.

A job-evaluation committee can help in the process of implementing and communicating about existing salary policies. When the committee is representative of different levels in the organizational hierarchy, each member becomes a natural spokesperson for his or her respective group. When decisions are made by that committee and are then approved by higher-level management, they are the starting point for a long-standing agreement between the parties involved.

Communication about pay policy should not end with the informal advocacy of a few committee members; rather, that is only a starting point. Effective communication is essential, especially because employees generally tend to overestimate what some people earn and underestimate what others earn.

In a classic and still-relevant treatment, Zimmerman (1984) suggests that the best approach to communicating about the compensation program is to

1. Study how communication is carried out in the organization. What are the common methods of communicating? How are compensation and benefit issues communicated, in particular?

2. Assess employee attitudes. How satisfied do employees seem to be with the compensation program?

3. Identify goals of the communication effort. What is it that people want to know about? What features of the compensation program do managers in the organization want to see emphasized?

4. Decide on what issues are to be communicated. What subjects are to be treated?

5. Select a way to communicate about issues. How can the desired message be sent to the appropriate audience? See Figure 17-2 for a few ideas.

By considering these issues, decision-makers can select ways to implement and communicate about compensation and benefits programs.

Problems with the Traditional Approach to Compensation/Benefits Programs

Compensation/benefit programs are not always part of an organization's HR Grand Strategy, but they should be. More often than not, they are based on

Figure 17-2: Methods of Communicating about Compensation: Advantages and Disadvantages

Method	Advantages	Disadvantages
Employee handbooks	I Allows for consistent presentation I Everyone receives a copy	I Might be difficult to keep up with changes in benefits
Brochures about the benefits	I Easy to pass out I Relatively easy to revise	I People might not read them I Individual benefits may differ as benefits change
Individualized statements	I Specific for each person hired	I Difficult to keep up to date I Expensive to prepare
Company newsletters/Magazines	I Wide distribution	I People may not read
Payroll notices	I Easily gets attention	I Easily lost or misplaced
Bulletin boards	I Low cost	I Not everyone will read
Group meetings	I Ensures feedback, questions and answers	I Not reduced to writing for subsequent reference
Orientation programs	I Everyone hears more or less the same presentation, thus ensuring consistency	I Employees may be overloaded with information

company tradition or past or standard business practice, rather than made an integral part of a long-range plan to encourage workers to develop and advance themselves in line with forecasted worker needs.

It should be obvious from the description of the traditional compensation/benefits process that the goal is to keep employees satisfied. The basis of most pay structures is current data from inside and outside the organization. People are remunerated on the kind of work (jobs) they do. After all, the duties that individuals perform are usually the foundation of most job evaluation methods used in establishing pay structures.

Individual progression through pay ranges, on the other hand, is typically based on performance or seniority. Pay-for-performance systems tend to reward *past performance* and rarely take into account the full difference between an exemplary and an average employee, which can be as much as a 500 percent difference in productivity. Seniority systems, while encouraging employee retention, ignore individual performance in order to reward individual longevity.

What is needed is a holistic approach to remuneration—compensation, benefits, and other rewards that together encourage long-term employee development and short-term performance. This holistic view might also include a reward system that goes beyond total compensation and an in-depth look at all factors that motivate (or demotivate) people to achieve results in the organization. It could consist also of a review of performance-management practices in the organization and an examination of so-called *alternative reward programs*—ways of recognizing outstanding performance, or outstanding suggestions that help the organization cut costs, increase profits, or make other bottom-line contributions to competitive success (Nadel, 1998).

Strategic Compensation/Benefit Programs

The Strategic Compensation Process

To re-orient the compensation and benefits process to the future, HRP practitioners work with managers in the organization to:

1. Consider priorities in a holistic remuneration program geared to support HR and organizational strategy.
2. Evaluate jobs in the organization as they *should be in the future* if they are being carried out in a way consistent with strategy.
3. Forecast compensation and benefit trends outside the organization.
4. Establish a flexible pay structure for jobs in the organization and prioritize jobs accordingly.
5. Administer the remuneration effort as part of a total reward strategy, emphasizing and taking into consideration group as well as individual development and productivity.

These steps are summarized in Figure 17-3.

Figure 17-3: Steps in the Strategic Compensation Process

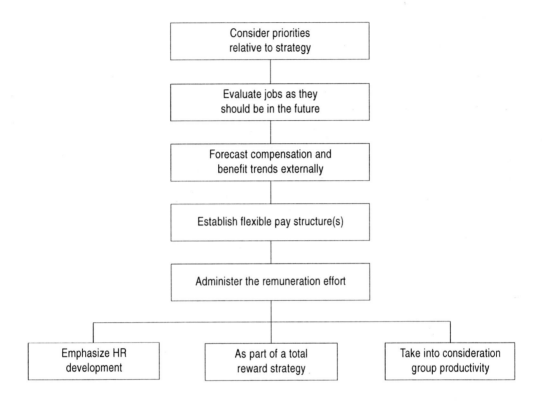

Considering Priorities

The first step in a strategic compensation program is to reassess purpose. In short, decision-makers need to decide whether they wish to lead or follow the labor market, and to what extent compensation/benefits should be factored into total HR Grand Strategy.

As noted earlier in the chapter, the traditional purpose of compensation/benefits tends to be maintenance: Decision-makers want to maintain competitiveness with other organizations seeking similar talent, and preserve equity between job classes inside the organization. The result is a reactive effort in which HRP practitioners examine existing pay rates and then strive to equal or surpass them.

The trouble is that this approach has very little to do with supporting future organizational plans. The focus is not on what compensation/benefits strategy will most effectively produce employee performance and development in line with plans; rather, it is on paying similar rates for similar jobs. As a consequence, what the organization does about compensation is not necessarily related to what should be in the future in order to help bring about plans.

Decision-makers need to consider compensation/benefits priorities against the backdrop of strategy. Will the HR plans require compensation/benefits that effectively attract newcomers to entry-level positions? Encourage employees to seek promotion or transfer? Facilitate individual training and development? Promote harmony within work groups and/or between work groups? Encourage job enrichment, job enlargement, autonomous work groups? Discourage unionization? Contribute to the personal, physical, and emotional well-being of employees? Naturally, some priorities should be more important than others in implementing a given HR plan. Priorities will also vary across different employee groups and company divisions.

Evaluating Jobs in the Future

The second step in a strategic compensation program is to establish norms about what jobs should be like in the future—not what they are at present—and then create an idealized (normative) evaluation of their importance relative to achievement of strategic objectives.

There are eight approaches to strategic job evaluation, each one corresponding to a traditional approach (summarized in Figure 17-4). Note that strategic job evaluation differs from its traditional counterpart in that it calls for inferences to be made about jobs in the future. In contrast, of course, traditional evaluation begins with present-oriented job analysis, followed by present-oriented assessment of job worth.

Forecasting Compensation/Benefit Trends

The third step in the strategic compensation process is to forecast future trends and their impacts on job worth. While this process is highly subjective, it is really no more nor less so than traditional surveys of external pay rates.

Various approaches can be used to forecast these trends. They include the Delphi procedure, nominal group technique, cross-impact analysis, scenarios, and even simple surveys and interviews. (See Figure 17-5 for brief descriptions of how they can be used.)

Establishing Flexible Pay Structures

If it is possible to carry out strategic job evaluation and forecast compensation and benefit trends, it is equally possible to use this information to prepare future pay structures using otherwise traditional methods.

Administering the Remuneration Effort

The final step in the strategic compensation process is administration. It involves implementing compensation strategy.

Individual progression through the pay structure is based on development rather than on pure pay-for-performance or seniority. The focus is thus on acquiring—in advance of need—new skills, knowledge, and abilities implicit in strategic-oriented job descriptions. The result is a highly talented workforce composed of people who think strategically because they are rewarded for doing so.

One way to make strategic-oriented pay decisions is to do strategic-oriented employee performance appraisals, described briefly in Chapter 4. The idea is to encourage performance for each job holder that is consistent with organizational strategy. In addition, various forms of incentive plans can be used (see Figure 17-6), depending on the HR Grand Strategy.

It is important to keep in mind that compensation and benefit strategy constitute only part of a total reward strategy. Direct and indirect compensation are each related to other types of rewards. Ideally, the reward system decision-makers will examine the strategy as a whole and make sure that component parts support each other, and not conflict.

Figure 17-4: Strategic Approaches to Job Evaluation

Approach	Description of Steps	Advantages	Disadvantages
Job ranking	To use the approach strategically ▪ Review strategic-oriented job descriptions ▪ Rank jobs in the organization in terms of their strategic importance	▪ Simple ▪ Easy to administer and to implement	▪ Highly subjective ▪ Potentially prone to abuse and personal favoritism
Job grading	To use the approach strategically ▪ Describe work in terms of its long-term impact, importance for achieving strategy, and development requirements over time ▪ Examine strategic-oriented job descriptions ▪ Place each job in a strategic classification grade	▪ Relatively simple ▪ Easy to administer	▪ Highly subjective
Job point method	To use the approach strategically ▪ Identify factors common to a broad range of jobs, which will help you relate them to HR and organizational strategy ▪ Identify subfactors (factors within factors) ▪ Identify rankings for each factor ▪ Determine points for subfactors ▪ Determine the relative value of jobs ▪ Rank jobs by points	▪ Allows for flexibility ▪ Helps make link between strategy and rewards explicit ▪ Helps show the relative contribution of jobs to organizational strategy, and HR plans in clear terms	▪ Takes lengthy period to install ▪ Rather complicated to work out factors and points, especially for unknown or merely desired factors rather than those actually existing
Job factor comparison	To use the approach strategically (complicated) ▪ Identify critical factors in jobs as they relate to organizational strategy ▪ Select "key" jobs that should emerge as most important over time in helping bring about strategy ▪ Allocate portions of each key job's strategic-oriented, future duties to wages/salary	▪ Allows for considerable reliability	▪ Very complicated ▪ Can only be used effectively when employees and managers understand it ▪ It must be used in conjunction with a strategic communication program that makes link between strategy and pay clear, even as it emerges

Figure 17-4: *(continued)*

Approach	Description of Steps	Advantages	Disadvantages
Job factor comparison (cont.)	▪ Compare key jobs by factors ▪ Assign every job in the organization a value relative to key jobs; maintain strategic orientation		
Job guide-chart method	To use the approach strategically ▪ Forecast, based on strategic-oriented job descriptions, what jobs should be like in the future, in terms of know-how, problem-solving, and accountability ▪ Assign point values to the jobs over time	▪ Helps to detect emerging problems with internal equity ▪ Especially suited to executive jobs, which are important for leadership in strategy	▪ Might not be suitable for jobs that must become more creative over time
Time span of discretion	To use the approach strategically ▪ Forecast maximum time a subordinate will be allowed to act before a superior checks the work ▪ Rank by expected-future time spans	▪ Very appropriate for distinguishing between jobs on the basis of strategic importance	▪ Not necessarily reliable because it is based on perceptions of the unknown
Job maturity curves	▪ To use strategically, simply project a trend line for earnings for each job class/occupation into the future	▪ Bases pay by job class in anticipation of market rates	▪ Too subjective ▪ Does not allow for differences of strategy between organizations

Figure 17-5: Forecasting Compensation/Benefit Trends

Approach	Inputs	Activities	Outputs
Delphi procedure	▪ Need information about present pay rates ▪ Need information about organizational strategy ▪ Need information about environmental conditions	▪ Conduct series of surveys with experts who never meet face-to-face ▪ List expected trends that are predicted to have greatest potential influence ▪ Conduct by occcupation, by organizational level, or by division (when a firm is diversified by industry)	▪ List of expected trends that are predicted to have greatest potential and/or influence ▪ Forecasts of how much influence on compensation/benefits will result from the trends
Nominal group technique	▪ Same inputs as needed for the Delphi procedure	▪ Conduct a meeting in which participants generate ideas, discuss them, vote on them	▪ Same outputs as derived from the Delphi procedure
Cross-impact analysis	▪ Requires results of a Delphi procedure or nominal group technique at the outset	▪ Array events in a matrix and then (subjectively) assess impact of one trend on others	▪ Assessment of how trends will interact, influencing each other; this information can, in turn, be used to refine forecasts about trends in compensation and benefits

Finally, the remuneration program must be viewed relative to desired future performance at several levels. Before and during implementation, HR planners must ask themselves: How much will new compensation/benefit initiatives affect

▪ *the organization?* (How well are employees in different job categories being rewarded for performance consistent with strategy?)

▪ *the job?* (How well is compensation/benefit strategy in line with changing job demands?)

▪ *the individual?* (How well is compensation/benefit strategy recognizing increasing knowledge, skills, and abilities? Recognizing special needs associated with different life cycle stages?)

Figure 17-5: *(continued)*

Approach	Inputs	Activities	Outputs
Scenarios	▪ Preparation of a short narrative description of a future situation	▪ Decision-makers draw inferences from the narrative about the importance of a person, occupation, or job in achieving organizational strategy	▪ Reconsideration of the relative placement of one job or occupation to others at some point in the future
Surveys	▪ Same information/ inputs needed as for the delphi procedure	▪ Survey managers inside the organization and/or experts outside the organization about important trends and their influence on future compensation/benefits	▪ Same outputs as derived from the Delphi procedure
Interviews	▪ Same information/ inputs needed as for the Delphi procedure	▪ Same activities as carried out for surveys except that managers/ external experts are talked to face-to-face rather than being asked questions in written form	▪ Same outputs as derived from the Delphi procedure

▪ *the work group?* (How well is compensation/benefit strategy encouraging cooperation among members of a work group?)

By posing these questions periodically, decision-makers can take care to identify and act on major problems in reward systems before they come up.

Figure 17-6: Incentive Plans

Name of Incentive Plan	Brief Description	Appropriate for HR Strategy	How to Use
Daywork	■ Simple approach to compensating individuals ■ Pay is based on expected daily production of an average worker progressing at an average rate ■ Not really an incentive plan, but a very common basis of pay plans	■ Only when the environment is very stable and the HR strategy reflects change in jobs ■ Will not be appropriate when the job will undergo future change or when there is need to improve teamwork	■ Use work measurement to assess daily production ■ Assess (evaluate) job ■ Pay on basis of hours worked at a set rate
Piece rate	■ Individuals are compensated for each unit produced	■ When quantity is prized over quality ■ When direct, short-term production is prized more than preparation for high-level responsibility	■ Determine number of units that must be produced or the number the worker must make in products, the same as daywork wage ■ Establish this number of units as a "standard" ■ Pay a bonus for each unit over "standard"
Commissions	■ Appropriate for salespersons ■ Pay for each unit sold	■ Same as piece rate	■ Same as piece rate, except "units sold" is used instead of "units produced"
Improshare	■ Incentives are based on work measurements ■ Company/employees share equally in gains	■ Increases accuracy of traditional job evaluation, thereby emphasizing internal equity between jobs	■ Compute total number of hours of work for all employees in an organization (i.e., total size of workforce times number of hours each employee works per week) ■ Compute hours needed to make each product ■ Multiply number of products made by hours needed to make each product to determine base productivity ■ Devise standard by multiplying $\dfrac{\text{total hours}}{\text{produced hours}} \times$ hours needed to make each product

Figure 17-6: *(continued)*

Name of Incentive Plan	Brief Description	Appropriate for HR Strategy	How to Use
			■ Compute hours gained in a week over hours expected ■ Convert productivity gains to percentage and give to workers
Scanlon	■ One of the earliest incentive plans ■ Incentives are based on reductions in payroll costs	■ Most appropriate for improving teamwork and encouraging creativity/innovation	■ Assess payroll costs ■ Determine historical average for payroll costs ■ Periodically compare actual to historical payroll costs ■ Distribute savings between actual and historical payroll costs to workers less a percentage (20–25%) to the company
Rucker	■ A refinement of the Scanlon plan ■ Incentives are based on value added	■ Same as Scanlon plan	■ Analyze cost of a product, breaking it down to materials cost, production costs (i.e., processing and labor) ■ Compute value added to the product by labor ■ Express value added by labor as a ratio of total cost ■ Use payroll costs to estimate total value added by labor ■ If actual sales exceed labor's added value, a productivity gain is apparent ■ Distribute savings/productivity gain less a company percentage

Figure 17-7: Types of Rewards

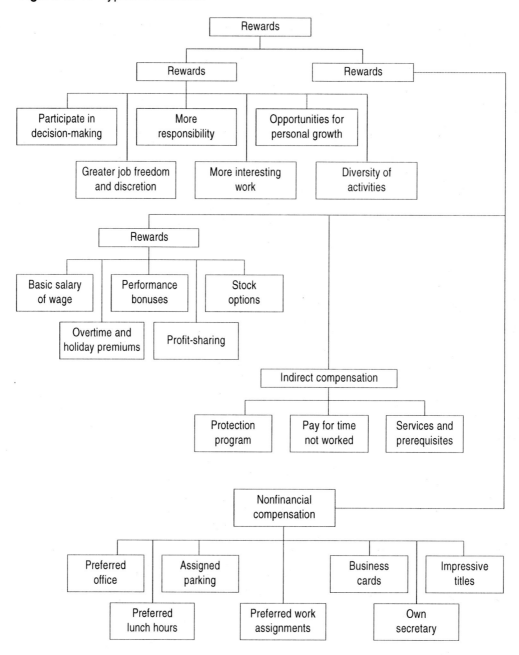

CHAPTER 18

THE HUMAN RESOURCES PLANNING MANAGER

What Does the HR Planning Manager Do?

The human resources (HR) planning manager is responsible for leading the human resources planning (HRP) department, unit, or function. The nature of this role varies widely, depending on how HRP is handled and where it is placed in the organization. It can also vary by corporate culture and by national culture.

In one sense, the chief HR executive—who typically bears a title like "vice president of human resources" is one kind of HR planning manager. He or she is responsible not just for HRP but also for all HR practice areas. If the organization is too small for a specialized unit devoted to HRP, then the chief HR executive is the HR planning manager.

On the other hand, larger organizations often do have specialized units that bear chief responsibility for HRP, whether comprehensive or limited. A *comprehensive HRP program* encompasses all activities described in this book; a *limited program* encompasses only some of these activities. In such cases, the HR Planning Manager is the supervisor in charge of the HRP unit.

Of course, there is a third alternative: The person or position responsible for HRP is also responsible for some other activity, such as training, organization development, or recruitment. In these cases, there is usually less emphasis placed on formal HRP and more emphasis placed on the HR practice area with which it is paired.

How Is the HR Planning Manager's Role Carried Out?

Think of the manager as one who:

1. Establishes goals and objectives of the HRP department or a specialized unit within the HR department.
2. Creates structure for the department.
3. Staffs the department.
4. Issues orders.
5. Resolves destructive conflicts.
6. Communicates with those inside and outside the department.
7. Plans for needed resources, particularly through budgeting.
8. Deals with power and political issues.

These activities are illustrated in Figure 18-1. Note that this role overlaps with others in some respects. More specifically, to the extent that the HRP manager interacts with those outside the unit and gears its activities to their needs, the role overlaps with the HR organizational coordinator. To the extent that the manager coordinates activities across HR practice areas and allocates work, the role overlaps with that of the integrator. Finally, the integrator, manager, and evaluator share interest in controlling and monitoring results against pre-established objectives and criteria.

The manager mobilizes departmental and unit resources and those of the organization in order to help implement HR Grand Strategy. To succeed in this process, he or she needs general management ability, technical knowledge of HRP, and expertise. He or she must also be "future agile"—that is, be able to react quickly when the need arises (Eichinger and Ulrich, 1995). We shall have more to say at the end of this chapter about the last of these issues—dealing with power, politics, and HRP.

Establishing HRP Department Goals and Objectives

A major responsibility of the HRP manager is to establish department goals and objectives based on departmental purpose and HR Grand Strategy. Management

Figure 18-1: The HRP Management Process

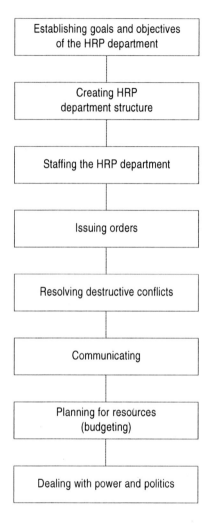

Establishing goals and objectives of the HRP department
Creating HRP department structure
Staffing the HRP department
Issuing orders
Resolving destructive conflicts
Communicating
Planning for resources (budgeting)
Dealing with power and politics

by objectives (MBO) is at once a way of (1) planning for implementation, (2) evaluating employee performance, and (3) controlling operations. Our focus at present is on MBO in planning and, more particularly, in managing.

MBO for a department involves eight steps:

1. The top executive meets in a group setting with supervisors in charge of each HR practice area. The meeting focuses on two questions:

What is the present status of the department? What should be the status of the department in the future?

2. The top HR executive meets with each supervisor, one-on-one, to negotiate individual objectives. This process helps integrate such practice areas as career planning and management, training, recruitment, organization development (OD), job redesign, employee assistance, labor relations, and compensation/benefits.

3. Each supervisor prepares goals to maintain the unit or practice area, deal with special problems, and improve operations of the unit.

4. Supervisors in each unit meet with their subordinates to continue the process.

5. The results of the meetings are formalized in writing and are expressed in measurable terms.

6. Periodically, the top executive meets with each subordinate to review results and discuss problems encountered in trying to achieve objectives and take advantage of new opportunities.

7. The process continues down the chain of command, with each supervisor meeting with each of the subordinates to review results and discuss problems/opportunities.

The results are evaluated at least once a year and then used as the basis for pay raises, bonuses, and determinations about individual promotability. The original process is then repeated in order to establish new objectives for the next year.

These steps help establish short-term departmental goals and objectives that are, in turn, linked to long-term organizational and HR strategy. They also coordinate activities of separate HR practice areas so that they constitute a whole greater than the sum of their respective parts.

Figure 18-2 illustrates these steps.

Creating Department Structure

How will the work of the department be allocated? This issue is an important one because allocation of work duties creates a framework for action and account-

Figure 18-2: Steps in Implementing Management-by-Objectives (MBO) in an HR Department

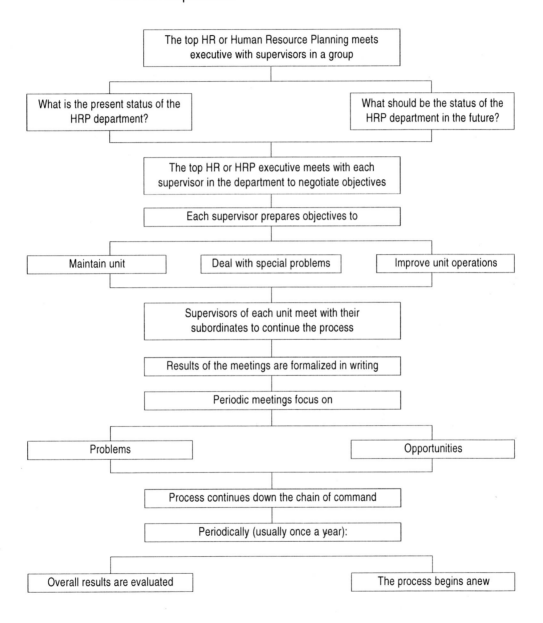

ability. To a significant degree, structure facilitates or hinders integration of activities and control of operations. Managers who do not understand how to effectively structure the development and its work put the company at a distinct disadvantage because structure—while serving as a constraint on strategic choice—can either help or hinder effective implementation of organizational strategy and, by inference, HR Grand Strategy.

There are three major issues to consider when structuring the HRP department or unit: complexity, formalization, and centralization. The process of reviewing structure is important in managing a department and is thus worth mention. If the department or unit is not set up adequately, it will likely be the chief reason why the strategy fails.

Complexity

To what extent should activities within the department be differentiated? In other words, (1) How many different units and occupations should be represented? (2) How many levels and kinds of supervision should exist? (3) How geographically dispersed should the department be? There is no right or wrong answer to any of these questions; rather, it is more useful to speak in terms of degrees of appropriateness or inappropriateness.

Generally speaking, the greater the size and/or complexity of HRP department operations, the greater the need for more units, levels of supervision, and geographical dispersion. In contrast, the smaller the size and the simpler the range of activities, the less the need for many units or levels of supervision.

Formalization

How much should jobs in the department be standardized? In other words, how interchangeable should people be, and how routine should jobs be? These questions deal with formalization.

Generally speaking, most jobs in the HRP department will be informally structured to encourage innovation and problem-solving. In practice, however, many low-level, highly formalized clerical jobs will still be needed, even in an age when personal computers are used to do work once handled by clerical help.

Standardizing jobs is one way to make it easier to recruit and train new HRP staff. As a practical matter, however, there are limits to how much standardization can be imposed on jobs of this kind. One strategy is to require employee cross-training so that, in the event of unexpected turnover, valuable skills and techniques will be preserved in the department.

Centralization

To what extent should decision-making be limited to higher-ups in the department or the organization? This question deals with centralization.

For most research-oriented jobs—such as roles associated with scanning, auditing, and forecasting human resources—high decentralization is probably appropriate. Professionals in any discipline resent tight control, authority, and the dependence associated with high centralization. Indeed, there is some evidence to suggest that research-oriented units *require* high degrees of decentralization in order to function effectively. HRP units often need to be decentralized.

The Process of Reviewing Department Structure

How does the HRP manager go about examining "goodness of fit" between the department's role, goals, objectives, and HR Grand Strategy? The answer to this question has to do with reviewing department structure.

In one classic treatment, Duncan (1985) suggested that there are eight steps in organization design. They serve as a useful point of departure for considering department structure. These eight design steps are

1. *Identify the system.* What will be structured?
2. *Examine the environment.* What are the surroundings? For an HRP unit, four environments are possible: (1) outside the organization; (2) inside the organization but outside the HRP department (for example, line departments); (3) inside the organization and inside the HR department, but outside the HRP unit, such as training,

recruitment, and labor relations), which is only applicable when the HRP unit is structurally distinct from other HR department activities; and (4) inside the HRP unit itself.

3. *State the purpose.* What is the role of the HRP unit?

4. *Specify what is done.* What are the activities of the HRP unit? What clients does it serve? How are they served?

5. *Assess activities.* Given the work to be done, how complex should the unit be? How formalized? How centralized?

6. *Identify controls.* How should long-term decisions be made? Is information acquired? Should short-term activities be monitored? Should coordination be facilitated within the unit? Should communication be carried out with outside groups? Should work be supervised?

7. *Design the structure.* On the basis of answers to the previous questions, how should the department be structured?

8. *Establish an authority system.* Who answers to whom? What kinds of decisions require higher approval? What kinds do not?

Each of these questions can and should be considered when you select a new HR Grand Strategy. Some organizations have been experimenting with a new structure for HR that positions some staff experts in each Strategic Business Unit, spins off routine tasks to a call center, and creates a cadre of experts at the corporate level (Kaschub, 1997). The aim of such a structure is to reduce bureaucracy and make the HR function more responsive to different needs and different groups within the organization.

Staffing the HRP Department

Staffing the HRP department involves specifying job requirements in HRP, recruiting and selecting people for those jobs, and evaluating and developing employees. It is a very important responsibility, because the aggregate knowledge, skills, and abilities of people in the department will determine, to a significant extent, what it does and will be capable of doing. One hopes that if there is a single task at which an HRP manager can excel, it will be this one.

The reason is that staffing advice for the entire organization emanates from the HRP department. It should thus be an area in which the manager sets an example that others will admire and will want to emulate.

Specifying Job Requirements

Staffing the HRP department begins with specifying job requirements. Too often, most operating managers tend to think of this activity on a position-by-position basis in which a vacancy triggers an examination of what the incumbent has been doing and what kind of person is needed to replace the incumbent. The assumption is that the same kind of person as the incumbent is needed. Of course, a one-for-one replacement will never be possible; no two individuals are ever alike. Moreover, such an approach is only appropriate when the match between incumbent and job has been a good one.

Perhaps a better approach is to think in terms of the entire HRP department. A vacancy presents an opportunity to reconsider allocation of overall work duties and skills that are needed. Consider:

1. What is the purpose of the position? What should it be?
2. What are the major goals and objectives of the current incumbent? What should they be, given the nature of the position as a part of the overall allocation of responsibilities in the HRP department?
3. What trends are likely to affect duties and responsibilities of the position over time? Consider: (1) What are the emerging trends outside the organization? (2) What are the emerging trends inside the organization but outside the HRP department? (3) What are the emerging trends within the HRP department? What group norms prevail?
4. What are the present strengths and weaknesses of the current position or the present incumbent?
5. What strategies exist to redesign the position relative to other positions in the HRP department? What should the position's duties be? What kind of education, experience, and personal characteristics are associated with those duties?

6. What decisions about the position are realistic, given the prevailing culture and skills existing in the department or work group? What decisions are appropriate, given strengths/weaknesses of the HRP department in its role of helping implement HR Grand Strategy?
7. How will success or failure be evaluated in redesigning the position or selecting a person for the position?

Of course, these questions are appropriate when there is need to change the HRP department in order to achieve a better match between what it does and what it should be doing. They are unnecessary when there is no discrepancy between what is and what should be.

The next step is preparation of a position description. Recall from Chapter 4 that position descriptions focus on only one person in one job. They are thus much more specific than job descriptions, which include only common duties across related positions. Indeed, position descriptions list not only what people should do but also indicate the relative importance of duties and how well they should be performed.

A position specification is logically related to this description. It sets forth the minimum education, experience, and essential personal characteristics necessary to learn the job. A person description is very much like a specification. However, it is more detailed and translates each task/duty on the position description into corresponding knowledge, skills, and abilities needed by an individual to perform the task.

Walker (1980) provides excerpts from representative position descriptions from HRP departments.

Recruiting and Selecting HRP Staff

HRP has traditionally tended to evolve from a short-term budgeting-oriented activity to a longer-term activity associated with the HR function in an organization. Research results generally support the idea that as an organization increases in size, its planning and HRP activities tend to become more formalized.

As noted in Chapter 11, there are two traditional sources of talent: the labor market inside the organization and the labor market outside the organization. These sources are not especially helpful when it comes to filling HR vacancies: Few formal academic programs exist to prepare people for the specific job of HR planner. Nor are internal career paths leading to the job always clear. To complicate matters, there is evidence that effective research units like HRP tend to attract personalities at odds with cultural characteristics found in some settings, such as manufacturing firms. Add to this fact that the HR field also attracts people who express allegiance to their profession first and the organization second. The result is that neither internal nor external recruitment sources can be relied on for a steady flow of talent into the HRP department.

For these reasons, it might be necessary to nurture talent from inside as well as outside the organization so that prospective HRP staff members are available when needed. Good "hunting grounds" within a firm include the corporate planning department; marketing specialists; HRP practitioners in practice areas outside HRP, such as training and recruitment; and, to a lesser extent, line managers. Outside the firm, sources of talent include public and private universities that have specialized majors in Human Resource Management (HRM), Human Resource Development (HRD), or Industrial Relations. Highly specialized search firms will also be useful for locating talent in other organizations. In each case, it is probably wise to establish long-term relationships with people who might need long-term development *before* they are ready to move into the HRP unit. College students can serve internships, in-house talent can rotate into the department for varying time periods, and employees within the department can train each other.

Selection is easier if people have been slowly developed for a transition into HRP. When long-term development is not possible, it will be necessary to prepare interview guides based on position descriptions, and then screen applicants carefully. However, the best that can be hoped for is that a newcomer will need only minimal training time. Substantial training in this area might even be unavoidable.

Evaluating and Developing HRP Staff

Evaluating and developing the staff of the HRP department or unit is at least as important as evaluating and developing those in other units. In fact, it is important for the HRP manager to set an example in managing staff for others in the organization. At the same time, the HRP staff can serve as guinea pigs for experimental studies of innovative practices in the HR field.

Management by objectives is probably the most appropriate employee appraisal system for HRP professionals. They should appreciate the opportunity to participate in decision-making and negotiate objectives. In addition, the HR manager, who is perhaps more keenly aware of the shortcomings in management-by-objectives than others typically are, can take steps such as holding staff brainstorming sessions to overcome them.

HRP professionals are likely to be somewhat more receptive to development than other employees. Specialized workshops in HRP are limited, but the HRP manager can make sure that staff members

1. Devise individualized development plans on at least a yearly basis, perhaps as part of their individualized MBO plans.

2. Keep abreast of new developments in the HRP field by encouraging attendance at important conferences in the field (for example, the annual conference of the HR Planning Society), publication of articles and delivery of presentations, and reviews and discussions of articles in relevant professional journals, such as *Human Resource Planning, Human Resource Management, HR Magazine, Personnel,* and *Personnel Journal.*

3. Establish ties, formal and informal, within the organization. One approach is to foster short-term transfers, as work load allows. Another approach is to rotate some newcomers, especially those on the fast-track, through the HRP unit.

4. Serve as mentors for less-experienced colleagues.

There is no absolute right or wrong approach to developing HRP staff. Take care of the basics—the same basics that are expected of line managers. Do them well. Then innovate and experiment. Try to balance the needs of the HRP unit with the career aspirations of the individual.

Issuing Orders

Issuing orders means directing and making short-term decisions, and guiding subordinates.

For most HRP professionals, the whole notion of giving and receiving "orders" is faintly unpleasant. If confronted with a direct order, they are quite likely to view it as "advice." They consider themselves professionals and their resistance to traditional authority is well known. Moreover, many specialists in this field are younger and better-educated than most employees. They share with other "new workers" an unwillingness to accept authority without question, a desire to participate in decision-making generally and in decisions affecting them specifically, an unwillingness to accept financial rewards as ends in themselves, and very little confidence in institutions. Hence, "issuing orders" to such a group presents special problems and opportunities.

A good place to start in thinking about orders is to look at models. Though various models of performance have been proposed, one way to think about performance is as a function of *situation*, *performer*, *behavior*, *consequence*, and *feedback*. Each factor needs to be considered before the supervisor ever opens his or her mouth to speak or takes up a pen to write a memo. Consider:

1. *Situation.* What is the situation, and how important is it? Is an order necessary to save time, money, and/or effort?
2. *Performer.* What kind of person is he/she? What kind of message is most likely to be effective?
3. *Behavior.* What is it, exactly, that needs to be done? How clearly does an order need to be so as to specify what action to take? Is it sufficient merely to remind workers what *results* are desired?
4. *Consequences.* What will be the results of action? To what extent is the performer aware of likely or desired results of his/her actions?
5. *Feedback.* What kind of results will be received by the performer? How will the performer know if results worked out as desired?

Issuing orders to a group such as an entire HRP staff is somewhat different from dealing with individuals. In groups, workers are pressured to conform to social norms and are bombarded with messages that thwart, change, or otherwise distort messages from superiors. It will probably be necessary to repeat messages, and back them up with feedback and control systems.

Many organizations tend to rely too heavily on written information to guide employees. They should issue orders and give advice face-to-face; it is faster and quite often more effective.

Resolving Destructive Conflicts

Conflict is usually understood to mean a disagreement between two or more people—usually a negative connotation. For HRP managers, conflict is possible in dealings with the external environment, with the organization's internal environment (that is, with units outside HRP), and within the HRP unit itself. Of course, conflict is also possible within an individual, but we shall not treat that topic here.

Conflict in an organizational setting usually stems from (1) *differences in goals* (owing to specialization of labor, different groups have different goals; the same principle applies to individuals enacting different roles); (2) *differences in values* (people vary in what they perceive as important); (3) *competition for resources* (organizations compete with each other for scarce resources; departments, work groups, and individuals within organizations also compete); (4) *interdependence* (to the extent that an individual or group depends on others, the opportunity for conflict exists in their interactions), and (5) *communication barriers*. Groups tend to grow more cohesive over time with their own special language and negative stereotypes of outsiders; this creates barriers between groups. Differences about issues can escalate to differences between individuals, partly because people tend to think of a disagreement as a personal matter.

Why are conflict issues of concern to the HRP manager? One reason has to do with the difference between line and staff employees. They focus on different goals: Staff specialists want to see things done "right." It is their job to provide advice and exert procedural control over line managers. They tend to be young and well educated, expressing allegiance to their profession first and to the organization second. In contrast, line managers are less interested in what is "right" and are more interested in getting the work out on time. Line and staff managers thus have quite different roles.

As shown in Figure 18-3, most major sources of conflict between people in general are found in line-staff relationships: They have different goals and values. They compete for resources. They are dependent on each other.

Since line and staff people are usually structurally separated, they are also prone to the effects of small-group formation.

What can be done to foster increased cooperation between line and staff?

1. Confront problems openly. It helps to discuss problems together and collaborate on solutions.
2. Develop common goals. One way to resolve parochial differences is to focus on "the big picture," such as shared objectives.
3. Increase available resources. One reason for the increasing number of mergers in corporate America is that expansion of an organization helps increase the pool of resources, thereby reducing conflict. A "rising tide lifts all boats" is an old saying that summarizes the value of mergers as a way to reduce dysfunctional conflict.
4. Alter leadership, structure, policies, and rewards. One way to deal with conflict is to identify cause and, to the extent that it is a result of one of these variables, act on it so as to reduce the conflict.
5. Find a "common enemy." Conflicting groups will unite to fight external threats. This is precisely what happened in Chrysler Corporation

Figure 18-3: Goal and Value Differences

Line Managers	*Staff Professionals*
▮ Focus on tasks	▮ Focus on employee morale, feelings
▮ Want more time to complete work	▮ Want more time for projects to improve productivity and morale
▮ Need advice regarding termination, legal compliance, etc.	▮ Need information from managers on staffing issues

several years ago, when unions and management temporarily halted their bickering to prevent bankruptcy.

The same principles are applicable to dealing with destructive interpersonal conflicts between individuals.

Communicating within and between Departments

Few topics warrant as much attention as the responsibility of the HRP manager to communicate with staff inside the department and with people outside the department. While this issue was briefly discussed in Chapter 2, it was not really treated fully at that time. It deserves some attention here.

Communication is not something that is an outgrowth of management; rather, it is the very essence of organized activity. Issuing orders and resolving destructive conflicts, which were treated in the previous sections, are really only unique applications of a manager's duty to inform, persuade, and influence others. Interaction with people is fundamental to a manager's role, and communication is of course an integral part of interaction.

For HRP managers, communication is particularly important. They depend on it to:

1. Obtain information of use in formulating HR plans, such as (1) the purpose, goals, and objectives of the HRP department; (2) the environment inside and outside the organization; and (3) strengths and weaknesses of the HRP department generally and HR practice areas specifically.
2. Provide information of use in implementing HR plans. What should be done? By whom? How often? Why?
3. Yield information about the relative success of HR strategies.
4. Direct, motivate, and provide feedback to employees within the HRP department.

In short, it is vital to all activities.

Most theorists agree that several factors are crucial in effective communication between and among individuals, groups, or departments: climate, trust, and motivation. These things can be identified, and corrective action can be taken to deal with them.

Climate, Trust, and Motivation

Organizational climate is the same as the "psychological feel" of the organization. It is not the same as culture, which has to do with shared values and norms. An individual can be *socialized* in a culture by learning the rules of behavior, but can only *experience* climate by feeling the amount of comfort and openness between people.

Trust is crucial in developing and maintaining effective communication. It is not a special term of art; rather, it refers to the willingness to be open, sincere, and truthful with others.

Motivation is also at the heart of the communication process. All communication really is based on motivation. People in organizational settings communicate so as to improve their status or condition. Hence, motivation—the willingness to exert effort—is strongly associated with communication.

Diagnosing Communication Problems

How can HRP managers diagnose the status of communication within their work units and between their units and others? A starting point is to examine climate, trust, and motivation. There are three fundamental approaches: informal diagnosis, the climate survey, and the communication audit.

Informal diagnosis is the simplest approach. Managers do soul searching by asking themselves these kinds of questions (1) Who do I seem to get along with? (2) Who do I feel uncomfortable with? (3) What accounts for this discomfort? (4) How do my feelings affect my behavior? (5) What groups or units in the organization appear interested in the HRP department? Disinterested? Why? It might well turn out that comfort is a function of familiarity and shared values, at least in part.

The same basic questions as those posed above can also be considered in the context of the HRP department itself. How well do staff members seem to get along? Is high turnover in the unit a possible indication of poor climate? Do staff members cooperate with each other, or do they spend time spreading rumors and backstabbing? To what extent is the supervisor sincere and open about problems confronting the organization, HRP department, himself or herself, or staff members? How is the supervisor perceived?

The organizational climate survey is more formal. It is a self-administered and typically anonymous questionnaire intended to gauge the feelings and perceptions of individuals about the organization or work group. A variation of this survey can be used to gauge communication between work groups or perceptions about those in other work groups. Space here does not allow for a complete description of how to go about conducting such a survey, but climate surveys can be easily purchased from other sources, or tailor-made.

A third and more ambitious approach is the *communication audit*. It is a comprehensive investigation of the present status of communication in an organization, between work groups, or within a department or work group. An audit, which helps diagnose existing communication strengths and weaknesses, is guided by a work plan. Of course, simpler plans are possible.

Taking Corrective Action

The results of informal diagnosis, climate surveys, and communication audits are used as a basis for identifying what corrective actions to take to improve communication. These actions include (1) small- or large-scale organization development interventions intended to improve trust, (2) increasing the quantity of information that flows between the HRP department and other parts of the organization or between the HRP manager and staff, (3) increasing the quality of information by improving identification of the information others need, (4) improving the range of methods used in communicating, and (5) taking steps to increase the status of the HRP department so that others will want to communicate with the HRP staff. Choosing an appropriate communication strategy is an important part of managing the department.

Planning for Needed Resources

Planning for needed resources on a short-term basis is often associated with budgeting. Most business firms and government agencies have some form of budget. It is during the budget process when resources are allocated. Hence, despite the highly rational and objective appearance of budgeting, it is really an opportunity for observing organizational politicking at work as groups and departments compete for resources.

Budgeting begins with a sales or revenue forecast. It indicates how many products the company expects to sell and the corresponding profits and expenses associated with products sold. From this forecast, the firm's decision-makers derive appropriate subsidiary budgets for capital expenditures and—among other items—labor costs. Quite often, labor represents the major expense of operations. In highly labor-intensive organizations—service firms and government agencies, for example—labor costs can be as high as 80 or 90 percent of total operating costs.

Organizations differ in the way that budgeting is handled. In some firms, top managers allocate resources from the top down. In others, budgets are prepared by the lowest-level supervisors and forwarded up the chain of command. Department heads combine budgets of each unit into an overall department budget, which is in turn forwarded to the highest levels. Middle and top managers can choose to change resource allocations and budget requests.

To a considerable extent, budget items reflect the purposes and objectives of departments. Decisions are made on what is to be done, and then budgets are prepared. HRP departments can vary in their purpose, objectives, and activities.

At one end of the continuum is what might be called the full-service HR department. It does much more than deal with HRP as a full-time activity. The top manager has a title like "vice president for human resources" or "personnel manager." The department handles such diverse practice areas as training, recruitment, and labor relations. There might not even be a formal forecasting function, which is typically equated with a specialized HRP unit.

In settings like this, the HR budget is often a cost-control device. The steps in preparing such a budget are relatively simple: (1) Specify organizational goals and objectives, (2) decide which goals/ objectives require action through HR plans and HR practice areas, (3) establish criteria in measurable terms, (4) create standards and staffing tables (standards are measured through tasks performed by the HR department; staffing tables indicate what kind and how many people will be needed by the department), (5) monitor costs of handling transactions, (6) provide feedback to each operating department regarding the services furnished by the HR department, (7) provide only those services requested by others, and (8) evaluate results, comparing historical averages to present ones. The important point is to think of results, not activities, programs, or practice areas (Bureau of National Affairs 1979, pp. 857 to 858).

At the other end of the continuum is the specialized HRP department. Usually only one unit or one division of a larger HR department, it deals solely with some or all activities associated with strategic planning for human resources (SPHR): work analysis, workforce analysis, environmental scanning, HR forecasting, HR auditing, and policy development/coordination for HRP, for example.

The steps in preparing a budget of this kind, focused on the HRP unit alone, involve estimating common expenditures. These expenditures include:

1. HRP staff costs (salaries, benefits, development/training, professional memberships)
2. Travel expenses
3. Consulting fees
4. Equipment costs (office equipment, data-processing equipment, photocopying)
5. Data-collection expenses (for example, postage)
6. Data-analysis expenses (for example, computer time)
7. Data-reporting expenses
8. Commodities (papers, pens)

One approach is to break down into categories all expenses from previous years and then plan next year's anticipated expenses, based on long-term (multiyear) and short-term (annual) objectives.

Some HRP managers find, as their corporate planning counterparts have, that data collection, analysis, and reporting expenses will increase year after year. As the external environment of the organization becomes more complex and managers become more familiar with services provided by the department, HR managers face increasing demand for services. HR managers from other practice areas and line managers might be interested in computer simulations that project expected HR costs over time, or project the impact of an HR program on some variable such as turnover. The process of creating cost-oriented simulations is called *shadow budgeting,* since the aim is to estimate future events and corresponding costs/revenues.

The traditional HRP budget has been cost-centered, as has been described. Other approaches are possible. One is to make a *profit center* of the HR department. All expenses for services rendered are billed to units requesting them. In addition, managers are given a free hand to market department products or services to outsiders. For example, training programs are packaged and sold to other companies. Even a specialized HRP unit can package and sell computer software for record keeping and HR forecasting. Training packages, books, and guides on such HRP activities as environmental scanning, forecasting, and HR auditing can be sold. This approach provides an incentive for working at peak productivity. The HR department becomes an autonomous entity, one that must produce to survive. A disadvantage is that the allure of external marketing and consulting can exceed that of providing services to the organization of which the HR department is part.

Dealing with Power and Politics

Politics and power are important for HRP managers. One reason is that staffing issues with which SPHR is concerned—plans and policies affecting pay, selection, development, retention, promotion, and transfer—are very much at the heart of organizational activities. Everyone is interested in these matters. Another reason is that to do their jobs, HRP managers need the wherewithal—the power—to influence. Yet they are seldom in a position to coerce others.

On what forms of power do HRP managers rely? How can they use politics to attain their ends? This section addresses these questions.

Types of Power

Most managers would probably agree that there are different types of power: power that stems from interpersonal relations, from placement within the organization, or from events, crises, and situations.

There are five kinds of interpersonal power (French and Raven, 1959). First is *legitimate power*. Responsibility brings with it authority, the right conferred by an organization to deal with certain issues. Authority is the same as legitimate power. Second is *reward power*. The ability to influence rewards is powerful indeed, because people tend to behave in ways that yield meaningful rewards to them. Third is *coercive power*. The ability to withhold rewards or impose punishment is another form of power. Fear is a motivator, though often one that produces unexpected results. Fourth is *expert power*. Those with knowledge that is highly regarded or precisely what is needed by the organization to avert an environmental threat or seize an opportunity possess power. Fifth is *referent power*. Association with other, more powerful people is a form of power. Generally speaking, line managers possess substantial legitimate power, reward power, and coercive power over their immediate subordinates. By virtue of position, they hold legitimate power. To the extent that their ratings of employee performance influence organizational pay practices and assignment of work, they exert reward or coercive power. Typically, their position gives them readier access to those in even higher positions, giving them referent power. Finally, to the extent that the line managers have more experience than subordinates, they possess expert power.

The placement of an individual or work unit within an organization is also a major determinant of power, perhaps the single most important one. Structure guides and controls behavior. Generally, the closer an individual or unit is to important stakeholders inside and outside the organization, the greater the power stemming from position.

Finally, events and crises can give power to those who have not otherwise enjoyed it before. The enactment of civil rights legislation increased the power of HRP practitioners, who were uniquely positioned to deal with the complexities introduced by it. Similarly, unionization of a nonunion firm increases the power of labor negotiators. Any number of events—planned or unplanned, anticipated or unanticipated—can empower those who have not enjoyed power before.

Power and the HRP Manager

What kinds of power do HRP managers possess?

Clearly, they are staff specialists whose principal role is to facilitate decision-making, provide information to others, and offer specialized HR services for line employees. They possess legitimate and expert power in HR planning. Through their role in consulting other managers, sometimes at the highest levels, they might also have referent power.

How can HRP managers increase their power and thereby increase their ability to influence the resources and time devoted to HRP?

Politics and HRP

Politics refers to behavior that is outside the organization's formal hierarchy of authority. It involves exerting influence and power over others, frequently to the self-serving benefit of one individual or group while to the detriment of other individuals or groups, or the organization as a whole. The aim of "playing politics" is thus to affect decision-making in a way that benefits some while not benefiting others. While most managers would undoubtedly prefer to think that playing politics is something that occurs everywhere else in the world except in their own organizations, available research evidence suggests that political behavior occurs everywhere.

Few can dispute the inherently political nature of strategic business planning. In fact, the whole process is ripe with opportunities for the astute organizational politician: Determining the organization's purpose, goals, and objectives presents a marvelous chance to insert self-seeking interests in the organizational charter; assessing strengths and weaknesses is a chance to make oneself look good to the detriment of others; scanning the external environment can mean fortuitous discovery of trends that require more resources for one's own work unit; and implementing strategy is a way to get the approval to follow one's own agenda or confuse and thwart others. While these points are somewhat exaggerated—particularly because more than one person is competing to achieve self-serving ends—most theorists concede that making strategy and then implementing it are highly political. Indeed, if lower-level managers are given a chance to participate in strategy formulation, they will do their best to reduce risk to themselves and consider parochial interests of their departments as chief criteria for offering and evaluating suggestions about strategy. As an organization's external environment becomes more volatile, managers tend to want more information before making strategic decisions, a fact reflected in the tendency of corporate planning departments to focus increasingly on gathering and evaluating information on proposed projects or courses of action.

What does politics have to do with the role of HR planners? A great deal. To the extent that SPHR really influences the actions of managers, it is apt to be the center of the same kind of attention as organizational strategy-making. An understanding of politics will enable HR planners to understand and analyze what's really going on.

Implementing HR plans, an activity closely associated with the role of the HRP manager, is one of the most difficult and political of jobs. It is really a long-term change effort, much like OD.

Expect resistance in any change effort. It is at times rational, at times emotional, and at times political. Expect managers to resist any long-term HR plan for such rational reasons as:

I The time needed to adjust to change
I The effort required to learn what to do
I The possible implications of change in terms of one's position (Will it mean a drop in status, real or perceived?)
I The costs needed to implement the plan
I The perceptions of what the plan "means" in operational terms ("Why that means we'll have to. . . . ")

Emotional resistance stems from

I   Fear of the uncertainty introduced by change
I   Dislike of those who proposed the change, are implementing it, or
     support it
I   Low levels of trust
I   A simple desire to preserve the status quo

Political resistance, on the other hand, stems from:

I   Vested interests in the status quo (Who benefits from present con-
     ditions?)
I   Coalitions (How will a proposed change affect certain interest groups?)
I   Narrow outlook (that is, thinking in terms of the HR plan's impact
     on a single group rather than on its broad, long-term, organizational
     impact)

While you formulate and implement HR plans, scan potential sources of resistance so that you can devise tactics in advance for dealing with them.

Political Strategies for Facilitating Implementation of HRP

What can HRP managers do to increase their power base in order to facilitate
successful implementation of HR plans, or, for that matter, obtain cooperation
for HR planning in general? They can use several specific strategies: (1) *Build
on expertise.* Do not be afraid to flaunt advanced degrees if they enhance one's
credibility and potential to influence. Be sure to recognize, however, that there
are times and/or situations when this strategy can have just the opposite effect.
(2) *Acquire information.* Take steps to learn about impending changes or contemplated moves in the organization, even if they do not appear to have immediate implications for affecting HR Plans. This shows that you are "in the know"
and enhances personal credibility through referent power. (3) *Eschew political
game-playing.* It might seem like a good idea to understand organizational politics, it is not at all worth risking your credibility or alienating one political

faction in favor of another. Work on acquiring an image as a non-combatant, especially if that means sacrificing short-term gain in favor of long-term endurance. (4) *Know the business.* Be an expert in HRP, but make a concerted effort to know the business and the industry of which it is part. (5) *Set an example.* The first rule of politics is to practice what one preaches. Nothing can be more damaging to credibility than accusations of hypocrisy. It also helps to make the example highly visible to others. (6) *Fight for beliefs, but be willing to compromise.* There is a time for debate and a time for action. Make your views known during debate. Once a decision has been made, however, accept it. (7) *Build alliances.* Establish informal and formal relationships with those at many levels. Use these relationships to gain information and sound out others. (8) *Gain support of staff.* A manager whose views are shared by his or her staff has a magnified impact. (9) *Appear nonthreatening.* Appear prudent, conservative, and interested in organizational improvement; the HRP manager who does is more likely to get a hearing than if perceived as a "staff weenie." (10) *Solicit ideas and suggestions.* Many new ideas are successful when others participate in and become committed to their formulation. Use this approach during implementation. (11) *Gain access to power.* If possible, find ways to gain access—directly or indirectly—to those who hold power. Association with the powerful helps in overcoming resistance. (12) *Use nonthreatening implementation strategies.* One way to gain acceptance is to introduce an idea to one work group, company location, or department to which one has ready access. After success is achieved on a limited scale, others will be ready to consider widespread implementation. (13) *Withhold support.* If another group is trying to compete with the HRP department or its programs, there are times when a highly visible *lack* of support will ultimately lead to more power.

By using these and other political strategies as conditions warrant, HRP managers can gain power in ways likely to contribute to successful formulation and implementation of HR plans.

Activity 18-1: The HRP Department Structure

Directions: Use this activity to help focus your thinking on HRP department structure. For each question in column 1, do some brainstorming on it in column 2. When applicable, consider how present conditions and/or future HR Grand Strategy should influence the structure of the department. There are no right or wrong answers.

Column 1	Column 2
Questions to consider:	Use this space for brainstorming
1. What will be structured?	
2. What are the environments like . . . a. Outside the organization? b. Inside the organization, but outside the HR department? c. Inside the organization and the HR department, but outside the HRP department? (Respond only if applicable.) d. Inside the HRP department?	
3. What is the role (purpose) of the HRP department?	
4. What are the activities in which the HRP unit is engaged?	
5. Who are the clients?	
6. How are clients served?	
7. How complex should the HRP department be? Why?	
8. How formalized should the HRP department be? Why?	
9. How centralized should decision-making be in the HRP department?	
10. How should a. Long-term decisions about the HRP department be made? b. Information be acquired by the department? c. Short-term activities be monitored? d. Coordination within the department be facilitated? e. Communication with outside groups be carried out? f. Work inside the HRP department be supervised?	

Activity 18-1: *(continued)*

Column 1	Column 2
Questions to consider	Use this space for brainstorming
11. How should the department be structured?	
12. What should the authority structure be like within the HRP department? a. Who should report to whom? b. What decisions require higher approval? c. What decisions do not require higher approval?	

Activity 18-2: Reducing Resistance to Implementation of HR Plans and Grand Strategy

Directions: Use this activity to do some brainstorming. For each source of potential resistance to implementation of HR plans and Grand Strategy listed in column 1, describe how it can be overcome or weakened in column 2.

Column 1	Column 2
Source of Resistance	How can it be overcome or weakened?
The time needed by people to adjust to change	
Effort/skill required to change	
Implications of change (i.e., loss of status, real or perceived)	
Costs associated with the change	
Perceptions of what the change will mean operationally	
Fear of uncertainty	
Personal dislike of those who engineered the change	
Personal dislike of those who are implementing the change	
Low levels of trust between groups or within them	
Desire to preserve the status quo	
Vested interest in the status quo	

Coalitions
   Within the organization
   Outside the organization	

Narrow (parochial) outlook	

CHAPTER 19

THE HUMAN RESOURCES PLANNING EVALUATOR

What Does the HR Planning Evaluator Do?

The planning evaluator is responsible for monitoring whether or not human resources (HR) strategy will work, is working, or has worked. Acting in this capacity, then, the HRP practitioner scans the environment inside and outside the organization before, during, and after implementation of plans to make sure that goals/objectives will be, are being, or have been achieved, that decisions and resources match strategy, and that things are turning out as expected.

How Is Evaluation Carried Out?

Think of the HRP evaluator's role as one in which incumbents:

1. Decide on the purpose(s) of evaluation.
2. Establish HR control systems.
3. Select criteria in line with the purpose.
4. Carry out evaluation before, during, and after implementation of HR Grand Strategy through various evaluative approaches.
5. Feed back the results of evaluation into the organization's strategic planning process, the HRP process, and the activities in HR practice areas.

These steps are illustrated in Figure 19-1.

Figure 19-1: Steps in the HRP Evaluation Process

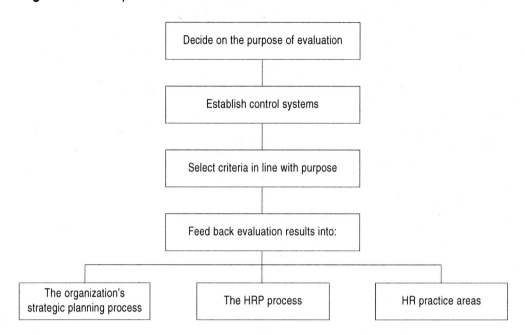

Purposes of HR Evaluation

In previous chapters, we explained the basic steps involved in comprehensive strategic planning for human resources. However, external and internal conditions change. People think of better ways of doing things. Some HR initiatives work out better than others. For these reasons, evaluation of strategic planning for human resources (SPHR) is necessary.

Evaluating SPHR is just as important as evaluating organizational strategy. Evaluation is useful to (1) make certain that strategy is consistent with organizational objectives and resources; (2) make certain that managers understand each other, their individual responsibilities, and the results for which they are held accountable; (3) assess tradeoffs between long-term and short-term use/ development of human resources; (4) forge agreements between managers about their respective roles in planning for and developing employees for the long-term benefit of the organization; (5) foster communication between the HR department and other departments in the organization; (6) negotiate critical HR issues especially pertinent to successful achievement of organizational objectives; (7) broaden knowledge about HR issues, plans, needs, and trends; and (8) provide an opportunity to assess other key players in the organization. Of course, the key concern should be to compare HR objectives and plans to other related issues. For instance, how well has the HR Grand Strategy contributed to achievement of organizational plans and objectives?

Evaluation of SPHR also provides opportunities to (1) review reasons for the original HR strategic choice, (2) identify what new conditions inside and outside the organization warrant complete or partial changes to existing strategy, (3) re-examine HR strengths and weaknesses, (4) re-examine HR opportunities and threats, (5) ponder timing and specific HR initiatives, and (6) select a way to alter HR Grand Strategy.

A classic model of strategy evaluation was devised by Tilles (1963). He suggested that the focus should be on purpose, environment, risk, time, and integration. When this classic model of strategy evaluation is focused on SPHR, Tilles's scheme suggests that HR planners and organizational strategists should ask the following questions:

1. Is there consistency between the HR Grand Strategy and business strategy?
2. Is the HR Grand Strategy appropriate for the current environment?
3. Is the HR Grand Strategy appropriate, given available resources?
4. How appropriate is the risk (if any) associated with the present HR Grand Strategy?
5. Are time schedules appropriate?
6. Does the present HR Grand Strategy "hang together"? In other words, does it contribute to effective integration across HR department practice areas and with other parts of the organization?

There are thus many potential reasons or purposes for evaluating HR plans, just as there are for evaluating strategic business plans. Important questions to ask about the evaluation process appear in Figure 19-2.

Figure 19-2: HRP Evaluation

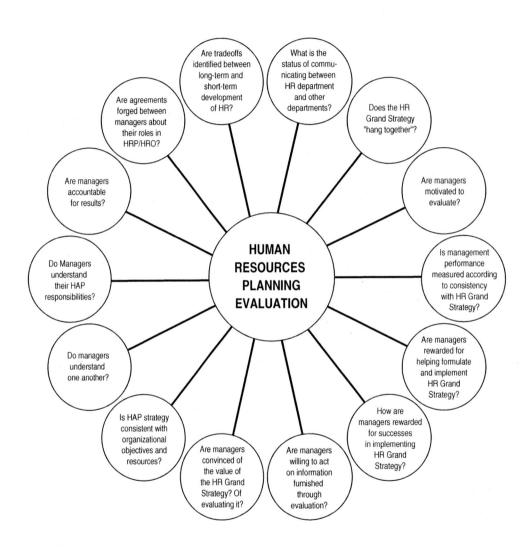

Figure 19-2: *(continued)*

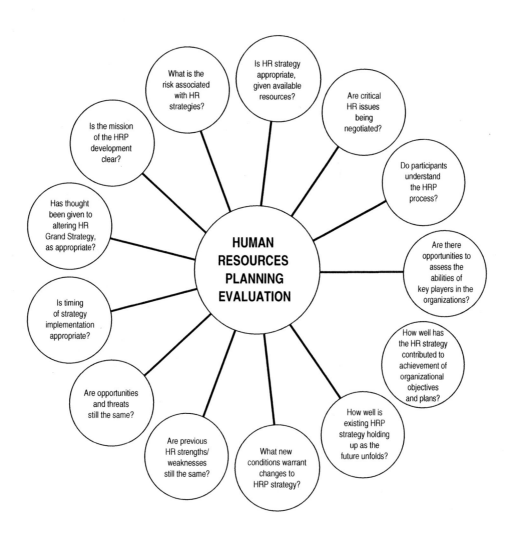

Of more recent vintage is the strategy evaluation scheme proposed by Robert S. Kaplan and David P. Norton in their book *The Balanced Scorecard* (1996). When applied to HR, their approach would suggest that HR planners should consider the following issues when evaluating HR strategy: (1) *financial issues* (What is the cost of people and HR practices, and what value-added do they bring to the organization in return for these expenditures?), (2) *operational issues* (How often or to what extent is HR doing the right things and doing things right?), (3) *customer* (How do the key stakeholders and customers of HR view it? How well linked and aligned is it with business goals?), and (4) *strategic capability* (How much and how well is the organization growing its capabilities to implement its strategic business plans?). Any HR strategy can be examined in light of these four key areas. These same four areas can also be examined during an HR audit.

Before undertaking any evaluation, however, HR planners should consider such issues as these:

1. *Motivation.* How motivated are managers to evaluate HR strategy? To what extent are they likely to be motivated to evaluate it as a result of events or conditions that have not yet occurred, but which will probably occur?

2. *Measurement.* To what extent is individual management performance evaluated according to success in recruiting, selecting, orienting, developing, assisting, and otherwise contributing to formulation and implementation of long-term HR Grand Strategy?

3. *Rewards.* How much, how well, and how often are managers rewarded for their success in implementing HR Grand Strategy? How are they rewarded? Do they value the rewards?

4. *Application.* How much are managers willing to act on information furnished through evaluation, and how convinced are they that evaluation is a worthwhile endeavor?

No evaluation process can be effective if it lacks motivation, effective measurement methods, rewards, and application.

Control Systems

Recall from Chapters 1 and 2 that the whole point of any strategy is to achieve objectives. Indeed, objectives represent the *ends;* strategy is only the *means.* In the process of implementing strategy, there needs to be some way to guide operational and short-term activities, decisions, and personnel actions in ways that ensure consistency with long-term strategy and objectives. Control systems serve this purpose.

There are two kinds of control systems: *strategic* and *operational.*

Strategic Control Systems

The focus of a strategic control system is on factors essential to the success of HR Grand Strategy. A control system of this kind is the appropriate concern of the organization's top management team and of the highest-level decision-maker in the HR department. The reason is that issues uncovered through strategic controls bear on the existence of the firm itself. These issues are within the rightful sphere of senior managers.

Pearce and Robinson (1985), writing about organizational strategy evaluation, list five success factors: The first factor is environmental. What results are sought relative to the organization's dealings with the outside world? How well are these results being achieved? The second factor is the industry. What issues are of key concern in a particular industry? Consider suppliers, competitors, and substitute products. What results do top managers hope to see in these areas? How well are these results being achieved? The third factor is strategy specific. What key issues are involved in a company's ability to implement a strategy? For example, a growth strategy calls for using greater plant capacity, increasing production, and sales. What results in these and related areas are sought? How well are they being achieved? The fourth factor involves the company. What are the company's key strengths and weaknesses? What results are sought in terms of avoiding environmental threats and taking advantage of opportunities posed by the environment? The fifth factor involves strategy success. What issues are of key concern to successful implementation of strategy? They include employee morale, succession systems, and productivity. What results are sought in these areas? What systems or methods are used to monitor them? How well are results turning out as desired?

Each factor, Pearce and Robinson assert, is an appropriate concern of top managers. They should take periodical stock of how well the organization has been measuring up to initial objectives as they pertain to these factors. In small- or medium-sized organizations, annual strategic planning meetings or retreats can be used to focus on yearly performance, reassess environmental conditions, and establish action plans to correct deficiencies. In large organizations, a full-time planning department can monitor information on a daily, weekly, monthly, quarterly, and/or yearly basis to pinpoint for senior managers deficiencies in performance that warrant their concern and action.

Many of these same factors are equally applicable to evaluation of HR Grand Strategy. (Remember that HR Grand Strategy supports and complements organizational strategy but is not necessarily driven by it.) For this reason, it should be reviewed at the same time as organizational strategy. Consider:

1. *Environmental factors.* What results are sought by the organization and its HR department relative to the external environment? More specifically, how much and how well are activities in the HR subsystem contributing to achievement of long-term plans? How much and how well are people being recruited, selected, and oriented in line with strategy? Trained and developed in line with future needs and strategic requirements? Encouraged to cooperate within their work groups? To cooperate with other groups? Motivated, through formal career management efforts, to meet future career objectives? Prepared for the future through job redesign initiatives, when appropriate? Assisted with personal problems that impede or are likely to impede performance? Supervised in accordance with formal labor contracts? Rewarded for performance in line with strategy?

2. *Industry factors.* What HR issues are of key concern in the industry? Consider: Are special regulations or laws applicable to occupations in the organization? What results do top managers and HR practitioners want to see in these areas? How well are results being achieved?

3. *Strategy-specific.* What key HR issues are involved in implementation of HR Grand Strategy? How good are relations between the HR department and line (operating) departments? What accounts for any problems in relations between them? How well has the structure of the HR department been contributing to achievement of HR planning objectives? What problems exist? How well have HR policies been contributing to achievement of HR planning objectives? How well have rewards been working for achievement of—and progress toward—HR planning objectives? How well have measurement methods been working for allocating rewards?

4. *Company factors.* What are the organization's existing HR strengths and weaknesses? For example: What skills, experience, and competencies are represented in the organization? How well are they matching up to needs created by the environment and by organizational plans as the future unfolds in the present? And what HR practice areas match up particularly well to desired future needs as envisioned in strategy? Which ones do not match up so well?

5. *Strategy success factors.* What specific issues are particularly pertinent to the HR Grand Strategy that has been chosen?

An appropriate time to evaluate HR Grand Strategy in a small- or medium-sized firm is when organizational strategy is reviewed. Senior-level managers can discuss how well HR activities are contributing to realization of strategic business plans.

In a larger firm, the task of evaluating HR strategy should probably be shared by top managers, HRP practitioners, and representatives of line management. A standing committee is formed to provide advice before, during, and after implementation of major programs of the HR department. It also serves as a vehicle for communicating about such programs, building support through participation, and helping control operations to keep them consistent with organizational and HR strategy.

Use Activity 19-1 at the end of the chapter to brainstorm on success factors associated with implementation of HR plans.

Operational Control Systems

The focus of an operational control system is on guiding short-term decisions and actions so that they do not conflict with long-term ones. "To be effective," write Pearce and Robinson (1985, p. 365), "operational control systems must incorporate standards of performance, measurement of performance, comparison/evaluation of performance, and the impetus for corrective action." Though this passage refers to organizational strategy evaluation, the same ideas are applicable to HR strategy.

Key operational controls include (1) budgets, (2) time schedules, (3) management by objectives (MBO) plans for a department, (3) performance appraisals, (4) measures of employee productivity, and (5) measures of employee satisfaction and morale.

Budgets are, of course, short-term in nature, based on annual forecasts of sales revenues. Personnel budgets are usually derived from such forecasts; the number and type of people needed are viewed as a function of production requirements, derived from sales forecasts. To state it in simpler terms, decision makers (1) estimate demand for organizational products and services, (2) estimate total revenues, (3) estimate the number of units that will have to be produced to meet demand, and (4) estimate the numbers and types of people and the salaries required to meet demand. The fourth step is associated with personnel or labor budgets and costs.

Actual and budgeted labor costs and production rates are compared at least quarterly. Deviations between actual and budgeted costs indicate a need for management attention to identify the cause of any discrepancy and its importance, and the corrective action.

Time schedules are quite important. In many cases, timing is crucial in strategy implementation. If a new machine is being purchased, have employees been trained to use it? If a new plant will open, have steps been taken in advance to hire and train employees?

Useful methods to control time include Gantt charts, the CPM (Critical Path Method), and the Project Evaluation Review Technique (PERT). More detailed descriptions of these methods can be found in books on production and operations management. The basic idea is to estimate in advance how much time will be needed for each step in a long-term effort. Results are then compared to estimates so as to control time.

Management by objectives (MBO) was previously discussed in Chapters 4 and 10. It can be used as a method of employee performance appraisal that focuses on individual results. Employees negotiate annual objectives with their supervisors. Quarterly review sessions monitor progress toward achievement of objectives.

The same approach can be used for operational control. The CEO and his or her immediate subordinates negotiate annual objectives, consistent with long-term plans, for the entire organization. Within each major division and department, meetings are held to establish objectives in line with those of the organization. Each quarter, supervisors of each department report progress to superiors. As a consequence, a formal control system exists to monitor results against intentions.

Employee performance appraisals serve a two-fold purpose. They compare actual results or behaviors of individuals to duties and responsibilities outlined on job descriptions. They are past-oriented and point out areas in which performance has exceeded or fallen behind expectations. They can also be future oriented, helping individuals identify skills they will need in the future, as well as plan for obtaining those skills.

Measures of employee productivity will be discussed at greater length in the next section of this chapter. However, they represent either (1) performance standards, which are minimally acceptable measures of daily production, staff retention, or scrap rates, or (2) performance objectives, which are desirable measures of production. Developing performance standards for each work group is an important starting point for an operational control system. Deviation from standards signals need for management attention to determine cause, significance, and remedial action.

Measures of employee satisfaction are of two kinds—*direct measures,* which are derived from employee attitude surveys, and *indirect measures,* which include avoidable turnover, absenteeism, employee suggestions, and supervisor perceptions. Both employee satisfaction and productivity measures are compared to criteria, a topic to which we will now turn.

Criteria

Throughout this book, we have used the term *criteria* to refer to *what should be.* Criteria are norms or standards, either what is minimally acceptable or what is desirable and realistically achievable. Choice of criteria is a major strategic decision in its own right. Generally speaking, two kinds of evaluative criteria exist: the quantitative kind of criteria and the qualitative.

Since criteria are so important to evaluation of HR strategy, they deserve more than passing attention. Let us begin with a brief overview of the literature on HR criteria and then describe quantitative and qualitative ones.

Most criteria for evaluating HR plans are nonexistent because relatively few firms carry out comprehensive SPHR as described in this book.

Traditionally, we think of evaluative criteria as relatively formal. Yet criteria can also be informal. If the criteria are informal, evaluation of otherwise informal HR plans will perhaps be equally informal, intuitive, and undocumented. Each manager compares his or her expectations of activities to expectations of results. The whole process is thus filtered through the mind informally. As a consequence, the real criterion for evaluation is (in the words of one corporate wit), "Are the dogs eating it?" This means, "Are managers accepting the plans and acting in a way consistent with them?" and "Do they like what they are getting?"

However, most HR managers would probably agree that at least some formal criteria are needed in order to lend credibility to the process and provide some way to hold line managers and themselves accountable for results. Without some formal criteria, it is easy for *goal displacement* to occur, in which activities take on their own purposes divorced from original intentions.

Stressing the importance of criteria for evaluation of HR management, Evans (1986) lists four in a classic treatment that is still relevant today:

1. *Internal equity,* having to do with managing the organization. More specifically: (1) How much do formal systems exist for establishing equality? How well are they functioning? (2) How much and how well are systems for negotiating collective-bargaining agreements

working? (3) How much and how well are systems working to improve human relations and quality of working life?

2. *Competitive performance,* having to do with dealing with competitive pressures. More specifically: (1) To what extent is the organization reducing payroll costs through staff reduction, automation, and training geared to increasing productivity? (2) To what extent is the organization developing a strong posture competitively by acquiring specialized competence by way of customer service, brand name recognition, technology, or other distinguishing features?

3. *Organization-environment interface,* having to do with matching performance to external demands. More specifically: (1) How much is the organization (generally) and the HR department (specifically) promoting innovation? (2) How much is the organization managing long-term employment and thereby facilitating the psychological security needed for adaptation to environmental change? (3) How much is the organization managing mobility so as to develop individuals over time?

4. *Inter-unit relationships,* having to do with relations between business units. It is most applicable to complex, multi-business corporations. More specifically: (1) How much is the organization working toward integration? (2) How much are inter-firm relationships fostered?

Each area identified represents, for Evans, a means to evaluate outcomes of HR management activities. They constitute large-scope strategic criteria.

Despite the appeal of broad-scope measures, the trend has been to evaluate HR efforts for their bottom-line (dollar) value more than their contribution to business strategy. Indeed, more attention has been directed to the dollar value of specific HR practice areas—such as training or recruitment—than to contributions of the entire HR effort to organizational requirements. One reason is that HRP practitioners face real problems in persuading operating managers that HR benefits outweigh their costs.

Several approaches have been suggested for placing dollar values on HR efforts:

1. *Human resources accounting* is one method. Flamholtz (1974 and 1985) distinguishes between placing a value on individuals and groups. For individuals, he suggests (a) "Defining the mutually exclusive set of 'states' an individual might occupy in the system (organization), (b) determining the value of each state to the organization, (c) estimating a person's expected tenure in an organization, and (d) finding the probability that a person will occupy each possible state at specified future times" (Flamholtz, 1974, pp. 168).

2. *Costing HR resources and programs.* Fitz-Enz (1984) recommends that HRP practitioners (1) collect information about costs of production and waste before implementing an HR change effort of any kind, (2) estimate the costs of operating the HR program, (3) select programs with high anticipated returns, and (4) follow up after the program to determine changes in production and scrap levels.

3. *Portfolio analysis.* Odiorne (1984) recommends handling human resources in a manner much like financial resources. Investments are matched to previous performance; results are examined by impact on work output. Generally speaking, evaluation of HR programs and results is rarely done.

Quantitative Measures

One approach to evaluating HR programs and their results is based on quantitative or numerical measures. It is perhaps the most commonly applied method of evaluation. Many such measures can be used.

It is simple enough to evaluate HR programs against quantitative measures. Working in concert with line managers, practitioners only need to:

1. Select the measures that they want to use. The choice can be highly subjective, depending on what managers value.

2. Decide whether to establish performance standards (What is the minimum acceptable performance?) or objectives (What kind of performance do we want?).

3. Decide whether or how much to measure against organizational strategy (Should measures be expressed in terms of how well or how much the outcomes of HR efforts are contributing to achievement of long-term organizational objectives?) and measure against costs versus benefits (Should measures focus on the dollar value of personnel/HR efforts?).

4. Determine units of analysis (At what level are measures to be applied: the entire organization, divisions, departments, work units, individuals?), frequency of measurement (How often will information be collected, reported, used as the basis for changing HR programs?), and the evaluator (Who is responsible for collecting information? Can the HR department do so, or will data be more credible if collected by third parties such as corporate planners, internal auditors, or external consultants?).

5. Establish methods for reassessing activities based on results of evaluation, reconsidering programs and HR Grand Strategy, and revising objectives and action plans.

These steps are reflected in Activity 19-2 at the end of the chapter.

Qualitative Measures

For those HRP practitioners who are skeptical of the value of quantitative measures, qualitative and thus non-numerical ones represent an alternative. They focus on perceptions and feelings, not on objective indices. Examples include (1) feelings of key managers, supervisors, and/or employees about the value of specific HR programs in such areas as recruitment, training, career management, job redesign, compensation, benefits, and health and safety; (2) global assessments about the value of the HR department in formulating and implementing organizational strategy, reducing costs, and increasing productivity; and (3) "welfare" measures, such as opinions expressed by employees on attitude surveys or exit interview questionnaires, or through quality circles or suggestion programs. See Activity 19-3 at the end of the chapter for an interview guide designed to collect information of this kind.

HRP practitioners follow the same basic steps in establishing qualitative measures that they do when establishing quantitative ones. In other words, they decide what information they want to collect for purposes of subsequent evaluation, what measures they wish to use (Supervisory feelings? Global assessments?), what they will base their comparisons on (Are evaluations intended to show contributions to achievement of HR objectives? Cost savings?), the unit of analysis on which they will focus (Will evaluation cover the entire organization? Only parts of it?), and the time schedule that will guide evaluation (Will there be need to collect anecdotal information before, during, or after implementation of a new HR program?). In addition, practitioners need to determine who will collect information and what uses will be made of it once it is collected.

Carrying Out the Evaluation Process

There are three points in time when it is appropriate to carry out an evaluation of HR plans: before, during, and after implementation. Let us consider each one.

Evaluation Before SPHR

Evaluation can be carried out before implementation of HR Grand Strategy to assess the current status or conditions in the organization and compare them to desired conditions (criteria).

The HR audit, described at some length in Chapter 5, is an example of this kind of evaluation. It can assess present strengths and weaknesses of any or all of the following:

1. The work presently being done versus what should be done, what will probably be done in the future, or what should be done in the future.
2. The workforce presently available versus the numbers/types of people who should be available, the numbers/types of people who will probably be available in the future, or the numbers/types of people who should be available in the future if organizational strategic objectives are to be achieved as envisioned by the strategists.

3. The present status of the HR department and its practice areas versus the desired status of the department and practice areas, the likely future status of the department and practice areas, or the desired future status of the departments and practice areas.

Evaluation During Implementation

Evaluation can also be carried out during implementation of HR Grand Strategy. It is basically a management control. Outcomes are monitored against objectives or intentions and any deviations from standards or criteria are signals for management attention and action. Many components of control systems were described in Chapter 10.

An effective human resource information system (HRIS) is a key ingredient of any control system. It is a tool for keeping records and organizing and sharing HR information. In addition to assisting in evaluation, an HR information system tracks personnel indices (quantitative criteria) on turnover, absenteeism, and attitude survey results. Organizations can design their own HRIS for a large (mainframe) or small (micro) computer, or can purchase predesigned systems. An effective HR information system is a tool to monitor HR progress in many areas: recruitment, career management, training, and more.

Evaluation after Strategic Planning

No HR Grand Strategy lasts forever, nor should it. There comes a time to reassess, in broad terms, how well the existing strategy has worked. An appropriate time for taking stock is often when a major change is announced in organizational Grand Strategy, when external environmental conditions change unexpectedly, or when a major change is experienced in HR, such as when a nonunion firm votes for unionization.

This is when you must do a full-scale strategy review. A *strategy review* is a meeting lasting over several days. Participants include top managers of the organization and others they see fit to invite. At this time, an in-depth assessment of company strategy is carried out.

Of course, other types of meetings are possible: planning cycle kickoff meetings, action plan review meetings, divisional review meetings, and environmental updates. They are described briefly in Figure 19-3.

On the other hand, a strategy review can be part of a planning cycle kickoff meeting or held separately. Its purpose is to take stock of the overall picture—organizational progress toward strategic objectives. It can help strategists consider whether a different *organizational* strategy is needed.

The HR planner is an appropriate participant in organizational strategy review. He or she can bring information about (1) numbers and types of people presently available, (2) specialized expertise available, (3) work being done and people doing it, (4) trends likely to affect the workforce and HR practice areas, and (5) the current direction of HR practice areas for career management, recruitment, training, job redesign, employee assistance, labor relations, compensation/benefits, and employee appraisal systems. Each matter obviously affects organizational strategy. Available human resources are opportunities for organizational strategy, but they can constrain strategy when available skills conflict with skills needed to implement new organizational plans. They provide opportunities for strategy because organizations rarely tap all of their human potential, which might be tapped to implement new plans.

To participate meaningfully in a strategy review, the HR planner needs to prepare ahead of time. Information from broad-scale HR audits are most useful for identifying organizational HR strengths, weaknesses, opportunities, and threats. Yet audits take time to commission and carry out.

Strategy review does not have to be limited to meetings on organizational plans. Meetings of the same kind can be limited to the HR department only. Indeed, each meeting described in the context of organizational strategy-making can also be used in HR strategy-making. The focus is different, however. One purpose of these meetings is to integrate activities across the department so that they are well coordinated. Another purpose is to make sure that initiatives of the HR department (as a whole) and practice areas (individually) are compatible with strategic business plans and objectives.

Figure 19-3: Meetings Associated with Strategy

Meeting	Purpose	Brief Description
Planning cycle kickoff meetings	▪ To begin a new, fresh examination of the organization's long-term direction	▪ Format can vary from a small group of top managers meeting at a retreat to a large-scale company conference ▪ Past strategy outcomes are assessed. In addition, organizational purpose, objectives, and environment are reviewed
Action plan review meetings	▪ To follow up on how well action plans are being achieved	▪ Format can vary from group meetings to one-on-one discussions ▪ Can occur at any level in the organizational hierarchy ▪ The focus is on follow up: How well are plans being achieved in each unit, division, etc.
Divisional review meetings	▪ To follow up on how well the division is progressing on achieving its long-term objectives	▪ Format can vary from group meetings to one-on-one discussions ▪ Can occur at any level within a division ▪ Focus is on follow-up
Environmental updates	▪ To re-examine the external environment, especially when there has been a major change or one is expected	▪ Format can vary ▪ Can occur at any level and in any part of the organization ▪ Focus is on finding out about new developments externally, assessing their impact, and deciding what to do about them

Feeding Back the Results of Evaluation

The role of HR evaluator is important because he/she (1) helps create HR strategy through feedback of information about past outcomes (i.e., results of each practice area); (2) helps establish control systems within the HR department and each practice area; (3) helps monitor results of strategy, reviewing it on a broad or a more limited scale; (4) helps collect information about results in each practice area, making sure that information about results lends itself to comparison across practice areas; and (5) helps feed back information to HR decision-makers and organizational strategists about results of the HR Grand Strategy and the outcomes of programs in each practice area.

HR evaluators serve as important linking pins, providing feedback up the chain of command about operational activities and results in each HR practice area. They convey information about operational outcomes for consideration in the review of HR plans and, in turn, in the review of organizational strategic plans as shown in Figure 19-4.

The process of data feedback is important in its own right because it energizes and directs behavior. It energizes by influencing beliefs about how behavior—and results—will be associated with rewards and punishments. It directs behavior because it pinpoints discrepancies between conditions/outcomes and criteria/objectives. When feedback prompts corrective action, outcomes will differ from objectives; an overall review of HR strategy will be needed as conditions change inside or outside the organization. In this sense, action taken is *anticipatory,* intended to counteract expected threats or take advantage of opportunities affecting the organization's human resources.

HR planning bears important resemblances to organizational development, which is concerned with facilitating long-term, broad-scale change and adaptations to change. Feedback is a key feature in OD. Organizations, like individuals, are information processing systems. Clearly, to the extent that HRP is strategic and geared to long-term change in the HR subsystem, it is like OD.

But what are the criteria for effective HR feedback systems? How can results be fed back? How can results be used to stimulate further planning? Let us turn to these questions.

According to Nadler (1977, pp. 148–149), effective feedback must be relevant, understandable, descriptive, verifiable, limited, "impact-able," comparable, and unfinalized. But what do these terms mean in the context of human resources planning? If feedback is to be helpful to decision-makers who review the results of evaluation, it must be: (1) *relevant to their concerns* (Have HR planners identified information that is important to decision-makers? Geared collection/feedback efforts accordingly?); (2) *Understandable to users* (Have HR planners cut through technical jargon and stated results clearly in terms a lay person is familiar with?); (3) *descriptive* (Has an effort been made to simplify and even dramatize specific instances or anecdotes that help demonstrate the importance of HR issues on the individual level?); (4) *verifiable* (Is it

Figure 19-4: The Strategy Hierarchy

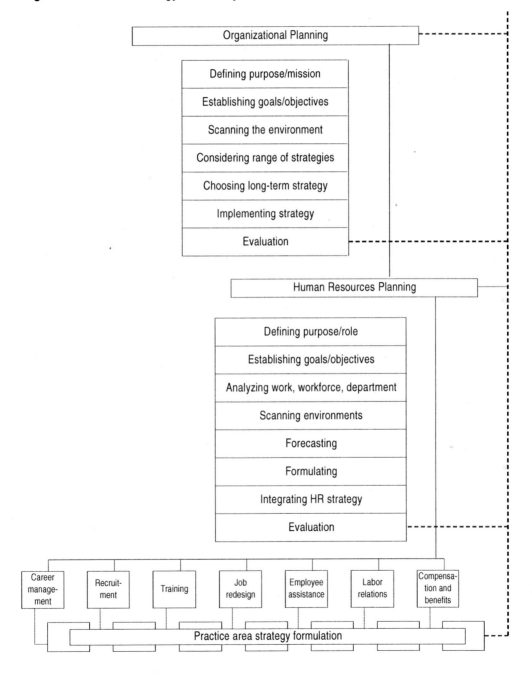

possible to go over the data again and come up with the same conclusion? Could a third party do so?); (5) *limited* (Has information been held to a minimum?); (6) *impactable* (Can receivers of feedback correct problems? How can feedback be tailored so that receivers get only that which they can use?); (7) *comparative* (How can feedback be given in such a way that it allows for comparison with standards, criteria, objectives, legal requirements, or other benchmarks?); and (8) *unfinalized* (Is feedback presented so that it implies that more investigation, problem identification, and problem resolution work needs to be done?).

Though each criterion above is important, the first one is perhaps most important. It is difficult to stimulate action—or even get attention—if feedback is not cast in terms pertinent to the concerns of those who receive it.

Methods of Feedback

Results are fed back to decision-makers through written memos, summaries, reports, meetings, and presentations. There are advantages and disadvantages to each one.

Memos meet the criterion of providing limited information. Short and focused on one issue or so, they can stimulate action. Since they are written, receivers have to consider responses carefully in a way that is not likely to be used in a meeting or at an oral presentation. However, memos are usually not appropriate for providing detailed feedback on complex issues, such as the current status of an entire corporation's HR Grand Strategy. The reason is that they are too short.

Summaries of detailed reports are appropriate for providing large amounts of information concisely. They are useful for meeting criteria such as "unfinalized" and "comparable." One way to summarize is to provide supervisors and managers with information about turnover, employee-attitude survey results, exit-interview data, training scores, and much more. Of course, it is important to establish in advance what information to report, *how much* of it should be reported, *how often* it should be reported, who should receive it, and *what kinds of criteria* to use for comparing current to desired conditions. The chief disadvantage of summaries is that they have a tendency to become more complex and detailed over time as managers ask for more information. As a result, summaries gradually become less relevant to all and fail to meet the criterion for providing limited data.

Reports are appropriate for large-scale initiatives, such as results of comprehensive HR audits, strategy review meetings, and in-depth cost-benefit studies. They meet most criteria for effective feedback except that they are rarely limited. Nor is it easy to make a long report relevant to the needs of all who need to read it.

Reports are probably most appropriate for comprehensive evaluations such as those undertaken for strategy formulation and overall reviews. To limit information, writers can prepare a summary of important points geared to issues of perceived relevance to key decision-makers. Memos and other shorter summaries are perhaps most appropriate for reporting evaluation results of specific programs and initiatives in specific HR practice areas.

Meetings and presentations are alternatives to written communication. Meetings are particularly appropriate for surfacing major issues and brainstorming about possible solutions. They can also help build consensus and support for major strategic HR decisions and far-reaching initiatives.

Presentations are not as useful for surfacing or solving problems because their structure is likely to be a reflection of presenter preferences. However, they serve to focus attention on a few issues or energize a group to action, and it is one way to be sure that everyone possesses at least a basic understanding of facts. This makes presentations superior to written memos, summaries, and reports, which are not always read or which contain information of key importance that is overlooked.

Ultimately, appropriate methods of feedback depend on such variables as (1) *audience preferences* (To what extent do members of the intended audience prefer one form of communication to others? What are the feelings of key decision-makers about memos, summaries, reports, meetings, and presentations?); (2) *communicator abilities* (How confident are those who prepare evaluative feedback about their ability to prepare effective memos, summaries, reports, and so on?); (3) *timing* (How much time is available?); and (4) *importance* (How important is it to provide sufficient information with which to make decisions?).

Using Results to Stimulate Planning

The value of evaluation and feedback depends on how much they serve to stimulate further thought, planning, and action. Even if results are turning out as desired or objectives are being met, feedback helps identify better approaches, better plans, and better objectives. For these reasons, it is important to establish channels of communication not only with those interested in immediate results, but also with those interested in longer-term results. Simply stated, some provision must be made to feed back information about outcomes in each practice area into evaluations of overall HR plans, and feed back information about the overall results of HR plans/Grand Strategy into organizational planning and strategy evaluation/formulation. In this way, constraints on future organizational and HR grand strategies can be identified. The outcomes of each HR practice area and the HR department as a whole can provide information about organizational strengths, weaknesses, opportunities, and threats.

All in all, the role of HR evaluator leads full-circle back to other roles (as shown in Figure 19-5). Information about outcomes feeds back into

1. *Coordinating HR-organizational relationships.* Given past practices and future opportunities, what should be the role of the HR department and its practice areas? Hence, feedback provided by the evaluator can and does influence the role of HR-organizational coordinator.

2. *Analyzing work.* How have HR practice areas individually and HR Grand Strategy as a whole contributed to what people do and how they do it?

3. *Analyzing the workforce.* How have HR practice areas individually and HR Grand Strategy as a whole contributed to the knowledge, skills, and abilities of people who do the work?

4. *Assessing the status of HR activities.* How do the strengths and weaknesses of the organization's programs factor in with human resources?

5. *Scanning the environment.* How accurate were past attempts to anticipate future problems and opportunities and changes in the work, the workforce, and the HR department?

6. *Formulating HR strategy.* How well have the organization's decision-makers selected HR strategy? How well has it been contributing to organizational objectives?

7. *Integrating HR strategy.* How well have HR practice areas been integrated into a whole that is greater than the sum of their respective parts? More specifically, how well has the organization dealt with career planning, career management, recruitment, training, organization development, job redesign, employee assistance, labor relations, compensation, and benefits?

8. *Evaluating HR strategy.* How well have evaluation efforts helped anticipate problems with HR strategy in advance, and how well have they helped guide HR implementation strategy, considering the objectives and intentions? How well has it provided the basis for reassessments and reformulations of overall HR strategy?

Through the evaluation cycle, then, the organization and its HR department can be prepared for the future.

Figure 19-5: The Evaluation Cycle in Strategic Human Resource Planning

HR Organizational Planning

Activity 19-1: Success Factors and HR Strategy

Directions: Use this activity to do some brainstorming. For each success factor listed in column 1, describe in column 2 what results are sought through HR activities (i.e., standards or objectives). Then describe in column 3 your perceptions about how well those results are being achieved through efforts of the HRP department. Finally, in column 4 describe what needs to be done (if anything) to improve results. There are no right or wrong answers.

Column 1 Success Factor	Column 2 What results are sought through HR activities?	Column 3 How well are results being achieved?	Column 4 What needs to be done to improve results?
1. Environmental			
2. Industry			
3. Strategy-specific			
4. Company factors			
5. Strategy success factors			

Activity 19-2: Evaluative Measures

Directions: Use this activity to help structure your thinking on evaluative measures for the HR department and for HR Grand Strategy. For each question in the left column below, write your ideas in the right column.

Questions	Thoughts
1. What measures of performance are desired? (Select from among those shown in Figure 19-2).	
2. Why these measures?	
3. Will the measures be expressed in terms of the *minimum* (standards) or the *desirable* (objectives)?	
4. What is the reasoning behind your answer to question 3?	
5. Will the measures be expressed in comparison to organizational strategy or costs versus benefits?	
6. What is the reasoning behind your answer to question 5?	
7. What will be the units of analysis— the entire organization? A division? Work units? Individuals?	
8. What is the reasoning behind your answer to question 7?	
9. How often will information about progress (actual versus measures) be . . . ? Why? 　a. Collected (Why?) 　b. Reported (Why?) 　c. Used to change programs (Why?)	
10. Who is responsible for collecting information?	
11. Why was this person or group chosen for collecting information?	
12. What methods will be used to . . . ? 　a. Reassess activities based on results of evaluation 　b. Reconsider HR programs and entire HR Grand Strategy 　c. Revise objectives or action plans	

Activity 19-3: An Interview Guide for the Evaluation of HR Practice Areas

Directions: Meet with randomly selected individuals from different segments of the organization. Solicit their opinions and perceptions on the questions below and on other matters pertinent to HR in the organization.

1. What is your overall opinion of the personnel department in the organization? Is it good, poor, or only so-so?

2. For what reason(s) do you feel this way?

3. What contacts have you had with personnel department–sponsored activities or programs over the past year? Examples can include training programs, recruitment, job postings, or employee performance appraisals. Simply describe the contacts you have had.

4. What specific strengths (or strong points) do you notice in the organization's personnel efforts?

5. What makes you feel they are strengths?

6. What specific weaknesses (or weak points) do you notice in the organization's personnel efforts?

7. What makes you feel they are weaknesses?

8. What suggestions for improvement would you like to give people in the personnel department?

Thank you for your cooperation.

Activity 19-4: Case Study

Directions: Read through the case that follows, and then answer questions at the end. (This case is entirely fictitious.)

Erica Smith, age 46, is vice president for personnel and human resources with the Lorton Company, a large and prominent manufacturing firm that employs 63,000 people in the United States and Europe. Smith's department is structured along functional and regional lines. About 135 people work in the HR department at the corporate level.

For the past five years, Lorton has been in the midst of retrenchment. The company, despite its size, is not diversified; rather, it manufactures a single line of heavy-duty farm and construction equipment. Economic conditions have been favorable for financing modest expansion and for replacing obsolete production machinery used in the manufacturing process. However, product demand for Lorton equipment has been disappointing. Demand for farm machinery is at an all-time low due to a catastrophic farm economy. Sales of construction equipment have increased substantially, but not enough to reduce Lorton's sizable inventory.

Lorton has been fighting for survival against overseas firms that enjoy government subsidies and low labor rates. In the United States and Europe, Lorton's strength is its maintenance system, one that foreign competitors have not yet matched. Company advertisements build on this strength, reminding consumers that they want not only quality-built but quality-maintained equipment. Farm and construction trade magazines are used for most of Lorton's advertising.

When the company's managers decided that retrenchment was necessary, the HR department responded with an HR Grand Strategy of retrenchment. More specifically,

1. They announced the beginning of widespread layoffs, particularly among blue-collar and unionized rank and file workers in the section of the firm dealing with the manufacture and sales of farm equipment.
2. They announced that there would be a hiring freeze, so that attrition could be used for additional staff reduction, at all levels, in order to reduce operating costs even more than the layoff.
3. All formal in-house training was eliminated. Only customer training, run on a fee basis (i.e., customer pays), was retained.
4. Employees near retirement were given special one-time inducements to accept early retirement.
5. Labor negotiators began requesting—and receiving—wage concessions from organized labor.
6. The company's model Employee Assistance Program, operated on a contractual basis with local hospitals, was eliminated.

A modest OD program, using quality circles, was the only HR department activity not substantially cut or eliminated. It was saved only through a direct and personal appeal for its continuation by the vice president of production.

There are signs that the U.S. farm economy will improve. A major farm subsidy program has been announced as a top priority of the newly elected president. Low interest rates are keeping the sales of construction equipment steady.

Activity 19-4: Case Study (*continued*)

Structure of the Human Resources Department at the Lorton Company

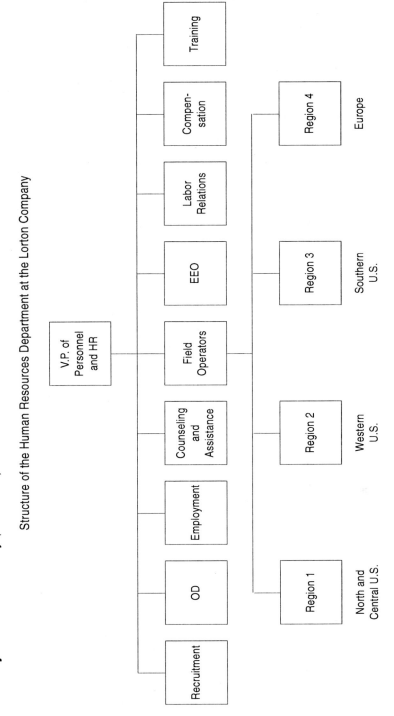

Activity 19-4: Case Study *(continued)*

Smith expects that any day now, the company's CEO will announce that he has set up a meeting to be hosted by the planning department. The purpose is to change organizational strategy.

Questions

1. What should Smith do in preparation for a meeting on organizational strategy?
2. What should the HR planning unit be doing while a retrenchment strategy for human resources is being implemented?
3. What kind of evaluation criteria would be appropriate in this setting: quantitative, qualitative, or a combination of the two?
4. Explain how results of an annual HR audit could be useful to Smith right now.
5. What *long-term* impact would you expect in the Lorton company as a result of each of the following:
   (a) widespread layoffs among blue-collar, unionized workers
   (b) layoffs in the section of the company producing farm machinery
   (c) a hiring freeze at all levels
   (d) elimination of all formal, in-house training
   (e) early retirement
   (f) wage concessions
   (g) elimination of the company's model Employee Assistance Program
6. Discuss how each item in #5 above introduces a constraint on the future choice of an *organizational* strategy and HR Grand Strategy. (For instance, how easily can a strategy of organizational growth be implemented when the farm machinery component of the firm has been so severely cut back?)
7. The chapter treated, quite briefly, the issue of cost-benefit analysis in terms of its potential applicability to *choosing* HR programs. How could the same technique have been used in Lorton to estimate the costs and benefits of *eliminating* HR programs?

REFERENCES

Abell, D. 1980. *Defining the business: The starting point of strategic planning.* Englewood Cliffs, N.J.: Prentice Hall.

Abernathy, D. Job hunting we will go. *Training and Development.* 54, no. 1 (2000):18.

Adler, R., and Coleman. 1999. Performance Management Profile: Example Audit of an HR Function. Unpublished SHRM whitepaper at http://www.shrm.org/whitepapers/documents/61123.asp

The aging baby boomers. (1996, October). *Workplace Visions.* Presented at a secured site at *http://www.shrm.org/issues/0996wv01.htm*

Alderman, L. How you can take control of your own career—Plus our exclusive job poll. *Money* 24, no. 7 (1995):37–38.

Altman, W. Recovery planning . . . for your career. *Management Accounting-London* 76, no. 3 (1998):64–66.

Atkinson, W. Award-winning advice. *Human Resource Executive* 14, no. 2 (2000):78–80.

At-Twaijri, M. I. An empirical investigation of the job design motivating factors: The Saudi case. *International Journal of Commerce and Management* 5, no. 4 (1995):24–32.

Banfield, P. Learning to reassess the role of training. *People Management* 3, no. 24 (1997):52.

Barney, J., and P. Wright. On becoming a strategic partner: The role of human resources in gaining competitive advantage. *Human Resource Management* 37, no. 1, (1998):31–46.

Baron, J., and D. Kreps. Consistent human resource practices. *California Management Review* 41, no. 3 (1999):29–53.

Bartlett, C., and S. Ghosal. Beyond strategic planning to organization learning: Lifeblood of the individualized corporation. *Strategy and Leadership* 26, no. 1 (1998):34–39.

Baytos, K. New developments in job design. *Business Credit* 97, no. 2 (1995):22–25.

Becker, B., and M. Huselid. Overview: Strategic human resource management in five leading firms. *Human Resource Management* 38, no. 4, (1999):287–301.

Belbin, M. , B.Watson, and C. West. True colours. *People Management* 3, no. 5 (1997):36–41.

Bennett, N., D. Ketchen, and E. Schultz. An examination of factors associated with the integration of human resource management and strategic decision-making. *Human Resource Management* 37, no. 1 (1998):3–16.

Birecree, A. M. A comparative analysis of cases of conflictual labor relations in the processing steel, paper, and coal industries. *Journal of Economic Issues* 31, no. 1 (1997):129–144.

Blancero, D. Key competencies for a transformed human resource organization: Results of a field study. *Human Resource Management* 35, no. 3 (1996, Fall):383–403.

Bohlander, G., and M. Campbell. Problem-solving bargaining and work redesign: Magma Copper's labor-management partnership. *National Productivity Review* 12, no. 4 (1993):519–533.

Bolman, L. G. Leadership and management effectiveness: A multi-frame, multi-sector analysis. *Human Resource Management* 30, no. 4 (1984, Winter):509–534.

Bowman, J. Performance appraisal: Verisimilitude trumps veracity. *Public Personnel Management* 28, no. 4 (2000):557–576.

Brew, P. Learning to plan and planning to learn: Resolving the planning school/learning school debate. *Strategic Management Journal* 20, no. 10 (1999):889–913.

Bridges, W. The end of the job. *Fortune* 130, no. 6 (1994):62–74.

Brockbank, W. If HR were really strategically proactive: Present and future directions in HR's contribution to competitive advantage. *Human Resource Management* 38, no. 4 (1999):337–352.

Brown, D. States of pay. *People Management* 5, no. 23 (1999):52–53.

Brown, T. My fair HR professional. *HR Focus* 74, no. 6 (1997):4–5.

Brown, T. My fair HR professional. *HR Focus* 74, no. 2 (1997):253–268.

Brown, T. Ringing up intellectual capital. *Management Review* 87, no. 1 (1998):47–51.

Burke, W. The new agenda for organization development. *Organizational Dynamics* 26: no. 1 (1997):6–20.

Bureau of Labor Statistics. 1995. *New data on contingent and alternative employment examined by BLS.* Unpublished work. Presented at *http://stats.bls.gov/pub/news.release/conemp.txt.*

Bureau of Labor Statistics. 1996. *Tomorrow's jobs.* Unpublished work. Presented at *http://stats.bls.gov/oco/oco2003.htm.* Washington, D.C.: U.S. Department of Labor.

Bursch, J., and A. Van Strander. Well-structured employee reward/recognition programs yield positive results. *HRFocus* 76, no. 11 (1999):1, 14–15.

Campbell, D. Task complexity: A review and analysis. *Academy of Management Review* 13, no. 1 (1998):40–52.

Campbell, D., K. Campbell, and H. Chia. Merit pay, performance appraisal, and individual motivation: An analysis and alternative. *Human Resource Management* 37, no. 2 (1998):131–146.

Capron, J. M. No good deed goes unpunished: Employee assistance programs as sources of liability. *Employee Relations Law Journal* 24, no. 3 (1998):79–99.

Case, M. S. Case study: How Owens Corning uses cash-equivalent benefits to tie compensation to performance. *Compensation and Benefits Review* 28, no. 3(1996):69–74.

Caudron, S. Team staffing requires new HR role. *Personnel Journal* 73, no. 5 (1994):88–94.

Chew, I., and P. Chon. Effects of strategic human resource management on strategic vision. *International Journal of Human Resource Management* 10, no. 6 (1999): 1030–1045.

Churchman, C. 1968. *The systems approach.* New York: Delacorte Press.

Clifford, J. Job analysis: Why do it, and how should it be done? *Public Personnel Management* 23, no. 2(1994):321–340.

Clifford, J. Manage work better to better manage human resources: A comparative study of two approaches to job analysis. *Public Personnel Management* 25, no. 1(1996): 89–102.

Cohen, G. Employee assistance programs: A preventive, cost-effective benefit. *Journal of Health Care Finance* 24, no. 3(1998):45–53.

Condodina, J. Echoes from the line: HR lacks strategic initiative. *HR Focus* 74, no. 7 (1997, July):2.

Conner, J. and D. Ulrich. Human resource roles: Creating value, not rhetoric. *The Journal of the Human Resource Planning Society* 19, no. 3 (1996):16–17.

Cordery, J. Work redesign: Rhetoric vs. reality. *Asia Pacific Journal of Human Resources* 33, no. 2 (1995):3–19.

Cross, R., and L. Baird. Technology is not enough: Improving performance by building organizational memory. *Sloan Management Review* 41, no. 3(2000):69–78.

Cutcher-Gershenfeld, J. Collective bargaining in small firms: Preliminary evidence of fundamental change. *Industrial and Labor Relations Review* 49, no. 2(1996a):195–212.

Cutcher-Gershenfeld, J. Global implications of recent innovations in U.S. collective bargaining. *Industrial Relations-Quebec* 51, no. 2 (1996b):281–301.

Cutcher-Gershenfeld, J. How do labor and management view collective bargaining? *Monthly Labor Review* 121, no. 10 (1998):23–31.

Dantico, J. 1994. Skill-based pay. Presented at *http://www.shrm.org/whitepapers/ documents/61404.asp*

Davis, S. Corporate culture and human resource management: Two keys to implementing strategy. *Human Resource Planning* 6, no. 3 (1983):159–167.

Deal, T., and A. Kennedy. 1982. *Corporate cultures: The rites and rituals of corporate life.* Reading, Mass.: Addison-Wesley.

Dolmat-Connell, J. A new paradigm for compensation and benefits competitiveness. *Compensation and Benefits Review* 26, no. 5 (1994):51–64.

Drucker, P. 1954. *The practice of management.* New York: Harper and Row.

Duane, M. 1996. *Customized human resource planning: Different practices for different organizations.* Westport, Conn.: Quorum Books.

Dubois, D. and W. Rothwell. 2000. *The competency toolkit.* 2 vols. Amherst, Mass.: Human Resource Development Press.

Duncan, D. 1985. Organization design. In W. Tracey (ed.), *Human resources management and development handbook.* New York: Amacom.

Dyer, L. Linking human resource and strategic planning, *Human Resource Planning* 7, no. 2 (1984):79–84.

Edmonstone, J. The death (and rebirth?) of organization development. *Health Manpower Management* 21, no. 1 (1995):28–33.

Edwards, J. R. The measurement of work: Hierarchical representation of the multimethod job design questionnaire. *Personnel Psychology* 52, no. 2 (1999):305–334.

Eichinger, B., and D. Ulrich. Are you future agile? *Human Resource Planning* 18, no. 4 (1995):30–41.

Emde, E. Why go for compliance when you need commitment? *Journal for Quality and Participation* 20, no. 1 (1997):30–33.

Evans, P. The strategic outcomes of human resource management. *Human Resource Management* 25, no. 1 (1986):149–67.

Farrell, J. Long live c-learning. *Training and Development* 54, no. 9 (2000):43–46.

Fayol, H. 1930. *Industrial and general administration.* Translated by J. Coubrough. Geneva: International Management Institute.

Fenwick, M., and H. De Cieri. Building an integrated approach to performance management using critical incident technique. *Asia Pacific Journal of Human Resources* 33, no. 3 (1995):76–91.

Fields, D., A. Chan, and S. Akhtar. Organizational context and human resource management strategy: A structural equation analysis of Hong Kong firms. *International Journal of Human Resource Management* 11, no. 2 (2000):264–277.

Fitz-enz, J. 1984. *How to measure human resource management.* New York: McGraw-Hill.

Flamholtz, E. 1974. *Human resource accounting.* Encino, Calif.: Dickenson Publishing.

Flamholtz, E. 1985. *Human resource accounting* (2nd ed.). San Francisco, Calif.: Jossey-Bass.

Flanagan, J. The critical incident technique. *Psychological Bulletin* 51, no. 4 (1954):327–358.

Fletcher, C. Circular argument. *People Management* 4, no. 19 (1998):46–49.

Flynn, G. It takes values to capitalize on change. *Workforce* 76, no. 4 (1997):27–34.

Fordyce, J., and R. Weil. 1971. *Managing with people.* Reading, Mass.: Addison-Wesley.

French, W., and B. Raven. 1959. The basis of social power. In D. Cartwright (ed.), *Studies in social power.* Ann Arbor: University of Michigan.

Fryer, B. Who's got the skill? *Inside Technology Training* 3, no. 5 (1999):40–44.

Fuller, J. The effect of labor relations climate on the union participation process. *Journal of Labor Research* 19, no. 1 (1998):173–187.

Gatewood, R., and E. Gatewood. The use of expert data in human resource planning: Guidelines from strategic planning. *Human Resources Planning* 6, no. 2 (1983):83–94.

Gilbert, T. Praxeonomy: A systematic approach to identifying training needs. *Management of Personnel Quarterly* 20 (1967, Fall):30–38.

Globalization. (1996, July). *Workplace Visions.* Presented at *http://www.shrm.org/issues/0796c.htm*

Glueck, W. 1980. *Business policy and strategic management* (3rd ed.). New York: McGraw-Hill.

Gorsline, K. A competency profile for human resources: No more shoemaker's children. *Human Resource Management* 35, no. 1(1996):53–66.

Grant, P. 1989. *Multiple-use job descriptions: A guide to analysis, preparation, and applications for human resources managers.* New York: Quorum.

Gratton, L. et al. Linking individual performance to business strategy: The people process model. *Human Resource Management* 38, no. 1 (1999):17–31.

Greengard, S. Economic forces are squeezing growth potential, but HR can unlock a prosperous future. *Workforce* 77, no. 3 (1998):44–54.

Grensing-Pophal, L. Follow me. *HR Magazine* 45, no. 2 (2000):36–41.

Grote, D. The secrets of performance appraisal: Best practices from the masters. *Across the Board* 37, no. 5 (2000):14–20.

Hackett, T., and V. Williams. 1993. *Documenting job content: An approach to job and work analysis.* Scottsdale, Arizona: The American Compensation Association.

Hackman, J., and G. Oldham. 1980. *Work redesign.* Reading, Mass.: Addison-Wesley.

Harper, E. Collective bargaining practices in the health care industry: An empirical analysis. *Health Care Supervisor* 13, no. 1 (1994):31–42.

Harrington, A. Anybody here want a job? *Fortune* 141, no. 10 (2000):489–498.

Hays, S. Generation X and the art of the reward. *Workforce* 78, no. 11 (1999):44–48.

Hirsh, W. Spinal accord. *People Management* 6, no. 11 (2000):40–46.

Hodges, T., ed. 1999. *In action: Measuring learning and performance.* Alexandria, Va.: The American Society for Training and Development.

Hornstein, H., and N. Tichy. 1973. *Organization diagnosis and improvement strategies.* New York: Behavioral Science Associates.

Hodges, T., ed. 1999. *In action: Measuring learning and performance.* Alexandria, Va.: The American Society for Training and Development.

Hulme, G. Using software for worker reviews. *Nation's Business* 86, no. 9 (1998):35–36.

Hupp, T. 1995. *Designing work groups, jobs, and work flow.* San Francisco: Jossey-Bass.

Hussey, D. Human resources: A strategic audit. *International Review of Strategic Management* 6 (1995):157–195.

Ingham, T. How to implement management by objectives in the workplace. *TQM Magazine* 6, no. 4 (1994):53–54.

Ingham, T. Management by objectives—A lesson in commitment and co-operation. *Managing Service Quality* 5, no. 6 (1995):35–38.

Jaques, E. 1964. *Time-span handbook*. London: Heinemann.

Jaques, E. 1972. *Measurement of responsibility*. New York: Halsted.

Johnson, S. 1983. Critical Incident. In F. Ulschak (ed.), *Human resource development: The theory and practice of needs assessment*. Reston, Va.: Reston Publishing.

Kahn, L. M. Collective bargaining and the interindustry wage structure: International evidence. *Economica* 65, no. 260 (1998):507–534.

Kaplan, R., and D. Norton. 1996. *The balanced scorecard: Translating strategy into action*. Boston: Harvard Business School.

Kaschub, W. PECO energy redesigns HR. *HR Focus* 74, no. 3 (1997):3.

Katz, D., and R. Kahn. 1978. *The social psychology of organizations* (2nd ed.). New York: John Wiley.

Kemske, F. HR 2008: A forecast based on our exclusive study. *Workforce* 77, no. 1 (1998):46–48.

Kerr, S. Organizational rewards: Practical, cost-neutral alternatives that you may know, but don't practice. *Organizational Dynamics* 28, no. 1 (1999):61–70.

Kikoski, J. Effective communication in the performance appraisal interview: Face-to-face communication for public managers in the culturally diverse workplace. *Public Personnel Management* 28, no. 2 (1999):301–322.

Kochanski, J. T. Introduction to special issues on human resource competencies. *Human Resource Management* 35, no. 1 (1996):3–6.

Koonce, R. Using the Internet as a career planning tool. *Training and Development* 51, no. 9 (1997):15.

Kotter, J. 1978. *Organizational dynamics: Diagnosis and intervention*. Reading, Mass.: Addison-Wesley.

Laabs, J. Boeing announces plans to overhaul exec pay structure. *Workforce* 77, no. 4 (1998):13.

Laabs, J. Rating jobs against new values. *Workforce* 76, no. 5 (1997):38–49.

Lam, L, and L. White. Human resource orientation and corporate performance. *Human Resource Development Quarterly* 9, no. 4 (1998):351–364.

Lawler, E. 1977. Reward Systems. In J. Hackman and J. Suttle (eds.), *Improving life at work*. Santa Monica, Calif.: Goodyear.

Lawler, E. 2000. *Rewarding excellence: Pay strategies for the new economy*. San Francisco: Jossey-Bass.

Lawrence, P., and J. Lorsch. 1967. *Organization and environment: Managing differentiation and integration*. Boston, Mass.: Harvard Business School.

Lawson, T. E. Critical competencies and developmental experiences for top HR executives. *Human Resource Management* 35, no. 1 (1996):67–85.

Lecky-Thompson, R. 1999. *Constructive appraisals*. New York: Amacom.

Leibman, M., R. Bruer, and B. Maki. Succession management: The next generation of succession planning. *Human Resource Planning* 19, no. 3 (1996):16–29.

Leonard, B. INS reports significant climb in job-based immigration. *HR Magazine* 42 (1997):10.

Lepsinger, R., and A. Lucia. 360° feedback and performance appraisal. *Training* 34, no. 9 (1997):62–70.

Levinson, H. 1972. *Organizational diagnosis.* Cambridge, Mass.: Harvard University Press.

Lewin, K. 1948. *Resolving social conflicts.* New York: Harper and Row.

Lewin, K. 1951. *Field theory in social science.* New York: Harper and Row.

Linstone, H. 1978. The Delphi technique. In J. Fowles (ed.), *Handbook of futures research.* Westport, Conn.: Greenwood Press.

Lippitt, G., Lancseth, P. and J. Mossop. 1985. *Implementing organizational change.* San Francisco, Calif.: Jossey-Bass.

Logan, J. Retention tangibles and intangibles. *Training and Development* 54, no. 4 (2000):48–50.

London, M., E. Bassman, and J. Fernandez (eds.). 1990. *Human resource forecasting and strategy development: Guidelines for analyzing and fulfilling organizational needs.* Westport, Conn.: Quorum Books.

Luthans, F., and A. Stajkovic. Reinforce for performance: The need to go beyond pay and even rewards. *Academy of Management Executives* 13, no. 2 (1999):49–57.

Maier, N. 1976. *The appraisal interview: Three basic approaches.* LaJolla, Calif.: University Associates.

Makridakis, S. 1990. *Forecasting, planning, and strategy for the 21st century.* New York: The Free Press.

March, J., and H. Simon. 1985. *Organizations.* New York: John Wiley.

Martell, K. How strategic is HRM? *Human Resource Management* 34, no. 2 (1995):253–268.

Martin, D., and K. Bartol. Performance appraisal: Maintaining system effectiveness. *Public Personnel Management* 27, no. 2 (1998):223–234.

Martinko, M., and J. Gepson. 1983. Nominal grouping and needs analysis. In F. Ulschak (ed.), *Human Resource Development: The theory and practice of needs assessment.* Reston, Va.: Reston Publishing.

McCann, J., and M. Buckner. Redesigning work: Motivations, challenges, and practices in 181 companies. *Human Resource Planning* 17, no. 4 (1994):23–41.

McClellan, K. The changing nature of EAP practice. *Personnel Administrator* 30, no. 8 (1985):29–38.

McCormick, E. (1976). Job and task analysis. In M. Dunnette (ed.), *Handbook of industrial and organizational psychology.* New York: Rand McNally.

McCormick, E. (1979). *Job analysis: Methods and applications.* New York: Amacom.

McCormick, E. (1979). Job Information: Its development and applications. In *ASPA Handbook of Personnel and Industrial Relations,* edited by D. Yoder and H. Heneman Jr. Washington, D.C.: Bureau of National Affairs.

McGehee, W., and P. Thayer. 1961. *Training in business and industry*. New York: John Wiley.

McMahan, G. C. The current practice of the human resources function. *Human Resource Planning* 19, no. 4 (1996):11–13.

Meade, J. Visual 360: A performance appraisal system that's "fun." *HR Magazine* 44, no. 7 (1999):118–122.

Meehan, R., and S. Ahmed. 1990. Forecasting human resources requirements: A demand model. *Human Resource Planning* 13, no. 4 (1999):297–307.

Meeker, C. Defining "ministerial aid": Union decertification under the National Labor Relations Act. *University of Chicago Law Review* 66, no. 3 (1999):999–1028.

Miller, L. Supporting the human resources function. *Internal Auditor* 54, no. 3 (1997): 20–21.

Mintzberg, H. 1979. Organizational power and goals: A skeletal theory. In *Strategic management: A new view of business policy and planning*, edited by C. Hofer and D. Schendel. Boston. Mass.: Little Brown.

Mintzberg, H. The fall and rise of strategic planning. *Harvard Business Review* 72, no. 1 (1994):107–114.

Morris, D. Using competency development tools as a strategy for change in the human resource function: A case study. *Human Resource Management* 35, no. 1 (1996):35–51.

Morrisey, G. 1976. *Management by objectives and results in the public sector*. Reading, Mass.: Addison-Wesley.

Murray, C., and A. Lopez, eds. 1996. *The global burden of disease: A comprehensive assessment of mortality and disability from diseases, injuries, and risk factors in 1990 and projected to 2020*. Cambridge, Mass.: Harvard School of Public Health.

Nadel, R. 1998. Compensation alternatives: Changes in business strategy, plans, and expectations. Presented at *http://www.shrm.org/whitepapers/documents/61440.asp*

Naditch, M. 1985. Industry-based wellness programs. In D. Myers (ed.), *Employee problem prevention and counseling: A guide for professionals*. Westport, Conn.: Quorum Books.

Nadler, D. 1977. *Feedback and organization development: Using data-based methods*. Reading, Mass.: Addison-Wesley.

Nadler, D., and M. Tushman. 1977. A diagnostic model for organization behavior. In J. Hackman, E. Lawler, and L. Porter (eds.), *Perspectives on behavior in organizations*. New York: Mcgraw-Hill.

National Academy of Public Administration. 1996. *A competency model for human resources professionals*. Washington D.C.: The Academy.

Odiorne, G. 1984. *Strategic management of human resources: A portfolio approach*. San Francisco: Jossey-Bass.

O'Neil, S. 1993. Broadbanding. Presented at *http://www.shrm.org/whitepapers/documents/61402.asp*

Pastin, M. The fallacy of long-range thinking. *Training* 23, no. 5 (1986):47–53.

Patton, C. Job swap. *Human Resource Executive* 14, no. 5 (2000):102–103.

Pauly, M. V. Using a total compensation approach for wage and benefits planning. *Benefits Quarterly* 12, no. 2 (1996):47–55.

Pearce, J., and R. Robinson Jr. 1985. *Strategic management: Strategy formulation and implementation* (2nd ed.). Homewood, Illinois: Richard D. Irwin.

Peter, L., and R. Hull. 1969. *The Peter principle*. New York: William Morrow.

Petrone, J. The organizational productivity process: Turning strategy into reality. *National Productivity Review* 18, no. 3 (1999):27–32.

Rabin, B. Measuring compensation structure: An application to executive pay. *Compensation and Benefits Management* 10, no. 4 (1994):30–39.

Rath, G., and K. Stoyanoff. 1983. The Delphi technique. In F. Ulschak (ed.), *Human resource development: The theory and practice of needs assessment*. Reston, Va.: Reston Publishing.

Reid, R. On target: Assessing technical skills. *Technical and Skills Training* 6, no. 4 (1995):6–8.

Reynolds, C. Global compensation and benefits in transition. *Compensation and Benefits Review* 32, no. 1 (2000):28–38.

Robertson, R. In-house certification. *Performance Improvement* 38, no. 9 (1999):26–34.

Rose, J. Attitudes toward collective bargaining and compulsory arbitration. *Journal of Collective Negotiations in the Public Sector* 25, no. 4 (1996):287–310.

Rothschild, W. 1976. *Putting it all together: A guide to strategic thinking*. New York: Amacom.

Rothwell, W. 1996. *Beyond training and development: State-of-the-art strategies for enhancing human performance*. New York: Amacom.

Rothwell, W. 2000. *ASTD models for human performance improvement: Roles, competencies, outputs*. (2nd ed.). Alexandria, Va.: The American Society for Training and Development.

Rothwell, W. 2000. *Effective succession planning: Ensuring leadership continuity and building talent from within* (2nd ed.). New York: Amacom.

Rothwell, W. 1999. *The action learning guidebook: A real-time strategy for problem-solving, training design, and employee development*. San Francisco: Jossey-Bass/Pfeiffer.

Rothwell, W. 1999. United States of America. In M. Zanko (ed.), *Global advantage through people: Human resource management policies and practices in ten APEC economies*. 483–550. Wollongong, Australia: International Business Research Institute, University of Wollongong.

Rothwell, W. Thinking strategically: The business of career decisions. *Training News* (May, 1984):19–20.

Rothwell, W., C. Hohne, and S. King. 2000. *Human performance improvement: Building practitioner competence.* Houston, Texas: Gulf Publishing.

Rothwell, W., and H. Kazanas. 1994. *Improving on-the-job training.* San Francisco: Jossey-Bass/Pfeiffer.

Rothwell, W., and H. Kazanas. 1998. *Mastering the instructional design process: A systematic approach* (2nd ed.). San Francisco: Jossey-Bass/Pfeiffer.

Rothwell, W., and H. Kazanas. 1999. *Building in-house leadership and management development programs.* Westport, Conn.: Quorum Books.

Rothwell, W., and J. Lindholm. Competency identification, modeling, and assessment in the USA. *International Journal of Training and Development* 3, no. 2 (1999):90–105.

Rothwell, W., R. Prescott, and M. Taylor. 1998. *Strategic HR leader: How to prepare your organization for the six key trends shaping the future.* Palo Alto, Calif.: Davies-Black Publishing.

Rothwell, W., and H. Sredl. 2000. *The ASTD reference guide to workplace learning and performance* (3rd ed.). 2 vols. Amherst, Mass.: HRD Press.

Saks, A. A psychological process investigation for the effects of recruitment source and organization information on job survival. *Journal of Organizational Behavior* 15, no. 3 (1994):225–244.

Schechter, S., W. Rothwell, and S. McLane. Think tank uses reverse Delphi process to reach consensus on top trends/competencies. *Issues and Trends in Personnel* (June, 1996):8–9.

Schleh, E. 1955. *Successful executive action.* Englewood Cliffs, N.J.: Prentice-Hall.

Schneider, B., and A. Konz. Strategic job analysis. *Human Resource Planning* 28, no. 1 (1989):51–63.

Siegel, G. Job analysis in the TQM Environment. *Public Personnel Management* 25, no. 4 (1996):485–494.

Solomon, M. Pre-employment tests: A scientific approach to hiring. *Credit Union Magazine* 63, no. 11 (1997):17.

Sperling, R. Trends in compensation and benefits strategies. *Employment Relations Today* 25, no. 2 (1998):85–99.

Spognardi, M. A. Conducting a human resources audit: A primer. *Employee Relations Law Journal* 23, no. 1 (1997):105–123.

Staffing Industry Report. 1997. *1997 Electronic recruiting index: Navigating the transition.* Unpublished work. Presented at *http://www.interbiznet.com/ern/1997eri/sireview.html.*

Stahl, D. Organizational diagnosis: A six-box model. *Nursing Management* 28, no. 4 (1997):18–20.

Starner, T. E-help. *Human Resource Executive* 14, no. 1 (2000):70–71.

Stevens, S. 1951. Mathematics, measurement, and psychophysics. In S. Stevens (ed.), *Handbook of Experimental Psychology*. New York: John Wiley.

Stieber, G. Crisis intervention: Preventing workplace homicide. *HR Focus* 76, no. 10 (1999):12.

Technology influences training needs. (1996, May-June). *Workplace Visions.* Presented at *http://www.shrm.org/issues/0596b.htm*

Tilles, S. How to evaluate corporate strategy. *Harvard Business Review* 41, no. 4 (1963):111–121.

Traynor, T. L. The impact of post-PATCO labor relations on U.S. union wages. *Eastern Economic Journal* 23, no. 1 (1997):61–72.

Tziner, A., C. Joanis, and K. Murphy. A comparison of three methods of performance appraisal with regard to goal properties, goal perception, and rate satisfaction. *Group and Organization Management* 25, no. 2 (2000):175–190.

Ulrich, D. Blue Cross of California: Human resources in a changing world. *Human Resource Management* 24, no. 1 (1985):69–80.

Ulrich, D. Human resource competencies: An empirical assessment. *Human Resource Management* 34, no. 4 (1995):473–495.

Ulrich, D., W. Brockbank, A. Yeung, and D. Lake. 1995. Human resource competencies: An empirical assessment. *Human Resource Management* 5, no. 4 (1995):473–496.

Urbanek, S. Job analysis: A local government's experience. *Public Personnel Management* 26, no. 3 (1997):423–429.

U.S. Population Soars. 2000. Presented at *http://dailynews.netscape.com/mynsnews/story.tmpl?table=50100andid=200012281427000227704).*

Utterback, J. 1979. Environmental analysis and forecasting. In C. Hofer and D. Schendel (eds.), *Strategic management: A new view of business policy and planning*. Boston, Mass.: Little Brown.

Wagner, S. Oh, Calcutta! *Training and Development* 52, no. 8 (1999):57.

Waldman, D., L. Atwater, and D. Antonioni. Has 360-degree feedback gone amok? *Academy of Management Executives* 12, no. 2 (1998):86–94.

Walker, J. 1980. *Human resource planning*. New York: McGraw-Hill.

Wang, R. Labor relations in Pacific Asia's four little tigers. *Government Union Review* 16, no. 1 (1995):20–31.

Ward, D. Workforce demand forecasting techniques. *Human Resource Planning* 19, no. 1 (1996):54–55.

Webster, E. 1964. *Decision-making in the employment interview*. Montreal: McGill University.

Webster, E. 1982. *The employment interview: A social judgment process*. Schomberg, Ontario: S.I.P. Publications.

Weisbord, M. Organizational diagnosis: Six places to look for trouble with or without a theory. *Group and Organization Studies* 1, no. 4 (1976):430–47.

Weisbord, M. 1978. *Organizational diagnosis: A workbook of theory and practice*. Reading, Mass.: Addison-Wesley.

Whelan-Berry, K., and J. Gordon. Strengthening human resource strategies: Insights from the experiences of midcareer professional women. *Human Resource Planning* 23, no. 1 (2000):26–37.

Wright, P. M. Strategy, core competence, and HR involvement as determinants of HR effectiveness and refinery performance. *Human Resource Management* 37, no. 1 (1998):17–29.

Yeung, A. Lower cost, higher value: Human resource function in transformation. *Human Resource Planning* 17, no. 3 (1994):1–16.

Yeung, A. Identifying and developing HR competencies for the future: Keys to sustaining the transformation of HR functions. *Human Resource Planning* 19, no. 4 (1996): 48–58.

Yeung, A. Introduction: Measuring human resource effectiveness and impact. *Human Resource Management* 36, no. 3 (1997):299–301.

Zemke, R. Don't fix that company. *Training* 36, no. 6 (1999):26–33.

Zemke, R., and T. Kramlinger. 1982. *Figuring things out: A trainer's guide to needs and task analysis*. Reading, Mass.: Addison-Wesley.

Zimmerman, L. 1984. Communicating the total compensation program to employees. In M. Rock (ed.), *Handbook of wage and salary administration* (2nd ed.). New York: McGraw-Hill.

Zinno, V. Fighting back. *Human Resource Executive* 9, no. 1 (1999):32–34.

INDEX

360-degree appraisal, 105, 123

360-feedback system, 105

Ability
work analysis and, 68, 69
workforce analysis and, 106, 107

Ability tests, 342–343

Ability to pay, 441

Absenteeism, 141, 153, 408, 517

Absorbing states, 218

Abuse, 416–417

Acceptance, self-improvement effort and, 421–422

Accident rates, 141, 153

Action, 385–388
delegated, 383–384
shared, 384
unilateral, 383, 384

Action planning, 51
meetings for, 391
for organization development, 383–385

Action plan review meetings, 524, 525

Action research process, 379

Actuarial model, 224

Advancement
career planning and, 305
employee performance appraisal and, 112

Affective objectives, 360

Affirmative action, 12, 13

Age, employee classification and, 213

Age Discrimination in Employment Act (1967), 13

Agency status, 442

Aging population, in U.S., 14–15

Albermarle Paper Co. v. Moody (1975), 13

Alcoholism, 415, 416
programs for, 425–426

Alternation, 121

Alternative employment arrangements, 14

Alternative reward programs, 465

American Council on Alcoholism (ACA), 415

American Federation of State, County, and Municipal Employees, 436

American Management Association, 452

Americans with Disabilities Act (1990), 12, 70, 393, 429

Analog models, 23

Analyzers, 282–283

Application form, 341

Appraisal interview
career-management programs and, 310
conducting, 133–134
employee performance, 126–127

Arbitration, 435

Assessment centers, 195

Assignment models, 220

AT&T, 77

Audience preferences, for type of feedback, 529

Authoritarian culture, human resources planning process and, 247

Authoritative criteria, 155, 157

Authority, degrees of, 67
Authorization cards, 439
Automatic pay increases, 462
Autonomous work groups, 406
Autonomy
  career planning and, 305
  intrinsic rewards and, 276
  task, 400, 401

Background checks, 344–345
Background information
  collecting in work analysis, 71–73
  for human resources audit, 144–148
Balanced Scorecard, The (Kaplan &
  Norton), 512
Balanced scorecard approach, to human
  resources audit, 138
Bargaining unit, 436
BCG growth/share matrix, portfolio
  analysis and, 238, 239–240
Behavior, culture and norms of, 53. *See
  also* Employee behavior problems
Behavior modeling, 128
Behavioral theorists, job redesign and,
  405–406
Behavioral theory, 395
Behaviorally anchored ratings, 116–118
  steps for, 116–117
Behaviorally anchored rating scale
  (BARS), 116–117
  sample, 117
Beliefs, culture and, 53
Benefits, 68, 282, 451
  evaluating, 462–463
  management control and, 277
  purposes of, 463
  types of, 462–463
  See also Compensation and benefits
Binding arbitration, 444

Biographical Information Blank, 341
Boston Consulting Group (BCG), 239
Bottom-line value, of human resources
  efforts, 519–520
Bribery, implementing job redesign and,
  408
Broadbanding, 461
Brochures, benefits, 466
Budget documents, position classification
  and, 213
Budgeting, 495–497, 516
  forecasting and, 214
Bulletin boards, 466
Business strategy, 6
Business strengths, 240, 241
Buzz groups, 365

Candidate data, 225
Capability
  work analysis and, 68, 69
  workforce analysis and, 106
Career, defined, 302
Career anchor, 305
Career counseling programs, 325–327
Career counselor, 312–313
Career development, 302
Career identity, 313
Career instruction, 310–311
Career management, 301–302
  compensation and benefits and, 453
  defined, 302
  employee assistance programs and, 417
  establishing programs for, 308–311
  labor relations and, 437
  recruitment and selection and, 334
  role in implementing human resources
    grand strategy, 301–303
  organization development and, 378
  strategic career management, 323–327

traditional approach to, 305–311
  problems with, 312
  worksheets, 328–332
Career path approach, 308
Career patterns
  identifying, 306–308
  identifying desired, 325
  identifying likely, 324
Career planning, 67, 281, 301–332
  compensation and benefits and, 453
  defined, 302
  employee assistance programs and, 417
  job redesign and, 394
  labor relations and, 437
  recruitment and selection and, 334
  role in implementing human resources
    grand strategy, 301–303
  stages of, 305
  strategic career planning, 312–323
  traditional approach to, 304–305
    problems with, 312
  worksheets, 328–332
Career progress, training and, 355
Career workshops, 325, 326
Case studies
  human resources auditor, 173
  human resources integrator, 298–299
  human resources organizational coordi-
    nator, 54, 56
  human resources planning evaluator,
    536–538
  human resources planning formulator,
    264–265
  strategic planning for human resources, 33
  workforce analyst, 135
Category formation, 196
Center for Substance Abuse Prevention
  (CSAP), 416

Change
  broad-scale, 376–378
  crisis and, 379
Change agent, role during action plan-
    ning, 384–385
Change orientation, for human resources
    practice areas, 280, 281
Chief executive
  choice of, 324
  role in human resources strategy leader-
    ship, 272
Chrysler Corporation, 491–492
Civil Rights Act (1964), 13
Classical theory, 395
Classification method, 457
Classroom learning, 364
Climate, 493
Coercion, implementing job redesign and,
    407–408
Coercive power, 498
Cognitive objectives, 360
Collective bargaining, 13, 435, 445–446
College-educated workers, underemploy-
    ment and, 19
Combination career strategy, 318, 320
Combination human resources grand
    strategy, 243, 245, 251
Commissions, 474
Communication
  about compensation, 466
  within and between departments,
    492–494
  diagnosing problems in, 493–494
  in workplace, 16
Communication audit, 494
Communication barriers, conflict and, 490
Company factors, strategy evaluation and,
    513, 515
Comparative analysis, 141

Compensation, 282
    administering program, 462
    defined, 451
    direct, 451
    indirect, 451
    total, 451
    See also Compensation and benefits
Compensation and benefits, 68, 451–476
    career management and, 303
    employee assistance programs and, 418
    job redesign and, 394
    labor relations and, 438
    organization development and, 379
    role in human resources grand strategy,
        453–454
    strategic, 465–476
    traditional approach to, 454–464
        problems with, 464–465
    training and, 356
    vocabulary of, 452
Compensatory process, 341
Competence
    career planning and, 305
    defined, 65
Competency
    identification of, 65, 89–90
Competitive advantage, unions and, 449
Competitive performance, 519
Competitiveness, people as asset for, 1, 4
Competitors, as impetus for change, 380
Compliance analysis, 141
Comprehensive human resources audit, 139
Comprehensive human resources plan-
    ning program, 477
Computer-based instruction, 365
Conflict resolution, 490–492
    organization development and, 378
Consultants, 14, 141
Consultative culture, human resources
    planning process and, 247

Content analysis
    document reviews and, 152, 154
    future-oriented work analysis and, 196
    in work analysis, 81, 86
Contingency theory, 406
Contingent workers, 14, 16–17, 345, 397
Continuous recruitment, 337–339
Contract, job, 346
Contract administration, 443, 449
Contract firms, 17
Contract issues, 441
Contract negotiation, 449
Control(s)
    human resources integrator and, 269
    matching to human resources strategy,
        274
    span of, 67
Control systems, 513–517
    operational control systems, 516–517
    strategic control systems, 513–515
Controlled conflict, in union–management
    relations, 445
Cooperation, fostering, 491–492
Coordinative human resources objectives,
    269, 270, 271
Core competency, 236
Cornell University School of Industrial
    and Labor Relations, 452
Cornell University/Human resources, 452
Corporate culture, 53
Corporate strategy, 6
Corrective action, 494
Cost efficiency, compensation and, 456
Costing human resources and programs,
    520
Counseling interview, 423–424
CPM (critical path method), 516
Creativity, career planning and, 305
Credibility, of human resources planners, 21

Credit investigation, of job candidates, 431
Crises, power and, 498
Criteria
    vs. discrepancies, 158
    evaluation of human resources plans
        and, 518–522
Criterion-referenced tests, 361
Critical incident
    defined, 115
    interview form, 172
Critical incident approach
    forecasting and, 220
    future-oriented employee performance
        appraisal and, 202
    future-oriented work analysis and,
        187–188, 197–199
    human resources audit and, 153–154
Critical incident rating, 115–116, 123
Critical incident training method, 365
Cronyism, 445
Cross-impact analysis (CIA)
    evaluating human resources grand
        strategies using, 246–247
    forecasting and, 220
    forecasting compensation trends, 469, 472
    future-oriented employee performance
        appraisal and, 202
    future-oriented work analysis and,
        190–192, 197, 197–199
Culture
    defined, 53
    human resources grand strategy and,
        375–376
    organization development and,
        374–375
Cunningham, William, 76
Customer, evaluation of human resources
    planning and, 512
Customer feedback survey, 126

Data-collection methods, for work
    analysis, 77–86
Daywork, 474
"Deadwood," 240
Decruitment, 334
Defenders, 280, 282
Degrees of authority, 67
Delegated action, 383–385
Delivery methods for training, 363–365
Delphi technique
    evaluating human resources grand
        strategies using, 246
    to forecast compensation trends, 469, 472
    forecasting and, 220
    future-oriented employee performance
        appraisal and, 202
    future-oriented work analysis and,
        188–189, 197, 198
    human resources audit and, 153, 155
Demand forecasting, 210, 215
    reasons for, 215
Demographic conditions, need for strate-
    gic planning and, 14–17
Demographic factors, 184
Destructive conflict, resolving, 490–492
Diaries, using in work analysis, 80, 85
Dictionary of Occupational Titles, 72
Direct compensation, 451
Direct observation, future-oriented work
    analysis and, 195
Directive training, 371
Disability-adjusted life year, 415
Discrepancies, vs. criteria, 157–158
Discussion meetings, 384
Disparate impact, 12
Disparate treatment, 12
Diversification career strategy, 317, 319
Diversification human resources grand
    strategy, 242, 245, 249–251

Diversity, appreciation of, 12
Divisional review meetings, 524, 525
Divisional structure, 289
    matching human resources grand
        strategy to, 286
Document reviews
    future-oriented employee performance
        appraisal and, 201–202
    future-oriented work analysis and,
        195–196, 199
    human resources audit and, 151–153
Domestic violence, 416–417
Dominant coalition, 146
Dominant culture, 374
Driving force, 376–377
Drucker, Peter, 118
Drug abuse, 416
    programs for, 426–427
Drug testing, 342
Dynamic homeostasis, 376

Economic conditions
    as impetus for change, 380
    need for strategic planning and, 7–9
    strategic career planning and, 315
    supply shifts and, 222
Economic factors, 183
Education
    to gain support for human resources
        strategy, 272
    implementing job redesign and, 408
    of top managers regarding strategic
        planning, 20
Educational level
    employee classification and, 213
    employment trends and, 11
    position classification and, 213
Effectiveness, 398
Efficiency, 397–398

e-learning, 364, 365
Element, defined, 75
Embedded test, 362
Emotional resistance, 501
Emotional wellness programs, 427
Employee assistance, 282
Employee assistance programs (EAPs),
        68, 415–434
    career management and, 303
    compensation and benefits and, 453
    evaluating, 428–429
    job redesign and, 394
    labor relations and, 437
    organization development and, 378
    program planning and, 433–434
    recruitment and selection and, 334
    role in human resources grand strategy,
        417–418
    strategic, 429–434
    traditional approach to, 418–429
        problems with, 429
    training and, 355
    types of, 425–428
Employee behavior problems
    employee assistance programs and,
        417
    identifying, 419–422
    pattern of, 422
Employee classification, 210, 212–213,
        239–240
    worksheet, 259
Employee dissatisfaction, causes of,
        438–439
Employee handbooks, 466
Employee performance appraisals. *See*
        Performance appraisals
Employee productivity, operational
        control and measures of, 516, 517
Employee ranking, 121

Employee satisfaction, measures of, 516, 517
Employment
change in, 1994–2005, 11
government effects on, 12
Employment-at-will, 12, 13–14
Employment tests, 342–343
Enabling behaviors, 361
English-only rule, 16
Enterprise Resource Planning (ERP) systems, 378
Entrepreneurial structure, 288
Entry test, 361–362
Environment, human resources grand strategy choice and, 243–244
Environmental factors
determining desired effects of, 205–207
strategy evaluation and, 513, 514
Environmental scanner, 29, 30
Environmental scanning, 228, 530
assessing effects of future trends, 186
conducting, 176–177
vs. forecasting, 209
future-oriented work analysis
conducting, 187–196
selecting means to conduct, 196–197
verifying results, 197–200
identifying future trends, 177–186
importance of, 176
problems with, 179–181
scanning for human resources department, 203–205
simplified model of, 178
strategic career planning and, 313–317
Environmental updates, 524, 525
Equal employment opportunity (EEO), 12, 67
Equal Employment Opportunity Commission, 12

Equal Pay Act (1963), 13
Equity, 441, 452
internal, 518–519
Essay test, 362
Evaluation
of benefits, 462–463
of career strategy, 322–323
cycle of in strategic human resources planning, 532
of employee assistance programs, 428–429, 434
of human resources planning staff, 488–489
of jobs in future, 467–468
measures for, 534
of pay rates, 460
in wellness programs, 430–431
See also Human resources evaluation
Evening program, 427
Execution deficiency, 358
Executive review, 202
Exemplars, 402
Expectations, workforce analysis and, 106, 107
Experience, employee classification and, 213
Expert power, 498
Exponential smoothing, 217
External analysis, 141
External environment
environmental scanning and, 183
human resources demand and, 216
External factors
in environmental scanning, 183–185
supply shifts and, 222
External labor market, 335, 337, 454, 456, 487
External labor supply, forecasting, 212, 226–228

Extrinsic rewards, 275–276
Factual data, 144
Fair Credit Reporting Act (1971), 431
Family
  decline of traditional, 19
  influence on career planning, 304
Family counseling, 427
Family Medical Leave Act, 12
Fayol, Henri, 3, 395
Federal Mediation and Conciliation
    Service (FMCS), 442–443
Feedback
  criteria for, 526, 528
  employee performance appraisal and, 112
  Job Diagnostic Survey, 401
  methods for, 528–529
  of results of human resources plan eval-
    uation, 525–532
  survey, 386
Financial counseling programs, 427–428
Financial issues, evaluation of human
    resources planning and, 512
Financial measurement methods, for
    strategic planning for human
    resources, 21–22
Findings sheet, 158, 159
First-order Markov model, 224
Five-point scale, 120
Flextime workers, 397
Flow models, 218–219
Focus, of intervention, 385
Focus groups, human resources audit and,
    151
Force fields, 376
Ford Motor Company, 425
Forecast error, 217
Forecasting
  compensation and benefit trends,
    468–469, 472–473

demand, 210, 215–216
vs. environmental scanning, 209
external labor supply, 212, 226–227
internal labor supply, 212
labor costs, 495
labor demand, 212
labor supply, 221
methods of, 216–221
models of, 210–215
sales/revenue, 495
strategic job redesign and, 411–412
supply, 210, 221–226
technological conditions, 9
work analysis and, 68, 69
Formal approaches to linking strategic
    business and human resources
    plans, 49–51
Formal instruction, 364, 366
Formal orientation, 346
Forum, 311
Four-factor condition/criteria analysis,
    231–236
  weighing human resources grand
    strategy alternatives using,
    244–253
  worksheets, 255–257
Four-point scale, 120
Front-end analysis, 358
Full-circle, multi-rater assessment, 123
Full-service human resources planning
    department, 495–496
Functional Job Analysis (FJA), 73, 74, 78
Functional strategy, 6
Functional structure, 288–289
  matching human resources grand
    strategy to, 285
Future trends
  assessing effects of, 186
  identifying, 176, 177–179

Future-oriented job specifications, 200–201
Future-oriented work analysis, 187–196, 207–208
    selecting means to conduct, 196–197
    verifying results, 197–200
Future-oriented workforce analysis, 200–202

Game training method, 365
Gantt charts, 516
Gaps, human resources audit and identification of, 234–235
General Aptitude Test Battery, 343
General Electric, 240
Generation X, 451
Genetic testing, 431
Geographic conditions, need for strategic planning and, 17–19
Geographic factors, 184
Geographical conditions, strategic career planning and, 316
Gerber company, 177
Gilbreth, Frank, 82, 397
Gilbreth, Lillian, 82, 397
Global business, future trends in, 184–185
Global managers, shortage of, 18–19
Glueck internal appraisal model, 147
Goal(s)
    conflict and differences in, 490, 491
    defined, 44
    human resources planning department, 478–480
    organizational, 42–46
    relation to purpose, 45
    strategic human resources plans, 46–48
Goal displacement, 518
Goal programming, 219

Government conditions, need for strategic planning and, 12–14
Government factors, 184
Governmental conditions
    strategic career planning and, 316
    supply shifts and, 222
Grassroots campaigning, human resources strategy and, 272
Grid organization development, 387
Grievance, 435, 444
Griggs v. Duke Power Co. (1971), 13
Group decision-making, shared action and, 384
Group interviews
    human resources audit and, 151
    in job analysis, 81
Group problem-solving, shared action and, 384
Group workshops for career instruction, 311
Growth career strategy, 317, 319
Growth employees, 238–239
Growth human resources grand strategy, 242, 245, 249–251

Hawthorne experiments, 398
Hay Group, 458
Hiring, forecasting and, 227
Historical data, forecasting and, 214
Holistic management, 432
Honesty tests, 342
Hornstein and Tichy model, for human resources audit, 146
HR Magazine, 488
HRP. *See* Strategic planning for human resources
Human creativity, 3
Human relations culture, human resources planning process and, 247

Human relations philosophy, 445
Human resources, 3
  forecasting in, 227–228
  short-term vs. long-term needs in, 22
Human resources accounting, 520
Human resources audit, 233, 522–523
  choosing issues to examine, 139,
      141–142
  collecting audit information, 150–161
  collecting background information,
      144–148
  compiling results, 160–161
  conducting, 138–139
  deciding how to conduct, 142–143
  diagnosis worksheet, 165–170
  finalizing audit plan, 148–149
  focus of, 150
  interview guides, 171, 172
  scope of, 150
  selecting people to assist with, 143
  simple plan, 148–149
  simplified model, 140
Human resources auditor, 29, 30,
      137–173
  case study, 173
  choosing issues to examine, 139,
      141–142
  collecting audit information, 150–161
  collecting background information,
      144–148
  compiling audit results, 160–161
  conducting human resources audit,
      138–139
  deciding how to conduct audit, 142–143
  diagnosis worksheet, 165–170
  finalizing audit plan, 148–149
  human resources environmental scanner
      and, 175
  interview guides, 171, 172

relation to human resources planning
      evaluator, 137
  responsibilities of, 137–138
  selecting people to assist with audit,
      143
Human resources competency models, 30
Human resources demand, causes of, 216
Human resources department
  classification worksheet, 259
  generic models of activities, 147–148
  scanning for, 203–205
    interview guide, 204
    outcomes, 204–205
  strengths and weaknesses, 155–157
    corrective action, 160–161
    determining causes of, 158, 160
    interview guide, 171
    summary, 162
Human resources department structure,
      287–291
  human resources integrator and, 269
  worksheet, 297–298
Human resources discrepancies
  conceptual model for, 155–156
  corrective action, 160–161
  determining causes, 158, 160
Human resources environmental scanner,
      175–208
  assessing effects of future trends,
      186
  conducting environmental scanning
      process, 176–177
  conducting future-oriented work
      analysis, 187–196
  conducting future-oriented workforce
      analysis, 200–202
  determining desired effects of
      environmental factors, 205–207
  identifying future trends, 177–186

importance of, 176
problems with environmental scanning, 179–181
responsibilities of, 175–176
scanning for the human resources department, 203–205
selecting means to conduct future-oriented work analysis, 196–197
verifying results of future-oriented work analysis, 197, 199–200
Human resources evaluation
cycle, 532
feeding back results, 525–532
how carried out, 507–508, 522–525
purposes of, 508–512
Human resources executive, role in human resources strategy leadership, 273
Human resources forecaster, 29, 30, 209–228
forecasting external labor supply, 226–228
forecasting methods, 216–221
forecasting models, 210, 212–215
reasons for demand forecasting, 215–216
reasons for supply forecasting, 221–223
responsibilities of, 209–210
supply forecasting methods, 223–225
Human resources grand strategy, 24
approaches to generating alternatives, 246–247
combination, 243, 245, 249–251
culture and, 375–376
devising human resources policies consistent with, 277–279
diversification, 242, 245, 249–251
environmental scanning role in, 182
evaluation of human resources plan after implementation, 523–524

during implementation, 523
prior to implementation, 248, 522–523
factors complicating choice of, 248, 252–253
growth, 242, 245, 249–251
integration, 242–243, 245, 249–251
matching to structure, 284–291
organizational strategy and, 248
range of, 241–244
retrenchment, 242, 245, 249–251
role of career planning and management in, 301–303
role of compensation and benefits in, 453–454
role of employee assistance programs, 417–418
role of job redesign in, 394–395
role of labor relations in, 437–438
role of organization development in, 374–379
role of recruitment and selection in, 333–334
role of training in, 354–356
selecting, 253–254
time of formulation, 248
turnabout, 243, 245, 249–251
weighing alternatives, 244–253
who to involve in formulation, 247
worksheets
for assessing management support for, 293
for considering, 260–261
for evaluating, 262–263
Human resources information system (HRIS), 105, 129–130, 523
Human resources integrator, 29, 30, 267–299
case study, 298–299

Human resources integrator *(continued)*
  coordinating human resources practice
    areas, 280–284
  developing human resources objectives,
    269–271, 292
  devising human resources policies con-
    sistent with strategy, 277–279
  matching rewards and controls to strat-
    egy, 274–277, 294–295
  matching structure to strategy, 284–291,
    297–298
  providing leadership, 271–274, 293
  responsibilities of, 267–269
Human resources inventory, recruitment
    and, 338
Human Resource Management, 488
Human resources objectives
  developing, 269–271
  worksheet, 292
Human resources organizational coordi-
    nator, 29, 30, 41–61
  alternative methods of linking strategic
    business and human resources
    plans, 48–53
  link between organizational and human
    resources plans and, 42
  purposes, goals, and objectives of
    organization and, 42–46
  purposes, goals, and objectives of
    strategic human resources plans
    and, 46–48
  responsibilities of, 41
Human resources philosophy, 445
Human resources planner, 29, 30
  defined, xviii
  roles of, 24, 26, 28–29
    conceptualization of, 29–31
    strategic planning for human
      resources model and, 31, 32
Human Resource Planning, 488

Human resources planning, 4
  employee performance appraisal results
    and, 128–130
  levels of, 270
  use of unions in, 448–449
  See also Strategic planning for human
    resources
Human resources planning department
  full-service, 495–496
  specialized, 496
Human resources planning evaluator, 29,
    30, 507–538
  carrying out evaluation process,
    522–525
  control systems, 513–517
  criteria, 518–522
  cycle, 532
  feeding back results of evaluation,
    525–532
  how evaluation is carried out,
    507–508
  purposes of evaluation, 508–512
  relation to human resources auditor, 137
  responsibilities of, 507
Human resources planning formulator,
    229–265
  case studies, 264–265
  conceptual models for strategic plan-
    ning for human resources, 230–231
  evaluating a human resources grand
    strategy, 262–263
  human resources grand strategies,
    241–244
  responsibilities of, 229–230
  selecting human resources grand strat-
    egy, 253–254, 260–261
  weighing strategic alternatives,
    244–253
Human resources planning manager, 29,
    30, 477–505

communicating within and between departments, 492–494

creating department structure, 480, 482–484, 503–504

dealing with power and politics, 497–502

establishing human resources planning department goals and objectives, 478–480

how role is carried out, 478

issuing orders, 489–490

planning for needed resources, 495–497

power and, 499

resolving destructive conflicts, 490–492

responsibilities of, 477

staffing department, 484–489

Human Resource Planning Society, 488

Human resources planning staff
evaluating and developing, 488–489
recruiting and selecting, 486–487

Human resources planning unit, 41

Human resources plans
link with organizational plans, 42
linking with strategic business plans, 42–48
alternative methods, 48–53

Human resources policies, consistent with human resources strategy, 277–279

Human resources practice areas
assessing influence of new initiative on, 296
coordinating, 280–284
evaluation of, 535
organization development and, 378–379

Human resources practitioners. *See* Human resources planner

Human resources programming, 230

Human resources strategy, success factors in, 533

Human resources work analyst, 63–101
approaches to work analysis, 73–77, 78
assessing values, 89–90
collecting general background information, 71–73
data-collection methods, 77, 79–86
identifying competencies, 89–90
importance of work analysis, 66–68
interview guide form for job analysis, 99–101
monitoring internal and external conditions, 88–89
responsibilities of, 63–64
results of work analysis, 73, 87–88
subject of work analysis, 68–71
traditional work analysis, 71
vocabulary of work analysis, 64–65
work analysis process, 87
work analysis role play, 91–98

Human resources workforce analyst, 103–135
appraisal interview, 133–134
case study, 135
focus of analysis, 106–107
focus of evaluation, 113–119
importance of employee performance appraisals, 112–113
importance of workforce analysis, 106
link between workforce and work analysis, 110–111
overcoming problems with employee appraisals, 125–128
preparing job specifications, 109–110
problems with traditional employee-appraisal methods, 123–125
process of evaluation, 119–123
responsibilities of, 104
sample employee performance-appraisal form, 131–132

Human resources workforce analyst (*continued*)
    traditional workforce analysis, 107–108
    using appraisal results in human resources planning, 128–130
    vocabulary for, 104–105
Human rights, major laws and cases, 13

Immigrants, as part of workforce, 16
Improshare, 474–475
Incentive plans, 474–475
Independent contractors, 17. *See also* Contingent workers
Indirect compensation, 451
Indirect observation, future-oriented work analysis and, 195
Individual, strategic human resources planning for, 2
Individual analysis, 359
Individual attributes, role behavior and, 27, 28
Individual development plans, 225
Individual interviews, in work analysis, 80, 84–85
Individual performance, assessing, 106. *See also* Performance appraisals
Individual stress forecasting, 432, 433
Industries, fastest-growing, 10
Industry attractiveness factors, 240–241
Industry factors, strategy evaluation and, 513, 514
Informal approaches to linking strategic business and human resources plans, 51–52
Informal employee performance-appraisal system, 111
Information input, 74

Information-processing approach, 82
Inputs, 177
Institutional memory, 374
Instructional content, designing, 363
Instructional objectives, 360–361, 369–371
Integration career strategy, 317, 320
Integration human resources grand strategy, 242–243, 245, 249–251
Integrative bargaining, 449
Intensive day program, 426
Interdependence, conflict and, 490
Interlocking conference approach, 118
Internal appraisal model, for human resources audit, 147
Internal environment, environmental scanning and, 182, 183
Internal equity, 518–519
Internal factors
    in environmental scanning, 185–186
    supply shifts and, 222
Internal functions, 5
Internal labor market, 335, 337, 454, 456, 487
Internal labor supply, forecasting, 212
International business, strategic business planning and, 5–6
Interpersonal factors, role behavior and, 27, 28
Interpersonal power, 498
Interpersonal skills, decline of traditional family and, 19
Interpretation, 51
Inter-unit relationships, 519
Interval scale, 120
Interventions, 358
Interview(s)
    appraisal, 133–134, 310
    counseling, 423–424

employee performance appraisal,
126–127
evaluating human resources grand
strategies using, 247
to forecast compensation trends, 469,
473
forecasting and, 220
future-oriented employee performance
appraisal and, 202
in future-oriented work analysis, 194,
197, 198
group, 81, 151
human resources audit and, 151, 152
individual, 80, 84–85
knock-out, 342
oral, 194
partially structured, 84
partially unstructured, 84
selection, 343–344
structured, 80, 81, 84
unstructured, 80, 81, 84
Interview guides, 84
critical incidents, 172
evaluation of human resources practice
areas, 535
human resources department scanning,
204
human resources department strengths
and weaknesses, 171
job analysis, 99–101
Interview schedule, 84
Intrinsic rewards, 275–276
Intuitive predictors, 214

Jaques, Elliot, 459
Jefferson, Thomas, 438
Job(s)
defined, 64
evaluating in future, 468

future trends in definition of, 185
monitoring factors influencing, 199–200
Job analysis, 409, 452
defined, 65
interview guide form for, 99–101
job evaluation and, 456
strategic job redesign and, 411–412
Job-analysis surveys, 84
Job characteristics, 74–75
Job classification, worksheet, 259
Job context, 74
Job cycle, defined, 65
Job descriptions, 88, 103
bias in, 69–70
converting to person descriptions, 110
defined, 65
future- vs. strategic-oriented, 206–207
human resources planner role and, 30
past-oriented, 347–348, 350
using in work analysis, 72
Job design, 394
employee assistance programs and,
418–419
recruitment and selection and, 334
Job diagnosis, 411
Job Diagnostic Survey (JDS), 399–401
Job Element Approach, 74, 75–76, 78
Job enlargement, 402, 403
Job enrichment, 402–403, 404
Job evaluation, 452, 456–460
Job-evaluation committee, 463–464
Job factor comparison, 457, 458, 460,
470–471
Job family, 64, 233, 234
Job grading, 457, 459–460, 470
Job grouping, 286
Job guide-chart method, 457, 458–459,
460, 471
Job guideline method, 457, 459

Job incumbent, 65, 73
  in employee performance appraisals, 122
  in work analysis, 87–88
Job Information Matrix System (JIMS),
    74, 75, 78
Job maturity curves, 457, 459, 460, 471
Job performance standard, 104
Job placement, power and, 498
Job point method, 457–458, 460, 470
Job posting, 338
Job ranking, 457, 459, 470
Job redesign, 393–413
  compensation and benefits and, 453
  defined, 394
  forecasting and, 227
  goal of, 397–398
  implementing, 407–408, 413
  initiatives, 355
  monitoring results, 408–409, 413
  organization and, 395
  role in human resources grand strategy,
    394–395
  strategic, 409–413
  traditional approaches to, 396–409
    problems with, 409
Job requirements, specifying, 485–486
Job restructuring, 70, 393
Job rotation, 404–405
Job satisfaction, 3
Job security, 441
Job sharing, 345, 406
Job specifications, 88, 104
  defined, 65
  future-oriented, 200–201
    vs. strategic-oriented, 207
  planning and, 233
  preparing, 109–110
Job standard, 114
Job structure, 67

Job title, 73
  defined, 64
  future-oriented work analysis and, 187
  vs. role, 31
  work analysis and, 63
Job transfer, 302–303
Johari window, conceptualizing
    differences in perception about
    work activities using, 70–71

Kaplan, Robert S., 512
Knock-out interview, 342
Know-how, 458
Kotter seven circle model, 146

Labor availability, 18–19
Labor demand, assessing, 212
Labor laws, 12–14
Labor-Management Relations Act, 441
Labor market
  external, 335, 337, 454, 456, 487
  internal, 335, 337, 454, 456, 487
Labor negotiation, 442
  job redesign and, 394
Labor relations, 282, 435–450
  avoidance of unionization, 446–448
  compensation and benefits and,
    453–454
  eliminating the union, 449–450
  employee assistance programs and, 418
  labor relations program, 68, 441–444
  organization development and, 378–379
  organizing campaign, 439–441
  reasons for unionization, 438–439
  role in human resources grand strategy,
    437–438
  strategic, 446–450
  traditional approach, 438–444
    problems with, 445–446

use of unions in organizational and
human resources planning,
448–449
Labor supply, forecasting, 221, 226–227
Lattice approach, to identifying career
patterns, 308
Lawrence and Lorsch model, for human
resources audit, 146
Layoffs, 7
Leadership
providing, 271–274
strategic career planning and, 316
strategy formulation and implementation
and, 20
Leadership factors, 185
Lecture, 363, 365
Legal assistance programs, 427–428
Legal conditions
strategic career planning and, 12–14, 316
supply shifts and, 222
Legal factors, 184
Legitimate power, 498
Lesson plan, 363
Levinson clinical approach, for human
resources audit, 144–145
Lewin Group, 416
Liability, employee assistance programs
and, 429
Life-cycle stage
of human resources planning, 47–48
portfolio analysis and, 238–239
Life stages, career planning and, 304–305
Likert, Rensis, 118
Limited contract, 425
Limited human resources planning
program, 477
Line managers
organization development and, 388
power of, 498

Linear programming, 219
Lobbying, to gain support for human
resources strategy, 272
Localization, 19
Location, position classification and, 213
Lockout, 436
Long-range planning, 5

Macy's department store, 425
Management by objectives (MBO),
118–119, 123–124
human resources audit and, 142
human resources strategy and, 277
implementing in human resources
department, 478–480, 481, 488
for operational control, 516–517
Management control, human resources
strategy and, 276–277
Management-development program, 309
Management philosophy and culture,
human resources planner role and, 26
Management rights, 442
Managers, role in human resources
strategy leadership, 273–274
Manpower planning, 3–4, 47
Marital counseling, 427, 428
Market, share, 42
Market conditions, strategic career
planning and, 316
Marketing/competitive factors, 184
Markov model, 218–219
first-order, 224
Mathematical models, 23
Matrix structure, 289, 291
matching human resources grand
strategy to, 286
Mature employees, 239
Maturity curves, 457, 459, 460, 471
Meaningful work, 401

Mediation, 436
Meetings, feedback, 529
Memos, feedback, 529
Mental disorders, 417
Mental health programs, 427
Mental models, 23
Mental processes, 74
Mentoring, 309, 325, 488
Merit pay, 462
Microcultures, 374
Minimal acceptable performance, 157
Missions. *See* Purpose(s)
Models
   decision making and, 23
   forecasting, 210–215
   strategic planning, 22–23, 25
Morale
   career management and, 305–306
   recruitment from within and, 347
Motivation, 493
   work analysis and, 68, 69
   workforce analysis and, 106
Moving average, 217
Multinational corporations, labor
      practices and, 436
Multiple hurdles process, 341
Multiple raters, in work analysis, 88
Myers-Briggs Type Inventory (MBTI), 343

Nadler and Tushman model, for human
      resources audit, 145–146
National Domestic Violence Hotline,
      416
National Institute on Alcohol Abuse, 416
National Institute on Drug Abuse, 416
National Labor Relations Board (NLRB),
      12, 439
Needs
   defined, 359

future human resource, 181–183
training, 357, 358–360
Negative discrepancies
   in human resources audit, 235–236
   human resources grand strategy and,
      254
New hires, 238
Newsletters, 466
Nine cell planning grid, 240–241
Nominal group technique (NGT)
   evaluating human resources grand
      strategies using, 246
   forecasting and, 220
   forecasting compensation trends, 469,
      472
   future-oriented employee performance
      appraisal and, 202
   future-oriented work analysis and,
      189–190, 197, 198
Nominal scale, 120
Nonabsorbing states, 218
Nondirective training, 371
Norm referenced tests, 361
Norms
   work analysis and, 68, 69
   workforce analysis and, 106, 107
Norms of behavior, 53
Norton, David P., 512

Objectives
   affective, 360
   cognitive, 360
   defined, 44
   human resources demand and, 216
   human resources integrator and
      development of, 267–269
   human resources planning department,
      478–480
   instructional, 360–361

management by. *See* Management by objectives
of organization, 42–46
psychomotor, 360
relation to purpose, 45
of strategic human resources plans, 46–48
Observation(s)
future-oriented employee performance appraisal and, 202
future-oriented work analysis and, 195, 197, 199
human resources audit and, 150–151
in work analysis, 79, 82–83
Occupational Analysis Inventory (OAI), 74, 76–77, 78
Occupational Health and Safety Administration, 12
Occupations, with largest job growth, 8–9
Offer, extending job, 345–346
Office of Federal Contract Compliance, 12
Old boy network, 347
Older workers, 14–15
On call workers, 16–17
Online sources
job hunting/career changing, 302
recruitment, 337
On-the-job (OJT) training, 364, 366
Open-ended questions, employee performance appraisal and, 127
Operational control systems, 516–517
Operational human resources objectives, 269, 270, 271
Operational human resources planning, 2
Operational issues, evaluation of human resources planning and, 512
Opportunities
defined, 235
organizational, 43

in WOTS-UP analysis, 236–237
Oral interview, in future-oriented work analysis, 194
Oral objective test, 362
Orders, issuing, 489–490
Ordinal scale, 120
Organization(s)
barriers to strategic planning in, 20–22
career management influences, 303
job redesign and, 395
purposes, goals, and objectives of, 42–46
as role systems, 28
strategic human resources planning for, 2
Organization chart
human resources audit and, 145, 147
position classification and, 213
Organization development, 67, 281, 373–391
compensation and benefits and, 453–454
defined, 373
employee assistance programs and, 417
evaluation of, 388
human resources plan evaluation feedback and, 526
human resources practice areas and, 378–379
job redesign and, 394
labor relations and, 437
role in human resources grand strategy, 374–379
strategic, 389–391
summary of interventions, 387
traditional approach, 379–388
problems with, 389
Organization development intervention, 379–388
action planning, 383–385

Organization development intervention
　(*continued*)
　data collection, 381–382
　feedback of data and diagnosis,
　　382–383
　preliminary focusing, 381
　problem recognition, 379–381
Organization-environment interface, 519
Organization job design, 281
Organization mirror, 153, 154–155, 387
Organization planning
　link with human resources planning, 42
　use of unions in, 448–449
Organization structure, strategic career
　　planning and, 316
Organization theory, 395
Organizational analysis, 359
Organizational career-management
　　process, 306–311
Organizational climate survey, 494
Organizational culture
　linking strategic business and human
　　resources plans and, 49, 52–53
　who to involve in human resources
　　planning process, 247
Organizational design, 67, 394
Organizational factors, role behavior and,
　　27, 28
Organizational goals, employee perform-
　　ance appraisal and, 111, 124
Organizational redesign, 394
Organizational resources, allocation of,
　　5–6
Organizational size, human resources
　　planner role and, 26
Organizational strategy, relation to human
　　resources grand strategy, 248,
　　249–251
Organizational strategy review, 523–524

meetings, 524, 525
Organizational structure, 67
　gaining support for human resources
　　strategy and, 272
　matching to strategy, 284–291
Orientation, 346–347, 359–360, 466
Outpatient program, 426–427
Outplacement, 334
Output(s), 177
　defined, 114
　staffing and, 213–215
Output ratings, 114–115, 123
Outside information, 144
Outside strategy, 274
Outsourcing, 14, 345, 397

Paired comparison, 121
Panel discussion, 365
Paper-and-pencil test, 362
Partially structured interview, 84
Partially structured observation sheets, 83
Partially structured surveys, 83–84
Partially unstructured interview, 84
Partially unstructured observation sheets,
　　83
Partially unstructured surveys, 83–84
Participative culture, human resources
　　planning process and, 247
Part-time workers, 14, 345, 397
Pay equity, 441
Pay for knowledge, 461
Pay-for-performance, 462, 465
Pay for skills, 461
Pay rates, evaluating, 460
Payroll notices, 466
Pay structure, 452
　establishing and updating, 461
　placing jobs in, 461–462
　See also Compensation and benefits

Peer appraisals, 122
Peer counseling, 424
Peer mentoring program, 309, 346–347
People, competitiveness and, 1, 4
Perceptions
  work analysis and, 68, 69, 70
  workforce analysis and, 106, 107
Performance, observation of, 419,
    421–422
Performance analysis, 358
Performance appraisals, 105, 325
  career-management programs and
    309–310
  carrying out, 119–123
  determining who handles evaluations,
    121–123
  focus of, 113–119
  formal, 111, 113
  future-oriented, 202, 370
    vs. strategic-oriented, 206–207
  human resources planning and,
    128–130
  human resources strategy and, 277
  importance of, 111, 112–113
  individual, 106
  operational control and, 516, 517
  performance characteristics, 201
  problems with, 125–126
  sample form, 131–132
Performance appraisal interview, 126–127
Performance contracting, 425
Performance evaluation, 105
Performance management, 105
Performance management system, 125
Performance models, 398–399, 400
  for strategic job redesign, 410
Performance standards, 67
Performance test, 362
Person descriptions, 104, 109–110,

    200–201, 325, 486
  future vs. strategic-oriented, 206–207
  planning and, 233
Personality tests, 342, 343
Personalization, 346
Personnel, 488
Personnel, stability of tenure of, 3
Personnel department, 4, 47
Personnel Journal, 488
Persuasion
  to gain support for human resources
    strategy, 272
  implementing job redesign and, 408
Peter principle, 22
Physical employment tests, 342
Piece rate, 474
Planning cycle kickoff meetings, 524,
    525
Planning gap, 180–181
Planning gap in the work, 23
Planning gap in the workforce, 23
Plans
  work analysis and, 68, 69
  workforce analysis and, 106, 107
Policy, 277
  strategic career planning and, 316
Policy making, 5
Political resistance, 501
Politics
  human resources planning and,
    497–501
  political strategies for implementing
    human resources planning,
    501–502
Population shift, workforce and, 17
Portfolio, defined, 237
Portfolio analysis, 237–240, 520
Position, defined, 64
Position analysis, 64

Position Analysis Questionnaire (PAQ), 73, 74–75, 76, 78, 83
Position classification, 210, 212–213
Position description, 486
  defined, 65
Position Description Questionnaire (PDQ), 73–74, 75, 78, 83
Position requirements, 225
Position specification, 104, 486
  defined, 65
Positive confrontation, 423
Positive discrepancies, human resources grand strategy and, 253
Post-test, 362
Power, 497–499
  coercive, 498
  expert, 498
  human resources planning manager and, 499
  interpersonal, 498
  legitimate, 498
  referent, 498
  reward, 498
  types of, 498–499
Practitioner skills, human resources planner role and, 26
Predictors, forecasting and, 214
Preretirees, 239
Presentations, feedback, 529
Pretest, 362
Primoff, Ernest, 75
Principles of resource analysis, 147
Priorities, in compensation and benefits, 467
Probability matrix, 224
Problem employees, 240
Problem recognition, 379–381
Problem-solving approach, 126, 423
Process consultation, 385–386

Process factors, 185
Productivity
  compensation and, 454–455
  forecasting and increases in, 227
  human resources demand and, 216
  job redesign and, 398
  operational control and measures of, 517
  training and, 356
Productivity changes, forecasting and, 214
Product/service life cycle, portfolio analysis and, 238–239
Professional Air Traffic Controllers Organization (PATCO), 445
Professional counseling, 425
Professional career-counseling program, 311
Professional career-planning counselors, 326
Profit center, 497
Programmatic human resources audit, 139, 141
Project evaluation review technique (PERT), 516
Project structure, 289, 291
  matching human resources grand strategy to, 286
Promotion, 302–303, 438
  employee performance appraisal and, 112
  forecasting and, 227
Property rights, in employment, 14
Prospectors, 282
Psychomotor objectives, 360
Purpose(s)
  of organization, 42–46
  relation to goals and objectives, 45
  of strategic human resources plans, 46–48
  in strategic planning, 46–47
Purpose statement, 43–44

preparing, 44–45

Qualifications inflation, 109
Qualitative/descriptive forecasting models, 220
Qualitative measures, evaluation of human resources plans and, 521–522
Qualitative methods, supply forecasting, 223–225
Qualitative/normative forecasting models, 220–221
Quantitative/descriptive forecasting methods, 216–219
Quantitative measures, evaluation of human resources plans and, 520–521
Quantitative methods, supply forecasting, 223, 224
Quantitative/normative forecasting models, 219–220
Questionnaires
  Delphi technique and, 189
  evaluating human resources grand strategies using, 247
  forecasting and, 221
  future-oriented employee performance appraisal and, 202
  future-oriented work analysis and, 193–194, 197, 198
  strategic organization development, 391

Race, employee classification and, 213
Rand Corporation, 188, 190
Rater bias, 123
Rating error, 106
Ratings test, 362
Ratio scale, 120
Reagan, Ronald, 445
Reality
  work analysis and, 68, 69

workforce analysis and, 106, 107
Reality shock, 347
Reasonable accommodation, 70, 393
Recruitment, 280, 281, 333–351
  attracting individuals, 339–341
  as cause of employee dissatisfaction, 438
  compensation and benefits and, 453–454
  defined, 333
  employee assistance programs and, 417
  establishing continuous, 337–339
  establishing specific requirements, 339
  forecasting and, 227
  of human resources planning staff, 486–487
  in-house, 338, 340–341
  labor relations and, 437
  organization development and, 378
  role in human resources grand strategy, 333–334
  screening, 341–342
  strategic, 348–351
  traditional approach, 335–347
    problems with, 347–348
  training as alternative to, 355
Referent power, 498
Referrals, recruitment and, 339
Regression models, 218
Reliability, 343
  defined, 65
Remuneration, administering, 469, 472–473
Reorientation of assignments, 274
Replacement chart, 225
Replacement summaries, 225
Reports, feedback, 529
Resistance, to change effort, 500–501, 505
Resource analysis, principles of, 147
Resources, conflict and competition for, 490

Restraining force, 376–378
Restricted human resources audit, 139, 141
Results of work analysis, deciding on, 73
Retention, 3
Retirement programs, 427
Retrenchment, 317, 319
Retrenchment human resources grand strategy, 242, 245, 249–251
Reward(s)
  employee performance appraisal and allocation of, 112
  matching to human resources grand strategy, 294–295
  matching to human resources strategy, 274–276
  types of, 476
Reward factors, 185
Reward power, 498
Reward strategy, 469
Reward systems, 451
  alternative, 465
  recruitment and selection and, 334
  strategic career planning and, 316–317
Risk
  career strategy and, 323
  portfolio analysis and, 237
Risk screening, of job candidates, 431
Rituals, organizational, 374–375
Role(s)
  defined, 27
  vs. job titles, 31
Role analysis, 387
Role behavior, 27, 28
Role play, 365
  work analysis, 91–98
Role receivers, 27, 28
Role senders, 27, 28
Role theory, 26–28

Rothschild principles of resource analysis, 147
Rucker, 475
Rumors, identifying employee behavior problems and, 421

Salary/wages, evaluating, 460. *See also* Compensation and benefits
Sales forecast, 495
Scale models, 22–23
Scaling, 119–121
Scanlon, 475
Scenario analysis, evaluating human resources grand strategies using, 247
Scenarios
  to forecast compensation trends, 469, 473
  future-oriented employee performance appraisal and, 202
  future-oriented work analysis and, 192–193, 197, 198
Schleh, Edward, 118
Scope
  of human resources audit, 139, 150
  of intervention, 385
Screening, 341–342
  job specifications and, 109
Security, career planning and, 305
Selection, 333–351
  checking applicant background, 344–345
  compensation and benefits and, 453
  conducting interviews, 343–344
  defined, 333–334
  employee assistance programs and, 417
  employee performance appraisal and, 112
  extending offer, 345–346
  of human resources planning staff, 486–487

index   **575**

Selection criteria, 67

Selection instruments, 30–31

Self-appraisal, of employee performance, 122

Self-diagnosis, of human resources planning skills, 34–39

Self-diagnostic survey, on linking strategic business planning to strategic human resources planning, 58–61

Self-directed teams, 394, 406

Self-help books, on career planning, 313

Self-improvement effort, 421–422

Self-study career instruction, 310

Sell approach, to recruitment, 340

Semi-Markov model, 218–219, 224

Seniority systems, 465

Sensitivity training, 385

Seven circle model, for human resources audit, 146–147

Seven-point scale, 120

Sex, employee classification and, 213

Shadow budgeting, 497

Shared action, 384

Simulation, 224, 365, 371

Simulation models, 23

Situational theory, 395

Six-box model, for human resources audit, 145

Skill and achievement tests, 342, 343

Skill deficiency, 358

Skill inventories, 105, 129, 225

Skill mastery, 358

Skill repertory, 358

Skill variety, 400, 401

Small-group decision-making

Social conditions

Social equity, compensation and, 455, 456

Social factors, 184

Social norms, 346

Social system, human resources audit and, 146–147

Socialization, 346

Society for Human Resource Management, 452

Sociotechnical systems, 378

Span of control, 67

Specialized human resources planning department, 496

Stability of tenure of personnel, 3

Stability strategy, 274

Staff leaseback arrangements, 406

Staffing, output and, 213–215

Staffing alternatives, 345

Staffing chart, 223

Staffing cycles, 214

Stakeholder analysis, 144

Stakeholder needs, human resources audit and, 150
Stakeholders, human resources grand strategy and, 253
"Stars," 240
States, 218
Statistical analysis, 141, 142
Status, of human resources department, 287
Strategic business planning, (SBP), 1, 50
    human resources grand strategy and, 253
    linking with human resources plans, 42–48
        alternative methods, 48–53
        self-diagnostic survey, 58–61
    work analysis and, 66
Strategic business unit (SBU), 6, 237, 484
Strategic career management, 323–327
Strategic career planning, 312–323
    assessing career strengths and weaknesses, 313–314
    clarifying individual identity, 313
    evaluating career strategy, 322–323, 332
    identifying range of career strategies, 317–318, 330
    implementing career strategy, 321–322, 331
    scanning the environment, 314–317, 329
    selecting a long-term career strategy, 318, 321
Strategic compensation and benefits, 465–476
Strategic control systems, 513–515
Strategic employee assistance programs, 429–434
Strategic four-factor analysis, 44–45
Strategic gap, 181
Strategic human resources objectives, 269–271

Strategic human resources plans, 182
    purposes, goals, and objectives of, 46–48
Strategic job redesign, 409–413
Strategic labor relations, 446–450
Strategic organization development, 389–391
Strategic-oriented human resources department scanning, 205–206
Strategic-oriented work analysis, 205–206
Strategic-oriented workforce analysis, 205–206
Strategic planning for human resources (SPHR), 1–39
    conceptual models, 230–231
        four-factor condition/criteria analysis, 231–236
        nine cell planning grid, 240–241
        portfolio analysis, 237–240
        WOTS-UP analysis, 236–237
    defined, xvii, 2
    demographic conditions and, 14–17
    economic conditions and, 7–9, 10, 11
    evaluation of, 508–512
    geographic conditions and, 17–19
    government/legal conditions and, 12–14
    human resources planner roles, 24, 26, 28–31, 32
    human resources planning and, 48
    meaning of strategy, 4–6
    model of, 22–24, 25
    need for, 6
    organizational obstacles to, 20–22
    origins of, 3–4
    process of, 22–24
    role theory, 26–28
    self-diagnostic survey on linking with strategic business planning, 58–61
    social conditions and, 19
    technological conditions and, 9

worksheet for identifying purpose of, 55–56

using human resources plan evaluation results to stimulate, 530–532

Strategic recruitment, 348–351

Strategic selection, 348–351

Strategic training, 368–372

Strategy
meaning of, 4–6
types of, 6

Strategy evaluation model, 509

Strategy hierarchy, 527

Strategy review, 523–524
meetings, 524, 525

Strategy-specific factors, strategy evaluation and, 513, 515

Strategy success factors, 513–514
strategy evaluation and, 513, 515

Strengths
assessing career, 313–314, 328
defined, 235
in WOTS-UP analysis, 236–237

Stress forecasting, 432

Strike, 436, 442

Strike fund, 442

Structural factors, 185

Structured content analysis, 81, 86

Structured diaries, 80, 85

Structured group interviews, 81

Structured individual interviews, 80, 84

Structured observations, in work analysis, 79, 82–83

Structured selection interviews, 343–344

Structured surveys, in work analysis, 79, 83–84

Subcultures, 374

Subordinate appraisals, 122

Substance abuse, 416

Succession charts, 225

Succession plans, 67, 225

Succession system, 202

Summaries, feedback, 528–529

Summary statistics, 216–217

Supervisors, employee performance appraisals and, 122

Supervisory training, job redesign and, 407

Supplier conditions, strategic career planning and, 316

Supplier factors, 184

Supply forecasting, 210
methods, 223–225
reasons for, 221–223

Supply shifts, causes of, 222–223

Survey(s)
benefits, 463
forecasting compensation trends, 469, 473
human resources audit and, 151
human resources planning skills, 34–39
job-analysis, 84
linking strategic business planning to strategic human resources planning, 58–61
organizational climate, 493–494
pay rate, 460
work analysis, 79, 83–84

Survey feedback, 386
strategic organization development and, 391

Talent, identifying sources of, 335–337

Task, defined, 64

Task analysis, defined, 64

Task autonomy, 400, 401

Task depth, 402

Task effectiveness, 402

Task efficiency, 402

Task grouping, 286, 401–404

Task identity, 400, 401
Task Inventory Approach, 74, 76, 78
Task patterns, 145
Task range, 402
Task relationships, 402
Task significance, 400, 401
Taylor, Frederick, 82, 114–115, 397,
    401–402
Team building, 385
Teams, 406
    for human resources audit, 143
Teamsters, 436
Technological conditions
    as impetus for change, 380
    need for strategic planning and, 9
    strategic career planning and, 315
    supply shifts and, 222
Technology factors, 183
Telecommuters, 14, 345, 397
Telecommuting capabilities, 18
Tell and listen approach, 126, 423
Tell and sell approach, 126, 423
Temporary-help agencies, 17
Tentative audit plan, 142–143
Tenure
    employee classification and, 213
    semi-Markov model and, 218
    supply shifts and, 223
Terminal behaviors, 361
Termination, 14
Tests
    formats, 362
    preparing test items, 361–363
T-group meetings, 384, 387
Thematic Apperception Tests (TAT),
    343
Third-party peace-making, 387
Threats
    defined, 235

to organization, 43
    in WOTS-UP analysis, 236–237
Time and motion study, 82
Time frames, for human resources
    practice areas, 280, 281
Time schedules, 516–517
Time span, 402
Time span of discretion, 457, 459, 471
Timing, of feedback, 529
Total compensation, 451
    purposes of, 454–456
Trade unions, 436
Traffic signal grid, 240–241
Training, 281, 353–372
    analyzing performance problems, 358
    choosing delivery methods, 363-364,
        365
    compensation and benefits and, 453
    to conduct employee performance
        appraisals, 127–128
    defined, 353–354
    directive, 371
    employee assistance programs and,
        417
    forecasting and, 227
    identifying needs, 358–360
    job redesign and, 394
    labor relations and, 437
    nondirective, 371
    offering instruction, 364, 366
    organization development and, 378
    preparing instructional objectives,
        360–361
    preparing test items, 361–363
    to recognize employee behavior
        problems, 423
    recruitment and selection and, 334
    role in implementing human resources
        grand strategy, 354–356

selecting/designing instructional
    content, 363
sensitivity, 385
strategic, 368–372
traditional approach, 356–367
    problems with, 367–368
training process, 356–357
transferring learning, 366–367, 372
Training category, change in employment
    and, 11
Training curriculum, 360
Training needs, employee performance
    appraisal and, 112
Training period, compensation and,
    455
Training plans, 67
Training requirements, position
    classification and, 213
Trait, defined, 113
Trait rating, 113–114, 123
Transfers, forecasting and, 227
Transformation processes, 177
Trend projections, 218
Trends. *See* Future trends
Trust, 493
Turnabout career strategy, 317, 320
Turnabout human resources grand
    strategy, 243, 245, 249–251
Turnover
    employee satisfaction and, 517
    forecasting and reduction in, 227
    human resources audit and, 141, 153
    job redesign and, 408
    supply shifts and, 222, 223
    training and, 355
Tutorial, 365

Underemployment, 19
Undue burden, 70

Undue hardship, 393
Unfair labor practice, 436, 440
Unfair treatment, 439
*Uniform Guidelines for Employee Selection
    Procedures,* 342, 344
Unilateral action, 383, 384
Union(s),
    advantages of, 446
    avoiding unionization, 445, 446–448
    decertification of, 440, 449–450
    management responses to, 445
    organizing campaign, 439–441
    reasons for unionization, 438–439
    recruitment and selection and, 334
    use in organizational and human
        resources planning, 448–449
Union agreements, career management
    and, 303
Union security, 442
Union stewards, 443
Unionization, 13
Unit, 363
United Auto Workers, 436
United States
    aging population in, 14–15
    economic changes in, 7–9
    population shift in, 17
U.S. Bureau of Labor Statistics, 16, 226
U.S. Department of Defense, 291
U.S. Equal Employment Opportunity
    Commission, 213
Unobtrusive measures
    human resources audit and, 153
Unstructured content analysis, 81, 86
Unstructured diaries, 80, 85
Unstructured group interviews, 81
Unstructured individual interviews, 80, 84
Unstructured observations, in work
    analysis, 79, 83

Unstructured selection interviews, 344
Unstructured surveys, in work analysis,
    79, 83–84

Vacancy model, 219
Validity, 343
    defined, 65
Value(s)
    career strategy and, 318, 322
    conflict and differences in, 490, 491
    culture and, 53
    defined, 65
    of top managers and planning, 44, 51
Value-added, building, 43
Values identification, 90
Videotape training, 365
Vietnam Era Veterans Readjustment Act
    (1974), 13
Violence
    domestic, 416–417
    workplace, 419
Vocabulary
    compensation and benefits, 452
    work analysis, 64
    workforce analysis, 104–105
Vocational Rehabilitation Act of 1973,
    13

Wagner Act (1935), 14
Walkout, 436
Washington v. Davis (1976), 13
Weaknesses
    assessing career, 313–314, 328
    defined, 235
    in WOTS-UP analysis, 236–237
Web-based career planning, 302
Web-based data collection, full-circle,
    multi-rater assessment and, 123
Web-based sources of labor, 337

Websites
    compensation and benefits, 452
    work analysis, 72
Weber, Max, 395
Weber v. Kaiser Aluminum (1976), 13
Wechsler Adult Intelligence Scale, 343
Weighted Application Blank, 341
Wellness programs, 429–431, 432
Wildcat strike, 436
Women, in workforce, 16
Work
    defined, 64
    planning gap in, 23
Work analysis, 233, 359, 399–401
    defined, 64, 103
    focus of, 68–71
    frequency of, 88–89
    future-oriented, 205–208
    importance of, 66–68
    initiation of, 89
    link with workforce analysis, 110–111
    role play, 91–98
    strategic business planning and, 66
    strategic-oriented, 205–206
    traditional, 63–64, 71
        carrying out work analysis, 87
        collecting general background
            information, 71–73
        compiling information and verify
            results, 87–88
        deciding on desired results, 73
        monitoring conditions, 88–89
        selecting approach, 73–77, 78
        selecting data-collection method, 77,
            79–86
    uses of, 88
    vocabulary of, 64–65
    See also Future-oriented work analysis
Work analyst, 29, 30

human resources environmental scanner and, 175
Work-context stress forecasting, 432, 433
Work flow rearrangement, 402, 403–404, 405
Work group
  changing, 401–407
    in strategic job redesign, 412
  organization development and, 378
  performance model, 399
Work log, 85
Work measurement, 82, 397–398
Work methods, 27
Work modeling, 405
Work observation, 82–83
Work output, 74
Work Performance Survey System (WPSS), 74, 77, 78
Work results, 27
Work rules, 346
Work scheduling, 406–407
Work standard, 104
Workforce
  planning gap in, 23
  transfer of jobs outside United States, 18–19
  trends in United States, 14–17
Workforce analysis, 233
  focus of, 106–107
  importance of, 106
  overcoming problems with employee appraisals, 125–128
  strategic-oriented, 206
  traditional, 107–108
    carrying out employee performance appraisals, 119–123
    focus of employee performance appraisals, 113–119
    importance of employee performance

appraisals, 112–113
    link between workforce and work analysis, 110–111
    preparing job specifications, 109–110
    problems with traditional employee-appraisal methods, 123–125
  using appraisal results in human resources planning, 128–130
  vocabulary for, 104–105
Workforce analyst, 29, 30
  human resources environmental scanner and, 175
Workforce development, future trends in, 185
Workforce factors, supply shifts and, 222
"Workhorses," 240
Working conditions, 439
Workplace flexibility, future trends in, 184
Workplace regulations, 12
Workplace violence, 419
Worksheets
  assessing career strengths and weakness, 328
  assessing influence of new initiative on human resources practice areas, 296
  assessing management support for human resources grand strategy, 293
  classification of jobs, people, and human resources department, 259
  considering human resources grand strategy, 260–261
  developing human resources objectives, 292
  evaluating a career strategy, 332
  evaluating human resources grand strategy, 262–263
  four-factor condition/criteria analysis, 255–257
  human resources audit, 165–170

Worksheets *(continued)*
  human resources department structure,
      297–298
  identifying purpose of strategic plan-
      ning for human resources, 55–56
  identifying range of career strategies, 330
  implementing individual career strategy,
      331
  matching rewards to human resources
      grand strategy, 294–295
  scanning career environment, 329
  WOTS-UP analysis, 258

Workshops, career, 311, 325, 326
World at Work, 452
Worth, compensation and, 454–455
WOTS-UP analysis, 236–237
  worksheet, 258
Written policies, 279
Written surveys
  human resources audit and, 151
  in work analysis, 83–84

Xerox Corporation, 177, 179